First published in Great Britain in 2007 by

The Policy Press
University of Bristol
Fourth Floor
Beacon House
Queen's Road
Bristol BS8 1QU
UK

Tel +44 (0)117 331 4054
Fax +44 (0)117 331 4093
e-mail tpp-info@bristol.ac.uk
www.policypress.org.uk

British Library Cataloguing in Publication Data
A catalogue record for this book is available from the British Library.

Library of Congress Cataloging-in-Publication Data
A catalog record for this book has been requested.

ISBN 978 1 86134 941 5 hardcover

Cover design by Qube Design Associates, Bristol.
Front cover: photograph kindly supplied by www.alamy.com
Printed and bound in Great Britain by Hobbs the Printers, Southampton.

Dedication

Just as this review was going to press we received the sad news of the sudden death of Eithne McLaughlin, who, with Gerry Boucher, has made a contribution, one of her last, to this volume. Eithne trained as a social anthropologist at Queen's University Belfast and the University of Cambridge, where she specialised in historical anthropology and museology. She spent several years working at the Social Policy Research Unit at the University of York before returning to Belfast as a lecturer at Queen's University, where she was appointed to a Chair of Social Policy in 1995. Eithne was an active member of the Social Policy Association (SPA) (one of the sponsors of this review), serving as a member of the Executive Committee in the early 1990s and as Chair between 1998 and 1999. She was President of the Sociology & Social Policy section of the British Association for the Advancement of Science (1999) and was elected as a Fellow of the UK's Academy of the Social Sciences in 2000. She made a valuable intellectual contribution to social policy as an academic discipline and to the development and practice of social policy at governmental level in the UK and in Ireland. She will be greatly missed by her friends and colleagues within the SPA and beyond. This issue of the *Social Policy Review* is dedicated to her memory.

KC TM PK

Contents

List of tables and figures

Tables

Figures

Notes on contributors

Louise Ackers is Professor of Socio-Legal Studies, Liverpool Law School, University of Liverpool, UK.

Stephen J. Ball is Karl Mannheim Professor of Sociology of Education at the Institute of Education, University of London, UK.

Fran Bennett is Senior Research Fellow in the Department of Social Policy and Social Work, University of Oxford, UK.

Gerry Boucher is Lecturer in Sociology in the School of Sociology and Social Policy at Queen's University Belfast, UK.

Henglien (Lisa) Chen is a social worker and postgraduate research student in the Department of Social Sciences, University of Loughborough, UK.

Harriet Churchill is Lecturer in Public and Social Policy in the School of Social Sciences, University of Manchester, UK.

Karen Clarke is Senior Lecturer in Social Policy in the School of Social Sciences, University of Manchester, UK.

Patricia Kennett is Senior Lecturer in Comparative Policy Studies in the School for Policy Studies, University of Bristol, UK.

Eleonore Kofman is Professor of Gender, Migration and Citizenship in the School of Health and Social Sciences, Middlesex University, UK.

Adrian Lee is Teaching Fellow at the Centre for Lifelong Learning, University of York, UK.

Stephen McKay is Professor of Social Research in the Institute of Applied Social Studies at the University of Birmingham, UK.

Eithne McLaughlin was Professor of Social Policy in the School of Sociology and Social Policy at Queen's University Belfast, UK.

Tony Maltby is Research Fellow and Deputy Director with the Centre for Research into the Older Workforce at the National Institute for Adult and Continuing Education (NIACE), Leicester, UK.

Alan Murie is Professor of Urban and Regional Studies at the Centre for Urban and Regional Studies, University of Birmingham, UK.

Stephen Peckham is Senior Lecturer in Health Service Delivery and Organisation in the Department of Public Health and Policy at the London School of Hygiene and Tropical Medicine, UK.

Kirstein Rummery is Senior Lecturer in Social Policy in the School of Social Sciences, University of Manchester, UK.

Dhananjayan Sriskandarajah is Associate Director and Head of Migration, Equalities and Citizenship at the Institute for Public Policy Research, UK.

Helen Stalford is Senior Lecturer in Law in the Liverpool Law School at the University of Liverpool, UK.

Sirin Sung is Lecturer in Social Policy in the School of Sociology, Social Policy and Social Work, Queen's University Belfast, UK.

Joanne Warner is Senior Lecturer in Social Work in the School of Social Policy, Sociology and Social Research at the University of Kent, UK.

Anthony M. Warnes is Professor of Social Gerontology at the Sheffield Institute for Studies on Ageing at the University of Sheffield, UK.

Introduction

Karen Clarke, Tony Maltby and Patricia Kennett

As in previous years, this volume of *Social Policy Review* is organised
into three sections. Part One reviews developments in key areas of
social policy during 2006: education, health, housing, adult social care,
children's services and social security. The introduction of a chapter
on children's services for the first time this year reflects the substantial
transformation that has taken place in recent years in the organisation
of social services. The emphasis on partnership working has resulted
in the reappearance of services organised around the characteristics of
particular client groups, replacing the Seebohm vision in which local
authority social services departments were responsible for providing a
service that offered support to all vulnerable groups.

The chapters in Part Two are by authors who presented papers at
the annual international conference of the Social Policy Association
held at Birmingham University in July 2006. Because the conference
produced a large number of papers on a wide range of topics, the
selection criteria for the chapters in Part Two were not simply to fit
them to some synthetically derived theme, but reflect an attempt to
represent this breadth. The selection has been made primarily on the
basis of the interest and topicality of the material presented, while equally
demonstrating the vitality of the discipline of social policy. The chapters
have in common a focus on the less often discussed and 'difficult to
research' challenges encountered within empirical research.

The theme for the chapters in Part Three is migration and social
policy. This is an issue that has provoked substantial debate and is high
on the political agenda both nationally and internationally. The chapters
in this section connect with, and expand on, key contemporary policy
debates in the field of migration – recent enlargement of the European
Union and the scale and impact of migration from new member states,
in particular Eastern Europe; the challenges brought about by the
migration of older people not only in terms of their ability to access
adequate and appropriate welfare services, but also to the existing systems
of welfare provision and the principles on which they were built; and
finally migration processes as the management of complex and multiple
life courses with a particular focus on children.

Part One: Current services

A number of common themes emerge from these reviews of developments in key social policy areas in 2006. Individual choice continued to be seen by the Labour government as central to driving service development in education and health. An emphasis on individual responsibility for welfare and an increasingly residual role for the state characterised developments in housing policy, education, some aspects of social security policy and policies on public health and adult social care. Partnership between the public, private and voluntary sectors continued to be the preferred arrangement for welfare provision across a range of different services. Such partnerships raise important questions about the place of local democratic mechanisms in the emerging governance arrangements: in education, in children's services, in adult social care and in health.

Stephen J. Ball examines developments in education policy in Chapter One, focusing on the transformation of the proposals in the 2005 White Paper *Higher standards, better schools for all* (DfES, 2005) into the 2006 Education and Inspections Act. He maps the continuity in policy between the City Technology Colleges (CTCs) and grant-maintained schools introduced by the Conservatives in the 1990s, the Labour government's Academies programme and the provision in the Act for all schools to become trusts, drawing in private sponsorship and operating relatively independently of local government control. The role of business sponsorship and the power of sponsors within the governance arrangements for Academies and for trust schools in the future, signal a new importance for business philanthropy in shaping policy, and introduced an 'enterprise narrative' into state education, which is increasingly focused on promoting future competitiveness in the global economy. The Act promotes parental responsibility for children's education in two different ways. Parental choice of school will continue to be the principal means of encouraging schools to improve pupils' educational attainment; at the same time, there are several provisions to increase parents' responsibility to the state for their children's behaviour in school, through measures such as parenting orders, where parents are seen as failing to exercise adequate control over their children. This is part of what Ball identifies as a moral agenda in education policy, which is also reflected in the provisions for regulating children's diet through school meals and restrictions on what can be sold in school tuck-shops and vending machines.

In Chapter Two, Stephen Peckham identifies a continuing divergence in 2006 between the four national health services within the UK as a result of devolution. Different solutions are emerging to common problems across England, Wales, Scotland and Northern Ireland about how to ensure both responsiveness to local need and equity of provision. While the solution within the English NHS has been a continued reliance on market mechanisms and a central role for individual patient choice, the other three countries within the UK have adopted approaches in which there is a greater role for central planning, organisational partnerships and professional engagement, giving a different role to patient choice. In all four contexts there is a tension between allowing policy to be made at the local level to suit local circumstances and maintaining some degree of central control over healthcare provision, through target setting and performance management. The different solutions offered in these national contexts, Peckham argues, offer an interesting natural experiment in which alternative approaches to common problems can be evaluated against each other.

Alan Murie's review of housing policy in 2006 (Chapter Three) places it in the context of the development of housing policy since 1945. The Labour governments since 1997 have continued their predecessors' policy of residualising social housing and offering no real long-term alternative to home ownership. Policy has focused on interventions to extend forms of home ownership to groups that have hitherto been prevented from entering the housing market. Problems of affordability and housing supply have been addressed primarily through the use of the planning system as a means of influencing the supply of housing through the market at 'arm's length'. This approach to housing policy has a number of important consequences in the context of the central place given to asset ownership in the government's welfare policy. The capital value of housing is taking on increasing importance as a resource that individuals can use to pay for services previously provided by the state. Long-term residential care for older people is the most obvious example, but Murie points to other examples, such as the maintenance of income in old age or paying for higher education through equity release schemes. This means that the significance of housing policy increasingly extends beyond the provision of shelter and places individual home ownership in a central position for the future funding of welfare, with important implications for the way in which differences in the capital value of housing transfer into inequalities in individual access to welfare provision.

Chapter Four provides an analysis by Kirstein Rummery of policy developments in adult social care in 2006. She identifies a tension within New Labour's modernisation agenda for social care, between the promotion of user empowerment in adult services and the development of a closer partnership between the health service and social services. The focus of policy has moved from attention to the needs of service users in the 2005 Green Paper, *Independence, well-being and choice* (DH, 2005) to the promotion of partnership working and identification of performance indicators to measure this in the health and social care White Paper published in 2006 (DH, 2006). Health, which, Rummery shows, emerges as the dominant partner in the White Paper proposals, has a much less well-developed culture of user empowerment than social services, both in terms of the voice of individual service users and in terms of local democratic accountability. She argues that although the White Paper addresses user empowerment issues such as choice, flexibility and information, these take the concept of empowerment as primarily a question of promoting individual autonomy. Collective empowerment and attention to other issues of importance to users of adult social care services, such as fairness, the cost of services and respect for service users, receive little attention in the 2006 proposals.

Children's services in Britain have undergone a major reorganisation following the publication of the *Every Child Matters* Green Paper in 2003 (DfES, 2003). Policy emphasis has shifted to the provision of universal family support services through Sure Start children's centres and extended schools, and to prevention and early intervention as the preferred means of promoting the well-being of children. Harriet Churchill (Chapter Five) summarises and analyses the principal developments in children's services in 2006. These include the implementation of new structures to promote joint working across the different services involved with children and families, and attention to issues of workforce training and retention, as well as important proposals to address the well-being of children in local authority care. Churchill identifies a number of different discourses within policy in relation to children and families: a social investment discourse, a social threat discourse and a social justice discourse. These discourses have different implications in terms of the problem to be addressed and the most appropriate means of doing so. Important questions remain about the adequacy of the resources that have been allocated to implementing the reforms in children's services, of the mechanisms established to promote partnership working across a wide range of local services and of the procedures for engaging children and parents in more participatory ways of working.

Steven McKay in Chapter Six examines a number of important developments in social security policy during 2006. He argues that while there were continuities with Labour's previous approach to welfare provision for adults of working age outside the labour market, developments in relation to pensions and child support established some important new principles for social security provision. The 2006 welfare reform Green Paper (DWP, 2006) continued the earlier policy emphasis on drawing those on benefits into paid work, using a combination of support from personal advisors and increasing compulsion to attend an interview with an advisor, as a condition of benefit receipt. Pension reform proposals in 2006 provided for an important extension of state pension entitlement on the basis of a smaller number of years of contributions and acceptance that state pension increases should be linked to earnings growth rather than price inflation. However, as McKay argues, the aim of this extension of state provision is to build a broader minimum platform from which to encourage more extensive provision for income security in old age through individual saving. A similar emphasis on private arrangements is apparent in the proposed reforms to child support. Parents are to be encouraged to arrive at voluntary agreements on child support, with a new Child Maintenance and Enforcement Commission (to replace the Child Support Agency), vested with significantly increased enforcement powers, but reserved for ex-partners who are unable to arrive at a voluntary agreement.

Part Two: Current issues

Adrian Lee's chapter (Chapter Seven) offers an analysis of older gay men and the ways in which their sexual identity affects their lives in the context of access to and provision of healthcare. He provides a short introductory overview of the recent work in this under-researched area, placing this within what he refers to as "a discourse of sexual citizenship". The main focus of the chapter, however, is a discussion of his recent work, which investigated healthcare decision making among older gay men and their interaction and discourse within healthcare settings. The central focus of this discussion is on their active or passive disclosure of their sexuality. He suggests that the manner of this disclosure and their subsequent experiences colours our understanding of sexual citizenship and their fair access as citizens. Furthermore, he suggests that there is a need for inclusiveness and a "greater sense of comfort" for older gay men. He proposes a number of pragmatic solutions for local service provision within primary care trusts, for healthcare policy more generally, and more widely for the *Opportunity Age* and *National Service Framework* agendas.

Sirin Sung and Fran Bennett (Chapter Eight) discuss another

'difficult-to-research' area. Indeed, they suggest that the "(re)distribution – of money, time and other resources" within the household is often neglected by researchers, moreover, "equality is assumed". The chapter offers an analysis of a recent Economic and Social Research Council (ESRC)-funded project considering the difficulties associated with researching the complexities of the management of household money and budgeting within long-term heterosexual relationships. Their interview sample comprised heterosexual couples living on means-tested benefits or tax credits and considered how they received, organised and used such income, and how this affected gender relations and inequalities within the household. They acknowledge the key work in this area of study, particularly that of Pahl, and provide the reader with a useful précis of this literature. Their chapter builds on this previous work to reveal the continuing complexity alongside the continuing gendered nature of the management of household finance. The discussion of their qualitative interviews makes fascinating reading. To elucidate the complexity of household financial arrangements, the analysis focuses on three areas: "big financial decisions, management of the joint bank account (where relevant), and personal spending". Previous work in this area (for example, Pahl) has attempted to offer a typology, breaking down styles and practices of management. However, Sung and Bennett argue that in their research deriving a typology was more difficult. The more likely arrangement was a reflection of the nature of the couple's relationship expressed as marriage as an equal partnership. Household income was seen as a united, 'one pot' resource, despite the dominance of the prevailing male breadwinning ideology. This research has therefore a wider importance for the continuing debate on the shift towards individualisation within social policy.

Henglien (Lisa) Chen (Chapter Nine) presents some of the complexities in undertaking cross-national research. Additionally, she addresses the issue of using international comparison ('lesson learning') as the basis for making policy on long-term healthcare for older people more effective in England, the Netherlands and Taiwan. These countries were selected "because each represents a different welfare arrangement" (even though there are some close similarities). Yet importantly, the selection was made because these countries show evidence of lesson learning intrinsic to the process of globalisation. A clear example of this process (not cited here) is that of Japan learning much from the German long-term care insurance system for their policy in this area. Chen's chapter provides us with an insight into the key issues through a case study approach that is supplemented by interviews with care providers (formal and informal), service users and professionals in their own languages. These are illuminating since they not only consider how long-term care is provided, but equally importantly consider issues of power and autonomy. Among her more important findings she argues that, "the gap of responsibility between the state, individual and family is closing". She makes the important point as evidence of this shift (citing Bengtson and Putney, 2000) that the 'family' as a source of care is becoming increasingly important in western societies, and support by the state in eastern societies. This transposes the historically observed trends. She also presents a list of key recommendations that might form the basis of further research but equally might be considered by government. The 'lesson learning' should continue.

Joanne Warner then offers us a useful critical analysis of mental health policy in the UK (Chapter Ten). As she notes, her chapter is set within a context where economic and social costs associated with poor mental health are rising in the EU. Currently, claims for incapacity benefits as a result of mental illness account for more than those who are unemployed and claiming Jobseeker's Allowance. She argues that there has hitherto been an emphasis on 'risk and dangerousness' that has led to the stigmatisation of those with poor mental health. Indeed, she suggests that the current trends within UK mental health policy will undermine efforts in support of those who develop mental health problems in their workplace. For her, the policy dilemma is how to achieve a balance between reducing the social stigma associated with poor mental health against the implementation of policies to improve mental health in the workplace. Her important and interesting chapter explores the current debate and some of the possibilities for future policy.

In Chapter Eleven Eithne McLaughlin and Gerry Boucher offer us a more theoretically based piece that reflects on Bauman's *Wasted lives, modernity and its outcasts* (2004) to consider how social policy might contribute to "harmonious intergroup relations" and to a socially just citizenship. They identify some important contradictions and tensions within EU policies, which lead to negative differentiated citizenship. They argue that this results in threats to peace and democracy that can ultimately only be countered by policies that promise greater social justice and an appreciation that "security of the individual and the polity" is achieved by social "rather than through criminal justice or military means". This they call the new social security. Through an analysis of the role of the nation state in globalisation, and immigration and integration policy, they suggest that a discourse on the relationship of social justice policies and differentiated citizenship will help meet the challenges imposed by the increasing broadly based diversity in Europe.

Part Three: Migration and social policy

The themes of migration and citizenship are continued in the final section of this volume. In May 2004 10 new member states acceded to the EU, followed in 2006 by Romania and Bulgaria. The first chapter in this part, by Dhananjayan Sriskandarajah, explores the nature and impact of and policy response to migration to the UK in the context of an enlarged Europe. The chapter highlights the tensions between the fundamental EU principle of freedom of movement and the domestic contexts in which political and policy decisions are made. The author is also keen to stress that, in relation to managing migration and responding to popular concerns about (and in some quarters hostility to) migration, "numbers matter". During the first phase of enlargement the UK government was one of only three member states not to impose restrictions on the freedom of movement of workers from the eight Central and Eastern European member states. However, the UK government's approach to the free movement of workers from Romania and Bulgaria has been somewhat different, and has included 'transitional' arrangements and the application of a quota on the number of positions open to lower-skilled workers. In setting out to explore this 'dramatic policy reversal' the author draws out some of the fundamental challenges facing policy makers in the UK. He highlights the tensions between national and supranational policy regimes; between an enlarged Europe and the free movement of workers; and the domestic political context in which governments are subject to popular pressure and perceptions. Sriskandarajah argues that there is little evidence to indicate that the latest wave of migration has had a detrimental effect on the UK and suggests that the government's increasing emphasis on enforcement, removals and barriers to access is an attempt to regain political legitimacy, public confidence and appear 'in control' of immigration policy in the UK.

Eleanore Kofman, in Chapter Thirteen, explores the gendered dimensions of immigration policies in the context of rising levels and more diversified forms of immigration and net migration, as well as a more complex policy regime. Kofman begins her analysis by recognising that women are present in all forms of entry into the UK, with family migration the most common form of settlement and asylum the least feminised category. She then goes on to map out and explain the enormous variation to be found in the proportion of women in each category and the implications for the different groups of women in terms of access to rights and citizenship. Kofman argues that the gendered perceptions of specific forms of migration influence the formation of policy just as the criteria applied to different channels of immigration shape the "gendered nature of these flows". The focus on 'managed migration' and the increasing emphasis on privileging more highly skilled, young workers has, according to Kofman, served to more sharply differentiate between and stratify different categories of migrants. Managed migration is more likely to favour men, while the more restrictive aspects of the policy regime will most likely impact on women whose channels of entry, skills, earning power and age put them at a severe disadvantage.

In Chapter Fourteen, Tony Warnes explores the development of and access to welfare policies for older foreign migrants in Europe. As demonstrated in this chapter this is a heterogeneous group, with diverse histories and motivations, residential status and needs. Warnes is particularly interested in the contradictions and conflict between migration policy and social welfare, and between the fundamental principles of intergenerational solidarity and closed national boundaries and populations that underpin European welfare systems, and the increasing mobility that undermines them. Drawing on the latest research on older migrants he highlights the different strands and explanations that have emerged in the migration literature. He then goes on to consider the development of and prospects for the cross-border portability of social security rights among the EU member states, and to argue for the integration of migration and social policy as a strategy for improving the living and welfare standards of migrants across Europe.

In Chapter Fifteen Louise Ackers and Helen Stalford consider the impact of personal and family relationships and obligations on migration behaviour. Their analysis seeks to add to debates that move beyond the 'male breadwinner' and economic rationality models of migration. Instead, they highlight the complexity and multiplicity of factors involved in the migration process with a particular focus on the life course and the influence of children. This analysis draws on qualitative research carried out among highly skilled (science) professionals moving within the EU, with Bulgaria and Poland identified as 'sending' countries and the UK and Germany as two 'destination' countries. Ackers and Stalford demonstrate that those who migrate with children are strongly influenced by their families' needs, particularly those of their children. However, the nature of these needs is not static but dynamic and will vary over the life course, just as strategies and options for meeting these needs will change. The authors highlight the importance of context for understanding the migration process, particularly in relation to domestic welfare regimes, access to and affordability of childcare provision, and education. Parents constantly re-negotiate and re-evaluate their coping strategies at different stages of the life cycle, balancing their own needs with the needs of their children. This chapter highlights that in a global age migration processes often lead to the transnational separation and dispersal of the nuclear family as a strategy for accommodating multiple life courses and contribute to the increasing complexity of patterns of family life.

References

Bauman, Z. (2004) *Wasted lives, modernity and its outcasts*, Cambridge: Polity Press.

Bengtson, V.L. and Putney, N.M. (2000) 'Who will care for tomorrow's elderly? Consequences of population aging East and West', in V.L. Bengtson, K.D. Kim, G.C. Myers and K.S. Eun (eds) *Aging in East and West: Families, states, and the elderly*, New York, NY: Springer Publishing Company.

DfES (Department for Education and Skills) (2003) *Every Child Matters*, Cm 5860, London: The Stationery Office.

DfES (2005) *Higher standards, better schools for all: More choice for parents and pupils*, Cm 6677, London: The Stationery Office.

DH (Department of Health) (2005) *Independence, well-being and choice: Our vision for the future of social care for adults in England*, Cm 6299, London: The Stationery Office.

DH (2006) *Our health, our care, our say: A new direction for community services*, Cm 6737, London: The Stationery Office.

DWP (Department for Work and Pensions) (2006) *A New Deal for Welfare: Empowering people to work*, Cm 6730, London: The Stationery Office.

Part One
Current services

ONE

'Going further?' Tony Blair and New Labour education policies

Stephen J. Ball

Introduction

Any account of education policy in 2006 has to be dominated by the content and process of the 2006 Education and Inspections Act. Within the Act almost all of the key themes of the New Labour public sector reform project are played out in and through education policy, building on, extending and reworking previous policies and previous legislation. The Act was also a significant moment in the history of Tony Blair.

In the run-up to the 1997 General Election Tony Blair (1996) announced 'education, education, education' as his key priority. In 2006 education policy may have played a not insignificant role in bringing his leadership of the Labour Party to an ignominious end. The Prime Minister has made an enormous personal investment in education policy and he himself has made many key policy announcements rather than the Secretary of State[1]. Education is a recurring theme in his speeches and press conferences, he makes many visits to schools and personally praises and rewards 'excellent' teachers. The 2005 White Paper (DfES, 2005a), the 2006 Act and the compromises that became necessary to achieve Party support were clearly identified with this commitment and his credibility. Blair also often speaks about education from the point of view of a parent.

In their review of English education policy in 2005 (and again here the focus is very directly on England) Dyson and colleagues (2006), borrowing a phrase from Tony Blair (2005a), posed the question as to whether that year marked a 'pivotal moment' in the New Labour programme of 'fundamental and irreversible' educational reforms. They went on to conclude, while acknowledging the significance of what had been 'achieved', that 2005 was pivotal in a different sense and that the fragility of and tensions within New Labour education policy were becoming ever more apparent. These tensions and fragilities are again very much in evidence in education policy in 2006 and serve to highlight both the extent and the limits of New Labour's reform agenda. Nonetheless, the longer-term significance of the 2006 Act, especially the provisions relating to trust schools, should not be under-estimated.

More broadly the Act exemplifies both New Labour's overall project of education reform (and public service reform generally) and concomitant changes in educational governance (and New Labour's governance strategies generally). It is also possible to see in the Act facets of New Labour's agenda around citizen behaviour and responsibility. The Act plays out in a particular way Tony Blair's commitment to an educational reform process that is about "standards not structures" (Labour Party, 1997). Indeed the 2005 White Paper, and the Act in a more watered-down version, suggest the deconstruction of a "national system of education locally delivered" and its replacement with a set of independent self-governing, not-for-profit trust schools. This, together with parental choice (for example, the provision of 'choice advisers' and free transport) and voice, is aimed at bringing further contestability and competition into the delivery of education services as a means of raising standards and bringing about 'improvement'. However, in various parts of the Act we also see the government acting to set targets (for example, for food standards and student health) in its top-down performance management role and installing tougher measures to improve failing schools by direct intervention (although these aspects of the Act are not dealt with here). Autonomy, contestability, competition and choice were central to Secretary of State Ruth Kelly's argument for the 2006 Act (see below) as ways of addressing school failures, combating under-achievement and raising standards, and these are set within a framework of benchmarks, targets and performance indicators, key mechanisms in *The UK government's approach to public service reform* (Cabinet Office, 2006). At a practical level this double move of greater localism (and institutionalism) and greater centralism is intended to replace the administrative, bureaucratic and indeed democratic procedures of local government delivery of services with more responsive, innovative and adaptable forms of provision:

> The purpose of the reforms is to create a modern education system and a modern NHS where within levels of investment at last coming up to the average of our competitors, real power is put in the hands of those who use the service – the patient and the parent; where the changes becoming self-

sustaining; the system, open, diverse, flexible, able to adjust and adapt to the changing world. (Blair, 2005a)

The new infrastructure of policy and delivery is made up of competitive providers (including private sector contractors and 'partners', and philanthropists and voluntary organisations), and various 'lead' and 'linkage' organisations (Jessop, 2002) whose members are appointed rather than elected – an 'appointed state' (Skelcher, 1998). This is part of a shift from "the government of a unitary state to governance in and by networks" (Bevir and Rhodes, 2003, p 41). Again, a move away from structures. This is discussed and illustrated further below in relation to the Academies programme. However, running alongside these mechanisms of educational and governance reform is another aspect of New Labour, and another personal project of Tony Blair – a version of moral authoritarianism that couples the rights of citizens with their responsibilities, for example through the *Respect action plan* (Home Office, 2006):

> Social democratic thought was always the application of morality to political philosophy. One of the basic insights of the left, one of its distinguishing features, is to caution against too excessive an individualism. People must live together and one of the basic tasks of government is to facilitate this living together.... As Tawney once put it: 'what we have been witnessing ... is the breakdown of society on the basis of rights divorced from obligations'. (Blair, 2005b)

Education and Inspections Act 2006

The substantial point of policy continuity between 2005 and 2006 is the move from an education White Paper, *Higher standards, better schools for all* (DfES, 2005a), to the Education and Inspections Bill that passed into law in November 2006. The Bill received its Third Reading in the House of Commons on 24 May, at which time, despite various concessions, 46 Labour MPs voted against it – the biggest government rebellion since 1924. The *Daily Mail* (01/03/06) had already proclaimed 28 February, the day on which the concessions were announced, as "the day Blair lost power". Ruth Kelly, the Secretary of State for Education who led the Bill through the Commons, was perhaps a 'credibility' casualty of the in-fighting over the Bill and in May 2006 was replaced by Alan Johnson.

She moved on to become Secretary of State for Communities and Local Government and Minister for Women and Equality.

The 2006 Act contains 10 Parts, including one that gives Wales a framework power to make its own secondary legislation in a number of areas. Most of the provisions can be understood as being embedded in various trends and themes within the New Labour education project of schools reform and raising educational standards. In particular, they involve further moves and tactics in relation to the 'liberalisation' and deregulation of the school system, the introduction of a greater diversity of types of school and extending the range of participants in the delivery of education services with a concomitant redefinition of the role of local authorities. There are further elements of the moral and social agenda around parenting – parental choice and parents' responsibilities towards schools on behalf of their children (parenting contracts, reintegration interviews, fines) – and greater disciplinary powers for teachers (Saturday detentions, confiscations). Also included are new regulations for, and specification of, aspects of curriculum, inspections and school meals, and new powers to close 'failing schools'.

Not all of these provisions can be attended to here. Attention will be focused on four main aspects: trust schools (and their relationship to the Academies programme), the role of local authorities and *Fair Access* (that is, admissions to schools), parents and parenting and the school food provisions.

Trust schools and Academies

The trust schools provisions of the 2006 Act arguably mark (or could have marked) the end of the modern era of state school provision that stretches back at least as far as 1902. Modelled on the Academies programme (and to some extent a reinvention of the Conservative's grant-maintained schools, which Labour abolished and renamed foundation schools), and also drawing on and extending aspects of other previous policy moves by Labour (specialist schools, education action zones and federations), the trust school initiative was signalled in the 2005 education White Paper as the next move in the attempt to raise educational standards. It is also a good example of a third way policy and network governance: "catalyzing all sectors – public, private and voluntary – into action to solve their community's problems" (Osborne and Gaelber, 1992, p 20).

Outlining the rationale for trust schools, Ruth Kelly, Secretary of State for Education, explained:

Specialist schools have become a mass movement for higher standards, now outperforming non-specialists by 11 percentage points at GCSE. Attainment at academies, which have replaced failing schools, is rising at a much faster rate than in other schools. These schools and their pupils have benefited from greater autonomy, greater freedom, a strong individual ethos, and the involvement of community partners from business, charities and higher education institutions.... The time is right to move to the next level building on these achievements and enabling every school to adopt these benefits to raise standards. (DfES press release, 28/02/06)

Trust schools, as initially conceived in the 2005 White Paper, would have had unprecedented freedoms from central and local authority control in almost all areas of their functioning. Even now they will own their own assets, may contract or procure their own building projects and may be established by, or in the case of existing schools, may establish partnerships with, external groups. If the school chooses, those external partners will be able to appoint the majority of the governing body. Schools may join together to form a trust.

The Department for Education and Skills' (DfES) guide to the Act asserts that:

Schools work best when they tailor their curriculum to meet their pupils' needs and take responsibility for their own school improvement, working closely with other schools and external partners. The Act will empower schools by devolving as much decision-making to them as possible, while giving local authorities an enhanced strategic role as the champions of pupils and parents. We expect that many schools will acquire shared trusts that can foster and deepen collaboration and help to deliver improved children's services and a new offer for 14–19-year-olds. Trusts will also be able to apply for additional flexibilities which can be used by all the schools with which they are associated. (DfES, 2006)

There is no single blueprint for becoming a trust – schools can choose who they work with, in order to "best meet the needs of their pupils" (DfES press release, 23/02/06). In effect, through this mechanism a whole new range of players can become involved in the 'ownership' and running of state schools – private companies, charitable foundations, religious organisations, voluntary associations, local community groups or groups of parents. We will return to the role of local authorities in relation to trust schools and the related issue of school admissions shortly. According to the 2005 White Paper, partners would offer to trust schools "external support and a success culture, bringing innovative and stronger leadership to the school, improving standards and extending choice" (DfES, 2005a, pp 24-5). As indicated above, two key dynamics of New Labour's reforms come together here, as a means to raise standards and create 'a world class education system' (for example, Blair 1999): autonomy, flexibility and business-like innovation on the one hand, and consumer choice and the freedom to respond to parent 'demand' in terms of substance or scale on the other.

While these kinds of possibilities were signalled in earlier legislation, which, for instance, gave non-statutory organisations the right to 'bid' to establish new state schools, the major precedent and driver for this development is clearly the Academies programme, which was itself a continuing controversial policy and political issue during 2006. The programme builds on the Conservatives' City Technology Colleges (CTCs) initiative, which was informed by the development and experience of charter schools in the US (PriceWaterhouseCooper, 2005). The programme is expensive – the House of Commons Education and Skills Select Committee (2005) estimated a cost of £5 billion – but it is not very large; there was an initial target of 200 such schools by 2010, 60 of these in the London boroughs. In November 2006 Tony Blair announced that the target would be raised to 400. By the end of September 2006 46 Academies were open.

Academies are run by their sponsors on the basis of the terms of a funding agreement with the DfES. These agreements are negotiated separately in each case. The Academies are "publicly funded independent schools" (DfES, 2005a) outside of local education authority (LEA) control and relate directly to the DfES Academies Division. They have, as the 2005 White Paper describes it, "freedom to shape their own destiny in the interest of parents and children" (DfES, 2005a, p 24). Sponsors provide 10% of the capital costs (or now a 'cash' fund) up to a maximum of £2 million, although the actual costs are much more. The average cost of an academy is £25-£30 million (against a typical new school building cost of £20-£25 million). The most expensive, the Bexley Business Academy, sponsored by property developer and Labour Party financial backer David Garrard, cost £38 million. Sponsors may choose their own headteacher and staff and appoint the majority of governors. There is one LEA governor and one elected by parents. Addressing potential sponsors the DfES/Academy Sponsors Trust brochure states: "Issues of ethos, specialism and uniform are entirely for you" (DfES, 2005b, p 5). Schools are exempt from the specific requirements of the national curriculum but are subject to Ofsted inspections. They also have the opportunity to set aside existing national agreements on the pay, conditions and certification of teachers, that is to say, they can employ non-qualified teachers. These are significant moves in the 'flexibilisation' of the teaching workforce. This builds on a more general policy impetus for the 'modernisation' of the school workforce and 'workforce re-modelling'.

Academies also specialise; they are, in effect, specialist schools writ large (and by the end of 2006 over 80% of all secondary schools in England were specialist), with 'business and enterprise' being the most popular specialism. The Academies involve a self-conscious attempt to promote entrepreneurism and competitiveness – 'the enterprise narrative'. This involves, in some cases, both the curriculum content and an organisational orientation towards entrepreneurism – for example, in the commercial exploitation of innovations and in relationships with commercial companies.

Sponsors of Academies include 'philanthropic' individuals (for example, Eric Payne, Jack Petchey, John Aisbitt, Clive Bourne), companies (for example, Tarmac, HSBC, WBA), charities (for example, Grieg, EduAction, Absolute Return for Kids [ARK]), religious groups (for example, Church of England, Catholic Church, Oasis Trust), and some universities (for example, Brunel, Manchester, University of the West of England, Wolverhampton). The largest sponsor in terms of number of schools is the Church of England charity, the United Learning Trust. Many of the individual sponsors are what we might call 'hero entrepreneurs' who embody key values of New Labour: in particular, the possibilities of meritocracy, of achieving individual success from modest beginnings and wealth creation from innovative ideas and knowledge. These include Alex Reed (Reed Recruitment), Frank Lowe (Lowe Group, advertising agency), Roger de Haan (Saga Holidays) and Rod Aldridge (Capita). In effect, these are new policy agents, proselytisers for a new kind of capitalism and 'responsible capitalists', espousing new values and 'putting something back in the community'. Not all sponsors are Labour supporters (for example, Robert Edmiston, EIM, and Lord Harris of Peckham, Carpetright).

In many respects the programme stands as a condensate of New Labour education policies. Academies are an experiment in and a symbol of education policy beyond the welfare state and an example and indicator of the more general shifts taking place in governance and regulatory structures (the move from government to governance). In other words, the programme signals a discursive–strategic shift towards a new kind of regulatory regime. Academies indicate a re-articulation and re-scaling of the state, they are part of a new localism and a new centralism, bypassing local democratic structures. They encompass new kinds of autonomy and new forms of control, controlled-decontrol. They stand in an open relation to their communities and often provide community facilities of various kinds. Innovation, inclusion and regeneration are tied together in the rhetoric of the Academies and to some extent at least are realised in practice, focused on a commitment to address local social problems and inequalities and histories of 'under-achievement'. A National Foundation for Educational Reform (NFER) study (Chamberlain et al, 2006) published in 2006, based on the first 17 Academies, found they were more socially diverse, in terms of children receiving free school meals, than the make-up of the locality in which they were set, but admitted a lower proportion of children who achieved Level 4 in Key Stage 2 Maths tests (that is, they admitted fewer children performing below their expected level in national tests). Finally, in a variety of ways, they drastically blur the demarcations in welfare provision between state and market, public and private, government and business.

However, the programme has not gone smoothly or unopposed. At the local level several proposed Academies have been 'seen off' by groups of local parents and trades unions campaigns, including two in London proposed by ARK, a charity founded by hedge-fund millionaire Arpad Busson; one in Coniston put forward by Peter Vardy (Christian fundamentalist car dealer who has opened three other Academies in the North East of England); and another proposed by fashion designer Jasper Conran. Several Academy proposals, including those in Merton, Islington and the Isle of Sheppey, have been subject to a legal challenge coordinated by lawyers from Matrix, the human rights chambers (that includes Cherie Blair), on behalf of parents and at least one has gone to judicial review (*The Guardian*, 13/06/06).

Academies (and trust and specialist schools) are indicative generally of a 're-agenting' (Jones, 2003) of education policy through the creation of new policy networks and involving the legitimation of new voices within policy and in the processes of governance (see Ball, 2007). These new policy networks draw in and on the 'energies' of entrepreneurial and policy 'heroes' and social entrepreneurs, and mobilise business philanthropy in ways that are intended to avoid both bureaucratic and market difficulties in bringing about change. These new agents facilitate 'faster', less durable and often very personal policy action. Some of the participants in this constitute a philanthropic elite that is engaged with government, party and state in a numbers of ways as part of new policy networks[2]. The networks contain flows of influence as well as flows of people, and influence is carried back and forth across the boundaries between the public and private and voluntary sectors – resources are exchanged, interests are served and rewards achieved, trust is established and views and discourses are legitimated. They structure and constrain and enable the circulation of ideas and give 'institutional force' to policy utterances, ensuring what can count as policy and limiting the possibilities of policy – specifically in this case, as noted already, the 'enterprise narrative', a new hegemonic vision that inserts competition and entrepreneurialism into the heart of the project of state education. These actors are, in Jessop's terms, the bearers of a new accumulation strategy; he also notes their "increasing participation ... in shaping education mission statements" (Jessop, 2002, p 186).

Trusts and local authorities

The trust school proposals in the 2005 White Paper appeared to take directly aspects of the Academy model and apply them, at least as a set of possibilities, to the school system as a whole, making it possible for any school to become 'an independent state school', outside of the oversight of the local authority – in a way very similar to grant-maintained schools. This would have been a further and perhaps decisive move in a longer-term process of the residualisation of LEAs and the eradication of local democratic influence over the provision and quality of schools. In effect the White Paper proposed that all local authority schools would be Academies, voluntary-aided, foundation or trust schools. LEAs would work alongside a newly created national 'schools commissioner' to promote choice, diversity and better access for disadvantaged groups to good schools. Again this can be seen as part of a general shift taking place across the whole public sector from administrative 'government' to network 'governance', where the latter is accomplished through 'informal authority' rather than bureaucracy. As Jessop puts it, this is a move towards the "polycentric state" and "a shift in the centre of gravity around which policy cycles move" (Jessop, 1998, p 32).

However, for many Labour MPs (a figure of 90 was mentioned in press reports) the trust proposals in the 2005 White Paper and the Bill were a step too far in the reform of education. They were unwilling either to give up on the principle of comprehensive education entirely or to see the powers of LEAs diminished further. Or, as Mathew D'Ancona put it, writing in the *Daily Telegraph*, "The Labour malcontents want to extend town hall control even further, and protect what Mr Blair has called the 'deadening uniformity' of the comprehensive system" (*Daily Telegraph*, 01/03/06). There were at least two bases of opposition within the Labour Party that are represented in the principle of 'a national education system locally administered'. Opposition was to both the 'break-up' of a national system, and the eradication of democratic local control, although, as already noted, both effects had been begun and advanced by previous legislation and reform moves. As Troyna (1995) noted, in the mid-1990s the Conservatives' twin track approach to reform, centralisation and devolution, "coalesce[d] around ... the weakening, and ultimately dismantling, of LEA influence" (p 174). However, it was here that the main compromises were made and the authority of the Prime Minister was tested, and perhaps seriously damaged. At a monthly No 10 press conference Tony Blair described pushing through 'his' school reforms, and they were presented very much as his vision, in the face of backbench opposition, as "a high-wire act" (Blair, 2006). Despite the use of what were called 'bully boy' tactics, a core of opposition among Labour MPs remained, although the final version of the Bill reflected a series of "uneasy compromises", which reduced the numbers of "rebels" (*Guardian Unlimited*, 28/02/06). The Conservative Shadow Education Secretary accused the Prime Minister of appeasing "the Labour left" at the expense of children's education (*Guardian Unlimited*, 03/02/06).

Where the White Paper had offered trusts control over their own admissions and signalled a shift in the role of LEAs from responsibility for local schooling arrangements and providers to that of "champions" of higher standards and "commissioners of services", the compromise version of the Bill gave local authorities "strategic oversight" of local admissions procedures, strengthened the role of local admissions forums and required the trust schools to "act in accordance" with a new code of practice for admissions. As part of the compromise arrangements LEAs remained as the decision makers on issues like school expansion and new school establishment and were given new powers to intervene in 'coasting or failing' schools. Critics of the White Paper, including Deputy Prime Minister John Prescott, former Labour Leader Neil Kinnock and the House of Commons Education and Skills Select Committee, believed that safeguards of this kind were needed to avoid the creation of a 'two-tier system', with middle-class children monopolising popular schools. The House of Commons Education and Skills Select Committee report on the White Paper was also wary (the Conservative members published their own Minority report) and called for LEAs to have a "new vigorous role" monitoring admissions, a complete ban on interviewing and selection by 'aptitude' and 'benchmarks' for the recruitment of 'poor' children to all schools (House of Commons Education and Skills Select Committee, 2006). The chair of the Committee argued that: "if we are serious about delivering good education to all our kids, you've got to make sure that admissions are fair and you've got to pay attention to the social mix that goes into schools" (BBC Radio 4 *Today* programme, 27/01/06).

Despite the compromises, the Act remains a significant extension of the New Labour 'modernisation' and 'transformation' agenda, albeit in less radical forms than originally intended, but the principle and possibility of trust schools was established. Perhaps more important in the short term is the role that the 'uneasy compromises' and 'tight-rope walking' played in the Prime Minister's loss of authority and credibility within his own Party and the country at large.

Parents and parenting

The White Paper, Bill and Act also have interesting things to say about parents, which again build on and elaborate existing trajectories in New Labour's education and social policy. They do so in two different respects. The trust schools and other provisions of the Act give greater powers and new 'voice' to parents in relation to schools, although this was more the case before the compromises than after. Describing the provisions of the Bill the Labour Party website asserted that:

> Labour will give parents a real say in how schools are run ... and hold parents accountable for the behaviour of their children.... In our first two terms, Labour pushed higher standards from the centre: for those standards to be maintained and built upon, they must now become self-sustaining within schools, owned and driven by teachers and parents.... Parents will be able to set up new schools supported by a dedicated capital funding.... Parents will have access to better and clearer information about local schools, and dedicated advisers to help the least well-off parents to choose the best school.... Poorer families (on free school meals or maximum Working Families Tax Credit)

will have new rights to free school transport.... (Labour Party, 2006)

Here parents are offered new opportunities and responsibilities as consumers of education. In other provisions of the Act, on 'Parental responsibilities and excluded pupils', sections 97-9 extend the reach of parenting contracts and parents are given specific responsibility for the behaviour of children (Guidance notes on the 2006 Act, DfES website, www.dfes.gov.uk). Parents are also required to take responsibility for pupils excluded for more than three days and are subject to prosecution or penalty notices if excluded pupils are found in a public place during school hours without a reasonable excuse. This builds on existing regulations relating to truancy that have seen a small number of parents imprisoned, and relates to legislation on 'anti-social behaviour'. In New Labour policy discourses parents are key to the regeneration of social morality, and lack of parental discipline is linked to problems of truancy, anti-social behaviour, offending and obesity (see below). Alongside the legal procedures addressed to 'failing' parents, efforts have also been made to offer parents professional health and child-rearing help and support, particularly through Sure Start schemes and Parentline (a confidential telephone counselling service aimed at providing professional counselling and support for parents and all who have the care of children), but parents deemed in need can also be sanctioned to attend parenting education classes (Home Office, 2003). In earlier measures the Labour government also introduced home–school contracts, homework guidelines and after-school homework centres. More generally all of this can be traced back to New Labour's 'new moralism' agenda, or what McCaig (2001) calls "social authoritarianism" and the "remoralisation" of society by strengthening civil institutions like the family. This is also very much 'third way' practice, the 'proactive state' addressing itself to 'causes' rather than 'effects', prevention rather than 'repair'.

These different aspects of the Act, greater 'voice' and increased parental responsibility, articulate two very different forms of relation between citizen and state, the first a neoliberal or market relation (although this also has elements of the bolstering of civil society) and the other a disciplinary relationship of normalisation. In each case the family is individualised either as a 'site of consumption' or a 'site of failure'. This dualism of responsibilities is embodied in the family Blair and self-reference is a commonly used trope when Blair is speaking about education policy. As he explained in one of his monthly news conferences during the passage of the Bill:

> Whenever I look at education, I speak as a parent first and as a politician second. I know what I wanted for my own children, and that is what I expect other parents to want and our job should be to help them get it, not to stand in the way of them and say we know better than you do what's good for your child. (Blair, 2006)

The contradiction here between 'expecting' and 'knowing' is telling and in relation to the final issue for discussion, knowing 'better than you do what's good for your child' is exactly what the government is saying.

School meals

The provisions on school meals in the Education Act may seem at first sight to be among the least important of its contributions to education reform and yet in a variety of ways they are fascinating both as a policy phenomenon and as part of a more general extension of state powers over the management of the bodies of citizens, that is, what Foucault called 'bio-politics' – the use of political technologies of surveillance, analysis, intervention and correction (1979). In one respect, these provisions can be viewed as a 'success' for campaigning celebrity chef Jamie Oliver, who put the quality of school food on the political agenda in 2005 via his television series *Jamie's school dinners*:

> The nation gasped as cameras filmed classrooms of children who were addicted to chips and unable to recognise a leek, while the dinner ladies were monotonously opening packets of processed food rather than cooking nutritious food from fresh ingredients. (BBC, 2006)

The Act paved the way for new minimum food-based standards introduced in all schools by September 2006, which effectively banned low-quality foods high in fat, salt and sugar – crisps, chocolate, fizzy drinks and 'low-quality' meat. Children would be served at least two portions of fruit and vegetables with every meal and deep-fried foods like chips would be limited to twice a week. Funding for meals also increased from 37p per child to 50p per child in primary schools and 60p in secondaries. From September 2007 additional rules will limit what can be sold in school tuck-shops and vending machines as recommended by the School Meal Review Panel. Even more stringent nutrient-based standards, stipulating essential nutrients, vitamins and minerals, will follow from 2008. All of this is backed by £220 million of new funding (FSA, 2006). Local authorities will be allowed to offer all pupils free meals, fresh fruit, milk or other refreshments during the school day, regardless of family income, in a bid to encourage children to eat healthily in school, although also in 2006 Hull LEA announced that it would be abandoning its policy of free school meals for all children (Johnson, 2006). Nutritional standards for school meals were abandoned and eligibility for free school meals reduced in 1971 by the then Secretary of State for Education, Margaret Thatcher.

Again these provisions build on previous policy moves including the establishment of the National Healthy Schools programme in 1999, which aimed to "engage staff, pupils, governors, parents and the wider community in a whole school approach to educational achievement, health and emotional well-being" (teachernet, 2006), including addressing students' 'food choices'. The programme encouraged schools to develop action plans, targets and audits in relation to healthy eating. Furthermore, since 2005 healthy schools initiatives are evaluated and 'supported' in England through the work of Ofsted inspections that report on the contribution that every school makes to specified education and health 'outcomes'. Proposals have been discussed that would extend the remit of Ofsted inspections to include evaluation of schools' performances in relation to overall health targets, even possibly including reduction in the aggregate Body Mass Index scores of every school (John Evans, personal communication). The government has set itself the target of stopping the year-on-year rise in obesity among children under the age of 11 by 2010. Evans et al (2007: forthcoming) refer to such initiatives as 'body policies' and 'body pedagogies', that is "actions designed to foster particular corporeal orientations to one's own and others' bodies in time, place and space", defining not only what children should eat but also "what shape they should be and how much they should weigh". In Foucault's words, the regime of disciplinary power "measures in quantitative terms and hierarchizes individuals. It introduces, through this 'value-giving' measure, the constraint of a conformity that must be achieved. Lastly, it traces the limit that will define difference in relation to all other differences, the external frontier of the abnormal. ..." (1979, p 183).

In more general terms the school meals provisions can be seen as a response to a national moral panic about children's weight and the issue of obesity, what Rich and Evans (2005) call the "obesity discourse", which is, they argue, both moralising and normalising. As one of many headlines of its type in 2006, *The Guardian*, responding to an Organisation for Economic Co-operation and Development (OECD) report, reported, "Fears for the future as figures reveal Britons are fattest people in Europe" (*The Guardian*, 11/10/06, p 17). The article went on to assert that "Being overweight or obese is now the norm in the UK". The OECD report itself noted that in England "Levels of obesity in children aged two to 10 rose from 9.9% in 1995 to 14.3% in 2004. In 2003 22% of men and 23% of women were obese" (OECD, 2004). This is part of what Evans (2003, p 96) calls "a cacophony of alarmist literature", which draws on "simplified and sanitized research" that is recycled in official reports.

Conclusion

Education policy in 2006 and the 2006 Education and Inspections Act display a set of policy trends and policy increments, some of which are specific to New Labour and some that can be traced back to the Conservative education reforms begun in 1988. The marginalisation of LEAs and local administrative and democratic controls, the emphasis on parental power and parental choice and the introduction of a greater diversity of and autonomy for schools, trusts (modelled on grant-maintained schools) and Academies (modelled on CTCs), all take up where the Conservatives left off and indeed go much further. However, in contrast to the Conservatives, these policies are presented not as ideological or political commitments but rather as pragmatic strategies towards school improvement and raising educational standards, ultimately in the cause of international economic competitiveness. They are particular manifestations of the Labour government's 'approach' to public sector reform – to the modernisation and transformation of the public services as a whole (Cabinet Office, 2006). Nonetheless, in place of political ideology these policies are invested with and expressed through the personal project and commitments and very hands-on involvements of Prime Minister and model parent Tony Blair – "Every time I've introduced a reform in Government, I wish in retrospect I had gone further" (Blair, 2005c). Given the rebellions and compromises that surrounded the 2006 Act it might be said that this time Blair has gone too far; the full extent of the damage done to his personal standing and credibility remains to be seen. On the other hand, as previously, these policy moves may lay the groundwork for further, more radical changes in the future. Ideas that start out as radical or unthinkable are made possible and sensible, and then obvious and necessary through this incremental process and the attendant reiterations of the rhetorics of reform.

The New Labour policies, like the Academies programme and trust schools (and there are many other examples in other areas of education policy), are also indicative of more general shifts taking place in the modalities of the state. Shifts wherein governance is increasingly accomplished through the 'informal authority' of networks – 'independent' state schools and federations of schools, private sponsors, voluntary organisations – rather than through bureaucratic hierarchies or local democratic structures. The state is by no means becoming impotent, but "is now dependent upon a vast array of state and non-state policy actors" (Marinetto, 2003, p 599) to accomplish its ends. In the process new voices are given space within policy talk and the spaces of policy are diversified and dissociated. New narratives about what counts as a 'good' education are articulated and validated in these new spaces by these new voices. New 'linkage' devices that bridge between the state and private and voluntary sectors (like the Specialist Schools and Academies Trust) are being created, excluding or circumventing but not always obliterating more traditional sites and voices of government.

However, as is also clear in the education policies of 2006, the development of new modalities does not mean giving up older ones. The 2006 Act demonstrates the state exercising both bio-power, in the management of the health and diet of the bodies of the population, as further extension of the "entry of life into history", as Foucault put it, and its moral guardianship, in the disciplining of unsatisfactory parents through "a whole set of instruments, techniques, procedures, levels of application; targets" (Foucault, 1979, p 170).

Acknowledgements

I am very grateful to Karen Clarke, John Evans, Meg Maguire and Carol Vincent for their comments on drafts of the chapter.

Notes

[1] Blair's approach and commitment has been emulated by Chancellor Gordon Brown. In his 2006 pre-Budget report (06/12/06) Brown announced a spending and policy package that he said was part of a programme to make Britain "the most educated nation in the world" so that it could challenge the emerging powers of China and India.

Education was the top priority "now and into the future" (HM Treasury, 2006).

[2] Three Academy school sponsors, Townsley, Garrard and Aldridge, were also involved in making loans to the Labour Party and another, Robert Edmiston, to the Conservatives. In the ensuing 'cash for loans' scandal, Aldridge, chair of Capita plc, a major government contractor, resigned.

References

BBC (2006) 'Jamie's school dinners' (www.bbc.co.uk/food).

Ball, S.J. (2007) *Education plc: Understanding private sector participation in public sector education*, London: Routledge.

Bevir, M. and Rhodes, R.A.W. (2003) 'Searching for civil society: changing patterns of governance in Britain', *Public Administration*, vol 81, no 1, pp 41-62.

Blair, T. (1996) Speech to the Labour Party Annual Conference, September.

Blair, T. (1999) Speech to the National Association of Headteachers, June.

Blair, T. (2005a) Monthly press conference, No 10 Downing Street, October.

Blair, T. (2005b) 'Our citizens should not live in fear', *The Observer*, 11 December.

Blair, T. (2005c) Speech to the Labour Party Annual Conference, September.

Blair, T. (2006) Monthly press conference, No 10 Downing Street, January.

Cabinet Office (2006) *The UK government's approach to public service reform*, London: Prime Minister's Strategy Unit, Public Service Reform Team.

Chamberlain, T., Rutt, S. and Fletcher-Campbell, F. (2006) *Admissions: Who goes where? Messages from the statistics*, Slough: NFER.

DfES (Department for Education and Skills) (2005a) *Higher standards, better schools for all: More choice for parents and pupils*, Cm 6677, London: The Stationery Office.

DfES (2005b) *Academy sponsors prospectus*, London: DfES.

DfES (2006) *Education and Inspections Act*, London: The Stationery Office.

Dyson, A., Kerr, K. and Ainscow, M. (2006) 'A "pivotal moment"? Education policy in England, 2005', in L. Bauld, K. Clarke and T. Maltby (eds) *Social Policy Review 18: Analysis and debate in social policy*, Bristol: The Policy Press, pp 49-64.

Evans, J. (2003) 'Physical education and health: apolemic or "let them eat cake!"', *European Physical Education Review*, vol 9, no 1, pp 87-101.

Evans, J., Rich, E., Alwood, R. and Davies, B. (2007: forthcoming) 'Body pedagogies, p/policy, health and gender', *British Educational Research Journal*.

Foucault, M. (1979) *Discipline and punish*, Harmondsworth: Penguin.

FSA (Food Standards Agency) (2006) *Putting the consumer first: Annual report to Parliament 2005/2006*, London: FSA.

HM Treasury (2006) *Pre-budget report statement to the House of Commons, delivered by the Rt Hon Gordon Brown MP, Chancellor of the Exchequer*, Treasury website (www.hm-treasury.gov.uk).

Home Office (2003) *Respect and responsibility: Taking a stand against anti-social behaviour*, London: The Stationery Office.

Home Office (2006) *Respect action plan*, London: Home Office.

House of Commons Education and Skills Select Committee (2005) *First report*, London: House of Commons.

Jessop, B. (1998) 'The rise of governance and the risks of failure', *International Social Science Journal*, vol 50, no 155, pp 29-45.

Jessop, B. (2002) *The future of the capitalist state*, Cambridge: Polity.

Johnson, D. (2006) (www.dianajohnson.labour.co.uk).

Jones, K. (2003) *Education in Britain: 1944 to the present*, Cambridge: Polity Press.

Labour Party (1997) *Election manifesto: New Labour because Britain deserves better*, London: Labour Party.

Labour Party (2006) White Paper briefing, London: Labour Party.

McCaig, C. (2001) 'New Labour and education, education, education', in S. Ludlam and M.J. Smith (eds) *New Labour in government*, Basingstoke: Macmillan.

Marinetto, M. (2003) 'Governing beyond the centre: a critique of the Anglo-governance school', *Political Studies*, vol 51, no 3, pp 592-608.

OECD (Organisation for Economic Co-operation and Development) (2004) *Health report*, Paris: OECD.

Osborne, D. and Gaebler, T. (1992) *Re-inventing government*, Reading, MA: Addison-Wesley.

PriceWaterhouseCooper (2005) *Academies evaluation: Second annual report*, London: DfES.

Rich, E. and Evans, J. (2005) 'Fat ethics – the obesity discourse', *Social Theory and Health*, vol 3, no 4, pp 341-58.

Skelcher, C. (1998) *The appointed state*, Buckingham: Open University Press.

teachernet (2006) 'What is emotional health and well-being' (www.wiredforhealth.gov.uk).

Troyna, B. (1995) 'The local management of schools and racial equality', in S. Tomlinson and M. Craft (eds) *Ethnic relations and schooling*, London: Athlone.

TWO

One, or four? The National Health Service in 2006

Stephen Peckham

Introduction

Since the early part of the 20th century there has been a continuing debate in the UK about the nature of a national health service. The establishment of the NHS in 1948 did little to end this debate that has continued over the past 60 years. The NHS was itself a compromise of interests – both political and medical – and discussion has repeatedly returned to whether the NHS should be a local or centralised service, what relationship it should have with local government, whether doctors, managers or politicians should run the service, whether it is affordable as a tax-funded service and so on. These debates remain as potent today as they were in 1948 and while it is unlikely that such debates will go away in the future it is perhaps a good time to examine the nature of the NHS 10 years after the election of the Labour government that has introduced political devolution, and towards the end of a three-year period when there has been substantial investment in NHS resources.

In 2006 the Welsh Assembly received devolved authority, providing the potential for wresting policy control of the Welsh NHS from Westminster and highlighting the increasing importance of political devolution in the UK. In addition, 2006 saw calls from the Conservative Party for an 'independent NHS' and from within the Labour Party for an independent NHS board and constitution. Health policy in England emphasised developing the role of the private and not-for-profit sectors in healthcare and further embedding a healthcare market, and so highlighted continuing debates about autonomy for, and within, the NHS. Yet, at the same time, in Northern Ireland, Scotland and Wales the emphasis has been on partnerships, professional engagement and central planning – often to overcome fragmentation and improve integration. Contributions to *Social Policy Review* over the past two years by Rudolf Klein (2005) and Ruth McDonald (2006) highlighted the development of patient choice and marketisation of healthcare. Developments through 2006 suggest that these are continuing themes, certainly within the English healthcare system. Recently there has also been an increasing concern with the relationship between the NHS and patients, service users and carers with an emphasis on self care and the role of health systems and the professionals who work within them in supporting self care (Kerr, 2005; DH, 2006a). This raises important questions about the nature and role of health systems and, in the UK context, questions about the poor performance of traditional managed and personal care services at a primary and community care level. Finally, despite generous increases in NHS resources, the dominant topic on the political agenda has been finance. Since the last few months of 2005 the media have been reporting problems of deficits. The English NHS reported a huge increase in year-end deficits in 2006 and this financial situation is thought to have contributed to the exit of Sir Nigel Crisp as Chief Executive of the NHS in March 2006. Although attention has been focused primarily on England, there has also been concern in Wales that the NHS is slipping deeper into the red. Recent proposals in Scotland for service reconfiguration also highlight the fact that despite being in overall balance there is a need to achieve significant system change to maintain affordability. While the focus has been on NHS deficits there has also been attention to why funding is not available for new drugs such as Herceptin® and Aricept®, renewing debates about the postcode lottery and NHS funding in England and Wales.

So what does all this mean for the NHS? In fact what is the NHS in 2006, and can we meaningfully talk about a *national* health service? Undoubtedly there are common problems faced by all healthcare systems and therefore shared across the UK's four health services but increasingly there appears to be variation in the solutions, especially between England and the other home countries. The clear direction of English policy towards market-based solutions sets it apart from the other systems where, despite the continuing purchaser–provider split, there is more emphasis on central planning, organisational partnerships and professional engagement. Other important differences are appearing, including the imminent abolition of prescription charges in Wales (already at levels well below charges in England) and the provision of free long-term care in Scotland. Yet the political reluctance to shed central controls remains a feature of the devolved NHS. In England, responses to tackling NHS deficits and ensuring financial balance have led to increased central intervention in NHS trusts (including job cuts) and primary care trusts (PCTs) (where mergers have been imposed) with an acknowledgement that more central control may be required in future. In Scotland and Wales, the response to concerns about poor performance has been the imposition of more central targets and performance criteria (SEHD, 2005; WAG, 2005).

It is true to say that the NHS has always embodied both diversity and uniformity. Nationally the pressures for uniformity appear strong as the health service is financed from general taxation and provides reasonably equitable access to hospital-based and primary care services. Yet the NHS can also be seen as a series of *local* health services, rather than a single *national* one, or more correctly, four national health services (Mohan, 1995; Greer, 2005). The pressures encouraging diversity include the forces for political devolution, with four separate foci for health policy development reflecting territorial cultures and traditions, different implementation processes, different governance structures and the restructuring of the state in the light of broader pressures (Greer, 2005). This diversity may provide locally contingent services and local horizontal integration but it may also result in inequality (such as the recent resurgence of concerns about the postcode lottery and drug availability) and fragmentation (Peckham and Exworthy, 2003; Peckham et al, 2005a). Despite this diversity, there still remain strong political and institutional forces that provide limits to local policy innovation across the UK (Greer, 2005). Factors tending to maintain uniformity across the UK include historical commitments, pressure group activity from professional bodies (for example, the British Medical Association and trades unions), UK-wide agreements such as on pay, terms and conditions, and regulatory processes including clinical audit, assessment of healthcare interventions and effectiveness guidance – from the National Institute for Health and Clinical Excellence (NICE) (for England and Wales) and NHS Quality Improvement Scotland (Greer, 2005). There are clearly simultaneous movements of decentralisation and centralisation occurring at any time within the NHS and, while some aspects of the NHS are decentralised, others remain centralised (Peckham et al, 2005a, 2005b).

Another key area of debate has been the nature of the relationship between the NHS and patients and the public, the delivery of quality health services and the promotion of health. There are important differences between the different NHS systems and between different stakeholder groups in how patient and public engagement has been addressed. Is quality of care improved through patient choice as in England, through greater patient and public involvement as in Wales, or through greater professional engagement as in Scotland? Questions about what is meant by quality and who should define quality are highly pertinent to current policy development. Will the roll-out of practice-based commissioning (PbC) improve patient care? What is the role of government in public health and what is the balance between central initiatives to protect and promote health and individual responsibility?

Four aspects of health policy during 2006 will be examined. These are: the continuing preoccupation with structural reform; the emphasis on the individual in relation to self care and patient choice; and two key changes in primary care: the developing system of quality targets in the General Medical Services (GMS) contract and the roll-out of PbC in England.

Structural change

Organisational change continues to be a prime health policy activity throughout the UK. Comparison between England, Scotland and Wales provides an interesting insight into whether small or large solutions are best for providing healthcare services. In England the fitness for purpose review has led to a reduction in the number of strategic health authorities (SHAs) and PCTs (DH, 2005a). The introduction of SHAs was always thought to be a stepping-stone to fewer, larger authorities and this consolidation finally occurred in 2006. The reduction in the number of PCTs was also widely anticipated for a number of years, completing a consolidation of commissioning that started with the move from primary care groups (PCGs) to PCTs between 2000 and 2003. The key argument is that small commissioners were failing and lacked the skills and resources to commission effectively. Concerns about the quality and strength of PCT commissioning have also been highlighted given the accelerated expansion of foundation trust status to all NHS trusts in the next few years and the introduction of payment by results. The changes that these developments will bring to NHS contracts and financial flows (especially coupled with patient choice) present enormous challenges to healthcare commissioners. There are now half the number of PCTs (152) and there has been some rationalisation of boundaries to bring greater coterminosity between social services departments and PCTs. However, it is hard to see any clear rationale for the changes across the country. The smallest PCT (Hartlepool) has a population of 90,000 while the largest (Hampshire) has a population of 1.2 million.

Concerns about size and capacity have also been of concern in Wales and this has resulted in the amalgamation of the activities of the 22 local health boards into three regions (resembling the old health authority boundaries) in order to develop commissioning capacity in the wake of poor performance reports and financial problems (Audit Commission in Wales, 2004; Healthcare Commission, 2005; WAG, 2005). While the proposed regions are an attempt to create better service integration and avoid fragmentation in Wales, the response to similar concerns in Scotland has resulted in changes at a more local level. The NHS in Scotland has just completed development of a more formal localised structure with the establishment of community health partnerships – bringing together community healthcare service providers and coordinating a wide range of primary medical and community health resources – to provide the delivery and planning of health services at a local level (SEHD, 2005). Greater integration and reduction of fragmentation are cornerstones of Welsh and Scottish health policy across both commissioning and provision. This is at odds with England, where the need for larger commissioning organisations is developing alongside a greater fragmentation of healthcare provision with an emphasis on greater provider plurality and patient choice (DH, 2006a).

Focusing attention on the individual

Apart from finance, two themes have dominated the NHS in 2006. Patient choice reflects an increasing emphasis on choice and consumerism in public services while self care highlights individual responsibility and limits to the role of public services in the maintenance of health and well-being. The choice and self care agendas appear, in England, to be separate from changes to the structures and processes for patient and public engagement while in Wales and Scotland the development of patient and public involvement seems to be central to these areas (SEHD, 2005; WAG, 2005). The self care agenda focuses on the contribution of patients (and their carers) to their own health and well-being. Essentially this means individuals taking responsibility for staying fit and maintaining good physical and mental health; meeting social, emotional and psychological needs; preventing illness or accidents; caring for minor ailments and long-term conditions; and maintaining health and well-being after an acute illness or discharge from hospital.

In England *Our health, our care, our say* (DH, 2006a) stressed the importance of self care and the support role of the NHS; this built on the earlier *Choosing health*, which introduced health trainers and placed a greater emphasis on individual skills for preventing ill health (DH, 2004) while the Green Paper on adult social services, *Independence, well-*

being and choice, highlighted the need to support people with long-term conditions to manage independently (DH, 2005b) (for further discussion of policy in this area, see Chapter Four by Kirstein Rummery, this volume). In Scotland and Wales current plans for service development also emphasise the need for NHS organisations to improve support for patients with long-term conditions as well as supporting their carers (Audit Commission in Wales, 2004; NHS Scotland, 2005).

In England, over 50% of the population have some form of chronic health problem. They are intensive users of health services and it is estimated that as many as 40% of general practice consultations and 70% of Accident & Emergency (A&E) visits are for minor ailments that could be taken care of by people themselves, while 10% of inpatients account for 55% of inpatient days (DH, 2005c). The benefits of supporting self care have been shown to be improved health outcomes, a better quality of life for those with long-term conditions, increased patient satisfaction and effective use of what is an enormous healthcare resource – patients and the public (DH, 2005c). However, to date the NHS has not been particularly good at supporting this process and it will be interesting to see whether a shift to self care creates further problems for patients and their carers if responsibility for self care is pursued by the NHS without providing appropriate support, especially for more vulnerable groups such as older people (DH, 2005d; Ellins and Coulter, 2005; Coulter, 2006).

As explored in previous Social Policy Reviews, patient choice is a common theme in UK health policy in all four countries and is represented as part of the consumerist project of New Labour, reflecting a wider emphasis on choice in public services (Clarke et al, 2005; Fotaki et al, 2005; McDonald, 2006). Choice in public services is central to Labour's modernisation agenda. It is seen as a means to achieving a number of objectives: to meet individual needs with more responsive services; challenge the power of professionals; drive quality improvements and improve equity; as well as being a good thing in its own right (DH, 2003, 2006a; Newman and Vidler, 2006). The rhetoric of choice is about giving patients more control and shifting decisions about care from the NHS and professionals. In this sense it represents a decentralist shift within health policy (Peckham et al, 2005b). Patient choice raises important questions about the way healthcare is accessed, delivered and experienced and needs to be seen within a web of factors that influence access to, and the use of, healthcare services in order to see whether there has been a real increase in patient autonomy or control (Exworthy and Peckham, 2006).

Policy on choice differs between England, Northern Ireland, Scotland and Wales reflecting differences in the ideological underpinning of how choices are constructed. For example, in England the emphasis is on consumerism and the use of choice as a driver for improving quality and efficiency alongside other supply-side developments to create contestability, such as payment by results and private sector treatment. This approach to patient choice is also seen to provide patients with opportunities for 'exit' in addition to policies that have emphasised 'voice' (Hirschmann, 1970). In England, patient choice is based on the belief that giving patients appropriate information on service providers will achieve greater responsiveness to patient needs, will increase technical and allocative efficiency, enhance quality of services and, most contentious of all, improve equity (Fotaki et al, 2005). Together with payment by results and PbC, patient choice aims to introduce a market-type competitive environment in healthcare provision that will drive health service improvements. Elements of choice already exist within the English NHS with NHS Direct and walk-in centres providing alternative access points to primary care. Current policies for increasing the range and type of providers (such as private and voluntary hospitals and GP specialists) and offering patients additional choices of access (for example, self-referral to physiotherapists) will, however, create a more fragmented health system within which choices are made (DH, 2006b; Exworthy and Peckham, 2006).

Governments in Northern Ireland, Wales and Scotland have not been so determined to widen choices of service providers and have tended not to be in favour of introducing a consumer market approach. The focus has been more on the demand-side in less overtly competitive environments but, particularly in Wales, with an increasing emphasis on patient and public 'voice' (Audit Commission in Wales, 2004; Fotaki et al, 2005; Healthcare Commission, 2005). In Wales the NHS Plan identified the need to develop health services that comply with patient preferences and there is now a second offer scheme where patients can be offered a second choice of treatment and/or location if they have waited for more than the national waiting time targets. The Welsh choice scheme is centrally driven and is specifically aimed at reducing waiting times following criticism about the poor performance of the Welsh healthcare system (Wanless, 2003; Audit Commission in Wales, 2004). In addition, the emphasis in the Welsh government's strategy is to "... empower the community to have its voice heard and heeded, rather than simply being given a choice of treatment location" (WAG, 2005, p 14). The Welsh Assembly has thus invested in patient and public involvement by creating a network across the country and establishing a central support service to develop patient and public engagement in service development and planning. In Scotland, the NHS Plan also stressed the need to be responsive to patients' views. The emphasis here has been on providing information on the quality of provider services (including the development of clinical performance indicators) so that clinical choices are made in consultation with patients (NHS Scotland, 2000). Patient choice of secondary provider is now facilitated by the National Waiting Times Database, which provides service users and their GPs with information to support GP referral decisions. In addition, the recent introduction of GP specialists and the establishment of the referral information service have increased the availability of alternative routes to treatment and information aimed at increasing patient choice (NHS Scotland, 2005). Finally, in Northern Ireland the opportunity for choice is more limited given the size of the health system. The recent proposal to introduce a second offer scheme (similar to Wales) has been welcomed and a recent review of health and social care services recommends further expansion of choice for specific treatments and specialties (Appleby, 2005). The Northern Ireland scheme will, as in the Welsh scheme, be centrally driven, providing location of treatment choice only for patients waiting nine months or more for hip and knee operations and six months for cardiac and cataract operations.

Current policies reflect an optimism that choice will yield a range of health service and patient benefits including improved performance (and faster treatment) through competition (England), reduction of waiting times (Wales and Northern Ireland) or better clinical outcomes for patients (Scotland), as well as an assumption that choice is a good thing in its own right and thus an important indicator of health services quality. Studies of patient choice in the English and London choice pilots found that the majority of people opted for a different provider rather than wait (Coulter et al, 2004; Burge et al, 2005). Operation of the Welsh second offer scheme also suggests that patients are willing to choose different treatments and providers rather than wait for treatment (Audit Commission in Wales, 2004). However, these studies show limitations to choice depending on sociodemographic characteristics and in relation to geographical location (Fotaki et al, 2005; Exworthy and Peckham, 2006). There is some evidence to support the view that patients benefit from being involved in treatment decisions and from the provision of information on treatment options, but there is also evidence to suggest that it is not necessarily the offering of a choice per se that generates the benefit (Fotaki et al, 2005). However, attempts to increase the extent to which patients are offered treatment choices may have negative as well as positive effects, especially if there is a lack of information for patients to base decisions on, if patients feel inadequately supported by health professionals, receive conflicting advice from different healthcare professionals or are distressed by the responsibility of being asked to make choices for themselves (Entwistle et al, 1998; Healthcare Commission, 2005). Results from a Department of Health survey in May 2006 also found that only 30% of patients recall being offered a choice of hospital for their first outpatient appointment (DH, 2006b). Such limited treatment choices and actual provision of choice suggest that there is less real patient choice and autonomy than is suggested by the policy rhetoric.

Changing role of primary care: tensions between autonomy and control?

The need to develop a stronger public health approach in primary care has long been recognised but activity has been slow despite changes to GP contracts in 1990 and despite public health being a key objective of primary care organisations from the mid-1990s (Peckham and Exworthy, 2003). One important aspect of the new GP contract introduced in April 2005 has been the Quality and Outcomes Framework (QOF). This has received relatively little general media coverage, although its operation has caused headlines in medical circles and a high degree of congratulatory medical press coverage. QOF has been described as offering a unique experiment in the use of incentives to reward quality, providing financial rewards to general practices based on a points system of over 150 quality indicators covering clinical, organisational and patient-focused aspects of practice (Smith and York, 2004).

While it is still too early to identify the full impact of the new contract, two aspects of QOF are of wider policy interest. The first is the use of financial targets to change GPs' clinical behaviour and the second is the unintended impacts of target systems on practice. There is some indication that both these factors are likely to be of increasing importance in the development of primary care services. Previous research examining the relationship between financial incentives and public health, following the introduction of new GP contract in 1990, found that financial reward for practices bore no relation to local need (Langham et al, 1995). Recent research in Scotland found that there are small inequalities between practices in the provision of simple monitoring interventions (for example, blood pressure, asthma checks), but larger inequalities for diagnostic, outcome and treatment measures, with poorer areas being more disadvantaged (McClean et al, 2006). In addition QOF may skew practice to labour-intensive interventions rather than interventions with greater potential for health gain (Fleetcroft and Cookson, 2006). Early analysis of QOF also suggests there is a correlation between exception reporting (the exclusion of patients from reported figures) and social deprivation indices (Galvin, 2006; Sigfrid et al, 2006). So even if practices in deprived populations are performing above average on public health indicators within QOF, if exclusion rates are higher, this may reduce the impact on reductions in health inequalities.

Studies have also found that financial reward is not necessarily the main incentive for practitioners to engage in quality improvement and, while targets clearly deliver changes in behaviour, they may also lead to goal misplacement in which rule following becomes an end in itself, rather than the means to an end (Harrison and Smith, 2004; Marshall and Harrison, 2005). While progress on improving clinical care in general practice has been substantial there are still gaps, with a wide variation in the quality of care for different patients (Seddon et al, 2001). There have been major successes in areas where targets have been set or additional resources have been provided but there are already concerns about the processes being developed to manage QOF and whether some non-targeted areas of practice are being ignored (Campbell et al, 2005). There is emerging evidence, however, that the use of the QOF is changing relationships in practices, with responses to the QOF being seen by those professionals affected as primarily a technical problem requiring attention to the design of information systems in order to rationalise practice and collect the relevant data, rather than being seen as the basis for guiding clinical practice (Checkland, 2006). What impact this will have on the quality of care is not clear at the present time but despite these concerns the QOF process should lead to improvements in clinical care as it provides targets associated with additional funding.

The increasing numbers of practitioners dealing with the care of an individual patient as a result of meeting the 24- or 48-hour targets for GP appointments raises questions about continuity of care and clinical quality, since the risk of error increases as more practitioners are involved in a patient's care (Blendon et al, 2002). As with many performance systems, the evidence of two years' data suggests that practices will prioritise maximising their performance against targets. These continue to be centrally negotiated and include an expanded range of clinical areas and more emphasis on health promotion activities. Discussions are under way between the British Medical Association (negotiating on behalf of

GPs) and the Department of Health on focusing QOF more on self care support and interventions to reduce demand in primary care.

The other major innovation, although some may see this as a further adaptation of primary care purchasing introduced in the 1990s through fundholding and total purchasing, is the introduction of practice-based or practice-led commissioning in England as an important component of NHS modernisation. The purpose of PbC is to achieve better patient care, make financial savings and reconfigure services by shifting investment to primary care. Since April 2005, all practices in England have been able to hold an indicative budget that covers their commissioning activity and, progressively, practices are allowed to take control over the commissioning of services starting with elective surgery and outpatient appointments but eventually covering a large element of all commissioned healthcare. Success will be dependent on practices being appropriately resourced, having the right level and mix of skills in practices (technical and clinical), having good healthcare professional support and engaging clinicians in the commissioning process (Smith et al, 2004). Certainly the fact that PbC is in reality a mandatory approach (although technically voluntary) means that practices must have a different attitude to PbC and the government expects all practices to engage in PbC at some level by the end of 2006. How far PbC will deliver practice autonomy is also in doubt as it is likely that PbC will operate within practice networks as well as within the overall strategic framework of the PCT and the NHS, introducing new tensions between the different levels of the NHS but also introducing a key distinction between England and the rest of the UK.

General practice in the UK also faces a number of other challenges and changes resulting from changes in the workforce, greater pressure to apply evidence-based medicine and treatment protocols and meet centrally set targets. It is into this complex context that the new contract has been introduced. These challenges are not unrecognised by the profession and the need for general practice to respond to social change was the topic of a Royal College of General Practitioners working group on the future of general practice (Wilson et al, 2006).

Conclusion

In the national media the tendency is always to focus on England and the dominance of privatisation, patient choice, the postcode lottery and the private finance initiative (PFI) despite the rapidly changing context of a devolved health system in the UK. Alongside devolution, decentralisation remains a key feature of UK health systems and UK health policy although, as identified above, the degree of decentralisation varies and there are still strong pressures for centralisation, especially around target setting (Peckham et al, 2005a). David Nicholson, the new Chief Executive of NHS England, has announced greater decentralisation of NHS resources and fewer central targets. How far this will really localise decision making is not as yet clear given continuing budgetary concerns and a focus on targets such as the 'Selbie 6' (named after Duncan Selbie, the Department of Health's Director of Programmes and Performance) identified in the current 2006/07 operating priorities for the NHS: (i) health inequalities (especially smoking); (ii) cancer 31- and 62-day waits; (iii) MRSA (methicillin-resistant staphylococcus aureus) rates; (iv) 18-week waits from referral to treatment; (v) implementing choose and book; and (vi) improving access to GUM (genito-urinary medicine) clinics. In Scotland the impact of the Kerr Report (Kerr, 2005) on reorganisation is moving slowly ahead and represents a continuation of the tradition of a centrally planned NHS economy while central control in Wales appears to be driven by concerns that local management is under-performing and unable to deliver patient services.

Interestingly politicians of all persuasions were not slow in the autumn of 2006 to put forward their solutions for the problems in the NHS – all championing greater freedom for the NHS, although it was not clear whether their comments reflected concern with the English system or the NHS in each of the four countries. Andy Burnham (Minister of State for Health in England) put forward a proposal for an NHS constitution rather like that of the BBC charter (Burnham, 2006). This is not a new idea as it surfaced a number of years ago in the Association of Community Health Councils in England and Wales' report on the NHS chaired by Will Hutton (Hutton, 2000). At the same time Gordon Brown called for an independent NHS board to remove decisions from the political arena (*The Guardian*, 25/09/2006), while the Conservatives argued for a fully independent NHS (*The Guardian*, 9/10/2006). However, during the 1990s the separation of the policy and delivery sections of the Department of Health led to the establishment of the NHS Executive with an NHS board of management – a structure reorganised by the current government to bring greater policy control back to the Department of Health. One further interesting development also emerged from the Health Services Management Centre in Birmingham, where it has been suggested that healthcare commissioning should be taken over by local government (Glasby et al, 2006), a variation on a long-standing debate about whether local authorities should deliver healthcare, echoing arguments in the 1940s between Morrison and Bevan.

While the NHS remains funded from central taxation it is difficult to see how central government cannot be involved in the health service. Recent discussion of higher NHS spending per head in Scotland (due to the Barnett formula) may in fact add another dimension to the health policy debate across the UK with pressures for greater devolution and independence, as politicians in Wales look at this 'generous' settlement (Christie and Swales, 2005). The discussion in this chapter demonstrates that while political and organisational structures change, the NHS remains embroiled in the same kinds of debates as it did in the 1940s, and is likely to remain so. Devolution has not only added an extra layer to the debates but has also provided the basis for a natural experiment in UK health policy.

References

Appleby, J. (2005) *Independent review of health and social care services in Northern Ireland*, Report to the Northern Ireland Office. Belfast: Department of Health for Northern Ireland.

Audit Commission in Wales (2004) *Transforming health and social care in Wales*, Cardiff: Audit Commission in Wales.

Blendon, R.J., Schoen, C., DesRoches, C., Osborn, R. and Zapert, K. (2002) 'Common concerns amid diverse systems: health care experiences in five countries', *Health Affairs*, vol 22, no 3, pp 106-21.

Burge, P., Devlin, N. and Appleby, J. (2005) *London Patient Choice project evaluation: A model of patients' choices of hospital from stated and revealed preference choice data*, London: Rand Europe/King's Fund/City University.

Burnham, A. (2006) 'A health constitutional', *Progress*, September (http://progressonline.org.uk/Magazine/article.asp?a=1399).

Campbell, S., Roland, M., Middleton, E. and Reeves, D. (2005) 'Improvements in quality of clinical care in English general practice 1998-2003: longitudinal observational study', *British Medical Journal*, vol 331, p 1121.

Checkland, K. (2006) 'Collecting data or shaping practice? Evidence from case studies in general practice about the impact of technology associated with the new GMS contract', PSA Annual Health Group Conference, Oxford, September.

Christie, A. and Swales, J.K. (2005) *The Barnett allocation mechanism: Formula plus influence?*, Glasgow: Centre for Public Policy for Regions.

Clarke, J., Smith, N. and Vidler, E. (2005) 'Consumerism and the reform of public services: inequalities and instabilities', in M. Powell, L. Bauld and K. Clarke (eds) *Social Policy Review 17*, Bristol: The Policy Press/ Social Policy Association, pp 167–82.

Coulter, A. (2006) *Engaging patients in their healthcare*, Oxford: Picker Institute Europe.

Coulter, A., Henderson, L. and Le Maistre, N. (2004) *Hospital choices: Patients' experience of the London Patient Choice project*, Oxford: Picker Institute Europe.

DH (Department of Health) (2003) *Building on the best: Choice, responsiveness and equity in the NHS*, London: DH.

DH (2004) *Choosing health: Making healthy choices easier*, Cm 6374, London: The Stationery Office.

DH (2005a) *Commissioning a patient-led NHS: Developing the NHS Improvement Plan*, London: DH.

DH (2005b) *Independence, well-being and choice: Our vision for the future of social care for adults in England*, Cm 6499, London: The Stationery Office.

DH (2005c) *Self care – A real choice: Self care support – A practical option*, London: DH.

DH (2005d) *Public attitudes to self care – Baseline Survey*, London: DH, February.

DH (2006a) *Our health, our care, our say: A new direction for community services*, Cm 6737, London: The Stationery Office.

DH (2006b) *Report on the results of the Patient Choice Survey, England – May/June 2006 and headline figures for July 2006*, London: DH.

Ellins, J. and Coulter, A. (2005) *How engaged are people in their health care? Findings of a national telephone survey*, London: The Health Foundation.

Entwistle, V.A., Sheldon, T.A., Sowden, A.J. and Watt, I.S. (1998) 'Evidence informed patient choice: practical issues of involving patients in decisions about health care technologies', *International Journal of Technology Assessment in Health Care*, vol 14, pp 212–25.

Exworthy, M. and Peckham, S. (2006) 'Access, choice and travel: implications for health policy', *Social Policy and Administration*, vol 40, no 3, pp 267–87.

Fleetcroft, R. and Cookson, R. (2006) 'Do incentive payments in the new NHS contract for primary care reflect likely population health gains?', *Journal of Health Services Research and Policy*, vol 11, no 1, pp 27–31.

Fotaki, M., Boyd, A., Smith, L., McDonald, R., Roland, M., Sheaff, R., Edwards, A. and Elwyn, G. (2005) *Patient choice and the organisation and delivery of health services: Scoping review*, Manchester: University of Manchester.

Galvin, R. (2006) 'Pay-for-performance: too much of a good thing? A conversation with Martin Roland', *Health Affairs*, vol 25, pp 412-19.

Glasby, J., Smith, J. and Dickinson, H. (2006) *Creating NHS Local: A new relationship between PCTs and local government*, Birmingham: Health Services Management Centre, University of Birmingham.

Greer, S. (2005) *Territorial politics and health policy: UK health policy in comparative perspective*, Manchester: Manchester University Press.

Harrison, S. and Smith, C. (2004) 'Trust and moral motivation; redundant resources in health and social care?', *Policy & Politics*, vol 32, no 3, pp 371-86.

Healthcare Commission (2005) *State of healthcare 2005*, London: Healthcare Commission.

Hirschmann, A. (1970) *Exit, voice and loyalty*, Cambridge, MA: Harvard University Press.

Hutton, W. (2000) *New life for health: The Commission on the NHS*, London: Virgin Books.

Kerr, D. (2005) *Building a health service fit for the future*, Edinburgh: Scottish Executive.

Klein, R. (2005) 'Transforming the NHS: the story in 2004', in M. Powell, L. Bauld and K. Clarke (eds) *Social Policy Review 17*, Bristol: The Policy Press/Social Policy Association, pp 51-68.

Langham, S., Gillam, S. and Thorogood, M. (1995) 'The carrot, the stick and the general practitioner: how have changes in financial incentives affected health promotion activity in general practice?', *British Journal of General Practice*, vol 45, pp 665-8.

McClean, G., Sutton, M. and Guthrie, B. (2006) 'Deprivation and quality of primary care services: evidence for persistence of the inverse care law from the UK Quality and Outcomes Framework', *Journal of Epidemiology and Community Health*, vol 60, no 11, pp 917-22.

McDonald, R. (2006) 'Creating a patient-led NHS: empowering "consumers" or shrinking the state?', in L. Bauld, K. Clarke and T. Maltby (eds) *Social Policy Review 18*, Bristol: The Policy Press/Social Policy Association, pp 33-48.

Marshall, M. and Harrison, S. (2005) 'It's about more than money: financial incentives and internal motivation', *Quality and Safety in Health Care*, vol 14, pp 4-5.

Mohan, J. (1995) *A national health service?*, Basingstoke: Macmillan.

Newman, J. and Vidler, E. (2006) 'Discriminating customers, responsible patients, empowered users: consumerism and the modernisation of health care', *Journal of Social Policy*, vol 35, no 2, pp 193-210.

NHS Scotland (2000) *Our national health: A plan for action, a plan for change*, Edinburgh: Scottish Executive Health Department.

NHS Scotland (2005) *The national framework for service change in NHS Scotland: Elective care action team – Final report*, Edinburgh: Scottish Executive Health Department.

Peckham, S. and Exworthy, M. (2003) *Primary care in the UK: Policy, organisation and management*, Basingstoke: Palgrave/Macmillan.

Peckham, S., Exworthy, M., Greener, I. and Powell, M. (2005b) 'Decentralising health services: more accountability or just more central control?', *Public Money and Management*, vol 25, no 4, pp 221-8.

Peckham, S., Exworthy, M., Powell, M. and Greener, I. (2005a) *Decentralisation as an organisational model for health care in England*, Report to NCCSDO (National Co-ordinating Centre for NHS Service Delivery and Organisation Research and Development), London: NCCSDO.

Seddon, M., Marshall, M., Campbell, S. and Roland, M. (2001) 'Systematic review of studies of quality of clinical care in general practice in the UK, Australia and New Zealand', *Quality in Health Care*, vol 10, pp 152-8.

SEHD (Scottish Executive Health Department) (2005) *Delivering for health*, Edinburgh: SEHD.

Sigfrid, L.A., Turner, C., Crook, D. and Ray, S. (2006) 'Using the UK primary care Quality and Outcomes Framework to audit health care equity: preliminary data on diabetes management', *Journal of Public Health*, vol 28, no 3, pp 221-5.

Smith, J., Mays, N., Dixon, J., Goodwin, N., Lewis, R., McCelland, S., McLeod, H. and Wyke, S. (2004) *A review of the effectiveness of primary care-led commissioning and its place in the NHS*, London: The Health Foundation.

Smith, P. and York, N. (2004) 'Quality incentives: the case of UK general practitioners', *Health Affairs*, vol 23, no 3, pp 112-18.

WAG (Welsh Assembly Government) (2005) *Designed for life: Creating world class health and social care for Wales in the 21st century*, Cardiff: WAG.

Wanless, D. (2003) *Review of health and social care in Wales*, Cardiff: Welsh Assembly Government.

Wilson, T., Roland, M. and Ham, C. (2006) 'The contribution of general practice and the general practitioner to NHS patients', *Journal of the Royal Society of Medicine*, vol 99, pp 24-8.

THREE

Housing policy, housing tenure and the housing market

Alan Murie

Introduction

Sixty years on from the end of the Second World War and the establishment of the post-war welfare state, more than 25 years on from the election of Margaret Thatcher's government and changes that reduced the size and role of public sector housing, and almost 10 years on from the election of a new Labour government, housing policy in Britain has home ownership at its heart. At the same time asset ownership is a more central element in the government's whole approach to public policy. Policy actions taken in 2006 confirm this direction and the importance of housing in the new asset-based welfare state.

Contrasting origins

Housing has been represented as the wobbly pillar under the post-war welfare state in Britain (see, for example, Malpass, 2003, 2005). During and after the Second World War the legislation and reorganisations that transformed the political and social rights of citizens and established the modern welfare state had less overt impact on housing policy than almost any other area. Although squalor was identified in the Beveridge report (Beveridge, 1942) as one of the main targets for the new welfare settlement, and although housing and housing costs were inextricably linked to problems of ill health and poverty, there was no dramatic reorganisation of the way that housing was provided or managed. There was no nationalisation of the housing service comparable with changes in health service provision and the state did not emerge as a monopoly or near monopoly provider of services comparable with health or education. While the changes were not so dramatic and local authorities continued to be the lead agencies for the government's direct provision of housing, the role of government in housing provision was, however, considerably increased. New towns and a new land use planning system combined with more generous subsidies for local authority housing meant that the state built new high quality housing that was superior to most of what was available in the private sector. At the same time rent control brought the bulk of the market within a managed system. Although it had not been so obviously reorganised, the private as well as the public sector operated in a very different way than in the past.

In the subsequent period housing has seen major changes (see Mullins and Murie, 2006). The private landlord who was still the majority provider of housing in 1946 has declined to become a minor player in percentage terms (10% of the market in England in 2006). A high quality public rented sector grew alongside an owner-occupied sector and both were much more popular than private renting. The promotion of home ownership and public (council and New Town) housing was a major success story not only because it transformed the way housing was owned and managed but because it dramatically reduced the housing shortage, squalor and bad housing – to the point where governments could regard the basic housing problem as solved. In the process, however, governments competed to become the advocates of home ownership that was increasingly seen as the preferred choice for housing among all sections of the population. The slum clearance drive from the 1950s to the 1970s speeded the decline of private renting and the reduction in housing that was unfit or deficient. At the same time it speeded the change in the role of public sector housing. The poorest sections of the community, who had generally been unable to afford to live in the higher rent and higher quality public sector and had consequently been concentrated in the lowest rent and lowest standard private rented housing, were displaced. They principally moved to the public sector where the extension of rent rebates (and subsequently Housing Benefit) enabled them to meet the housing costs involved. The residualisation of council housing, and the social rented sector more generally, refers to the narrowing of its social base and the greater concentration of lower income households in the sector (see Murie, 2006). Residualisation is associated with this shift from private renting and the changing role and reputation of an ageing public housing sector and with the promotion of home ownership and its increasing attractiveness to higher- and middle-income groups, as taxation treatment and the types and locations of housing involved made it more attractive by comparison. By the 1970s public sector housing was less exclusively the tenure for affluent working-class households and the era of mass home ownership was established.

Although there were major changes in the housing system and housing policy in earlier periods, most of the accounts of housing and planning policy identify the policies pursued by Margaret Thatcher's governments from 1979 onwards as marking something of a watershed in policy development (Malpass, 1990; Cole and Furbey, 1994; Malpass and Murie, 1999; Mullins and Murie, 2006). Most of them also acknowledge that the Labour government that preceded Margaret Thatcher's had already reduced housing capital expenditure and council house building and had introduced higher rents and identified itself with owner–occupation. Although it hesitated to embark on a policy of mass council house sales, the 1974–79 Labour government continued to enable sales to take place under a general ministerial consent. The Thatcher government took this one step further with a more active policy of privatisation through demunicipalisation. Rising council rents, a shift from object to subject subsidies (from General Exchequer subsidies attached to council dwellings to housing benefits where subsidy was attached to the household and determined in accordance with income and household needs) and the rapid run–down of new public sector house building programmes signalled the end of the period of parallel growth of owner–occupation and council housing. A period of growth for owner–occupation and decline for council housing followed. The deregulation of the private rented sector was intended to trigger a revival of that sector and housing associations, which had access to private finance, became the preferred vehicle for new social rented housing and the recipient of stock transferred from local authorities.

By the time a new Labour government had been elected in 1997 the policy pattern had dramatically changed. New Towns and the New Town programme had effectively been completed. Council house building had declined almost to zero. The council housing sector had declined mainly because of the sale, under the Right to Buy, of over two million council properties, but also with the continuing transfer of stock to housing associations. Rents had increased steadily and General Exchequer subsidies for council housing had substantially been replaced by housing benefits based on an assessment of household needs and incomes. Housing Benefit expenditure had escalated and local authorities' responsibility for administering the scheme changed their relationship with many tenants and left them appearing to be the source of problems that were intrinsic to the scheme devised by central government.

The housing system had been changed from the managed system established in the 1940s to a market system. Policy was centred on home ownership. All of these factors confirmed the impression that there was no long-term future in being a council tenant. The properties that were available were increasingly unattractive. If you were in a good property you were better to buy it under the Right to Buy with a massive discount rather than pay increasing rents. As the Right to Buy resulted in the sale of the best properties, the remaining sector was increasingly residual in its quality and dwelling type. It consisted of the dwellings and locations that were least preferred and this added to the changing social base (Forrest and Murie, 1990; Jones and Murie, 2006). More affluent, middle-aged tenants had bought properties and left the council housing sector much more like the sector that it had never previously been: as a welfare sector catering for low-income and benefit-dependent people, elderly households and people looking for short-term accommodation until they were able to move on to owner-occupation elsewhere.

One of the beliefs of the Conservative government in the 1980s was that the size of the public sector house building programme effectively crowded out private sector development. The theory was that a reduction in public sector programmes, combined with changes in planning and housing policy, would create the environment in which the private sector would expand and respond to need more completely. In practice the outcome had been very different. The private sector completion rate hardly increased as the amount of new building carried out by local authorities and housing associations declined. The consequence was reduced overall housing construction. To this extent, one of the legacies of Thatcherism was an increased shortage of affordable housing because of the impact of policies on the reduction in the amount of residential construction taking place nationally.

The Thatcher governments' negative view of council housing made the opportunity to use the planning system to fill the void doubly attractive – it involved less public expenditure and generated less municipal ownership. Local planning authorities were initially encouraged and then required to refer to affordable housing in their local plans and urban development plans. While housing tenure remained a matter that planning policy could not directly address, the term 'affordable' housing was regarded as including low-cost market housing as well as social rented housing. Whitehead and Crook (2000) concluded that the position was relatively straightforward. Once a planning authority had provided evidence of the need for affordable housing and defined an affordable housing policy, it could negotiate with developers of sites above a minimum threshold. These negotiations might result in provision elsewhere, but the presumption was increasingly that there should be mixed provision on site.

New Labour: continuity and change

During its long years in opposition between 1979 and 1997 the gap in relation to housing policy between the Labour Party and the Conservative government had narrowed. Labour's antagonism to the Right to Buy and the championing of municipal housing had given way to a more limited set of promises to give greater priority to increased housing expenditure. The early years of the Labour administration, after it came into office in 1997, were consequently marked by limited policy innovation in housing (Mullins and Murie, 2006). There were important developments related to homelessness with new legislation in 2002; and the introduction of the Decent Homes programme (to bring housing generally but particularly social rented housing up to a newly defined decency standard) backed by increased investment began to offset the years of under-investment in an ageing council housing stock. In addition the attention given to social exclusion meant some stronger reference to problems in the housing sector and to neighbourhoods. However, the central theme in policy was the promotion of home ownership.

It was not until 2000 that the new Labour government produced a housing Green Paper (DETR and DSS, 2000) and this document was more marked by continuity with the previous decades than radical change. The language of choice appeared throughout and connected choice-based lettings with the Right to Buy, an expanded stock transfer programme and the convergence of rents for both council and housing association properties on market-related levels. The increasing reference to quality of housing and the development of a Decent Homes standard and targets to reach this by 2010 had implications for council housing but also for stock transfers as it was evident that this was one of the ways of ensuring that funds would be available to meet the required standard. It is difficult to avoid the conclusion that the government had arrived at a genuinely residual view of social rented housing. It believed that the owner-occupied sector worked and that continued encouragement of that sector would be electorally popular and have limited costs to the public purse. Housing Benefit was not extended to lower-income owner-occupiers and mortgage interest tax relief had been successfully phased out. In the period of low interest rates this had been done with no political reaction. At the same time increases in stamp duty meant that the government could begin to tax the owner-occupied sector.

The government promoted home buyers' packs designed to require vendors to provide any potential purchaser with key information about the condition and other aspects of any property they were selling – and so protect the purchaser. They also attacked cowboy builders. Both of these are examples of the government intervening to reduce the risks associated with ownership. While the government did begin to take some steps to alter the Right to Buy (in 1998), there was no real attempt to reduce the flow of sales until 2005. Indeed, the uptake of the Right to Buy increased under the Labour government until 2006, fuelled partly by periodic speculation about its being replaced.

In the social rented sector audit and inspection altered the accountability framework and landlords' managerial failures were presented as the key source of problems. Concerns about anti-social behaviour were taken up by the government (and reiterated throughout 2006), but the difficulties of taking effective action continued to place local authorities in the position of appearing to be unable to manage problems effectively. They appeared to be adding to the problems of many tenants through the delays and bureaucracy associated with Housing Benefit and other programmes. The government continued to use housing associations as its preferred deliverer of social housing and local authorities were required to formally assess the merits of different options for future development (stock transfer, private finance initiative [PFI] and arm's-length management organisations [ALMOs], with the latter only possible for the best management performers).

The second period of office of the Blair government (from 2001) was associated with a more active approach to housing policy. Devolution in Scotland, Wales and Northern Ireland invigorated the housing agenda in each of these parts of the UK and a revival was also apparent with concerns about affordability in England. Rather than presiding over the end of housing policy the Blair government in this phase was responsible for a renaissance of housing policy. In England a series of task forces and policy papers began to give a greater priority and prominence to housing issues. Most notably the Urban Task Force (1999) identified the need for urban renaissance and the *Sustainable communities* White Paper (ODPM, 2003a) was produced by the newly formed Office of the Deputy Prime Minister (ODPM) that succeeded the Department of Transport, Local Government and the Regions (DTLR). This paper referred to a step-change in housing policy and focused on the problems associated with growth and affordability in London and South East England and low demand problems in the Midlands and Northern regions. The Communities Plan involved a regionalisation of housing policy with capital expenditures being determined regionally (by appointed regional housing boards) through a single housing pot combining the previously different channels from the ODPM and The Housing Corporation. The Communities Plan also brought into greater prominence concerns over the operation of the planning system and its responsiveness to the problems in different parts of England.

Home ownership and affordability

The revival of housing policy did not, however, imply any alteration to the primacy given to home ownership. In March 2003, the government had asked Baroness Dean, then chair of The Housing Corporation, to lead a home ownership task force to look at practical ideas to support home ownership, helping tenants and others on modest incomes to buy a home, while minimising the loss to social housing (Home Ownership Task Force, 2003). The government accepted the majority of the Task Force's recommendations in May 2004. These included measures to streamline the existing policies designed to improve access to home ownership and to provide more advice and information to individuals about sustainable home ownership.

In April 2003 the Chancellor of the Exchequer and the Deputy Prime Minister asked Kate Barker to conduct a review of issues affecting housing supply in the UK. An interim report, produced in December 2003 (Barker, 2003), identified the ways in which housing supply affected economic and social well-being and estimated the scale and causes of the housing shortage and the poor ability of new housing supply to respond to rising house prices. *Delivering stability: Securing our future housing needs: Barker Review of housing supply – Final report* (Barker, 2004) was published by the Treasury on the day of the Budget statement in March 2004 and welcomed by the Chancellor of the Exchequer. The Barker Review's remit was to consider the weak responsiveness of the new-build housing market in the face of rising house prices and the Treasury's concern that this feature of the UK housing market had several undesirable economic consequences (rising house prices leading to high demands for public subsidy towards new affordable homes, the inability of high price areas to attract workers on ordinary salaries and the leakage of equity into consumer spending leading to difficulties in controlling the money supply and with implications for the setting of interest rates and for inflation). This adversely affected economic growth and hindered the achievement of major macroeconomic and European policy objectives.

The Barker Review made recommendations relating to changes to the planning system but crucially asserted that the long-term stability of the housing market, with house price increases held to a low and pre-determined level, would require a substantial increase in house building. Existing levels of building were insufficient and an increase of between 70,000 to 120,000 units per annum in England was needed to improve affordability trends. The report acknowledged that this could raise problems of sustainability and environmental consequences and contained several recommendations aimed at changing the delivery processes for new house building. These included the provision of national guidance on housing market affordability drawn up by the government and changes to regional institutional arrangements including the merger of regional planning bodies and regional housing boards. The Review also recommended that additional funds would be needed to deliver additional social housing to meet projected future needs.

The new focus on affordability in the Communities Plan and the Barker Review continued the process of seeking to deliver housing policy through the planning system and largely through the market. Except for the identification of the need for more construction of social rented housing, the formula was much as before. In the lead-up to the General Election early in 2005, the government issued a five-year plan, setting out the next phase in the delivery of the Sustainable Communities Plan (ODPM, 2005a). This paper continued with the themes identified in the Communities Plan in 2003 but included a greater focus on first-time buyers and the availability of new Homebuy schemes to enable different groups to access home ownership. The focus of policies was still on further increasing home ownership over time. A new scheme to help first-time buyers involved using public land for new homes in order to keep costs down; in effect the costs of land would not be fully borne by initial costs of house purchase. The new package for social tenants was entitled 'Choice to Own' – an interesting development from 'Right to Buy'. Choice to Own emphasised giving all social tenants a choice about how to move into home ownership rather than the Right to Buy being the only route in (and only applying to people who were or had been secure council tenants). Public money could be used more effectively to give people alternatives in home ownership other than the Right to Buy, and Choice to Own included an extension to the Homebuy scheme to give council and housing association tenants the right to buy a share in their home and in time to buy the property outright. This in effect extended the Homebuy scheme to social rented tenants in a situation where the Right to Buy was not available or was less generous than in the past and the rent-to-mortgage scheme had not worked.

What was emerging was a wider series of interventions to enable different groups to access home ownership and to create different routes into the tenure available through different types of loan and by buying different proportions of the property so that the largest possible number of households would be able to make use of one scheme or another. This pattern has been described as a new comprehensive home ownership strategy (Mullins and Murie, 2006). The one hesitation in the rush to promote home ownership was the introduction of new legislation and discount ceilings affecting the Right to Buy. These were designed to prevent abuse of the Right to Buy and to improve 'value for money'. The abuses involved had been the subject of research (Jones, 2003) and included companies entering into arrangements with tenants who exercised the Right to Buy having previously agreed to transfer the ownership to these companies in exchange for cash. The value for money considerations related to whether the level of discount was unnecessarily high to enable tenants to buy and consequently reduced the receipts to the public purse without increasing the take-up of the scheme (see Jones and Murie, 2006).

Many of the schemes announced in the context of the Barker Review and the General Election of 2005 worked through to implementation in 2006. Plans to ensure that the Decent Homes target was met by 2010 continued to push ahead and there was a continuing major transfer of housing stock from local authorities to housing associations. The Social Homebuy scheme was launched and piloted but with very limited uptake by the end of the year. At the same time Right to Buy sales fell back to a very low level following the adjustment to discounts. The responsibility for housing and planning policy moved from the ODPM to a new Department for Communities and Local Government (and from John Prescott to Ruth Kelly). If there was any discernable change in emphasis it was to downplay regional housing initiatives and the Sustainable Communities Plan and to reaffirm the commitment to home ownership and its further expansion.

The changes in departments and ministers provided an opportunity to review and reaffirm. The new Department for Communities and Local Government was built on the old ODPM but had additional key responsibilities (including community cohesion and civic renewal from the Home Office). Housing was referred to as being at the centre of the Department's new focus and a particular emphasis was placed on trying to create mixed communities, on environmental sustainability and on the importance of housing for the economy. The new minister commented:

> When I was in the Bank of England and the Treasury I saw just how crucial housing was to economic performance. And so my department has a key role in the fundamental issues of labour supply, labour flexibility and ultimately Britain's productivity and prosperity. And these economic issues must be at the centre of the department's thinking. (Kelly, 2006, p 1)

The minister also reaffirmed the priority attached to home ownership:

> ... housing is an inspiration and opportunity. I want to see a society in which everyone has the opportunity to get on, fulfil their potential – no matter who they are or where they come from. A society that values and promotes social mobility. We all know how most people associate getting on with owning a home or getting a better one. People naturally value the sense of security that having an asset brings. Important points of progress in many of our lives come when we move out of the family home and start renting or get our first foot on the housing ladder – whether we buy outright or through some form of shared ownership. (Kelly, 2006, p 1)

Emphasis was placed on delivering on the overall housing targets set by Kate Barker and the commitment made to increase the supply of social housing with a target of 30,000 additional social homes a year by 2007/08. At the same time it was seen as important to ensure that the social housing policy was fit for purpose. While social housing must retain its role in supporting those in the most need, two other core objectives were identified: to see how social housing could help create genuinely mixed communities and to help achieve social mobility.

In the context of the second of these Ruth Kelly stated:

> While maintaining the important values of security and quality, we must maximise the opportunities that social housing brings for people to get on in their lives. It must give tenants greater choice and be a spring board into ownership

for those who only need it for a short period of time as well
as those who need it for life. (Kelly, 2006, p 3)

Following her earlier report Kate Barker had been invited in 2005 to
conduct an independent review of the land use planning system in
England. The terms of reference were to consider how, building on recent
reforms, the planning system could better deliver economic growth
alongside other sustainable development goals. Following the publication
of an interim report in July 2006 the final report was published in
December 2006. The final report emphasised the importance of the
planning system as a vital support to productivity and economic growth
and suggested reforms to increase the flexibility and responsiveness
of the system, the efficiency of the process and more efficient use of
land (Barker, 2006). The emphasis was placed on a positive approach
to development, and the economic benefits associated with it, and
reform of the planning process for major infrastructure projects with
final decisions taken by a new independent Planning Commission. The
proposals related to land included a review of Green Belt boundaries as
well as action to improve the quality of Green Belt land and to incentivise
the use of previously developed land. The reaction to these proposals
was mixed and the government's response was not immediately clear.
However, there is significance in the approach to policy continuing to
be driven through the Treasury rather than the government departments
with explicit housing and planning policy responsibilities, the emphasis
placed on economic development and the preference for appointed
commissions and depoliticised processes.

The outline of policy development above has emphasised the
continuing focus on home ownership. But as the government has
more and more enthusiastically embraced home ownership as the way
forward for housing so the increasing inflation of house prices in the
home ownership market has been the focus of comment. The year
2006 saw a continuation of the stream of media and research reports
highlighting the consequences of increasing prices for different sections
of the community and emphasising an affordability crisis across much
of the UK. The government itself repeatedly referred to affordability
problems and the actions taken following the original Barker Review
reflected the government's approach to the crisis and the need to increase
housing supply. However, the affordability debate remains fraught. Just
as it is true that "over the last decade it has become progressively more
difficult for households to access home ownership as house prices
have risen sharply" (Wilcox, 2006, p 2), so it is also true that over the

past decade the significant growth of income experienced by some households coupled with low direct taxation and low interest rates has generated an increased demand for investment in housing. It is the ability of some households to afford to pay more for housing and to choose to do so that has pushed prices up to levels that others may find unaffordable. To this extent the affordability problem is endemic in a housing provision system dominated by the market and where inequalities of incomes are reflected in house prices. The price that one group is prepared to pay for housing, and sees as a good housing and investment decision, represents an affordability crisis for another group. Affordability problems are not a surprising feature of the housing market and of a long-established home ownership sector. Indeed it would be surprising if the welfare restructuring and economic and demographic changes over three decades did not generate this outcome and if the maturation of the home ownership market was not associated with greater differentiation and stratification.

The recent favourable investment performance of housing when compared with other options for those with income to invest (notably when compared with private pensions) has added to the extent to which housing has attracted investors in a period of widening income inequality. In this context the development of the buy-to-let market – facilitated by the earlier deregulation of the private rented sector – has become a significant factor in the development of the housing market. Whether or not they are buying second homes, investors with high incomes that are rising much more rapidly than inflation compete with first-time buyers and existing owners seeking to move house, and add to affordability pressures. This is especially so if the incomes of the first-time buyers and existing owners involved are lower and rising more slowly. In this context the view that adding to the supply of private housing will expand home ownership, or that increased supply in high demand areas (as suggested by Barker) will have the effect of reducing house prices, is open to challenge. Increased supply in some cases may result in a growth in the buy-to-let market and result in an expansion of the private rented sector and this has been a feature of some developments of urban mixed tenure housing (see Rowlands et al, 2006); or increased supply in high demand areas may simply enable more people to trade up to such areas and find an opportunity to invest more of their resources in housing. As long as there is a significant group of households experiencing rising disposable incomes and if the alternative investments are less attractive there is likely to be a growth in willingness to invest in housing – a willingness to 'over-consume' housing, to trade up for investment reasons and to buy-to-let. Those with higher incomes will be able not just to pay more by committing the same proportion of their (higher) incomes to housing but to commit a higher proportion of their income. The consequence may be to price others out of the home ownership market. In this context the absence of an attractive alternative in social housing becomes the problem. The failure of the government to regard social housing as other than a residual pathway towards home ownership has a different implication against this background than in the context of the 1970s or 1980s. It leaves an intermediate group unable to access the housing they want within the home ownership sector without overextending their household budgets but with no sustainable alternative.

Conclusion

Housing policy in the UK in the 21st century is not built around decommodified social or public sector housing. Three decades of policy – from the International Monetary Fund cuts of 1976 through to 2006 – have envisaged a declining role for the public sector. In the intervening period privatisation, demunicipalisation and residualisation have been important. But the government has not withdrawn from housing or ceased to intervene. The promotion of home ownership has become the sole dominating concern and has been pursued through different policies – including the privatisation of public housing under the Right to Buy, deregulation and fiscal incentives and special schemes aimed at first-time buyers and other households. Public and social rented housing is no longer the cornerstone of housing policy and ownership of housing assets has become more important in the government's overall welfare strategy. By 2006 home ownership was no longer competing with state housing in a two-pronged housing strategy, nor was it the favoured method in a confused policy agenda. It was the dominant element in a new, comprehensive approach to housing. The government had begun to see home ownership not just as a popular form of housing tenure but as a pillar on which other policies could be built.

During the 1990s and subsequently, the government has increasingly begun to look at the possibilities of funding a variety of welfare services, partly through the release of equity from home ownership. As the costs of the welfare state have been seen to be disproportionate, so governments have looked to individuals to make provision for the purchase of services that were previously provided by the state. The growth of equity held in the form of home ownership has attracted the attention of different parts of government, which have seen the opportunity to offload a difficult financing problem by calling into play the potential of equity release.

The accumulation of wealth through home ownership, rather than being a byproduct of the primary role of housing as shelter, or being an end in itself, was increasingly seen by the government as a means to an end, and a device to assist in the financing of a range of services. In 1998 the government took steps that made it possible to increase equity release type loans and subsequent steps by the government have shown a further willingness to encourage equity release.

Asset ownership has been identified as a key part of the government's welfare policy (HM Treasury, 2001) and within this housing plays a role in providing long-term independence and opportunity. Increased home ownership is critical to the longer-term agenda for the Labour government along with new asset-based welfare policies – the Saving Gateway and the Child Trust Fund. Housing represents the most important asset for all groups except the very wealthy and its importance in the distribution of wealth has been recognised for some decades. In setting out its proposals to expand the opportunity to own, the government referred to "enabling more people to share in increasing asset wealth". It stated "homes are not just places to live. They are also assets" and went on to state that "support for home ownership will enable more people on lower incomes to benefit from any further increases in the value of housing assets" (ODPM, 2005b, p 9). Expanding home ownership was presented as a way of reducing the wealth gap (ODPM, 2005a) and the gap between owners and non-owners had triggered a debate about schemes to provide equity stakes for tenants (Hill et al, 2002; ODPM, 2003b), perhaps involving the building of an entitlement linked to the numbers of years of rent payment.

The ownership of property involving an initial home and additional buy-to-let properties has been increasingly built into the government's thinking. The clearest examples relate to provision for older people in long-term care. Home owners moving into long-term residential care in England are effectively expected to fund their long-term care out of the equity held in their home. How this is done is a matter for the older person and their family, but only when the value of the asset has diminished enormously is the government willing to fund long-term care rather than draw on this source.

Equity release has also been referred to in other contexts: to maintain income in older age, to support work to improve energy efficiency in homes, and to meet the costs associated with further and higher education provision. In a political environment where increasing taxation is difficult for any government to contemplate, even if they were to regard it as desirable economically, equity release becomes the funding of last resort for many schemes that, in the past, the state would have aspired to fund. The citizen, rather than being guaranteed a range of social benefits as a right of citizenship, is being reminded that they could afford to purchase these services through the market by drawing on the wealth that they have accumulated in home ownership.

The asset-based welfare state puts housing in a much more central position than it was before, but this is a position that is less to do with the provision of shelter alone and more to do with its role as the basis for financing (and individualising responsibility for) a range of other forms of welfare provision. It involves a very significant shift away from the principles of uniformity and universality that are associated with social insurance provisions emerging from the Beveridge report (1942). The provision that the government now encourages people to make will not yield the same level of benefit to all households. The lottery of the market will continue to apply. For some people their own property or buy-to-let properties will provide them with very substantial assets and possibly incomes in older age; for others with much lower incomes there will be no housing asset or a very limited one. And the division between those with sufficiently large assets to be released through trading down in the housing market or through equity release and those with insufficient assets are divisions among home owners as well as between home owners and tenants. They relate to occupational histories, social class and lifetime earnings as well as where people live (and have lived) and what their housing strategies have been. In proclaiming the merits of asset-based welfare the government is less concerned with uniformity of provision or outcome or with the form of provision than with encouraging people to make provision to meet their material welfare needs.

References

Barker, K. (2003) *Review of housing supply: Interim report*, London: The Stationery Office.

Barker, K. (2004) *Delivering stability: Securing our future housing needs. Barker Review of housing supply – Final report: Recommendations*, London: The Stationery Office.

Barker, K. (2006) *Barker Review of land use planning: Final report*, London: The Stationery Office.

Beveridge, W. (1942) *Social insurance and allied services* (The Beveridge Report) Cmd 6404, London: HMSO.

Cole, I. and Furbey, R. (1994) *The eclipse of council housing*, London: Routledge.

DETR (Department of the Environment, Transport and the Regions) and DSS (Department of Social Security) (2000) *Quality and choice: A decent home for all*, Housing Green Paper, London: DETR and DSS.

Forrest, R. and Murie, A. (1990) *Selling the welfare state*, London: Routledge.

Hill, S., Lupton, M., Moody, G. and Regan, S. (2002) *A stake worth having*, London: Chartered Institute of Housing and Institute for Public Policy Research.

HM Treasury (2001) *Savings and assets for all*, London: The Stationery Office.

Home Ownership Task Force (2003) *A home of my own* (www.housingcorp.gov.uk/upload/pdf/HOTF_web.pdf).

Jones, C. (2003) *Exploitation of the Right to Buy scheme by companies*, London: Office of the Deputy Prime Minister.

Jones, C. and Murie, A. (2006) *The Right to Buy*, Oxford: Blackwell.

Kelly, R. (2006) 'Housing, community and opportunity', Speech to the Chartered Institute of Housing Conference, 20 June, Department for Communities and Local Government (www.communities.gov.uk).

Malpass, P. (1990) *Reshaping housing policy: Subsidies, rents and residualisation*, London: Routledge.

Malpass, P. (2003) 'The wobbly pillar? Housing policy and the British postwar welfare state', *Journal of Social Policy*, vol 32, no 4, pp 589–606.

Malpass, P. (2005) *Housing and the welfare state: The development of housing policy in Britain*, Basingstoke: Palgrave.

Malpass, P. and Murie, A. (1999) *Housing policy and practice*, Basingstoke: Macmillan.

Mullins, D. and Murie, A. (2006) *Housing policy in the UK*, Basingstoke: Palgrave Macmillan.

Murie, A. (2006) 'Moving with the times: changing frameworks for housing research and policy', in P. Malpass and L. Cairncross (eds) *Building on the past*, Bristol: The Policy Press, pp 15–50.

ODPM (Office of the Deputy Prime Minister) (2003a) *Sustainable communities: Building for the future*, London: ODPM.

ODPM (2003b) *Equity shares for social housing*, London: ODPM.

ODPM (2005a) *Sustainable communities: Homes for all. A five-year plan of the Office of the Deputy Prime Minister*, Cm 6424, London: The Stationery Office.

ODPM (2005b) *Homebuy – Expanding the opportunity to own*, London: ODPM.

Rowlands, R., Murie, A. and Tice, A. (2006) *More than tenure mix*, York: Joseph Rowntree Foundation.

Urban Task Force (1999) *Towards an urban renaissance: Final report of the Urban Task Force*, London: E & FN Spon.

Whitehead, C. and Crook, A. (2000) 'The achievement of affordable housing through the planning system', in S. Monk and C. Whitehead (eds) *Restructuring housing systems*, York: York Publishing Services.

Wilcox, S. (2006) *The geography of affordable and unaffordable housing*, York: Joseph Rowntree Foundation.

FOUR

Modernising services, empowering users? Adult social care in 2006

Kirstein Rummery

Introduction

The implementation in 1993 of the 1990 National Health Service (NHS) and Community Care Act was one of the most fundamental upheavals social services in the UK had ever experienced, introducing splits between the purchasing and direct provision of care services for adults, and implementing a 'quasi-market' in social care (Le Grand and Bartlett, 1993; Lewis and Glennerster, 1996). These reforms aimed to control public expenditure, facilitate joint working between health and social care and empower service users. This legacy remains a powerful driver in social services: policies designed and implemented by the New Labour government since 1997 have never strayed too far from these themes. Within the policy discourse of 'modernisation' efforts have been concentrated on addressing problems associated with the implementation of the legacy of the 1990s changes, rather than changing the vision or the discourse of the policy itself (Newman, 2001).

Adult social care services have always struggled with the sometimes conflicting aims of community care policy. Analyses of the implementation of the 1990 changes have shown how frontline workers have become compelled to prioritise the overarching aim of controlling expenditure, acting as gatekeepers and rationers, rather than facilitating user empowerment (Lewis and Glennerster, 1996; Rummery, 2002a). Development of the mixed market in care has resulted in an increase in the proportion of services being delivered by the independent sector, without any evidence that this has necessarily increased choice and control for service users (Hardy et al, 1999; Tanner, 2003; Clarke 2006). In some respects the gatekeeping and mixed market elements of community care policy started in the 1990s have continued unabated under New Labour, albeit under the discourse of modernisation rather than the discourse of new managerialism (Newman, 2001).

Where New Labour has differed significantly from the previous Conservative administration is in the emphasis given to joint, or partnership, working with health. This has moved from a marginal activity to the mainstream of business for both organisations, with the removal of structural barriers to integration at various levels with the 1999 Health Act, to various organisational changes, performance objectives and cross-cutting policy initiatives since. Adult social care organisations have, sometimes with good reason, been wary of increasing pressure to work in partnership with health. As I have stated elsewhere, "partnership working New Labour style benefits powerful partners" (Rummery, 2002b, p 243), enabling the more powerful partner to achieve their own goals more effectively, but this can sometimes be at the expense of the less powerful partner. Despite the evidence that adult social services organisations have delivered on key elements of the community care agenda, and that the NHS has been slow to change and less accountable to patients than social services are to service users (Callaghan and Wistow, 2006a; Glasby et al, 2006; Wistow, 2006), health is still the dominant partner, with important implications for the extent to which user empowerment is likely to be achieved.

This chapter examines the way in which the overarching discourse of modernisation of adult care services has masked some of the conflicts inherent in policy developments in 2006, particularly those concerning partnerships and user empowerment. The first part of the chapter concentrates on the proposals set out in *Our health, Our care, Our say* (DH, 2006a), the joint health and social care White Paper that followed the social care Green Paper *Independence, well-being and choice* (DH, 2005). The second part concentrates on wider policy developments in 2006 that were of concern to specific groups of users of adult care services, particularly older people, disabled people and mental health service users.

Our health, Our care, Our say

In 2005 a lengthy consultation process over the future of adult social care services culminated in the publication of the social care Green Paper *Independence, well-being and choice* (DH, 2005), details of which were discussed in Glendinning and Means (2006). *Independence, well-being and choice* focused on outcomes for users in a much more coherent and systematic way than is apparent in the White Paper. The Green Paper identified seven policy objectives for users of adult social care services: improved health and emotional well-being, improved quality of life, making a positive contribution, choice and control, freedom from discrimination, economic well-being and personal dignity. Henwood (2006) has argued that these objectives have become diluted in the White Paper, with overarching attention focusing on improving joint working with health and with performance indicators tailored accordingly.

After a promising front cover and tagline (*Our health, Our care, Our say: A new direction for community services – Health and social care working in partnership*), analysis of the proposals reveals that health, and the role of the NHS, takes precedence over the role of social services. Sections outlining plans for community-based services, enabling healthy independence and well-being, access to primary care, access to community services and shifting the locus of care closer to people's homes all concentrate on changes to the way healthcare is commissioned and delivered. Only in the section on support for people with long-term needs is social services given a prominent role. One of the few explicit social care goals within this section is that by 2008 everyone who is eligible should be able to receive an integrated care plan, involving health and social care services and building on work to provide a single assessment process for health and social care for older people. By 2008 all primary care trusts (PCTs) and social services departments must have established joint health and care managed networks, following models used in mental health and intermediate care teams, and it is estimated that around 250,000 service users with complex needs will benefit from integrated case management.

There are plans to set up at least one large-scale pilot with an emphasis on patient education, joint health and social care teams, good local community health and care services, and health and social care commissioners with the right incentives to deliver improved care: in other words, to bring together what is already known about past failures to provide adequately for people with complex long-term needs (DH, 2006a, p 120). It is envisaged that the demonstration pilot will cover a population of at least one million, and that there will not only be significant improvements in patient outcomes, but crucially that there will be reduced use of acute hospital care. Nineteen 'Partnerships for Older People' Projects (POPPs) went live in May 2006 and a further 12 sites were announced in December 2006, again with the explicit aim of reducing hospital admissions. This is further evidence that an apparently 'joint' policy is in fact dominated by NHS concerns and that these will possibly override the interests of social services and, potentially, service users (Glasby, 2006). *Our health* clearly takes precedence over *our care*. So what has happened to *our say*?

Empowering users, or delegating care?

In comparison to the NHS, social services organisations in the UK, particularly since the implementation of the 1990 community care reforms, have a much more distinguished history of empowering users. This is a reflection, in part, of key differences in the funding, structures, aims and professional ethos of the relevant organisations. Since their creation in the early 1970s, social services departments have come under the control of local, rather than national, government: they are funded by, and accountable to, the local population through the democratic mechanism of elected local authorities. While this has disadvantages for users, in that the provision of services (and correspondingly ease of access to those services) can vary considerably across localities, it does mean that users have input into the funding and organisation of services through democratic means. Organisationally there are also a host of mechanisms in place to ensure that social services departments involve service users in the planning, commissioning and delivery of services, with very few levers of comparable strength in health organisations (Wistow, 2006).

The community care changes, and the subsequent emphasis on joint working with health, have meant that dominance of the social work profession in social services organisations has come under threat (Hudson, 2006). Nevertheless, social workers retain a key role in social care, and of all the professions associated with the provision of social care they have the strongest ethical and professional commitment to empowering service users. Along with democratic accountability, organisational commitments to user consultation in planning and commissioning services, individual social workers' commitment to user empowerment remains a relatively powerful protection of users' interests (Cheetham, 1993; Shepherd, 1995).

In contrast, the NHS has always been funded through national taxation, with comparatively weak accountability mechanisms to local patients (Rowe and Shepherd, 2002). Some progress has been made on this under New Labour, with the strengthening of patients' voices through the National Institute for Health and Clinical Excellence (NICE) (Davies et al, 2006) and at a more local level through PCTs (Pickard et al, 2006). Greater emphasis on patient involvement in healthcare commissioning has been encouraged through provisions in the consultation exercise *A stronger local voice* (DH, 2006b), and legal challenges have established that patients must be fully consulted over changes in service provision (*R [Smith] v North Eastern Derbyshire Primary Care Trust [Secretary of State for Health intervening]*, Court of Appeal, 23 August 2006). However, despite the evidence that patient involvement in the NHS significantly improves outcomes, both policy makers and practitioners in the NHS have been slow to act on the evidence of best practice in this area (Callaghan and Wistow, 2006b; Coulter and Ellins, 2006). There is also evidence that patients feel disengaged from healthcare commissioning and relatively uninvolved in decisions about their own healthcare, compared to other developed nations (Coulter, 2006). The erosion of social services' power in relation to health, alongside the relatively weak outcome and performance measures for users in the White Paper, is therefore of concern. Some commentators have gone as far as to suggest that health's dominance should be reversed, and that, given their better record on user accountability and managing tight budgets, local authorities should be given the opportunity to manage PCTs and other parts of the NHS (Glasby et al, 2006; Wistow, 2006).

This is not to say that the provision of social care has been particularly user-focused in the past. The power imbalance inherent in the relationships between users and practitioners was made worse by the introduction of assessment and care management and the mixed economy of care, which gave social services the ability to commission services on behalf of users, but users themselves were not able to exercise the crucial options of choice, voice or exit that make marketised systems responsive to purchasers (Barnes, 1997). It has been noted that personalised or user-centred care is difficult to attain under present commissioning arrangements (CSCI, 2006a). Among the most successful attempts to counteract this lack of user-responsiveness has been to place more control over the way in which services are purchased and delivered directly in the hands of users themselves. This usually takes the form of enabling users to purchase their own services through cash mechanisms (such as direct payments or personal budgets).

There are problems with individualised cash systems, some of which are relatively minor and procedural (such as problems with implementation, the recruitment and employment of personal assistants, and training and pay issues) and some of which are more complex (such as the diversion of resources away from core service provision, their unsuitability in times of crisis, the lack of protection for vulnerable disabled people and workers, and the reliance on market mechanisms to provide social rights) (Spandler, 2004; Rummery, 2006). Nevertheless there is an overwhelming amount of evidence that shows that purchasing their own care gives users of adult social care services a much greater degree of choice and control, and therefore independence, than using state-commissioned services (Leece and Bornat, 2006). The consultation exercise that culminated in the publication of the Green Paper *Independence, well-being and choice* (DH, 2005) showed that users were in support of extending direct payments, and there are currently individual budget pilots under way whereby cash is pooled from a variety of sources (local authority, community equipment and independent living funds, among others). These started in March 2006 and are due to run for two years. Without pre-empting the results of ongoing evaluations, if these pilots prove successful it will mean a fundamental challenge to traditional methods of social care service delivery. The role of social workers and social services organisations, already substantially changed through the 1990 community care changes, looks set to be further challenged by the extension of direct payments and self-assessment: the need for professional assessors and service commissioners is set to diminish significantly the more these roles are played by users themselves.

In looking at ways to support people with long-term needs, the White Paper emphasises facilitating self care, support for carers and facilitating multidisciplinary networks. However, even within this focus, the bulk of investment appears to be in areas such as the Expert Patients Programme (designed to facilitate self care among people with long-term and chronic health conditions) and improving information services for patients and carers. While this may go some way towards challenging professional hegemonies and empowering people with complex needs to become more informed and better able to manage their own health, this is nowhere near the level of choice and control over social care services that is exercised by the users of direct payments and personal budgets. Investing in information services is not the same as investing directly in service provision: rather, it places even greater emphasis on the role that individuals and families play in providing support for vulnerable people. Financial incentives designed to 'take money closer to the patient', enabling increased investment in primary and community-based health services, are not the same as money directly under the control of the patient, and the policy challenge of moving from a "fragmented and acute care dominated system to one that is coordinated and community oriented" (Hudson, 2006, p 4) should not be underestimated.

Users' concerns

Our health, Our care, Our say can be seen as further disenfranchising social services departments in two ways. First, it places great emphasis on joint working with health, but, as was seen above, this is very much on health's terms. Second, particularly through self-assessment and individual budgets, it places greater control over service commissioning and delivery in the hands of users. Arguably, the latter focus is more in line with social services' own aims and values, both organisationally and professionally, than the former, and so this element of disenfranchisement can be seen as a mixed blessing rather than an overwhelmingly negative development.

However, it should be remembered that any organisation within the welfare state is a means to the end of achieving the well-being of citizens, and social services are no exception: we should be wary of the protection of organisational interests per se. From the wider perspective of the well-being of citizens, particularly the users of adult social care services and their families, carers and supporters, it is clear there have been several salient developments in social care outside of the organisational changes outlined in *Our health, Our care, Our say*, and the remainder of this chapter will be devoted to discussing them.

Older people

The year 2006 saw a continuation in the decline of residential care use, with numbers falling by around 3% compared to previous years (Community Care Statistics, 2006), although demand is predicted to rise by 6% by 2016 (Laing & Buisson, 2006). The government reached its target number of older people being supported to live at home through the provision of intensive home care (30% of the number in residential care) by March 2006 and has extended the target to 34% by March 2008 (Summary of the Public Service Agreement on Home Care, 2006). In the light of that evidence, it is a concern that research still highlights how unresponsive to users' needs such services are, with the Social Care Inspectorate highlighting issues around the length and quality of home care, with users perceiving visits as being too rushed to provide adequate care (CSCI, 2006b). Concerns also continue around the considerable variations in costs for domiciliary services, with users faced with a 'triple lottery' on charges, based on where they live; how their local authority applied the eligibility criteria for care services; and the charging policy of their local authority (Counsel and Care, 2006).

Given the ongoing complexity of community care assessment and care provision systems, it is also of concern that older people often do not have access to advocacy services to support challenges to the system (Kitchen, 2006).

Paying for care is an ongoing issue for older people. The Scottish Parliament's brave decision to break with England and follow the Royal Commission's recommendations on providing personal and nursing care free of charge came under review, with research indicating that this fairer and more popular approach to funding care had not resulted in significant rises in costs (Bell and Bowes, 2006), although the Scottish Parliament has warned of the risk of demand outstripping supply and the need for clarity about costs (Scottish Executive, 2006). In the light of the recommendations of the Wanless Report (Wanless, 2002) that spending on social care will have to treble by 2026 to meet rising demand, and marked reluctance from the Welsh Assembly to follow the Scottish example, it is worth keeping the Scottish evidence under review. Options for paying for long-term care have always struggled with the thorny issue of how to take into account people's personal wealth, with the present system of treating housing as an asset being seen as inconsistent and leading to resentment and unfair outcomes (Joseph Rowntree Foundation, 2006). There is strong support for state funding of social care, with increased taxation or insurance contributions if necessary, rather than the divisiveness of means testing and asset stripping (Age Concern, 2006; Croucher and Rhodes, 2006).

The year 2006 marked the halfway point in New Labour's 10-year plan to improve older people's services, set out under the *National Service Framework for older people* (DH, 2001). The lack of consultation and user involvement in services was highlighted as a reason for some slow progress in achieving improvements (Commission for Healthcare Audit and Inspection, 2006), which is perhaps why patient involvement has featured fairly prominently in *Our health, Our care, Our say*. The next phase is set to focus on the involvement of older people in service planning and improving the integration of services. As health and social care service integration has featured prominently in New Labour's policies for older people, it is notable that there is as yet a distinct lack of evidence to suggest that service integration leads to demonstrable benefits for service users (Rummery, 2005); for example, services provided through integrated health and social care teams do not result in a greater proportion of older people living independently in the community (Brown and Cullis, 2006). Service integration may well prove to be an interesting exercise in how to reduce costs without actually improving outcomes for older people.

Disabled people

The past few years have given rise to several policy developments in social care that have had a considerable impact on the lives of disabled people. Proposals in *Our health, Our care, Our say* to build on the perceived success of direct payments – whereby users receive cash in lieu of services and purchase their own care, usually through the employment of personal assistants – will be welcomed by many users, who have highlighted the considerable improvements in choice and control over services that are experienced by the users of direct payments (Leece and Bornat, 2006). However, research evidence published in 2006 has reiterated concerns about the variations in take-up and governance arrangements and their implications for equity and social justice (Riddell et al, 2005; Scourfield, 2005; Leece and Bornat, 2006), and issues remain unresolved about diverting resources away from core service provision, low levels of funding and the potential for abuse and exploitation of both users and care workers (Spandler, 2004; Ungerson, 2004). In this respect *Our health, Our care, Our say* represents something of a missed opportunity to radically overhaul social care for disabled people. In the light of the evidence that suggests that using cash to purchase services gives disabled people much greater levels of independence than can be achieved through the direct provision of services, the need to improve funding, enable equitable access and improve information and support in these systems urgently needs to be addressed. These issues are not going to be solved by the addition of several more 'pilots' with varying funding and governance arrangements, even if those pilots do manage to address some of the complex organisational issues that have prevented efficient use of funds. In order to achieve social justice direct payments need to be properly funded, and universally and systematically accessible, and *Our health, Our care, Our say* does not go nearly far enough in addressing those objectives.

Of course, direct payments are not the only policy development in social care that has the potential to improve disabled people's lives – indeed, direct payments in their present form are not necessarily suitable for many disabled people, particularly those with learning disabilities. Efforts to move away from a 'personal gift' model of service delivery (whereby disabled people are the passive recipients of services) towards a 'self-directed support' model (whereby disabled people control how the funding to meet their needs is used, for example through employing a personal care assistant in the same way as a user of direct payments would) have been piloted in six councils in the In Control Project, and the results have shown that people with learning disabilities experience considerable benefits in levels of independence and social inclusion (Poll et al, 2006). Researchers have argued that these results are replicable both across localities (with around half of English local authorities now adopting some of the measures in the In Control system) and across user groups. In contrast to these positive developments, 2006 saw some worrying evidence emerge about the quality and safety of care services provided to adults with learning disabilities, with one NHS trust in Cornwall providing "unacceptable levels of care" and several others coming under inspection (CSCI, 2006c). Many of the concerns highlighted were in NHS settings. At the same time the Disability Rights Commission highlighted the shortfalls in access to health services and inequitable outcomes experienced by people with learning disabilities (Disability Rights Commission, 2006). In the light of that evidence, the ongoing precedence given to the organisational interests of health over social care should be scrutinised with care.

Mental health service users

In 2004 the European Court of Human Rights found that a severely autistic man, who lacked capacity and had been kept at Bournewood hospital against the will of his carers, had been unlawfully detained. The court found that his detention had not been carried out in accordance with a procedure prescribed by law and there was no process by which the man (or those acting for him) could have the lawfulness of the decision to deprive him of his liberty speedily decided (DH, 2006c). This gave rise to the so-called Bournewood gap, whereby people who lack capacity to consent to treatment are detained under common law, rather than under the Mental Health Act. After consultation the government published key proposals to close that gap, including the commitment to ensure that:

- all involved will have to act in the best interests of the person in care and in the least restrictive manner;
- the criteria under which someone can be detained will be strengthened;
- an individual's rights will have to be respected and it will be easier to challenge the decision once someone has been detained;

- every person will have someone 'independent' to represent their interests; and
- the proposals will cover both care homes and those being treated in hospital (*Hansard*, 29 June 2006).

Concerns also continue about the level of choice and control that mental health service users are able to exercise over community-based services and research indicates that involvement of mental health service users in health and social care is poor (Warner et al, 2006). Gaps in service provision for particularly vulnerable groups of mental health service users were highlighted by research published in 2006, with children from minority ethnic backgrounds, children in care and young offenders being highlighted as particularly poorly served (BMA, 2006; Chitsabesan et al, 2006).

Modernising services, or empowering users?

In promising to 'modernise' public services (Cabinet Office, 1999) New Labour has pursued a distinctive agenda that has had a relatively narrow focus but an enormous impact on health and social care organisations. The narrow focus has been to take up the legacy of new public management left by the previous Conservative administration and initiate a programme of institutional reform that has changed the discourse but appears to have left the policy framework the same: focusing on performance management, drivers to improve effectiveness and efficiency in public services, service restructuring and the involvement of outside partners in the commissioning and delivery of services (Newman, 2001). Scourfield has argued that the discourse of modernisation in social care has become so powerful that policy developments that do not follow the route of increased outsourcing and quasi-markets are almost 'unsayable' (Scourfield, 2006). However, if social services organisations retained more control over the delivery of services they would arguably be able to exercise much more powerful levers to make them both more responsive to users and integrate them more effectively with health services, the twin aims of *Our health, Our care, Our say*.

'Modernisation' clearly continued to be the dominant discourse in social care in 2006. We can see elements of service restructuring and enhanced performance management (again) in the White Paper, as well as the overarching push towards greater integration and partnership working with health. These pressures, combined with moves in recent years towards hiving off children's services, have meant that the Seebohm vision of large, unified social services organisations within local government control meeting the needs of vulnerable groups of people is severely under threat (Birrell, 2006). In *Social Policy Review 18*, Glendinning and Means noted that the treble forces of user empowerment, corporate responsibilities and the demands of the NHS were leading to a "hollowing out" of social services departments (Glendinning and Means, 2006, p 27) and it is hard to find evidence from developments in 2006 to counter that view.

Nevertheless, some of the policies that threaten the power of social services organisations do appear to have the motive of user empowerment, including moves towards increased use of self-assessment and user-controlled services (for example, through individual budgets), as well as increasing user involvement in the planning and commissioning of healthcare services. However, user-defined outcomes often differ radically from service-defined ones, and the performance management agenda that comes under the policy imperative towards modernisation fails to place user-defined outcomes at its centre (Glasby and Beresford, 2006). Although there is acknowledgement that users' concerns include issues of choice, flexibility and information, which the White Paper does attempt to address (albeit leaving institutional power relatively untouched), other key issues acknowledged by policy makers to be important for users, such as respect, fairness and the cost of services, have not been addressed. Although empowering users in itself is cited as a key aim of the White Paper, it is only when that aim can be tied to the modernisation agenda that policy changes are discernible. *Our say* becomes significant when what users say they want is in line with the dominant policy agenda: more partnership working with health, more cost-effective use of services, shorter and less frequent stays in hospital. The voices become muted, however, when they say they want better and fairer funding of social care services, disregard of housing assets in assessing personal contributions to the cost of care, free personal care, and fairer and more consistent rules about service charges and access to individual budgets.

Conclusion

The power of social services organisations was further eroded in 2006, with moves towards greater integration with health and devolved power to service users being the twin drivers of the modernisation agenda. However, these twin drivers are not necessarily compatible, and social care users and workers should be wary of them, for several reasons. First, the evidence suggests that in any partnership, the needs and aims of the dominant partner will usually dictate the terms and achievements of the partnership: in this case, it is clear that the NHS, and therefore the medical model of care, is dominant (Rummery, 2005). This has worrying implications for user empowerment: it means that not only will users' interests be subservient to the organisational power and interests of health and social care, but also that the dominant partner in the partnership is one whose professional and organisational interests have historically been much less tied to user empowerment than social services'. Second, although the evidence of social services' success in achieving user empowerment remains patchy, analysis of the 1990 community care changes shows conclusively that social care professionals had to manage an impossible tension between user empowerment and resource rationing in their practice, and that organisational imperatives to ration access to resources and implement quasi-markets took precedence (Lewis and Glennerster, 1996). If we look at what the overarching imperative driving the policy changes in 2006 is, then it is clear that the modernisation agenda and the drive to contain service costs continues to dominate the policy discourse, and health and social care partnerships, and user empowerment, are seen as the route to that end, with the former a more powerful route than the latter.

If New Labour really wanted to achieve significant gains in user outcomes through modernising public services, then 2006 marks some significant lost opportunities for a bold vision for health and social care. If cost and demand containment really are so vital, why not let local authorities take over the running of health services, instead of the other way round? If user empowerment really is so vital, again, why not let local authorities take over the running of health services? Particularly since the 1990 community care changes, local authorities and social services departments have had years of experience of managing tight budgets and of being accountable to users through democratic and citizen-engagement means, and their core workers (professional social workers) have a professional and ethical commitment to user empowerment that surpasses anything health professionals have to offer (Wistow, 2006). *Our health, Our care, Our say* has made very little progress in addressing some of the key issues in social care that concern users: the unfairness of access to and the funding of social care services, the failure to properly address the issue of funding for long-term care, the failure to make personal care free of charge, and the failure to make direct payments properly funded and universally accessible. While there is nothing on the agenda from the Conservative or Liberal Democrat Parties to indicate that they have any brighter ideas or bolder visions, it does appear that New Labour has run out of steam in social care.

References

Age Concern (2006) *Who should pay for care? Paying for care in later life*, London: Age Concern.

Barnes, M. (1997) *Care, communities and citizens*, London: Longman.

Bell, A. and Bowes, D. (2006) *Financial care models in Scotland and the UK*, York: Joseph Rowntree Foundation.

Birrell, D. (2006) 'The disintegration of local authority social services departments', *Local Government Studies*, vol 32, no 2, pp 139-51.

BMA (British Medical Association) (2006) *Child and adolescent mental health*, London: BMA.

Brown, L. and Cullis, J. (2006) 'Team production and policy for the care of older people: problems with theory and evidence', *Policy Studies*, vol 27, no 1, pp 55-69.

Cabinet Office (1999) *Modernising government*, Cm 4310, London: The Stationery Office.

Callaghan, G. and Wistow, G. (2006a) 'Governance and public involvement in the British National Health Service: understanding difficulties and developments', *Social Science and Medicine*, vol 63, no 9, pp 2289-300.

Callaghan, G. and Wistow, G. (2006b) 'Publics, patients, citizens or consumers: power and decision making in primary health care', *Public Administration*, vol 84, no 3, pp 583-601.

Cheetham, J. (1993) 'Social work and community care in the 1990s: pitfalls and potentials', in R. Page and J. Baldock (eds) *Social Policy Review 5*, London: Social Policy Association, pp 155-77.

Chitsabesan, P., Kroll, L., Bailey, S., Kenning, C., MacDonald, W. and Theodosiou, L. (2006) 'Mental health needs of young offenders in custody and in the community', *British Journal of Psychiatry*, vol 188, pp 534-40.

Clarke, J. (2006) 'Consumer, clients or citizens? Politics, policy and practice in the reform of social care', *European Societies*, vol 8, no 3, pp 423-42.

Commission for Healthcare Audit and Inspection (2006) *Living well in later life: A review of progress against the National Service Framework for older people*, London: Commission for Healthcare Audit and Inspection.

Community Care Statistics (2006) *Community Care Statistics 2006: Supported residents (adults) England*, The Information Centre, Adult Social Care Statistics (www.ic.nhs.uk/pubs/ccs06suppres).

Coulter, A. (2006) *Engaging patients in their healthcare: How is the UK doing relative to other countries?*, Oxford: Picker Institute Europe.

Coulter, A. and Ellins, J. (2006) *Patient-focused interventions: A review of the evidence*, London: The Health Foundation.

Counsel and Care (2006) *Care contradictions: Higher charges and fewer services*, London: Counsel and Care.

Croucher, K. and Rhodes, P. (2006) *Testing consumer views on paying for long-term care*, York: Joseph Rowntree Foundation.

CSCI (Commission for Social Care Inspection) (2006a) *Relentless optimism: Creative commissioning for personalized care*, London: CSCI.

CSCI (2006b) *Time to care? An overview of home care services for older people in England, 2006*, London: CSCI.

CSCI (2006c) *Joint investigation into the provision of services for people with learning disabilities at Cornwall Partnership NHS Trust*, London: Commission for Healthcare Audit and Inspection.

Davies, C., Wetherell, M. and Barnett, E. (2006) *Citizens at the centre: Deliberative participation in healthcare decisions*, Bristol: The Policy Press.

DH (Department of Health) (2001) *National Service Framework for older people*, London: DH.

DH (2005) *Independence, well-being and choice: Our vision for the future of social care for adults in England*, Cm 6499, London: The Stationery Office.

DH (2006a) *Our health, Our care, Our say: A new direction for community services – Health and social care working in partnership*, Cm 6737, London: The Stationery Office.

DH (2006b) *A stronger local voice: A framework for creating a stronger local voice in the development of health and social care services*, London: DH.

DH (2006c) *Bournewood briefing sheet* (www.dh.gov.uk/assetRoot/ 04/13/68/45/04136845.pdf).

Disability Rights Commission (2006) *Equal treatment: Closing the gap – A formal investigation into physical health inequalities experienced by people with learning disabilities and/or mental health problems*, London: Disability Rights Commission.

Glasby, J. (2006) 'Whose agenda is it anyway', *Community Care*, 23 February-1 March, pp 34-5.

Glasby, J. and Beresford, P. (2006) 'Who knows best? Evidence-based practice and the service-user contribution', *Critical Social Policy*, vol 26, no 1, pp 268-84.

Glasby, J., Smith, J. and Dickinson, H. (2006) *Creating NHS Local: A new relationship between PCTs and local government*, Birmingham: Health Services Management Centre, University of Birmingham.

Glendinning, C. and Means, R. (2006) 'Personal social services: developments in adult social care', in L. Bauld, K. Clarke and T. Maltby (eds) *Social Policy Review 18*, Bristol: The Policy Press/Social Policy Association, pp 15-33.

Hardy, B., Young, R. and Wistow, G. (1999) 'Dimensions of choice in the assessment and care management process: the views of older people', *Health and Social Care in the Community*, vol 7, no 6, pp 483-91.

Henwood, M. (2006) 'Destination unknown', *Community Care*, 23 February-1 March, pp 36-7.

Hudson, B. (2006) 'Policy change and policy dilemmas: interpreting the community services White Paper in England', *International Journal of Integrated Care*, vol 6, 17 August (www.ijic.org).

Joseph Rowntree Foundation (2006) *Paying for long-term care*, York: Joseph Rowntree Foundation.

Kitchen, G. (2006) *Mapping older people's advocacy in the English regions*, Stoke on Trent: Older People's Advocacy Alliance.

Laing & Buisson (2006) *Care of elderly people: UK market report 2006*, London: Laing & Buisson.

Leece, J. and Bornat, J. (eds) (2006) *Developments in direct payments*, Bristol: The Policy Press.

Le Grand, J. and Bartlett, W. (eds) (1993) *Quasi-markets and social policy*, Basingstoke: Macmillan.

Lewis, J. and Glennerster, H. (1996) *Implementing the new community care*, Buckingham: Open University Press.

Newman, J. (2001) *Modernising governance: New Labour, policy and society*, London: Sage Publications.

Pickard, S., Sheaff, R. and Dowling, B. (2006) 'Exit, voice, governance and user-responsiveness: the case of English primary care trusts', *Social Science and Medicine*, vol 63, no 2, pp 373-83.

Poll, C., Duffy, S., Hatton, C., Sanderson, H. and Routledge, M. (2006) *A report on In Control's first phase 2003-2005*, London: In Control.

Riddell, S., Pearson, C., Jolly, D., Barnes, C., Priestly, M. and Mercer, G. (2005) 'The development of direct payments in the UK: implications for social justice', *Social Policy and Society*, vol 4, part 1, pp 75-87.

Rowe, R. and Shepherd, M. (2002) 'Public participation in the new NHS: no closer to citizen control?', *Social Policy and Administration*, vol 36, no 3, pp 275-90.

Rummery, K. (2002a) *Disability, citizenship and community care: A case for welfare rights?*, Aldershot: Ashgate.

Rummery, K. (2002b) 'Towards a theory of welfare partnerships', in C. Glendinning, M. Powell and K. Rummery (eds) *Partnerships, New Labour and the governance of welfare*, Bristol: The Policy Press, pp 229-47.

Rummery, K. (2005) 'Partnerships and collaborative governance in welfare: the citizenship challenge', *Social Policy and Society*, vol 5, part 2, pp 293-305.

Rummery, K. (2006) 'Disabled citizens and social exclusion: the role of direct payments', *Policy & Politics*, vol 34, no 4, pp 633-51.

Scottish Executive (2006) *Range and Capacity Group second report: The future care of older people in Scotland*, Edinburgh: Scottish Executive.

Scourfield, P. (2005) 'Implementing the Community Care (Direct Payments) Act: will the supply of personal assistants meet the demand and at what price?', *Journal of Social Policy*, vol 34, part 3, pp 469-89.

Scourfield, P. (2006) '"What matters is what works?": how discourses of modernisation have both silenced and limited debate on domiciliary care for older people', *Critical Social Policy*, vol 26, no 1, pp 5-30.

Shepherd, M. (1995) *Care management and the new social work: A critical analysis*, London: Whiting and Birch.

Spandler, H. (2004) 'Friend or foe? Towards a critical assessment of direct payments', *Critical Social Policy*, vol 24, no 2, pp 187-209.

Summary of the Public Service Agreement on Home Care (2006) *Summary of the Public Service Agreement (PSA) target on home care 2006*, The Information Centre (www.ic.nhs.uk/pubs/psahome).

Tanner, D. (2003) 'Older people and access to care', *British Journal of Social Work*, vol 33, no 4, pp 499-515.

Ungerson, C. (2004) 'Whose empowerment and independence? A cross-national perspective on cash for care schemes', *Ageing and Society*, vol 24, no 2, pp 189-212.

Wanless, D. (2002) *Securing our future health: Taking a long-term view*, www.hm-treasury.gov.uk/wanless, accessed 30/03/2007.

Warner, L., Mariathasan, J., Lawton-Smith, S. and Samele, C. (2006) *Choice literature review: A review of the literature and consultation on choice and decision-making for users and carers of mental health and social care services*, London: Sainsbury Centre for Mental Health/King's Fund.

Wistow, G. (2006) *Improving services, improving governance*, London: Local Government Association.

Children's services in 2006

Harriet Churchill

Introduction

This chapter examines the rapidly unfolding story of children's services reform in the UK in 2006. Those working in children's services are responding to multiple drivers of change inhabiting a fast-moving policy landscape. Major reorganisation is under way in response to the 2004 Children Act, which implemented the structural reforms put forward in the *Every Child Matters* Green Paper (DfES, 2003). The 2004 Children Act seeks comprehensive reform across the range of services for children aged 0-19 years and their families and has been described as constituting "the most radical transformation [of children's services] since the 1948 Children Act" (Hudson, 2006, p 86). The timing of such radical reform has been explained as the cumulative effect of huge concern over child protection failures (Laming, 2003), and ongoing policy agendas aiming to 'modernise' public services and reduce social exclusion (Parton, 2006). With imminent implementation targets and several new policy announcements in 2006, this chapter sets out to examine reform in two stages. First, the main tenets of the evolving national policy framework are summarised. Second, there is a discussion highlighting five key implementation concerns – competing policy agendas, realising the outcome-led approach, accountability gaps, joining up services and developing partnership working and resources and capabilities for implementation and development.

Children's services reform 2004-06: national policy framework

The *Every Child Matters* Green Paper sought to reduce the risk of child protection failures, by re-orientating children's services towards improving children's "lives as a whole", their "outcomes", "well-being" and "life chances", "maximising the opportunities open to them"

(DfES, 2003, pp 6-7). The Green Paper defines children's well-being in terms of five objectives that are to guide service review and reform: enhancing children's health, safety, contribution to society, enjoyment and achievements, and economic well-being (DfES, 2003, p 14). To advance these outcomes for children, several proposals were put forward envisaging more integrated, accessible and responsive services focused on prevention and supported by enhanced accountability, organisational reform, joined-up working and workforce development.

Integrated, preventative and responsive services

Every Child Matters proposed a comprehensive review of children's services, placing "children's needs at the heart" of provision (DfES, 2003, p 9). The Laming Report (2003) attributed the failure to protect Victoria Climbié from harm as a consequence of fragmentation between the 'hard end' of crisis intervention and the 'soft end' of general universal services for all, as well as a lack of clarity about professional responsibilities. *Every Child Matters* proposed that this fragmentation should be overcome by universal services meeting general needs in a tailored personalised way while also providing "the detection of problems at the earliest possible stage" and "seamless access to more specialist services" (DfES, 2003, pp 20-1). Children's centres and extended schools are two principal means of service reform, with a more recent additional spotlight on youth services reform (DfES, 2005; Home Office, 2006). Building on Sure Start Local Programmes (SSLPs), children's centres have initially been funded in economically deprived neighbourhoods. Extending the remit of SSLPs, they serve a wider community (children aged 0-19, carers and parents), provide more prescribed core services (mainly health, childcare and early education), are accountable to the new local children's authority and are inspected against the five outcomes for children in *Every Child Matters*. Extended schools work with other service providers to host a range of services, such as out-of-school childcare and activities, parental support, basic healthcare and referrals to specialist services. The Department for Education and Skills has set ambitious targets for 2,500 operational Sure Start children's centres by 2008 and every school to be an extended school by 2010. By December 2006 there were around 900 children's centres operational (DfES, 2006a). By October 2006 around 2,500 schools had become extended schools while 4,700 schools were in the process of becoming extended schools (Ofsted, 2006).

Table 5.1 provides a summary of the most recent policy developments in 2006. Announcements on health, education, social care, criminal justice and local government reform all support the shift towards more community-based and preventative services. The 2006 Department of Health White Paper, *Our health, Our care, Our say*, stressed the need for pre-natal and post-natal maternity and preventative health services, identifying children's centres and home visiting as critical mechanisms for improving access and responsiveness. The 2006 Childcare Act expands local authorities' duty to ensure enough childcare places are available for all working parents requiring provision, to provide information on childcare options to parents and to provide information, advice and staff development to childcare providers. A focus on improving services for disabled children and adults is also discernible with the Office for Disability Issues reviewing services for disabled children in line with the five outcomes of *Every Child Matters* (DfES, 2006a). Supporting parents 'as early as possible' has been highlighted as critical in preventing the "escalation of behaviour and health problems" (SEU, 2006, p 19). The *Respect action plan* suggested that "the small minority of families with multi-faceted problems" could benefit from intensive health-led family support and 'supernanny' style parenting courses (Home Office, 2006, p 21; Ward and Wintour, 2006). Additionally there were proposals to improve access to educational, volunteering and leisure opportunities for young people at risk (DfES, 2005; Home Office, 2006). Specific proposals included an Opportunity Card for young people from low-income families to access local leisure facilities, and £100 million investment in youth volunteering. Additionally, local authorities will soon be required to provide a more comprehensive package of services to young people found truanting from school (Home Office, 2006).

In 2006 the long-awaited *Care matters* Green Paper was published, setting out proposals for the reform of social care for children (DfES, 2006b). *Care matters* seeks to reduce the cost of providing social care for children and to improve children's outcomes. Looked-after children have much lower levels of educational attainment and are three times more likely than other children to be in the criminal justice system (DfES, 2006b). *Care matters* seeks to better prevent children entering care, improve the provision and stability of care, and support children leaving care. Emphasis is placed on more multiagency support services for families with children at risk of entering care. Improving foster care and adoption are also critical to the reforms. Proposals include a higher basic level of maintenance for carers, multiagency packages of family support services tailored to children's needs, improved training and support for carers, an emphasis on involving children in decisions and better inspection of provision. The role of social workers is to change in

Table 5.1: Significant policy announcements supporting children's services reform in 2006

Policy source	Announcements
Department of Health, *Our health, Our care, Our say: A new direction for community services*, January 2006	• Emphasis on preventative and community-based health and social care services • Stronger joint planning, commissioning, delivery and workforce development between health and social care services • Active role for citizens in service decisions and health choices • Audit of local services for disabled children and community health/social care resources
Home Office, *Respect action plan*, January 2006	• Aims to tackle "disruptive behaviour" and create "respect for each other" (Home Office, 2006, p 3) • Identifies a "minority" who "lack respect for normal values" and engage in anti-social behaviour, "alcohol, crime and drug misuse" (Home Office, 2006, pp 3, 21) • Focus on punitive and preventative measures aimed at parents, families, schools and communities • Extensions of legal powers for citizens and services to identify, monitor and reprimand anti-social behaviour • Enhanced information sharing between agencies • Investments in intensive parenting/family support schemes for parents in need • Reform of services to improve educational, volunteering and leisure opportunities for young people at risk

continued ...

Table 5.1 (continued)

Policy source	Announcements
2006 Childcare Act, July	• Local authorities and partners to improve outcomes for children under the age of five via improved childcare provision and standards • Local authorities to ensure childcare provision meets working parents' needs, supports childcare providers and ensures adequate information about local services • Strengthened role for service user feedback • New national integrated Early Years Foundation Stage; all service providers working with children under the age of eight to register and deliver against new framework
Social Exclusion Unit, *Reaching out: An action plan on social exclusion*, September 2006	• Focuses on the "most excluded" who suffer "lifelong disadvantage" and a "generational cycle of exclusion" (SEU, 2006, p 2) • Seeks early identification of problems, preventative and localised, tailored services • Advocates intensive home-based health-led services and parenting support for young children and parents with multiple needs based around children's centres • Additional focus on children in care, teenage parents, children with behavioural/mental health needs and adults with 'chaotic' lives • Highlights need for identification and dissemination of effective family support services

continued ....

Table 5.1 (continued)

Policy source	Announcements
Department for Communities and Local Government, *Strong and prosperous communities*, Local Government White Paper, October 2006	• Focus on central government, local government and community relations • Local councils and partner agencies have a duty to produce and deliver Local Area Agreements (LAAs) (actions plans and targets for delivery of strategic service plans) in agreement with central government • Structural reforms include the option of three local authority leadership structures (directly elected local mayor, directly elected councillor executive or councillor-elected leader), strengthened role for overview and scrutiny committees in monitoring service standards, review of access to councillor opportunities, strengthened role and local budget for councillors for neighbourhood improvement and a simplification of performance monitoring frameworks/targets • Citizen participation to be enabled via better information on services, standards and local council priorities, increased powers to hold service providers to account via 'action calls', better access to direct service management and increased duties on local authorities to involve community members

continued ...

Table 5.1 (continued)

Policy source	Announcements
Department for Education and Skills, *Care matters*, November 2006	• Seeks to prevent children entering care, improve the quality and stability of care placements and foster care, improve educational outcomes and support transitions out of care • Pilots intensive integrated family support and family therapy approaches for children at risk of entering care • Pilots social care practices with budget-holding lead social workers assigned to each child in care • Reform of foster care via better recruitment, support, regulation and procurement for foster carers • Increases social workers' budget and university financial support for educational opportunities; increases access and level of school transport, leisure and volunteering opportunities • Extends schools' duty to admit children in care and assigns a 'virtual' headteacher to review standards of education in area for children in care • Children in care: veto on extended care after the age of 18 • Workforce development and training for social care, health and educational professionals working with children in care, supported by better dissemination of good practice

order to enhance accountability and responsiveness to children in care. Once a child has entered the care system, a lead social worker, operating in a local social care practice with a local budget, will commission and oversee services and act as a consistent guardian advocate for the child. These GP-style 'social care practices', commissioned by but independent from local authorities, will be piloted and seek to enhance flexibility so that social workers have more 'freedom' to respond directly and quickly to children's needs. The duty of local authorities to enhance educational outcomes is also restated, with proposals for better school transport following a change in care placement, and financial support to access university. Access to health and leisure services will also be reviewed (DfES, 2006b).

A new framework of organisational structures, accountability and joined-up working

Every Child Matters sought to address vertical and horizontal accountability gaps occurring between central and local government, between different professions and organisations, and between managers and frontline practitioners. By 2008 local children's social services and education departments are to merge to become local children's authorities, under the leadership of a children's director, supported by a lead council member for children. By 2008, children's directors are to establish a local children's trust, made up of senior officers from health, social services and education, working in partnership with the voluntary and business sectors. This will become the strategic body steering the reform of children's services. Children's trusts will initially conduct a systematic review of services and local needs, in order to produce a Children and Young People's Plan (CYPP). This is to be agreed with central government and published by 2008. Children's trusts are able to jointly commission services facilitated by a degree of budget pooling. Local children's authorities are also to establish local safeguarding boards, specifically responsible for the review of services for children at risk. Such reorganisation alongside enhanced joint planning and commissioning is expected to deliver efficiency gains as duplication is reduced, budgets are pooled and services become more suitably targeted (DfES, 2003). However, it was not until 2006 that a Transformation Fund was announced to support these organisational reforms and efforts to secure more joined-up working.

The *Every Child Matters* initiatives also build on previous reforms aimed at developing a common needs assessment framework for health and care services and better information sharing. A controversial proposal included the development of a national children's database through which practitioners from across agencies could access and contribute to an electronic record of a child's involvement with services (DfES, 2003). By 2005 guidance to health practitioners set out a duty to share information at the point of 'concern' about risks to children rather than evidence of harm (DH, 2005), and national service plans have since stipulated responsibility for reporting child protection concerns across education, health, community and police services.

Performance monitoring has been reformed to improve service accountability against the *Every Child Matters* outcomes framework. The 2006 Childcare Act stipulates that Ofsted is to inspect all children's services and develop integrated standards frameworks. The local government White Paper supports the *Every Child Matters* outcomes framework, as local authorities are to be accountable for outcomes for children, young people and families as one of the four streams for local authority performance rating. LAAs are to include childcare and children's services targets and communities will be encouraged to take a more active role in service development and delivery (DCLG, 2006).

Workforce development

Staff shortages, inadequate training, lack of leadership, low staff morale and poor staff retention were cited as critical factors leading to poor service outcomes (DfES, 2003, 2006b). Workforce development has therefore been a major aspect of reform with initiatives to:

- improve workforce data;
- create an integrated qualification, skills and career framework across children's services, for example based on the Early Years Foundation Stage;
- improve recruitment and retention through campaigns, better training and improved support for foster carers and for health, social care and education professionals;
- improve leadership and management through schemes such as the 'virtual headteacher' (responsible for improving educational standards for children in care) and lead professionals for children and families most in need;
- identify and disseminate evidence-based good practice through organisations to be established for this purpose, such as the National Academy for Parenting Practitioners or the National Centre for

Excellence in Children's Services (DfES, 2006a; Home Office, 2006).

New bodies, such as the Children's Workforce Unit and the Sector Skills Council for Children, have been established to review the qualifications and skills required to develop the children's services workforce. Crucial to development is the need to identify and disseminate evidence-based good practice. For example, the National Academy for Parenting Practitioners, to be established in 2007, will develop evidence-based training programmes to support professionals across the statutory, third and private sectors in their delivery of family support services (SEU, 2006).

Policy responses and impacts

By the end of 2006 most local authorities had reorganised their education and social care services, established children's directors, children's trusts and local safeguarding boards, reviewed local services and set local priorities in line with achieving better outcomes for children. There are some indications of improvements in service standards and outcomes for children. The annual inspection of services found some rise in standards and meaningful improvements against the five *Every Child Matters* outcomes (Ofsted, 2006). Ofsted concluded that local authorities were giving greater priority to safeguarding children, progress had been made towards more integrated inter-agency working and children had a meaningful role in service planning (Ofsted, 2006). However, the pace and scale of reform varied greatly across localities, with some local authorities taking a leading role in the process of national reform, while others lagged behind and fell below national standards. In explaining the varied pace of change, five key implementation issues will be examined: competing policy agendas, realising the outcome-led approach, accountability gaps, joining up services and developing partnership working, and resources and capabilities for implementation and development.

Competing policy agendas

Across central and local government, as well as professional organisations, there are several competing agendas motivating those involved in children's services. These competing agendas can be described as tensions between social threat, social investment and social justice perspectives on the problems children, families and society face. Some commentators on policy change have identified a tension between a 'social investment' approach to addressing problems such as poor educational outcomes or anti-social behaviour among young people and an 'empowerment' or 'ethic of care' perspective that seeks to enhance children's rights, resources and well-being (Featherstone, 2004; Williams, 2004). A social investment approach seems to be dominant across the European Union, framing social policy reform around the need to contain welfare expenditure and address problems of unemployment, skills shortages and welfare dependency through investment in health, social care and educational services that support parenting and child development from a very early stage in a child's life (Lister, 2003; Williams, 2004). Claims that the current UK reforms demonstrate the ascendancy of social investment approaches to social policy and social problems refer to several key features of reform:

- the reforms are led by the Department for Education and Skills;
- children's directors have in practice mainly been drawn from educational professions;
- service inspection has become the responsibility of Ofsted;
- targets supporting the outcomes framework monitor physical health outcomes, numeracy and literacy targets, teenage pregnancy rates and social care data (rather than targets for user satisfaction, user involvement or a more diverse conception of well-being beyond health and education);
- reforms include an extension of data systems to monitor children's health and educational development (Williams, 2004; Parton, 2006).

While improved access to health and educational services is critical in addressing disadvantage, there is concern that reforming children's services primarily around health and educational outcomes can provide a narrow framework for services and lead to detrimental effects. The social investment approach can neglect children's rights and experiences as children, reformulate childhood as a public concern rather than a 'private matter' and can view childhood as a time of preparation for future employment. This approach goes hand in hand with increased regulation of children, young people and parents, in the interests of monitoring development and preventing problems.

Additionally, there is a significant social threat discourse, especially emanating from the Home Office focus on anti-social behaviour as an "intractable problem with the behaviour of some individuals and families" whereby "there is a lack of respect for values that almost everyone in the country shares" and a lack of parental teaching of such values (Home Office, 2006, p 9). The *Respect action plan* seeks a "new approach to tackle the behaviour of problem families by challenging them to accept support to change their behaviour, backed up by enforcement measures" (Respect Homepage, 2006). An element of mistrust towards parents pervades these policy discourses. Government and media announcements in 2006 have also expressed alarm over child health and development trends, with clear positioning of parents and professionals as at fault. Barratt has argued that alarmist policy discourses can increase parental anxiety over what constitutes good parenting and inhibit 'autonomous emotional expressions' within parent–child interactions (Barratt, 2006). Professionals may also prematurely label children as having problems and parents could fear such labelling (Brown, 2004). A narrow social investment approach to children's services reform, fused with social threat discourses, contributes to a negative representation of children focused primarily on narrow educational developmental targets.

However, it would be inaccurate to characterise New Labour's approach to children's services as exclusively driven by a social investment or social threat approach or to overlook the important expansion in services for children and families. It is the tensions between competing agendas and diverse conceptions of children's well-being shaping policy and practice that are significant. At every level of policy implementation individuals hold varied perspectives, utilising spaces and capacities for discretion and creativity in responding to national frameworks (Hudson, 2006). More holistic and social justice approaches to children's well-being are also evident. These approaches focus more on the need to redress the balance of power, resources and opportunities in society and services provision in children's favour. However, the social justice aims are undermined by a lack of emphasis on these in funding, in the evidence base and in institutional obligations to ensure user participation. Social threat discourses collide with social justice approaches. The former condemn disadvantaged groups as deviant, and result in punitive measures; the latter seek to understand people's own sense of their problems, dissent and needs while also investing in rehabilitation and opportunities for empowerment and cultural recognition. Local priorities and practice will be informed by whether local children's trusts adopt a social investment, social threat or social justice conception of local problems and needs.

Realising the outcome-led approach

Despite these competing conceptualisations, the reforms have gone some way to unify and clarify service goals. The shift towards outcome-led provision has been backed up by organisational and legal changes that facilitate more joint working towards the five *Every Child Matters* outcomes. However, beyond the tensions between the social investment, social threat and social justice discourses that inform policy objectives, there are difficulties with the *Every Child Matters* outcome-led approach. Here it is the methodological complexities and underlying theories of the determinants of children's well-being that will be the focus of discussion.

Translating the five outcomes into measurable indicators is an interpretive and technical process that, until recently, has not been supported by clear national guidelines (Ofsted, 2006). Children's trusts are developing diverse approaches. While Plymouth Children's Authority has recruited a researcher to develop its systems for 'data compiling and analysis' (DfES, 2006a), other authorities have compiled data from existing national and local sources. Data collection relies on practitioners to record the information and they may interpret the five outcomes in diverse ways. They also complain of a lack of time, expertise, resources and IT support, which inhibits their ability to keep comprehensive and up-to-date records (Ofsted, 2004).

The evidence base for achieving the five key outcomes is also somewhat limited. The government recognises that detailed cause and effect relationships are difficult to establish, but asserts the risk factors causing poor outcomes for children are 'well-known' (DfES, 2003; SEU, 2006). Evidence has been defined as those findings supported by "replicable, longitudinal, representative and random control trials" (SEU, 2006, p 30), which privileges certain research approaches, leading in particular to a lack of engagement with more qualitative, theoretical, contextualised or user perspective research. However, these latter approaches can contribute to service development. For example, Madge (2006) asked children about their lives at home, school and in the community. For respondents, "spending time with family and friends' and 'receiving love and attention' were two features of a 'good childhood' that remain hidden in the *Every Child Matters* framework (Madge, 2006). When asked to prioritise their school worries, the quality of their relationships with and treatment by their friends and teachers came before their concerns about their academic subjects (Madge, 2006). In serving an older age range, children's centres need to provide a more "inspirational range of activities for children and young people" and much more "meaningful involvement", according to a prominent campaign for investment in youth services (4Children, 2006).

Other research studies have argued that the affective quality of adult/parent–child relations are critical in buffering the detrimental psychological effects associated with poverty, stigma and low educational attainment (Gillies, 2005; Barratt, 2006). Additionally, a study concerned with the relationship between adults' and children's well-being within and beyond families has warned of a neglect of parental well-being within *Every Child Matters* reforms, with a lack of services catering for stressed parents, employed parents and parents vulnerable to mental health problems (Barratt, 2006). There is also an apparent contradiction between labour market and child-oriented policy developments, with New Labour criticised for increasing levels of work–family conflict through its advocacy of paid work as the best way out of poverty and its unimaginative support for employed parents (Williams, 2004). These problems may be resolved if the new LAAs adopt a more strategic approach to planning across adult, children and community services, as the local government White Paper recommends – as long as economic and social development are somehow considered together (DCLG, 2006). A more integrated approach of this kind could promote a more favourable economic and social environment for family well-being.

Accountability gaps

The new institutional frameworks for children's services do not seem to fully address accountability gaps. Children's directors are responsible for education and social care services for children, while the children's trusts, the key local strategic bodies, are composed of senior officials from a wider range of principal service providers. There potentially remain some limitations to the remit of children's directors in terms of responsibilities beyond care and education services, and questions about structures to allow an input to the local strategy from frontline professionals such as teachers and GPs whose role in reform is key. Headteachers, for example, have expressed a varied commitment to the extended schools initiative, and social workers are divided in response to *Care matters*. For Hudson, the reforms neglect the role of services such as the police and housing, as well as the relationship between frontline professionals and local strategic policy makers. He argues that the reforms need to go further to generate a stronger consensus, responsiveness and multifaceted joint working (Hudson, 2006). Responses to *Care matters* have also raised concerns about accountability in the proposed social care practices, which will require local authority regulation and need to remain linked to local authority support and guidance (*Community Care*, 2006a). Furthermore accountability directly to children, parents and citizens continues to be weak. Some commentators have responded to the *Care matters* proposals by arguing that a genuinely user-led service requires stronger legal powers to enable children, parents and communities to call for service changes (*Community Care*, 2006b). Again, the local government White Paper may lead to improvements in accountability to adult citizens via the emphasis on developing decentralised decision making and locally elected service representatives.

Joining up services and developing partnership working

When considering partnership working there are also many unresolved issues. While the 2004 Children Act has structurally integrated education and social services departments within local authorities, the majority of children's directors have been recruited from educational backgrounds and may be less aware of the objectives and perspectives of other services – an issue raised in a recent Audit Commission report (Hudson, 2006). The Audit Commission examined extended schools in 14 children's authorities and found that authorities were unclear how services other than mainstream social care and health could be supported via schools. The approach to joint planning at times involved merely asking partners to comment on draft proposals written by education officials (Audit Commission, 2006). Key services for children and families such as housing, community safety, youth services and community arts had weak links with schools, and were not well represented within children's authorities' strategic planning (Audit Commission, 2006). Voluntary organisations and youth workers have felt marginalised in the reform of the youth service. A report by the Youth Justice Board found that in seven out of ten local authorities examined, youth workers had little or no involvement in the decision that led to an Anti-Social Behaviour Order (ASBO), although they felt they could provide young people and parents with the support needed to improve behavioural outcomes (Roberts, 2006).

Investment of time and resources is needed to generate the conditions for effective joined-up working. A report on the development of integrated family support schemes concluded that resource, institutional and cultural constraints continued to inhibit joint working (Carpenter et al, 2005). For example, social workers were reluctant to refer families to services that they perceived as 'unspecialist' such as Sure Start services, while Sure Start workers were reluctant to involve social workers, because of fear of alarming parents or confusion over their responsibilities in child protection (Carpenter et al, 2005, p 37). Professionals wanted their specialism to be clarified and recognised alongside aspirations to develop partnership working. Ambitious government targets, frequent organisational and financial uncertainty and complex legal and technical issues in sharing information also hindered joint working in practice (Carpenter et al, 2005). To overcome these problems, the report recommended joint target setting, comprehensive resource assessment and allocation (in terms of time, staff and funding), more practitioner consultation, joint training and awareness events, local leadership from local authorities, clarification of specialist contributions to family support services and investment in professional development (Carpenter et al, 2005). One response to these problems has been to allocate a lead professional to oversee service delivery or to take the lead in locally establishing joint working initiatives (DfES, 2006a).

CYPPs will need to recognise and counter the possibility of continued accountability gaps between children's authorities and other agencies, and between frontline staff and local policy makers. Allocating clear responsibility and resources for developing linkages in information sharing and decision making across services and hierarchies will be very important. Further, while the *Every Child Matters* reforms aim to create an integrated and coherent set of 'children's services', fragmentation may reappear between children's and adult services. Different local authorities are developing different structural approaches to address this problem. While Surrey Council has merged children and adult social care services, others, such as Brighton Council, have merged education, social care and (some) health services for children within the children's trust structure.

The Department for Education and Skills has also published further guidance on working in more participatory ways with children. The guidance is based on a research report on participation approaches to service planning and provision that found participation was far from "embedded in service practice" (Kirby et al, 2005). It was in the voluntary sector, youth work and regeneration work that a more participatory approach occurred, with health and criminal justice services cited as much further behind (Kirby et al, 2005). However, even in the more progressive sectors, participation remains largely a matter concerned with service delivery options rather than strategic service decisions and tends to not be backed up by feedback to young people or training for adult decision makers (Kirby et al, 2005). An analysis of 20 CYPPs found that three quarters of children's authorities had not involved or consulted disabled children and their parents in drawing up their plans, even though this is a requirement and the government has issued specific guidance for involving disabled service users (*Community Care*, 2006c). The Department for Education and Skills' guidance advocates that local authorities draw on the skills of the progressive sectors (Kirby et al, 2005), and invest time and money in promoting participation. However, more in-depth guidance or national standards for involving children (or parents) has not been produced and there are major resource constraints.

Resources and capabilities for implementation and development

There are many understandably cynical voices, claiming that the reforms set out above are so severely under-resourced that in reality they either deliver more rhetoric than radical change or increase the responsibilities of local authorities under crippling financial conditions (*Community Care*, 2006b). The government was slow to respond to local authority requests for additional ring-fenced funds for implementing change, with the £250 million Transformation Grant not announced until mid-2006. In order to realise the ambitious targets for improving children's outcomes, many have argued that much more substantial investment will be needed. Even if the *Every Child Matters* outcomes framework is accepted, the targeted nature of investment means impact will be limited. For example, the focus on investing initially in neighbourhoods classed as the most economically deprived will limit impact on children's outcomes as around 44% of children living in relative poverty live outside of these localities (Parton, 2006). Further, a preventative approach aimed at 'maximising children's opportunities' and outcomes is far from a cheap option. Local authorities continue to face hard choices in juggling funding between adult and children's services, acute and preventative provisions (*Community Care*, 2006b). For example, health practitioners are concerned that funding for acute services is under threat, and youth workers have witnessed the closure of youth clubs, while investment is raised for anti-social behaviour detection (*Community Care*, 2006b; Roberts, 2006). The Association of Directors of Social Services claimed there was a £1.76 billion financial deficit in social services, limiting the capacity to implement the changes required in the health White Paper (DH, 2006) and *Care matters* (DfES, 2006b).

Workforce development is a particularly major challenge and was identified as a critical issue in *Care matters*. The data now collected on the social care workforce indicate that around 15% of care worker vacancies in children's homes remain unfilled, that there are too few qualified social workers in comparison to vacancies and that 30% of local authorities recruit from overseas to fill shortages in social care recruitment (DfES, 2006a). Without solving recruitment problems, stability of care for children remains a major challenge in the care system. The reforms also require new skills and qualifications. For example, social workers acting as social care practice managers will need to acquire business and budget management skills.

Local authorities have been quick to highlight the transaction costs involved in implementing reform. However, the government views reform as securing efficiency gains via the better use of existing funding and the flexibility of joint commissioning. For example, in October 2006, the new Skills for Care and Children's Workforce Development Council claimed that it was the role of local authorities to "take up their responsibilities for supporting human resources" (*Community Care*, 2006b, p 28). Hence lack of investment in staff development was seen as a consequence of inappropriate local authority use of resources rather than inadequate central funding. However, only 53% of councils planned to spend the transformation grant on training and development according to one source in 2006-07 (*Community Care*, 2006b). The 2006 pre-Budget speech announced increases in spending on education and financial support to families, but funding for social care and health remains tight.

Conclusion

This chapter set out to review the current reform of children's services in the UK with a focus on developments in 2006 and the implementation of the *Every Child Matters* initiatives. Multiple drivers of reform were identified including Lord Laming's review of child protection services, New Labour policy agendas to modernise public services and to invest in children's health and educational development, and campaigns to enhance children's rights and well-being. A number of legislative changes and policy initiatives have been introduced, emanating mainly from the Department for Education and Skills but supported by the Department of Health, the Home Office and the Department for Communities and Local Government. Key dimensions of change include a shift towards outcome-led, integrated, responsive and preventative services; improved vertical and horizontal service accountability; more joined-up working; and better workforce retention, recruitment and performance. Local children's authorities have responded to the quick pace of reform. However, major concerns and limitations remain. These include contradictory policy agendas, which represent conflicting values and conceptions of the 'problem' in relation to children, families and communities. In particular social threat, social investment and social justice perspectives provide different policy priorities and implications, which can translate to contradictory pressures for local policy actors. Another critical issue has been the limited evidence base informing policy and a lack of dialogue between policy makers and theoretical, qualitative and user perspectives research. Further, a number of problems and constraints remain in attempting to effectively integrate services and join up planning, commissioning and delivery. These include cultural and institutional factors as well as the need for adequate vision, resources and investment to generate the conditions for change. Accountability gaps may remain with some services less in touch with the children's trusts agendas, and many frontline practitioners feeling a lack of voice in the children's trust framework. Crucially many local authorities complain of inadequate investment to meet local needs and national targets. These factors are critical in shaping the practical implementation of reforms and ensuring that these initiatives succeed in improving the lives of those at the receiving end and those working in children's services.

References

4Children (2006) '4Children and the National Youth Agency unite to call on government to treble investment in young people', News and information (www.4children.org.uk/information/show/ref/770, 5/11/06).

Audit Commission (2006) *More than the sum: Mobilising the whole council and its partners to support school success*, London: Audit Commission.

Barratt, H. (2006) *Attachment and the perils of parenting*, London: NFPI.

Brown, A. (2004) 'Anti-social behaviour, crime control and social control', *The Howard Journal*, vol 43, no 2, pp 203-11.

Carpenter J., Griffin, M. and Brown, S. (2005) *The impact of Sure Start on social services*, Sure Start Unit Research Report FR015, London: DfES.

Community Care (2006a) 'Good idea or diversion?', 12 October, p 6.

Community Care (2006b) 'If we think we can relax on *Every Child Matters* we are deluded', 19 October, p 28.

Community Care (2006c) 'Plans fail to consult disabled children', 19 October, p 6.

DCLG (Department for Communities and Local Government) (2006) *Strong and prosperous communities: The local government White Paper*, Cm 6939, vol 1, London: The Stationery Office.

DfES (Department for Education and Skills) (2003) *Every Child Matters*, Cm 5860, London: The Stationery Office.

DfES (2005) *Youth matters: Next steps*, Cm 6629, London: DfES.

DfES (2006a) everychildmatters.gov.uk (17/10/06).

DfES (2006b) *Care matters: Transforming the lives of children and young people in care*, Cm 6932, London: The Stationery Office.

DH (Department of Health) (2005) *What to do if you have concerns about child protection*, London: The Stationery Office.

DH (2006) *Our health, Our care, Our say: Making it happen*, London: DH.

Featherstone, B. (2004) 'Rethinking family support in the current policy context', *British Journal of Social Work*, vol 36, no 1, pp 5-19.

Gillies, V. (2005) 'Raising the meritocracy: parenting and individualisation of social class', *Sociology*, vol 39, no 5, pp 835-53.

Home Office (2006) *Respect action plan*, London: Respect Task Force.

Hudson, B. (2006) 'Children and young people's strategic plans: we've been here before haven't we?', *Policy Studies*, vol 27, no 2, pp 86-99.

Kirby, P., Lanyon, C., Cronin, K. and Sinclair, R. (2005) *Building a culture of participation: Involving children and young people in policy, service planning, delivery and evaluation*, Research Report, London: DfES.

Laming, Lord (2003) *The Victoria Climbié Inquiry: A report of an inquiry*, Cm 5730, London: The Stationery Office.

Lister, R. (2003) 'Investing in the citizen-workers of the future: transformations in citizenship and the state under New Labour', *Social Policy and Administration*, vol 37, no 5, pp 427-43.

Madge, N. (2006) *Children these days*, Bristol: The Policy Press.

Ofsted (2004) *Strategic planning in LEAs: A technical report evaluating developments in LEAs' strategic planning and identifying good practice*, London: Ofsted.

Ofsted (2006) *The annual report of Her Majesty's Chief Inspector of Schools 2005/2006*, HC 78, London: The Stationery Office.

Parton, N. (2006) *Safeguarding children: Early intervention and surveillance in late modern society*, Basingstoke: Palgrave.

Respect Homepage (2006) *Respect action plan* (www.respect.gov.uk/article.aspx?id=9058, 17/1/06).

Roberts, Y. (2006) 'Casey fails to hear the voices of dissent', *Community Care*, 9 November, p 8.

SEU (Social Exclusion Unit) (2006) *Reaching out: An action plan on social exclusion*, London: SEU/Cabinet Office.

Ward, L. and Wintour, P. (2006) 'State supernannies to help struggling parents', *The Guardian*, 22 November.

Williams, F. (2004) 'Who works is what matters', *Critical Social Policy*, vol 24, no 3, pp 406-27.

SIX

Laying new foundations?
Social security reform in 2006

Stephen McKay

Introduction

In 2006 significant policy reforms were developed in the areas of child support, pensions, and more generally for recipients of out-of-work benefits. In each case the government set out agendas for reform that would have major long-term consequences, although with little happening immediately. To what extent, therefore, has New Labour been laying down new foundations for social security in the future? How far do the reforms imply a break with the past, and in what ways do they represent a continuation of key New Labour themes?

In this review we focus on the three main areas of reform, after setting out the relevant context. A later section more briefly discusses other policy developments taking place in 2006.

Background

Britain has long had a complex system of social security, with complex benefits (and tax credits) based on a range of different principles of eligibility (McKay and Rowlingson, 1998). Among its key features are a flat-rate system of contributory benefits, a high reliance on means-tested benefits to alleviate poverty (often set at levels exceeding contributory benefits), and universal benefits to meet some of the costs of children or disability. Over time, and particularly during the 1980s and 1990s, the emphasis on the contributory side of benefits was much reduced. These became a less important part of social security, which shifted towards income testing as the basis of eligibility.

Since Beveridge, social security has also tried to preserve people's incentives to provide for themselves. This has been particularly true for pensions. Voluntary private arrangements, through employer and personal pensions, have long been available for people to provide a higher level of retirement income. Where people are able to make their own provision, this is encouraged through generous tax breaks on the contributions made, and National Insurance rebates for those contracting out of the State Second Pension (previously the State Earnings Related Pension Scheme [SERPS]).

Policy since 1997

Academic discussion of social security under New Labour has tended to focus on their earlier years in office. The government's approach has been analysed as having strong degrees of both populism and pragmatism (Powell, 2000). It has also been notable for a strong emphasis on the role of paid work, and economic concerns more generally. A recent commentator described social security under New Labour as having become a "work-focused benefit regime" (Kemp, 2005, p 30).

An explicitly political or ideological approach has been substituted with an increased emphasis on technocratic solutions ('what works') and economic efficiency. One of the key themes has been a rejection of any thoroughgoing attempts to reduce inequality, or to consider redistribution as any part of the anti-poverty strategy (Lister, 2001).

Writers have often emphasised some ambivalence about an overall pattern of reform (especially Lister, 2001) that has also included significant increases in support for families with children, the introduction of a National Minimum Wage and considerable increases in support for older people. Driver and Martell (2002) discuss the possible tension that has arisen between support for the family and the emphasis on having more people move into paid work. Economists have also emphasised and measured the tension between encouraging people to move into work and increase their earnings, and the growth of means testing of benefits (Adam et al, 2006).

Brewer et al (2002) contrast the large number of reforms implemented under the first New Labour government (1997-2001) with their lack of explicit ideas about reform on taking office. They also remind us that the first two years were dedicated to following the tight spending plans set out by the previous Conservative government, so that major spending commitments could not really be enacted until 1999. Perhaps not surprisingly, education and the National Health Service (NHS)/ health were always ahead of social security in the competition for scarce funds. Even so, the New Deal for Young People was a key expensive ingredient of reform from the start.

Brewer et al (2002) characterise the main areas of change as being those of: encouraging paid work; reducing poverty for pensioners and, especially since 1999, for children; and an emphasis on means testing ('targeting') at the expense of contributory benefits. Perhaps a key theme underlying much of the change was attention to the very poorest (or most socially excluded) groups, and a denial that larger structures of inequality were related to the particular problems of the most disadvantaged. The earlier years of this administration were therefore particularly notable for:

- the introduction of welfare-to-work programmes, through various New Deals particularly for the young unemployed and for lone parents;
- the commitment (made in 1999) to end child poverty within 20 years, with various milestones in place before then;
- area-based targeting of services, such as through Sure Start (see Alcock, 2004);
- the replacement of in-work benefits delivered through the Department for Work and Pensions with tax credits delivered through the Inland Revenue (now Her Majesty's Revenue and Customs [HMRC]).

More recently the encouragement of paid work has been expressed in an aspiration for an 80% employment rate, rather than the prevailing 75% rate.

Social security reform has also been subject to the kinds of modernisation of social policy delivery seen in other parts of the welfare state. Efficiency savings were always bound to fall heavily on the Department for Work and Pensions, since it has a very large number of staff. The Department is projected to lose about 30,000 jobs over a three-year period, which has raised understandable concerns about its ability to deliver an efficient and customer-oriented benefits system.

Continuities and changes in 2006

In 2005, the Department for Work and Pensions had three different, arguably very different, Secretaries of State – Alan Johnson, David Blunkett and John Hutton. So, with John Hutton the Secretary of State throughout 2006, the Department for Work and Pensions has had a welcome degree of stability in its leadership. This has probably helped in the government's overall task of introducing some of the most important and far-reaching changes in social security made under Labour. It is perhaps too early to detect a specific Hutton-ite agenda, but 2006 was certainly a busy year for social security reform and two particularly significant areas of reform were tackled – pensions and child support. Arguably these are two of the most difficult challenges in the whole of social policy, let alone social security, and the reforms made in 2006 are certainly intended to signal a radical break with the past.

In some key areas the programme in 2006 is a continuation of the previous agenda – John Hutton reaffirmed the commitment to tackle child poverty and has made this the Department's number one priority[1]. The drive for efficiency savings continues, as in other departments. One of the key policy drivers continues to be to get people into work (and cease claiming benefits, at least in time), to assist both in controlling spending and in reducing poverty. This much continues past trends in policy development.

But 2006 has also seen large-scale reforms of significant areas long seen as overdue for change. A key principle that has affected reform across these is to remove the state from the process of service delivery, and for individuals to make their own arrangements (in terms of saving for retirement, and, for parents, agreeing levels of child support). The role of the state then becomes one of regulator, setting either default options (the new savings plans in the form of 'personal accounts': see DWP, 2006a) or a back-up service (child support: see DWP, 2006b).

Pensions reform, discussed below, puts renewed emphasis on the link between National Insurance contributions and entitlement to the state pension – a link long under pressure. The idea of a citizenship-based pension, once popular and partly recommended by the Pensions Commission (2005), was discarded in favour of a continued contributory approach. This reverses the policy direction taken over recent decades. Another major policy reversal was restoring the link between earnings growth and pensions, albeit this is subject to some fairly strong equivocation concerning affordability and the timing of its reintroduction. Moreover, the analysis and policy has at least half an eye trained on the proportion of pensioners subject to means testing, an area that has exercised commentators in the past without exciting much government interest.

Welfare reform Green Paper

This long-anticipated statement of policy direction was intended to speed the return of benefit recipients into work. It was particularly concerned with those people, not in work, who generally did *not* face an obligation to seek work (unlike unemployed jobseekers). The problem it addressed was that "there are groups of people locked into long-term dependency on benefits" (DWP, 2006c, p 3). The Green Paper was subtitled *Empowering people to work*, and the key objectives it set for policy change were to:

* reduce the numbers receiving Incapacity Benefit (IB) by one million over 10 years;
* increase the number of lone parents in work by 300,000;
* increase the numbers of people aged 50+ and working by one million.

Hutton said that the welfare Green Paper was "the beginning of what must be a national debate on the future direction of our welfare reforms" (DWP, 2006c, p iv). It was designed to do this through a whole raft of different policies, building on the experience of various New Deal programmes. IB is to be replaced by a new Employment and Support Allowance (ESA) by 2008. The ESA will be based on Jobseeker's Allowance (JSA) levels, with additional amounts following on from the Personal Capability Assessment (PCA). Work-focused interviews (with new IB claimants) will promote higher levels of work-related activity – with the threat of cuts in benefit for those who do not attend. The PCA is to focus on work-related factors, rather than being concerned with benefit entitlement. It is supposed to consider what people are able to do, rather than focusing on what they are unable to do. The reform also promises to look in detail at routes onto benefits for those with mental health problems, currently a significant proportion of those qualifying for IB. It is envisaged that financial support will continue for claimants who return to work. The private and voluntary sector are also to be invited to manage Pathways to Work schemes. Preston (2006) argues for a more critical examination of the role of employers, and their reluctance to recruit disabled workers. The Work and Pensions Select Committee report also addresses this issue, with additional concerns about the availability of funding for some elements (providing a good face-to-face service), the proposed changes that introduce a PCA and the adequacy of the proposed ESA (Work and Pensions Select Committee, 2006).

There is considerable overlap between IB recipients and the over-50s. For those older people outside IB, the Department for Work and Pensions plans to offer additional New Deal support for the over-50s including more intensive face-to-face guidance.

Some similar measures are proposed for lone parents. Lone parents with a youngest child aged 11 or older, will have a work-focused interview every three months, and other lone parents receiving benefit for more than a year will be seen every six months. A new additional payment, designed to reward work-related activities, is to be tested. In January 2007, John Hutton signalled a debate on whether lone parents should be expected to seek/take work when their youngest child reached 11, which would be a controversial step despite similar policies in most other countries.

Social security benefits for those of working age are increasingly oriented towards work. The expectation is that benefit recipients will be on the road to work, or at least actively engaging with ways of finding and remaining in paid work. With an aspiration of an 80% employment target, attention is focused on those groups less likely to be in paid work, with particular emphasis on lone parents and disabled people. More attention is also focused on older workers, with low but increasing rates of paid work. Those from minority ethnic groups also have lower rates of economic activity than their white counterparts, and are the subject of a specific government target, but receive less attention in the Green Paper.

The overall approach follows that of the earlier New Deal programmes. The key tool, for those groups not obliged to seek work, is one of intensive advice about work, training, childcare and the like. This is accompanied by a degree of increasing conditionality of entitlement to benefits for these groups – although for many the only new requirement is to attend (work-focused) interviews.

Pensions reform

Pensions reform and how people plan for incomes in retirement are firmly on the policy agenda, perhaps even at the top of that agenda. Part of the reason for the current interest in reform is the ageing of the population, which has resulted from rapid increases in life expectancy and the longer-term trend towards lower fertility. As a result, the percentage of the population aged 65+ is projected to double between 2000 and 2050 (Pensions Commission, 2004). This trend places greater stress on the means that people use to provide for their retirement, which in the UK involves an unusually wide array of choices. The Pensions Commission said that the UK had "the most complex pension system in the world" (Pensions Commission, 2004, p 210).

In addition to the trend towards an ageing population there have been signs that private pension provision is static or even declining, and in the UK the private sector plays an unusually large role. Many firms have closed their salary-related employer schemes to new members, and other forms of provision (such as stakeholder pensions) have often provided less generous employer contributions. Public trust in financial institutions and their products has been eroded following concerns about the mis-selling of personal pensions, and endowment policies. This has generated a large 'savings gap' and a perceived need to encourage greater private saving.

In April 2006 ('A' day), the wide variety of tax regimes affecting pensions changed. A series of eight sets of rules for different pension types were reduced to a single simplified set, including (notably) a lifetime limit on the size of individuals' retirement funds, no limit to pension funding just before retirement, and higher annual limits on pension contributions.

Other problems – in addition to those of affordability and adequacy – have also been given close attention. In particular:

- the different pension outcomes, prospects and choices of women compared to men (DWP, 2005);
- the incomplete take-up of Pension Credit; while this is the main means-tested benefit for pensioners (Adams et al, 2006), only around two thirds of those eligible for Pension Credit actually receive it (DWP, 2006d).

White Papers

The year 2006 saw two White Papers on pension reform. The first, *Security in retirement: Towards a new pensions system* (DWP 2006e), gave the structure for the entire reform agenda. The second, *Personal accounts: A new way to save* (DWP, 2006a), set out details of the new savings plan forming the central plank of the new strategy. The White Papers, and subsequent Pensions Bill, announced a number of key changes, including a new low-cost savings scheme ('personal accounts') into which employees are to be automatically enrolled. The Pensions Commission described this as a National Pensions and Savings Scheme (NPSS), before the Department for Work and Pensions adopted the simpler moniker of personal accounts. This is the ambitious centre-piece of the reforms. Up to 10 million people without access to occupational pensions may ultimately be included in this system.

These accounts have a number of key features. Employees are automatically entered into the savings scheme, unless they choose to opt out. This reversal of the usual joining process (opt-in) is designed to harness the power of inertia that often keeps people out of such schemes. In personal accounts, employees will contribute at least 4%, matched by a minimum 3% employer contribution and around 1% in the form of normal tax relief from the state. There will be choices of fund into which to invest the funds, and a default fund for those not making a selection (there are similarities here with the Child Trust Fund). The government is clearly a little concerned that such a scheme may lead to levelling-down among existing pension products. It intends to combat this possibility by having a maximum annual contribution and by preventing transfers into or out of personal accounts.

Personal accounts have received considerable attention, but we should not overlook other reforms affecting state pensions and discussed in the earlier of the two White Papers. Among the major elements of reform are:

- future increases in the state pension linked to earnings growth, rather than price inflation as at present;
- gradually raising the state pension age, reaching 66 by 2026, 67 by 2036 and 68 by 2046;
- a change to contributory conditions, particularly requiring 30 years' of contributions rather than 44 (for those retiring at 65) and a number of amendments and simplifications to contributory conditions. These changes retain a basic contributory element to the state pension, and avoid any changes based on either a more universal approach (such as a citizenship pensions) or moves towards greater means testing;
- enhancements to the value of deferred state pensions so it is more worthwhile for people to continue to work, taking their pension some months (or years) after state pension age. Those who defer may receive either a higher pension or a lump sum.

Age discrimination legislation

Age discrimination legislation came into force in October 2006. This may be seen as primarily an issue about equalities and rights. But it also serves as an encouragement for older people to retain contact with the labour market, and to consider their prospects (or rights) enhanced.

Defined benefit pension schemes: closures by firms

For some time, employers have been closing down their defined benefit schemes, which often have generous employer contributions. In most cases, this means that existing members may continue to contribute, but no new members are accepted. In their place most have introduced defined contribution arrangements, often attracting a lower level of employer contribution (see McKay, 2006).

In other highly visible cases, the closure of firms has sometimes resulted in occupational pension funds having large deficits. When this has happened in the past, rules dictated that any available money be used to pay current pensions. Those still of working age might then have much reduced pension rights – even though their own retirement could be quite close, and their ability to make up any savings very limited. To tackle this problem, a Pension Protection Fund was established to provide compensation for such people (with limits on levels of compensation). This fund is designed to restore confidence in employer (salary-related) schemes, and is funded by levies on the pensions industry. A new pensions regulator introduces wider powers to protect the benefits of work-based pensions.

Much of the approach to pension reform appears to be strongly based on the recommendations of the Pensions Commission (2004, 2005). It is clearly rather early to be evaluating reforms that will not have their full impact for several decades. However, while the overall package has commanded some support, the response from the independent Pensions Policy Institute (PPI), which has scrutinised most aspects of the reform, has been distinctly unenthusiastic:

> The White Paper proposals change the overall income distribution of older people very little, but if anything give more to higher income people than lower income.... The White Paper's estimate of the likely number of people eligible for the means-tested Pension Credit in future

(around one-third) looks to be at the bottom of a wide possible range. (PPI, 2006, p 3)

In other words, the government is assuming (or projecting) that fewer people will be eligible for means testing, a generally desirable aim, while the PPI is projecting rather higher numbers will still fall within the scope of Pension Credit. The PPI's analysis also suggests that few resources are involved in the reform: "There is no net cost to Government from the reforms in the short term.... From 2030 the White Paper proposals have an annual net cost to Government of around 0.1% of GDP" (PPI, 2006, p 3). Overall, they argue that the key pensions issues have been alleviated, to some extent, but not really solved. They also believe that the expectations being placed on personal accounts are much too high, and not likely to be realised.

Reforming child support, an end to the Child Support Agency

In 2006 the government lost patience with trying to make child support – and especially the Child Support Agency (CSA) – work as it was intended. Following an independent review (under Henshaw), the failure of its earlier reforms to make progress, and continued bad performance statistics, a new approach was thought to be needed. In December a White Paper set out a new direction for child support, with a greater emphasis on people making their own arrangements and the proposal for a new body with even stronger enforcement powers (Henshaw, 2006). The policy emphasis strongly shifted towards child poverty as an objective, and away from the earlier focus on making people face responsibilities.

While pensions policy has been the culmination of years of intensive work by an independent commission, and attempts at forging a national consensus, proposals for child support reform have taken less than a year from announcing an appetite for reform until the publication of a White Paper. It remains to be seen if the more rapid approach will deliver a sustainable programme of reform.

The CSA was created in 1993, with the role of implementing the 1991 Child Support Act and subsequent legislation. Previously child support had been dealt with through a mix of the courts and, more commonly for benefit recipient cases, by Department of Social Security liable relative officers. The 1991 Act introduced a complex formula for calculating maintenance, with an apparent aim of setting a 'fair' level of maintenance. Later reforms (following *Improving child support*: DSS, 1995) introduced further adjustments. The CSA did not have a successful record of either setting maintenance accurately or collecting it regularly. It was widely and openly despised by it clients, most of whom had no choice but to use its services. As a result, the Labour government decided to reform the system in a more thoroughgoing way.

The big attempt at reform, within the auspices of retaining the CSA and its customer bases, was embodied in the 2000 Child Support, Pensions and Social Security Act. The reforms included sweeping changes to the rules of the assessment formula (the 'scheme'), the telephone systems and the IT (the 'system'). Non-resident parents on the new scheme are required to pay simple percentages of net income in child support (15% for one child, 20% for two, 25% for three or more). One of the intended benefits of the simplified formula for calculating maintenance was that it would save time collecting information and therefore free up staff resources to spend more time ensuring compliance.

The reforms were implemented, late, in 2003, but initially only applied to new clients. While it was intended to move all clients over to the new rules, the system never attained that robustness and client compliance to enable this to happen.

In the first full year of operation of the reformed system, the CSA was responsible for collecting maintenance for around 1.4 million parents with care. But compliance actually fell, as did the accuracy of assessments. The number of non-resident parents making payments (as a percentage of all cases that had a current child support assessment) was 75% under the old scheme and 67% under the new, with accuracy rates of 85% (old scheme) and 81% (new scheme) (CSA, 2006).

Public attitudes

It has proved difficult to design a child maintenance system that commands widespread consensus. There are considerable differences in public attitudes towards child support, and these are not reflected in the rules. For instance, in British Social Attitudes, when asked what should happen to child support payments if a parent with care remarries: 51% think payments should continue (the actual policy), but 13% say they should stop, while 33% say it depends on the new husband's income (it does not) (Kiernan, 1992). Similarly, analysis by White (2002) found that many people believe the income of the parent with care should count in assessing child support (it does not), and very poor non-resident parents should be exempted from paying (few are).

The 2006 reforms

In 2006 the government came to the conclusion that further attempts to reform the system of child support were fruitless and an entirely new start had to be made. In February 2006, the Secretary of State for Work and Pensions announced a complete overhaul of the whole child support system and appointed former Chief Executive of Liverpool City Council Sir David Henshaw to consider the most effective future arrangements for an efficient child support system.

Henshaw concluded that there was a need for fundamental change in the way that child support was delivered in the UK. His principal recommendations were intended to facilitate a system that will be simpler to use and administer, tougher on parents who do not face up to their responsibilities, make a bigger impact on the reduction in child poverty, and deliver value for money for taxpayers. The proposals centred around the following key elements (Henshaw, 2006):

- allowing lone parents on benefit to be allowed to keep more maintenance through a significant increase in the extent to which child maintenance is disregarded in income-related benefits;
- a greater level of *personal responsibility*. Thus, wherever possible, separated parents should reach private maintenance agreements between themselves with effective state back-up in cases where amicable agreements cannot be reached;
- the introduction of new, tougher enforcement powers to be used for absent parents failing to take financial responsibility for their children.

The Department for Work and Pensions published an initial response to the Henshaw proposals (DWP, 2006f), mostly supporting the recommendations and establishing a public consultation prior to the White Paper that appeared in December 2006 (DWP, 2006b).

Child support White Paper: from Child Support Agency to Child Maintenance and Enforcement Commission

It had long been apparent that the child support system, and perhaps more crucially its administration via the CSA, was not functioning well – "From day one, however, the Child Support Agency has not delivered anywhere near what was expected of it" (DWP, 2006b, para 1). The more recent discussion and reforms have given greater priority to the child poverty objective than was ever envisaged with the CSA. The government has now set its reform agenda to make "tackling child poverty the first and most critical test for reform" (DWP, 2006b, para 16).

The 2006 White Paper sets out four clear principles for the reform of child maintenance. These are to:

- help tackle child poverty;
- promote parental responsibility;
- provide a cost-effective and professional service;
- be simple and transparent (DWP, 2006b, para 1.28).

From 2008 a new body, the Child Maintenance and Enforcement Commission (C-MEC) will be established as a non-departmental public body, led by a commissioner for child maintenance. This will take over responsibility from the CSA for the assessment and collection (and enforcement) of child maintenance. A new range of eye-catching enforcement powers is also proposed, including the power to remove people's passports and impose curfews on them, in cases of non-payment. Advance publicity correctly predicted a new feature where the names of those successfully prosecuted will appear on a 'name and shame' website.

There are also some rather technical but extremely important changes to the way that maintenance and maintenance arrears may be pursued. At present, and in line with the enforcement of debts of other kinds, much enforcement work requires the CSA to obtain, from a court, a Liability Order. This then opens up a wide range of measures, including imprisonment, the use of bailiffs, and powers to remove driving licences. In future it seems that C-MEC will have the power to act without going through the court. This gives them considerable powers, not available to others seeking to enforce civil debts.

Where people are unable to reach their own agreement, a new even simpler formula will be applied. It will be based on gross income, and use income data from the tax authorities. In a sentence that appears to belie years of problems with tax credits, the Department for Work and Pensions is happy to: "Believe that historic tax income information is close enough to the current financial position of most non-resident parents at the time to be an acceptable and sufficiently robust basis for assessment" (DWP, 2006b, p 61).

The new formula does not appear to have any provision for sharing of care, a radical departure from the past formulas used. Non-resident parents with overnight care could face quite substantial increases in the levels of child support expected, if their ex-partner opts to use the new C-MEC. It remains to be seen what their reactions to this change will be, and if the pattern of care changes as a result.

Other developments

These three major areas of change do not exhaust the long list of changes and developments in income maintenance policy and related areas in 2006.

Progress towards eliminating child poverty

In March the 2004/05 Households Below Average Income (HBAI) series was published, showing progress towards reducing and eliminating child poverty. It was noted at the time that the Department for Work and Pensions' press release announced "New figures show good progress on poverty" while the Institute of Fiscal Studies' (IFS) release of the same day preferred "Government misses child poverty targets": two messages consistent with the results but entirely different in emphasis.

In fact the target was to reduce the number of children in poverty by 25% between 1998/99 and 2004/05. The outturn was to cut poverty by 23% before housing costs and by 17% after housing costs. Almost half of all children in poverty are in households in which at least one adult works. Around two fifths live in lone-parent families. Other research, using household *spending* rather than *income*, suggests a *rise* in relative poverty rather than a *reduction* (Brewer et al, 2006).

It is clear that the child poverty commitment remains crucial to government policy. A review (Harker, 2006) outlines progress and challenges ahead, emphasising the need to raise skills to assist both movement into work and people remaining in paid work.

A Green Paper from the Department for Education and Skills (DfES, 2006) continues the emphasis on the most disadvantaged. It made clear the severe disadvantages faced by children in care – of whom 11% gain five good GCSEs, compared with 56% among all children. According to the consultation, "the childhood we are giving them has not been good enough" (DfES, 2006, p 1). The document suggests a range of ways of improving education for this group, and better managing the transition from care into adult life. It also calls for earlier intervention with families whose children are on the 'edge' of care (for further discussion, see Chapter Five by Churchill, this volume).

Tax credits

The main form of support for families with children is now tax credits, which are delivered via HMRC, formerly the Inland Revenue. The administration of tax credits has been subject to concerns, as the payments are based on historic income data (often from one to two years earlier) and revised in later years to deal with any under-payments or over-payments. This has created problems for some low-income families, who can receive less in a given year if they were 'overpaid' the previous year. The introduction of tax credits was also subject to long waiting times.

The Public Administration Select Committee pointed out that "regular and reliable payment is not a desirable budgeting convenience but a real necessity" (2006, para 27). A number of reforms have attempted to ameliorate some of the problems; in particular the threshold for making reassessments has been significantly increased. This makes the system less responsive to change, but reduces the likelihood of over-payments needing to be recovered.

Civil partnerships

The first civil partnership ceremonies for same-sex couples began in December 2005, with approaching 16,000 such partnerships formed by September 2006 (ONS, 2006). Within social security, there has been a long tradition of treating co-resident heterosexual couples as if they were married for the purposes of assessing benefit eligibility regardless of their formal marital status, so in principle same-sex couples could be treated as couples irrespective of their civil partnership status. Relevant changes have been made in many areas (pensions, child support) to recognise the general equivalence of civil partnership with marriage.

Conclusion

Much of the picture of social security reform under New Labour has been one of increased targeting of benefits, in particular through means testing (including the Pension Credit and Child Tax Credit). Reforms to IB also eat away at the idea of an unconditional contributory principle. The other main stream to reform has been the importance of work, moving benefit recipients into work – "paid work has been even more central as New Labour's welfare reforms have unfolded, and it is now predominant" (Kemp, 2005, p 29).

The changes made or announced in 2006 have some strong points of continuity with the agenda of targeting resources where need is greatest. In particular they emphasise the importance of private solutions rather than state provision. Changes to child support will see the abolition of the CSA, and an emphasis on private solutions. The replacement body will still be available to those unable to agree, and will have new, extremely strong enforcement powers. Only time will tell if this will turn the tide of disappointment with child maintenance collection.

After a long period of review, state pensions promise to be significant for some time to come – as long as the White Paper reforms are enacted. Pension increases will again be linked to earnings, not just prices – although there are key financial caveats to this (with costs offset by a higher state pension age). While this might appear to be a strengthening of the role of the state, such is the interaction of state and private pensions that reform of each must proceed together. Without having at least a basic platform of a secure basic pension the incentives to make private provision are diminished, "a successful system of private pension provision needed the sound foundation of a sustainable system of state pensions" (Work and Pensions Select Committee, 2003, p 6). Reform of the state pension is needed to promote private solutions to problems of pensions under-saving.

To return to the question posed in the title, will 2006 be seen as a watershed for establishing social security on a new basis, or as a simple continuation of the past? A strong case for identifying a break with the past may be made for pensions. A long review has opened the way to higher state pensions, a rare event in recent social security history, but prompted at least partly by concerns to encourage private provision. The courage to abolish the CSA was finally summoned, but the reforms do not look particularly radical or inspire confidence that much additional child maintenance will result. The welfare reform agenda continues the policy approaches of the past, albeit with renewed vigour. Only in pensions do we see the state continuing to play a major role as provider, rather than simply as enabler or as back-up.

Note

[1] Jim Murphy, Minister for Employment and Welfare Reform, established a child poverty web-log (blog) (www.dwp.gov.uk/welfarereform/blog). A quick read shows it is not exactly riveting stuff, and was attracting few comments at the time of writing (January 2007). Nevertheless the tone is more user friendly than the press releases, and continues to show the

Department for Work and Pensions' (and its ministers') keen interest in child poverty.

References

Adam, S., Brewer, M. and Shephard, A. (2006) *The poverty trade-off: Work incentives and income redistribution in Britain*, Bristol: The Policy Press.

Alcock, P. (2004) 'Participation and pathology: contradictory tensions in area-based policy', *Social Policy & Society*, vol 3, part 2, pp 87-96.

Brewer, A., Goodman, A. and Leicester, A. (2006) *Household spending in Britain: What can it teach us about poverty?*, York: Joseph Rowntree Foundation.

Brewer, M., Clark, T. and Wakefield, M. (2002) 'Social security under New Labour: what did the third way mean for welfare reform?', *Fiscal Studies*, vol 23, no 4, pp 505-37.

CSA (Child Support Agency) (2006) *Annual report and accounts 2005-6*, HC 1402, London: The Stationery Office.

DfES (Department for Education and Skills) (2006) *Care matters: Transforming the lives of children and young people in care*, Green Paper, London: DfES.

Driver, S. and Martell, L. (2002) 'New Labour, work and the family', *Social Policy & Administration*, vol 36, no 1, pp 46-61.

DSS (Department of Social Security) (1995) *Improving child support*, Cm 2745, London: HMSO.

DWP (Department for Work and Pensions) (2005) *Women and pensions: The evidence*, London: DWP.

DWP (2006a) *Personal accounts: A new way to save*, Cm 6975, London: The Stationery Office.

DWP (2006b) *A new system of child maintenance*, Cm 6979, London: The Stationery Office.

DWP (2006c) *A New Deal for welfare: Empowering people to work*, Cm 6730, London: The Stationery Office.

DWP (2006d) *Pension Credit estimates of take-up 2004/2005*, London: Statistics First Release.

DWP (2006e) *Security in retirement: Towards a new pension system*, Cm 6841, London: The Stationery Office.

DWP (2006f) *A fresh start: Child support redesign – The government's response to Sir David Henshaw*, Cm 6895, London: The Stationery Office.

Harker, L. (2006) *Delivering on child poverty: What would it take?*, London: The Stationery Office.

Henshaw, D. (2006) *Recovering child support: Routes to responsibility*, Cm 6894, London: DWP.

Kemp, P. (2005) 'Social security and welfare reform under New Labour', in M. Powell, L. Bauld and K. Clarke (eds) *Social Policy Review 17: Analysis and debate in social policy, 2005*, Bristol: The Policy Press/Social Policy Association, pp 15-32.

Kiernan, K. (1992) 'Men and women at work and at home', in R. Jowell (ed) *British social attitudes: Ninth report*, Aldershot: Dartmouth, pp 89-111.

Lister, R. (2001) 'New Labour: a study in ambiguity from a position of ambivalence', *Critical Social Policy*, vol 21, no 4, pp 425-47.

McKay, S. (2006) *Employers pension provision survey 2005*, DWP Research Report No 329, London: Corporate Document Services.

McKay, S. and Rowlingson, K. (1998) *Social security in Britain*, Basingstoke: Macmillan.

ONS (Office for National Statistics) (2006) *Civil partnerships news release*, London: ONS, 4 December.

Pensions Commission (2004) *Pensions: Challenges and choices: The first report of the Pensions Commission*, London: The Stationery Office.

Pensions Commission (2005) *A new pension settlement for the twenty-first century: The second report of the Pensions Commission*, London: The Stationery Office.

Powell, M. (2000) 'New Labour and the third way in the British welfare state: a new and distinctive approach?', *Critical Social Policy*, vol 20, no 1, pp 39-60.

PPI (Pensions Policy Institute) (2006) *An evaluation of the White Paper state pension reform proposals*, London: PPI.

Preston, G. (ed) (2006) *A route out of poverty? Disabled people, work and welfare reform*, London: CPAG.

Public Administration Select Committee (2006) *Tax Credits: Putting things right*, HC 577, London: The Stationery Office.

White, D. (2002) *Attitudes towards child support and the Child Support Agency*, In-house report 100, London: DWP/ASD.

Work and Pensions Select Committee (2003) *The future of UK pensions: Volumes I-III*, HC 92-I-III, London: The Stationery Office.

Work and Pensions Select Committee (2006) *Incapacity benefits and pathways to work*, May, HC 616-1, London: The Stationery Office.

Part Two
Current issues

"I can't ask that!": promoting discussion of sexuality and effective health service interactions with older non-heterosexual men

Adrian Lee

Introduction

This chapter aims to enhance the understanding of social policy academics and practitioners with regard to the homosexuality of older men, with whom they may interact on a professional basis or write about through their research, without actively and consciously considering how sexuality can substantially influence aspects of daily living. In order to fulfil this aim, I first outline research to date on the size of the older gay male population in order to argue that this is significant enough to warrant more wholehearted interest from policy makers and service providers. Then, the discourse of sexual citizenship is discussed as this also contextualises my work. Finally, the substantive sections of the chapter introduce the research and the participants, before exploring decision making regarding coming out in a healthcare setting and the implications of different scenarios for the well-being of older gay men. It is argued that healthcare professionals require greater information in order to recognise the wider relevance of knowing a person's sexual orientation and to gain a better understanding of how best to discuss such subjects with patients who might be reluctant to access care and discuss their sexuality and relationships.

A number of professional responses are subsequently discussed that have implications for macro-level policy making and local service provision within healthcare institutions. This is also relevant research in light of the active ageing agenda and the government's aim to ensure later life is lived through activity, good health, secure income and independence. The cross-departmental *Opportunity Age* initiative launched in 2005 (DWP, 2005) reflects this and lays out the responsibilities of central and local government and governmental agencies, as well as older people and communities themselves. Arguably the efforts under the *National Service Framework for older people* (DH, 2001) concerning the NHS, and *Opportunity Age* (DWP, 2005), can only succeed if all aspects of older people's social worlds are recognised and accounted for.

The population

Older men form a relatively small proportion of the UK population, with the number aged 65 and over standing at 4,143,300, and with 1,754,200 men aged over 75 (ONS, 2006). A limited body of gerontological work focuses specifically on older men, with contributions made by Thompson (1994), Neugebauer–Visano (1995) and Schiavi (1999), who offer substantial, albeit quite heterosexist, contributions about older men and their sexuality. This largely relates to physical changes and experiences of loss, bereavement and intimacy, although other texts are more androcentric and examine broad social issues more far removed from individual older people.

The size of the gay male population is impossible to accurately calculate, as data have only recently been collected on a large scale, and there are a number of methodological limitations. This is one of the most sensitive demographic issues to research (Jacobs et al, 1999; Cahill et al, 2000; Martin and Knox, 2000). The comprehensive British National Survey of Sexual Attitudes and Lifestyles (Wellings et al, 1994), which set an upper age limit of 59, still gave a detailed, if less than perfect, insight into British sexuality. The 2000 follow-up updated the statistics, while at the same time further adding to the confusions (Smith, 2006). Table 7.1 presents some of the varied UK and US estimates for lesbian, gay and bisexual (LGB) population sizes. However, the lack of uniformity about which groups of people the figures refer to is problematic. For reference, recent UK population figures are shown in Table 7.2, accompanied by calculations using some values from Table 7.1 to estimate the size of the older gay male population most relevant to this subject.

It is argued here that it is important in policy-making terms to be aware of a population's size, but also of its density. The 2001 Census confirmed suggestions that the LGB population is concentrated in certain areas of the country, where services will need to adapt, as with

Table 7.1: Estimates for the number of older LGB adults in the US and UK

Research	%	Reasoning/explanation	% refers to
Kinsey et al (1948) cited in Martin and Knox (2000) and Cahill et al (2000)	4 8–10 13	Lifelong pattern of exclusive homosexuality Predominantly homosexual More homosexual than heterosexual relationships	All US extrapolated from study sample
Wellings et al (1994)	1.4–6.1	1.4% men had a male sexual partner within the past two years 3.6% report some genital contact with a man 6.1% report some kind of homosexual experience	UK male population
ACE (2001)	6.5	Uses Kinsey range as 3–10% and 6.5 is the median value, assuming it applies to all ages	UK population gay or lesbian

Table 7.2: Population data for the UK male population aged 50+

Age group	Total male population (000s rounded)	10% total male population (000s rounded)	6% total male population (000s rounded)
Aged 50+	9,406	940	564
Aged 60+	5,662	566	339
Aged 70+	2,837	283	170
Aged 80+	915	91	54

Source: ONS (2006)

any other population changes, to accommodate the needs of ageing gay people.

All the figures mentioned earlier are indicative, but the government has adopted them for policy-making purposes. The Department of Trade and Industry used 5%-7% in its civil partnership White Paper (DTI, 2003), based on some of the evidence previously discussed, and HM Treasury has more recently decided on 6% as the size of the LGB population (rainbownetwork.com, 2005). Smith (2006, pp 44-5) has questioned the accuracy of all the estimates used. His plausible conclusion is that it is difficult to know the size of the gay male community, and he uses it as justification to more fully research the demographics for policy making about service provision, such as through the 2011 Census. However, it suffices to say that older gay men do live among us all, even though we do not know how many might identify themselves as homosexual[1]. These are "silent pioneers" in the gay community (Brown et al, 1997, p 4), and "older adult gay men and lesbians may be said to constitute the most invisible of an already invisible minority" (Blando, 2001, p 87). Therefore, there is a need to understand more about who these people are, what experiences they have had, what needs arise in later life and how these can be best met.

Policy context and sexual citizenship

A growing body of work is examining the interactions between homosexuals and health services (Caulfield and Platzer, 1998; Heath, 1999, 2002a, 2002b; Cant, 2002; Hinchliff et al, 2004). Since 1997 there has also been a wave of equality legislation and initiatives to encourage inclusion focused on incorporating sexual orientation. Furthermore, more attention has recently been paid to investigating the needs and experiences of older gays (ACE, 2001, 2002, 2003; Heaphy et al, 2003; Colling and Lee, 2004), hitherto invisible members of society. Such initiatives have highlighted the lack of knowledge among service providers and the gay community about specific challenges of gay ageing and they have presented accounts of service use interactions that have been far from ideal. In part, this research and debate has influenced the development of the *National Service Framework for older people* (DH, 2001), *Opportunity Age* (DWP, 2005), equality legislation such as the 2004 Civil Partnership Act and the 2005 Mental Capacity Act guidance on professional practice to develop sensitive and inclusive services (RCN/UNISON, 2004). Most recently, the 2006 Equality Act gave Ruth Kelly, as Secretary of State, the power to introduce secondary legislation to ensure LGB people (and heterosexuals) receive equal access to goods and services. In response to questions in Parliament, Ms Kelly stated that the government would take such steps in April 2007 (*Hansard*, 2006, col 1014).

The discussion of service needs and welfare experiences of older gay men takes place within the context of these recent reforms and the discourse of sexual citizenship. This growing stream of citizenship studies highlights how multiple issues of sexuality interact with multiple issues of citizenship (see Richardson, 1998). However, it is only more recently that, compared to other fields, social policy has begun to examine how its activity intersects with sexuality (Richardson, 2000).

British society is underpinned by, and access to full citizenship rights and recognition has been conditional on, assumed heterosexuality *and* the promotion of certain forms of heterosexuality. Richardson (1998) argues that married heterosexuals have been lauded and supported, to the exclusion of other heterosexuals and non-heterosexuals in civil, political, social, economic and cultural realms of citizenship. Donovan et al concur with this:

> Participation in society is premised on not only being heterosexual but for the most part belonging to a married heterosexual couple embedded within a particular type of family.... (Hetero)sexuality permeates the underpinnings of the legal, political and particularly social aspects of citizenship. (1999, p 694)

However, these views have begun to change, partly because of the New Labour government's efforts to push through civil partnership legislation and offer greater rights to sexual minorities, while at the same time others have argued their family policies might be responsible for an undervaluing of 'traditional' family types and social mores (Phillips, 2006). Among broad impacts, heterosexism affects older non-heterosexuals particularly, as their histories and identities were formed during periods of oppression. This can dissuade them from standing up against exclusion from care settings and affect retirement incomes and inheritances. The value of their relationships and unconventional support networks has also been undermined (Donovan et al, 1999). Recent changes to the law, such as the 2004 Civil Partnership Act and associated changes, have reduced some of the inequality, but the playing field is yet to be fully levelled.

Yet, inequality has not been wholly criticised because without recognition has come the freedom to experiment with new forms and dynamics of relationships within the private sphere (Richardson, 1998).This point is returned to later with regard to decision making in relation to coming out. Richardson argues that sexual citizenship has brought to the fore the false bifurcation of public and private spheres citizenship hitherto conceptualised. Weeks (1998) and Donovan et al (1999) also develop such observations about the changing public/private dichotomy.

Since early legislation criminalised sexual acts in private, non-heterosexuals have unequally seen the public regulation of rights and responsibilities come into their private spheres. Public spaces, when private spheres were liberated, were then draconically policed to ensure boundaries of toleration were not crossed (Richardson, 1998; McGhee, 2004): the lack of recognition of relationships, and measures negating homosexual couples and headed families (such as Section 28) continued to deny them full citizenship (Richardson, 1998). Richardson distinguishes two approaches to analysing sexual citizenship: first, rights of sexual expression and, second, how sexuality limits access (or not) to other forms of citizenship rights/freedoms (civil, political, etc) (Richardson, 1998, 2000). Both require recognition of how gays and lesbians are treated in the public and private spheres, whether fair boundaries exist allowing the necessary freedom, flexibility and choice (Weeks, 1998), and the recognition and valuing of the plurality of intimate relationships.

However, it is the second of Richardson's strands that this chapter focuses on. McGhee (2004, p 358) also argues that, in the discussion of the public/private divide, there has been too much focus on non-heterosexuals in domestic, familial settings, and that more focus is needed to examine the place of gays and lesbians and the costs, benefits, rights and responsibilities of them as citizens in a changing public society. McGhee's hint to avoid too insular a focus is relevant to older gay men and justifies my study of healthcare. This chapter aims to highlight the need for welfare provision to be more inclusive towards, and foster a sense of comfort for, older gay men as they go about their everyday lives, or when they face times of particular need. Research in this area is also essential in monitoring the government's efforts to develop public services that: "Will become increasingly focused on the promotion of well-being and independence; easy to access; customer focused; and aimed at tackling social exclusion" (DWP, 2005, para 33).

Examining post-1997 Labour government legal reforms following the publication of the cited literature on sexual citizenship suggests that Britain is moving forward. Yet, work remains to be done to ensure that policies are implemented and translate into changing social attitudes so that marginalised homosexuals (older individuals and couples included) can access services, arrange their affairs, have their partnerships recognised by state and society, and feel that their identities and cultural heritage are valued by others, thus including them in their communities.

The qualitative interview data explains how participants' perceptions of their sexual identity as older men and their life experiences have implications for our understanding of sexual citizenship. The intention is to highlight the limited entitlement and participation of the interviewees because of their homosexual identities, and how ageing as gay men impedes participants' abilities to have fair access to citizenship within the gay community. Furthermore, suggestions are made as to how positive steps can be taken within the healthcare field. In the demographic and sexual citizenship contexts, some of the issues affecting older gay men's health service use experiences are discussed.

Methods and participants

Fifteen self-defined gay/homosexual men took part in semi-structured in-depth interviews to generate data about the influence their sexual identity had on daily living and their welfare needs and how these needs were formally and informally met; they were aged from 57 to 84 years old (mean age 66.8 years). Two thirds lived in Yorkshire and many in rural to very remote locations. Participants had reached a range of educational achievements up to postgraduate level. Their employment backgrounds included the public sector, manual occupations, hospitality and religious ministry. Additionally, seven had served in the forces. The majority had retired, although several still undertook some paid work, engaged in gay-related and mainstream voluntary work and adult education classes.

Most participants were single, but two couples took part in one-to-one interviews, and another man lived with a long-term partner. In short, five interviewees were part of a long-term, interdependent relationship. These three relationships had lasted for between 25 and 30 years. One man was a (gay) widower, after the death of his partner of 29 years. Two men had been divorced in the past few years, one of whom had teenaged children. Four participants had never had a long-term relationship with another man. The participants had varied, but often minimal, contact with the gay community. However, 12 were currently involved in, or were on the mailing lists of, gay political and social groups of some kind. Others had previously been more involved in the gay scene of bars, clubs and saunas, but three men had virtually no contact with other gays or the gay community. Where geographical distances limited some men's contact, 'virtual' forms existed, via newsletters and the internet. Also, a minority of participants did not want to socialise with homosexuals.

The participants' financial circumstances were grouped by adapting a British Household Panel Survey (BHPS) question[2]. The majority were financially comfortable or very comfortable. However, four men were described as 'just about getting by' or as 'finding it difficult'. Participants' incomes came from state and occupational pensions, savings/investments, inheritances, state benefits and present paid work. This has potential significance for social researchers in light of civil partnership legislation as couples should be assessed as single benefit units, which could reduce the incomes of some couples.

Table 7.3 summarises each participant's health conditions. The men's health often necessitated regular consultation with GPs or other

Table 7.3: Participants' health conditions

Participant	Health conditions
P1 (77)[3]	Previously had cancer that now restricts diet; varicose veins
P2 (67)	Long-term effects of hepatitis; investigations regarding possible prostate problem
P3 (84)	Some difficulty walking; recently had prostate surgery and a hernia operation
P4 (62)	Arthritis
P5 (65)	Cardiac condition; irritable bowel syndrome
P6 (66)	Cardiac condition
P7 (58)	Born profoundly deaf; currently has a condition relating to balance and dizziness
P8 (67)	Varicose veins; diabetes; blood pressure condition; investigations for a possible prostate problem
P9 (63)	Mental health problems; high blood pressure
P10 (59)	Clinical depression; impaired mobility/neurological condition after adverse reaction to medication
P11 (65)	Possible cardiac condition
P12 (69)	Osteoarthritis and awaiting joint replacement surgery; high blood pressure
P13 (70)	Diabetes; blood pressure condition
P14 (64)	Cardiac condition; diabetes
P15 (57)	Arthritis; blood pressure condition

clinicians, for example, specialist diabetic clinic nurses, dieticians or chiropodists. Two men were also in receipt of benefits and had to be independently medically assessed at periodic intervals.

Coming out

A key research aim was to demonstrate how issues surrounding attitudes towards, and the expression of, a non-normative sexual identity influence the participants' daily circumstances and service use experiences. Coming out (disclosure of one's sexual identity or intimate relationships) is central to this, particularly in relation to health service interactions. Disclosure is an ongoing process involving a realisation and acceptance of one's own homosexuality, as well as disclosing it to others in different contexts and at different times throughout the life course. The data suggested that participants made active and passive disclosures (also observed by Eliason and Schope, 2001, in their data), but two types of active disclosure were distinguishable. Unprompted active disclosures were when a disclosure was made without first being asked about sexuality or relationships. For example, P10 (59) and P11 (65) told their new GP they were a couple when they registered with the practice. The second, prompted active disclosure, involves men answering a question about their sexual orientation that someone had asked. For example, P12 (69) had gone to his GP asking about (sexual) performance-enhancing medications; when his GP asked if he was trying to tell him he was gay, P12 said that he was.

Passive disclosure can be avoiding telling others about the nature of a relationship or lifestyle, but not hiding it either, not passing as heterosexual. Examples include choosing not to censor words and personal news to avoid disclosing telling information, or choosing not to hide copies of *Gay Times* if someone came to visit, something to which P2 (67) referred regarding his neighbours. Several participants believed they had passively disclosed their sexuality to others, including GPs. They were not certain their doctor knew they were gay, but felt they must have assumed it so there was no need to confirm or deny suspicions. Examples of such behaviour are discussed later. Assumptions played an important role in these participants' process of disclosure.

Interviewees gave numerous examples of how they assume friends, neighbours, and so on, know of their homosexuality and/or relationships. This affects, to some extent, how they behave within social interactions, which might include passively disclosing their sexual orientation in their conversation and behaviour. The participant's assumption can lead them to avoid making any sort of disclosure, leaving a person in the dark when knowing for certain the interviewee's sexual orientation could actually be relevant and useful. An example could be assuming a GP knows they are gay and therefore not mentioning it, when the doctor actually has no firm idea. P1 (77) highlighted where non-disclosure can create barriers in interactions that put older gay men at risk. He assumed his GP knew he was gay, but did not feel the need to openly discuss it. This meant he had reached his own conclusions about his health and risk of exposure to sexually transmitted infections, based on his recovery from another illness. During treatment for this, doctors had commented on his strong immune system that he now appeared to believe offered some protection. The role of assumptions in eliciting or 'avoiding' disclosure is, therefore, potentially detrimental. Coming to inaccurate assumptions or decisions about likely reactions to their homosexuality also generated barriers to informal support for some men, creating a greater, more active potential role for formal welfare services. This is because neighbours and friends were considered to be unlikely sources of support, despite my considered opinion that support might be offered to most participants. However, this in no way reduces the impact anxiety about sources of support might cause to older gay men (Heaphy et al, 2003).

Patient–doctor interactions

Disclosure decisions

The GP is often the first port of call for people when unwell, and the relationship can be very important, especially when regular consultations are needed. The degree of openness and the ability to which men felt they could talk freely to GPs and healthcare professionals about their concerns and lives is very important (Cant, 2002; Snowdon-Carr, 2005). Eleven men felt they were 'out' to some degree to their own doctor and sometimes other GPs in the practice, although this was usually based on assumptions. For example, P14 (64) and P15 (57) assumed that as their surgery knew they lived together they would reach an accurate conclusion. Only seven interviewees said they had (or suggested that they had) actively come out.

For several men, actively coming out had been an important early decision when registering with a doctor, especially if they had previously experienced homophobia. This gave them the opportunity to gauge attitudes before a real patient–doctor relationship developed. Other men, however, were less forthcoming. For participants who assumed their doctor's awareness of their homosexuality, there was no concern at them having such knowledge, yet they did not see the value of discussing it and ensuring assumptions were accurate. This was the case for P14 (64) and P15 (57), a cohabiting couple, but for single men there was less circumstantial evidence on which practitioners could base assumptions. P1 (77) did not recall telling his doctor himself, but felt she did know. He was happy with this situation, but would actively come out if the need arose, such as if he contracted an illness through sex. Two others said they would also disclose their sexuality in such circumstances, and a third came out to his doctor following an HIV scare. This suggested that the interviewees perceived that their sexuality was only relevant in relation to conditions or illnesses connected to (homo)sexual activity and not to their lives in general. However, there are a range of health issues for which knowing a person's sexuality can be most useful, including: dealing with stress through excessive tobacco, alcohol or drug use; cancers and prostate conditions; psychological conditions influenced by reactions to homosexuality; and the availability of informal care assistance (Dean et al, 2000; GMLA, 2003a, 2003b; Keogh et al, 2004). Furthermore, is a disclosure likely to be made when a man feels particularly vulnerable, such as following risky sexual behaviour? These, therefore, are important findings, suggesting the need for more proactive behaviour on the part of clinicians to facilitate open discussion of sexual identity and to recognise its potential wider clinical and social relevance (Keogh et al, 2004).

Non-disclosure was of particular concern. P6 (66) believed that his young GP would not react badly if he came out and he did not foresee that there were risks of experiencing discrimination in the current climate. Nevertheless, he still felt unable to make this disclosure. This was in line with his overall secrecy and discretion about this part of his life. However, as a sexually active man he could be faced with the need to come out when unplanned and when he was more vulnerable, rather than having done so at a considered, chosen time. His informal support network was also very small. P7 (58) also had quite deep anxieties about disclosure. He was "frightened" to come out to his GP. He thought that gossip and rumour spread quickly in his town and he could not trust the doctor to keep their oath of confidentiality, although he said various people in the town, including his family, already knew he was gay. P7 could see the benefits of both positions, but did not know which was the most risky to his health and well-being. The data bore close similarities to findings of Keogh et al (2004), and Webb and Wright (2001), who found that almost all their large LGB survey respondents had a GP. However, only 50.8% of those aged 65+ were 'out' to them, with older men being the most closeted. Heaphy et al (2003) also recorded a very similar figure.

When Webb and Wright (2001, pp 34-5) asked: "You could ask your GP not to write in your medical records that you are LGB", 24.8% were "not at all/not confident", and a third were "neither confident nor not confident". Furthermore, 15.4% were "not at all/not confident" and 29% were not sure that their GP had a non-judgemental approach to LGB people. These figures are concerning, as the survey was conducted among one of the largest UK LGB populations. Keogh et al (2004) found similar concerns in their national survey, as did Cant (2002) and Barlow (2003) in cosmopolitan London.

Healthcare experiences

As well as discussing disclosure to GPs, the interviews involved some detailed conversations about the experience, overall, of services delivered by healthcare professionals. The data paint, in most cases, a positive picture of service provision. No one spoke of having any major concerns about consulting their GP, despite those specific anxieties referred to previously. Some men recognised the value of their relationships more widely than for successful clinical outcomes. P5 (65) valued a good "bedside manner", as he received after a recent hospital appointment in which he had no prior knowledge he would be seeing a locum doctor and not who he expected. He spoke at length of the need for doctors to build a rapport with their patients. This was, perhaps, influenced by previous experiences he had had with less personable ones who he viewed as ageist or homophobic.

For P8 (67), his relationship with the doctor, practice nurse and receptionist also meant a lot. He assumed the GP was aware he was gay, but had not actively come out. He had been involved in caring for an older gay couple who had since died:

> P8: "I had to miss an appointment because 'James' was very poorly, and the nurse said 'oh we didn't expect you' you see, and then the first time I went to see a doctor after 'James' died, she said 'you're a friend of "James", I'm so sorry to hear about him', sorry about his death."

> R: "It sounds like you've got a good relationship with your GP...."

> P8: "I have a good [relationship] ... [and] good relationship with the nurse there ... and the receptionist."

These examples highlight the positive benefit of small considerations by healthcare professionals, to encourage older gay men to feel that they and their sexual identities are respected and accepted.

When consulting hospital services, there were more incidents of men not disclosing their sexuality to clinicians, and a general sense that it was not necessary because of the conditions for which they were being seen, although researchers would suggest that they were perhaps more relevant than they might first appear (see, for example, Dean et al, 2000; GMLA, 2003a, 2003b; Keogh et al, 2004). However, of concern was reluctance, even among quite confident and 'out' men, to disclose their homosexuality, because service providers might be homophobic. Coming out is always a matter for personal choice, but this chapter argues, in light of evidence elsewhere (Dean et al, 2000; Cant, 2002; GMLA, 2003a, 2003b), that service providers need to ensure their practice environment is welcoming enough so that users have the opportunity to make this decision free from any anxious motivations. Their sexuality and domestic circumstances might be relevant to their care or needs, without them themselves fully realising it as they have always 'made do'. Overall, a number of events were recounted from the relatively recent past that stuck with participants and had some continued influence over their attitudes and behaviour. Two such examples are particularly illustrative.

P2 (67) recalled an appointment approximately two years prior to the interview (circa 2001) where he felt a disclosure was relevant to his condition, which acts as a reminder that "even individuals who enjoy significant social support as openly gay men and lesbians may find it difficult or imprudent to reveal their sexuality in a doctor's office" (Dean et al, 2000, p 107):

> P2: "On my blood tests he put 'known homosexual' and I thought 'why have you done that if you think I'm a biohazard you should just stamp it biohazard, why is it important for all your staff to know that I'm homosexual?'. I don't mind being homosexual but I do object to you using homophobic literature and I reported him."
>
> R: "Did he explain himself?"

P2:"He said he was very sorry, he didn't realise that he was being homophobic.... I thought an apology wasn't enough so I reported him.... And they [hospital administration] said that they were going to look at all their policies, and I thought that was quite a useful bit of politics, and they sent me lots of letters.... I thought I should really make a statement so that the other doctors don't do it to other gay men.... I was quite pleased that I had the bottle to confront him."

P2 has long been an open, self-affirming and politically active gay man, and he had worked in healthcare for many years and he felt others would be less willing to stand up for their rights to equal treatment. Reassuringly, he said this incident had not altered his overall attitude about coming out and interacting with doctors.

A more closeted couple gave examples of difficulties in hospitals, which related to possible institutional-level ignorance of effective communication regarding the needs of homosexual couples. Having worked in a hospital for many years, P14 (64) had witnessed anti-HIV/AIDS and homophobic sentiments. He spoke of discrimination based on homophobia and 'AIDS-phobia' at the same time as having close friends in medicine and ostensibly promoting the professionalism of medical staff. This was during the AIDS epidemic's infancy, primarily, but had lasting ramifications. His account of his illness in the 1990s suggested his past witness outweighed his rational feelings of professionalism and tolerance when he himself was sick and vulnerable. He and his partner independently recalled a very distressing scenario:

P14:"I had my second heart attack [on holiday] and ... we were together ... and ... there was this young doctor and she was asking me questions, but you must respect I had two hours from getting [the heart attack], to getting sorted out, and er, I felt pretty lousy.... I don't know whether she said 'are you gay?' or what, but I couldn't see the other side of me saying 'yes' and dealing with the questions that might come, or feeling under pressure, I felt so ill. It came out, it wasn't deliberate, I wasn't expecting it, and I said 'no'. There was the feeling that, you know, at the end of the day, there are people who [are homophobic], I mean I have seen it in the hospital where I've taken action on it from time to time."

P15: "When he had his [first] heart attack, I wasn't allowed in, it was only immediate family, and I couldn't go until he was out of coronary care. Which is distressing, that's when it really hit home, you know, that you haven't got the same rights.... His family were 50 miles away, but they ... came over pretty quickly, and of course the second time he had his heart attack we were [on holiday], and I had to telephone his sisters and then flew up...."

R: "The family, were they alright with the visiting, did they sort of tell the doctors?"

P15: "No ... because ... I think they were aware, [but] as far as they were concerned, they were more interested in what was happening to him, not me. But [the second time] you see, I was the one that went in with him, so I was allowed in.... But I didn't want to go saying to his [family], you know, 'really I should be in because you know, we're a couple', I didn't say anything."

R: "What held you back...?"

P15: "Well because they're nice people, I mean they were very quick and explained what had happened. I mean, had he have gone onto the critical list and started to deteriorate, then I would have had to have said, 'look, now I'm going to have to tell you that I'm gay, that we're both gay, we've had a relationship, I think I should be allowed to see him', but, whether the authorities would allow me to see him, I don't know. The [staff] at that particular time said it was immediate family, next-of-kin only."

These are examples from the 1990s, but there is no reason to suggest similar events do not still occur, hence the necessity for guidance to be published on treating gay people and their significant others (RCN/UNISON, 2004), and for the provisions in the 2004 Civil Partnership Act, those relating to lasting power of attorney in the 2005 Mental Capacity Act[4] and the 2006 Equality Act. The example above outlines key concerns, relating to personal understandings of 'next-of-kin' and 'family', and the way in which people, when at their most vulnerable, may face difficult choices in their interactions with healthcare professionals.

The data illustrate general concerns of a significant minority of participants about fair, inclusive and positive treatment. They suggest a need to promote these issues to healthcare professionals at all levels and seek to improve service quality, which is expanded on later.

Professional responses

The views and experiences previously discussed suggest the need for action on a number of fronts to improve the present and future health services interactions of the interviewees and older gay men generally, and thus increase their access to social citizenship entitlements discussed as sexual citizenship. Concerns above about the levels of disclosure of gay men living in areas with large gay communities raise the question of what the experience might be like in less open-minded places, where clinicians might have less frequent overt contact with LGB people and their specific health needs. It was in such areas that many of the research participants lived. Therefore, proactive steps by healthcare professionals to indicate their attitude and the policies they are committed to upholding, could reduce individuals' concerns about confidentiality.

Gay men need to feel able to disclose their sexuality when relevant, as mentioned earlier, which has implications for the training of healthcare professionals in diversity, anti-discriminatory practice and communication. The barriers to disclosure and successful outcomes of medical interactions need to be appreciated and dismantled through a concerted approach to person-centred care (considering the individual's needs and involving them in the decision-making process regarding their care; see Pugh, 2005; Rivers, 2006). Health and social care has increasingly recognised this, for example: RCN (1994) reproduced in Wilton (2000), RCN/UNISON (2004), SSI (1995a, 1995b), the *National Service Framework for older people* (DH, 2001) and through the 2000 Care Standards Act (Clarke et al, 2002; DH, 2003). Although the *National Service Framework* did not mention sexuality, it is the measures on person-centred care that can arguably be used to push for recognition of the effects of a person's sexuality on their daily lives. Action by welfare professionals to more fully facilitate open disclosures and show more of an understanding of sexuality in broad terms similar to our understanding of ethnic and cultural identity, should aid their decision making, as they will have a fuller picture of the experiences of any illness and of the available care.

The data also concurs with a number of actions suggested elsewhere to encourage openness, feelings of acceptance and non-judgemental treatment. This includes displaying posters of gay community group activities and subtle gay-themed images in waiting or consultation rooms; introducing a 'kite mark' symbol to explicitly show a business or service is gay friendly; ensuring inclusive language is used in consultations and on forms, such as asking about 'partners' or 'significant relationships' like friendships; being gender neutral when asking questions; subtly rather than bluntly asking a person about their sexuality; and increasing staff awareness of sexuality and diverse sexualities through training and the promotion *and* enforcement of equality policies (Wilton, 2000; Eliason and Schope, 2001; Harrison, 2001; ACE, 2002; Brown, 2002; Clarke et al, 2002; Kitchen, 2003; GLMA, 2003a, 2003b; ODIT, 2003; Colling and Lee, 2004). It is also important that healthcare professionals are aware that, for example, next-of-kin has a very limited legal definition in healthcare and that a person should be free to designate who they wish as their next-of-kin to be contacted and involved in their medical treatment and decision making (Caulfield and Platzer, 1998; DTI, 2003; RCN/UNISON, 2004). Age Concern (ACE, 2001) proposes that such steps can cost little but greatly benefit all service users. Such steps taken in an individual surgery, on a micro-level, will, when undertaken on a macro-level across health and social services, have a larger impact when accounting for the estimated size of the LGB population.

However, practitioners might have difficulties in approaching this subject from the start (Hinchliff et al, 2004; Snowdon-Carr, 2005), and can be reluctant to discuss sexuality for fear of their intentions being misconstrued, damaging the rapport with patients. For example, doctors were referred to as using participants as informal sources of information. Taken into consideration with the lasting effects of past negative experiences of using health services, the data highlight a need for more formal training to increase awareness of how a person's sexual identity impacts on formal service use and regarding how it can be more sensitively discussed. Hicks and Watson (2003) give an overview and critique of the way in which sexuality is taught and discussed in the caring professions, and the data add to their calls for improvements in medical training. The experiences of P2 (67) and P4 (62) neatly demonstrate this.

P2 was one of the gay men similar to those Wilton (2000) mentions have been called on to help informally train professionals. He said his GP was "very good", but he seemed less comfortable because the GP was "always asking me to talk to his medical students". Additionally, P4 (62) suggested his GP lacked confidence to discuss sexuality:

P4:"I would say their [his GP's] attitude is cautious ... but I got on alright with them."

R:"How do you mean cautious?"

P4: "I don't think they're used to people saying to them 'yeah, well, I'm a homosexual'. Right?"

R:"Yeah."

P4:"They didn't immediately rush off and test me for AIDS if that's what you mean."

R:"They just don't really know what to say for risk of saying the wrong thing, or something like that?"

P4: "Yeah, yeah, I would say their attitude was cautious, right."

These examples support calls for sensitive professional training and practice including sexuality and communicating with diverse populations, from the early days of a medical student's career to continuing professional development of qualified and practising professionals.

Also, national policy initiatives relating to equality for staff might mean that those working in welfare services could be encouraged to be more open about their own sexuality and more aware of how such openness can positively facilitate disclosure by their service users and enhance their satisfaction with care (Brown, 2002; ODIT, 2003). It is reassuring that a number of statutory health agencies from the Department of Health, to strategic health authorities, to local NHS acute and primary care trusts have signed up to the Stonewall (2006) Workplace Equality Index, and are included in the top 81 employers in the index that scores bodies on their policies and practice with regard to LGB equality and diversity issues. Nevertheless, as with regard to encouraging participants to come out, I do not suggest professionals should feel compelled to disclose their sexuality, as this is their right according to the sexual citizenship discourse, but that their employers should do what is practicable to develop a safe environment into which staff can feel able to come out without anxiety, and knowing that measures such as the 2003 Employment Equality (Sexual Orientation) Regulations (OPSI, 2003) and other work-related equality laws will be monitored and enforced.

Conclusion

This chapter has suggested that older gay men are largely satisfied with their health service experiences. However, a significant proportion of participants felt unable to openly discuss their sexuality with clinicians, and others did not see its relevance to their health needs. Participants raised fears relating to confidentiality, mistreatment due to previous experience, or because of an awareness of the stigmatisation of homosexuality. Their attitudes and experiences suggested that healthcare professionals need to take a more proactive role to facilitate open discussion and feelings of acceptance among this still quite invisible section of the population, as opposed to expecting patients to instigate discussion themselves.

There is also an expectation of such action because of initiatives including the *National Service Framework for older people*, the 2004 Civil Partnership Act and *Opportunity Age*. The UK is an ageing society with a government that promotes the active ageing of citizens. Therefore, the older LGB population is also ageing at the same time as becoming more open and forthright in claiming equal opportunities to high-quality healthcare. This chapter argues that this creates a role for social policy analysts who can ensure their own work is inclusive and highlights inadequacies. There is also a need to maintain the post-1997 government momentum to push through equality measures enhancing sexual citizenship rights, particularly as the 2006 Equality Act continues to prove controversial. The government has offered assurances that it will use secondary legislation to ensure LGB people are protected from discrimination in the provision of goods and services, although not without scepticism from campaigners at the same time as causing much distress to potentially influential religious groups (Shoffman, 2006; thisislondon.co.uk, 2006). However, despite a key role for macro-level policy making and monitoring of service provision, participants suggested that it is on a very personal, individual, level that signs of acceptance and respect for their sexual identities can be most appreciated. The chapter has suggested a number of professional responses that could go a considerable way to achieving this.

Notes

[1] In this chapter 'gay' and 'homosexual' are used synonymously, although elsewhere (Lee, 2006) the contentions that arise regarding labelling male non-heterosexual identities are recognised, especially when conducting fieldwork. Here these contentions are not ignored, yet for

ease of reading the terms are used interchangeably unless referred to in a specific context.

[2] The BHPS Likert scale question asked is: "How well would you say you yourself are managing financially these days?" (BHPS, 2004).

[3] To ensure anonymity the interviewees are identified as Px = participant and the number corresponds to the order in which they were interviewed. Their age at the time of the interview appears in brackets.

[4] The 2005 Mental Capacity Act, to be implemented April 2007 (DH, 2006), was welcomed by campaigners, as gay carers can still struggle to obtain formal recognition:

> [We have] been informed of some appalling personal experiences where a ... carer of a lesbian or gay person has been denied his or her role as primary carer both by professionals and family members. A measure that will protect us in law ... will be of enormous benefit. (Alzheimer's Society, 2005, p 3)

References

ACE (Age Concern England) (2001) *Opening doors: Working with older lesbians and gay men*, Service development resource pack, London: ACE.

ACE (2002) *Opening doors ... to the needs of older lesbians, gay men and bisexuals: Report of the one-day conference held in London April 2002*, London: ACE.

ACE (2003) *Planning for life as an older lesbian, gay man, bisexual or transgendered person*, London: ACE (www.ageconcern.org.uk/AgeConcern/information_1323.htm, 31/3/05).

Alzheimer's Society (2005) 'The Mental Capacity Bill: its relevance for the gay community', *Lesbian and Gay Network Newsletter*, February, Alzheimer's Society Lesbian and Gay Network.

Barlow, P. (2003) *Speaking Out! Experiences of lesbians, gay men, bisexuals and transgender people in Newham and issues for public sector service providers*, London: London Borough of Newham.

BHPS (British Household Panel Survey) (2004) 'BHPS user documentation and questionnaires', Institute for Social and Economic Research (http://iserwww.essex.ac.uk/ulsc/bhps/doc/, 22/8/04).

Blando, J.A. (2001) 'Twice hidden: older gay and lesbian couples, friends and intimacy', *Generations (American Society of Aging)*, vol 25, no 2, pp 87-9.

Brown, E. (2002) *Lesbian and gay issues in residential care homes (Blackpool, Fylde, Preston and Wyre)*, Blackpool: Age Concern Blackpool and District.

Brown L.B., Sarosy, S.G., Cook, T.C. and Quarto, J.G. (1997) *Garland studies on the elderly in America: Gay men and aging*, New York, NY, and London: Garland.

Cahill, S., South, K. and Spade, J. (2000) *Outing age: Public policy issues affecting gay, lesbian, bisexual and transgender elders*, New York, NY: Policy Institute NGLTF.

Cant, B. (2002) 'An exploration of the views of gay and bisexual men in one London borough of both primary care needs and the practice of primary care practitioners', *Primary Health Care Research and Development*, vol 3, no 2, pp 124-30.

Caulfield, H. and Platzer, H. (1998) 'Next of kin', *Nursing Standard*, vol 13, no 7, pp 47-9.

Civil Partnership Act (2004) c 33, London: The Stationery Office.

Clarke, A., Bright, L. and Greenwood, C. (2002) *Sex and relationships: A guide for care homes*, London: Counsel and Care.

Colling, A. and Lee, A. (2004) *Gay and grey ... with dignity: The report of a one-day conference on older lesbian, gay, bisexual needs*, Scarborough: SGCN.

Dean, L., Meyer, I.H., Robinson, K., Sell, R.L., Sember, R., Silenzio, V.M.B., Bowen, D.J., Bradford, J., Rothblum, E., White, J., Dunn, P., Lawrence, A., Wolfe, D. and Xavier, J. (2000) 'Lesbian, gay, bisexual and transgender health: findings and concerns', *Journal of the Gay and Lesbian Medical Association*, vol 4, no 3, pp 102-51.

DH (Department of Health) (2001) *National Service Framework for older people*, London: DH.

DH (2003) *Care homes for older people: National minimum standards* (3rd edn), London: The Stationery Office.

DH (2006) 'New rights under the Mental Capacity Act, 20/1/2006' (www.dh.gov.uk/NewsHome/NewsArticle/fs/en?CONTENT_ID=4126681&chk=XWLXDq, 25/4/06).

Donovan, C., Heaphy, B. and Weeks, J. (1999) 'Citizenship and same sex relationships', *Journal of Social Policy*, vol 28, no 4, pp 689-709.

DTI (Department of Trade and Industry) (2003) *Civil partnership: A framework for the legal recognition of same-sex couples*, London: DTI.

DWP (Department for Work and Pensions) (2005) *Opportunity Age – Opportunity and security throughout life* (www.dwp.gov.uk/opportunity_ age/, 3/1/07).

Eliason, M.J. and Schope, R. (2001) 'Does "don't ask don't tell" apply to health care? Lesbian, gay, and bisexual people's disclosure to health care providers', *Journal of the Gay and Lesbian Medical Association*, vol 5, no 4, pp 25-134.

Equality Act (2006) c 3, London: The Stationery Office.

GMLA (2003a) 'Creating a safe clinical environment for LGBTI patients' (www.glma.org/medical/clinical/lgbti_clinical_guidelines. pdf, 24/10/05).

GMLA (2003b) 'Creating a safe clinical environment for men who have sex with men' (www.glma.org/medical/clinical/msm_safe_clinical. pdf, 24/10/05).

Hansard (2006) 'Sexual Orientation (Goods and Services) Regulations', 19 October 06, col 1014.

Harrison, J. (2001) '"It's none of my business": gay and lesbian invisibility in aged care', *Australian Occupational Therapy Journal*, vol 48, no 1, pp 42-145.

Heaphy, B., Yip, A. and Thompson, D. (2003) *Lesbian, gay and bisexual lives over 50*, Nottingham: York House Publications/Nottingham Trent University.

Heath, H. (1999) *Sexuality in old age*, Nursing Times Clinical Monographs No 40, London: Nursing Times Press.

Heath, H. (2002a) 'Out in the cold', *Nursing Standard*, vol 16, no 48, p 18.

Heath, H. (2002b) 'Opening doors', *Nursing Older People*, vol 14, no 4, pp 10-13.

Hicks, S. and Watson, K. (2003) 'Desire lines: "queering" health and social welfare', *Sociological Research Online*, vol 8, no 1 (www.socresonline. org.uk/8/1/hicks.html, 31/3/05).

Hinchliff, S., Gott, M. and Galena, E. (2004) 'GPs' perceptions of the gender-related barriers to discussing sexual health in consultations', *European Journal of General Practice*, 10, June, pp 56-60.

Jacobs, R.J., Rasmussen, L.A. and Hohman, M.M. (1999) 'Social support needs of older lesbians, gay men and bisexuals', *Journal of Gay and Lesbian Social Services*, vol 9, no 1, pp 1-30.

Keogh, P., Weatherburn, P., Henderson, L., Reid, D., Dodds, C. and Hickson, F. (2004) *Doctoring gay men: Exploring the contribution of general practice*, London: SIGMA Research.

Kitchen, G. (2003) *Social care needs of older gay men and lesbians on Merseyside*, Get Heard/Sefton Pensioners Advocacy Centre.

Lee, A.M. (2006) 'Exploring the identities, welfare needs, and service use experiences of gay men in later life', Unpublished PhD thesis, York: University or York.

McGhee, D. (2004) 'Beyond toleration: privacy, citizenship and sexual minorities in England and Wales', *The British Journal of Sociology*, vol 55, no 3, pp 357-75.

Martin, J.I. and Knox, J. (2000) 'Methodological and ethical issues in research on lesbians and gay men', *Social Work Research*, vol 24, no 1, pp 51-9.

Mental Capacity Act (2005) c 9, London: The Stationery Office.

Neugebauer-Visano, R. (ed) (1995) *Seniors and sexuality: Experiencing intimacy in later life*, Toronto: Canadian Scholars Press.

ODIT (Opening Doors in Thanet) (2003) *Equally different: Report on the situation of older lesbian, gay, bisexual and transgendered people in Thanet, Kent*, Thanet: ODIT.

ONS (Office for National Statistics) (2006) 'Mid-2005 population estimates: United Kingdom; estimated resident population by single year of age and sex' (www.statistics.gov.uk/STATBASE/Expodata/Spreadsheets/D9387.xls, 26/10/06).

OPSI (Office of Public Sector Information) (2003) *Employment Equality (Sexual Orientation) Regulations*, Statutory Instrument 2003 No 1661, London: The Stationery Office.

Phillips, M. (2006) 'Why Labour despises the family' (www.melaniephillips.com/articles-new/?p=440, 6/1/07).

Pugh, S. (2005) 'Assessing the cultural needs of older lesbians and gay men: implications for practice', *Practice*, vol 17, no 3, pp 207-18.

rainbownetwork.com (2005) '3.5 million British gays' (www.rainbownetwork.com/News/detail.asp?iData=24812&iChannel=2&nChannel=News, 4/4/06).

RCN (Royal College of Nursing)/UNISON (2004) *Not just a 'friend': Best practice guidance on health care for lesbian, gay and bisexual service users and their families*, London: RCN/UNISON.

Richardson, D. (1998) 'Sexuality and citizenship', *Sociology*, vol 32, no 1, pp 83-100.

Richardson, D. (2000) 'Constructing sexual citizenship: theorizing sexual rights', *Critical Social Policy*, vol 20, no 1, pp 105-35.

Rivers, L. (2006) 'Independent lives, care and carers', in A. Lee and A. Colling (eds) *Report on gay and grey … looking forward with hope: The report of a one-day conference on LGB ageing issues*, Scarborough: SGCN.

Schiavi, R.C. (1999) *Aging and male sexuality*, Cambridge: Cambridge University Press.

Shoffman, M. (2006) 'Gay campaigners attack Ruth Kelly over equality delay' (www.pinknews.co.uk/news/articles/2005-2735. html, 6/1/07).

Smith, R. (2006) 'Go figure', *Gay Times*, no 337, October, pp 44-5.

Snowdon-Carr, V. (2005) '"Coming out" to services', *Lesbian and Gay Network Newsletter*, February, Alzheimer's Society Lesbian and Gay Network.

SSI (Social Services Inspectorate) (1995a) *Responding to residents: A report of inspections of local authority residential care homes for older people*, Wetherby: SSI/DH.

SSI (1995b) *Responding to residents: Messages for staff from inspections of local authority residential care homes for older people*, Wetherby: SSI/DH.

Stonewall (2006) 'Workplace Equality Index 2006' (www.stonewall.org. uk/workplace/1477.asp, 3/1/07).

thisislondon.co.uk (2006) 'Christian lawyers to petition Queen to block gay rights bill' (www.thisislondon.co.uk/news/article-23380090-details/Christian%20lawyers%20to%20petition%20Queen%20to%20block%20gay%20rights%20bill/article.do, 6/1/07).

Thompson (Jr), E.H. (ed) (1994) *Older men's lives*, London: Sage Publications.

Webb, D. and Wright, D. (2001) *Count me in: Findings from the lesbian, gay, bisexual, transgender community needs assessment*, Brighton and Hove: Brighton and Hove Council.

Weeks, J. (1998) 'The sexual citizen', *Theory, Culture and Society*, vol 15, part 3-4, pp 35-52.

Wellings, K., Field, J., Johnson, A.M. and Wadsworth, J. (1994) *Sexual behaviour in Britain: The National Survey of Sexual Attitudes and Lifestyles*, London: Penguin.

Wilton, T. (2000) *Sexualities in health and social care: A textbook*, Buckingham: Open University Press.

EIGHT

Dealing with money in low- to moderate-income couples: insights from individual interviews

Sirin Sung and Fran Bennett

Introduction

> Research on the material aspects of family life is not easy because so much economic behaviour takes place (literally) behind closed doors. (Burgoyne et al, 2006, p 619)

As Cantillon et al (2004) argue, what happens within households is often neglected. The family is a key site of distribution – of money, time and labour (see, for example, Lister, 2005), as well as other resources – but is often a 'black box', which is not investigated and in which equality is assumed. The qualitative study drawn on in this chapter is one element of a research project funded by the Economic and Social Research Council (ESRC) as part of the Gender Equality Network that tries to help open up this 'black box'[1]. The research aims to find out more about what goes on within heterosexual couples[2] in relation to financial resources, and to use this to analyse the effects of changes in social security, tax credits and associated labour market policies. The project is timely given current policy changes in this area in the UK, which are affecting the resources available to men and women and the conditions under which these are given – and hence also gender relationships.

This chapter is based on some findings from semi-structured interviews with a sample made up of 30 low- to moderate-income heterosexual couples living in different areas of Britain, who had had children at some point, and where one or (mostly) both partners were of working age[3]. Most were on means-tested benefits or tax credits at the time of the interview and/or had been in the past. The sample was drawn from a 'booster' group of low- to moderate-income households added to the British Household Panel Survey (BHPS) in the late 1990s for the European Community Household Panel (ECHP). (They had last been interviewed for this purpose in 2001.) Interviews were carried out individually rather than jointly, in order to explore the different perceptions of men and women about factual information as well as views and feelings. This decision could be criticised as resulting in unnecessary duplication. But we found that in a number of cases, the man and woman had different degrees of knowledge about the facts of their household finances, as well as different views.

The interviews were intended to investigate any policy-relevant gendered power inequalities, and how benefits and tax credits may affect gender relations. In order to do this, some emphasis was placed on how couples received, organised and used money. There have now been many studies about how couples manage financial resources (for example, in the UK: Pahl, 1989, 1993; Vogler and Pahl, 1994; Rake and Jayatilaka, 2002; and in New Zealand: Fleming, 1997). Pahl (2006) also cites a range of studies from 'developing' countries. Some research in this area has focused on low-income households – the most relevant income group for this project, with its focus on benefits and tax credits (for example, Goode et al, 1998a, 1998b, 1998c; Snape et al, 1999). In this chapter, we explore some of the complexities of financial management in low- to moderate-income couples by highlighting some issues emerging from our interviews. This does not therefore represent a comprehensive account of all our findings.

The chapter is divided into four sections. The next, second, section outlines existing typologies of household financial management and research on gendered patterns of money management. The third section presents the main findings on money management from our research in the light of the existing literature. The themes of this section include complexity, continuity in traditional gendered patterns of money management, and teasing out the relationship between managing money day to day and control over household finances; we look at several potential indicators of financial control. The final section concludes by discussing some of the issues that emerged in a wider context.

Typologies of household financial management

Pahl (1989) suggested that it is possible to classify different patterns of organising and managing money in households. The different systems she identified included the whole wage system, the allowance system, the shared management/pooling system and the independent management system. Goode et al (1998a), among others, explain these systems. In the whole wage system, one partner manages all the household money except the other's personal spending money. In the housekeeping allowance system, one partner gives the other a housekeeping allowance and then keeps the rest of the money, from which some bills may be paid. In the pooling system, all the money is pooled and finances are managed jointly. In independent management, finances are kept completely separate.

Vogler and Pahl (1993) further developed Pahl's original classification into a seven-fold typology of household allocative systems, focusing on overall responsibility for financial management. This new typology added male and female versions of the whole wage system, and divided pooling into male, female and jointly managed pooling systems (for example, see Molloy and Snape, 1999). 'Partial pooling' was recognised as combining some features of pooling and independent management. Vogler et al (2006) cluster these systems into those in which the couple operates as more or less a single economic unit – whole wage, housekeeping allowance and joint pooling – and those that are more individualised/ privatised (independent management and partial pooling); Goode et al (1998a) described these as pooling versus segregated systems.

Different factors can influence financial management within the household, including the source of income and who receives it, the distribution of income and gendered patterns of allocation of financial resources (Pahl, 1989; Vogler and Pahl, 1994; Goode et al, 1998a; Molloy and Snape, 1999; Snape et al, 1999). Vogler (1998) argues that money management and distribution in the household have an independent effect on gendered power inequalities. We discuss this further below.

Complexity

Pahl's early work gave very valuable insights, in terms of how to analyse financial arrangements within households. As with any typology, however, it has been argued that in reality financial management and allocative systems are more complex than this might suggest (see, for example, Goode et al, 1998a and Nyman, 1999). This is particularly important, perhaps, in the light of current social changes. Pahl (2006), for example, emphasises the greater complexity of households in the UK today, and their increased permeability in terms of flows of money. Vogler et al (2006) say that the use of allocative systems may have gone as far as possible, as they are currently formulated; future research should explore further nuances within the joint and partial pooling and independent management systems, as these are least well understood.

Some of our interviews did demonstrate greater complexity than the standard typology might suggest. A particularly striking example was one couple in which the man's (weekly) wage was always paid into the woman's bank account and the woman's (monthly) salary into the man's. The rationale given by both for doing this was mainly the practicality of managing money efficiently between them, but this was based on clear gender roles in terms of spending, with the woman responsible for weekly shopping for food and other household needs, and the man responsible for paying the monthly bills.

> "My wages go into Emma's[4] bank and Emma's wages go into my bank ... the simple reason being because Emma is paid monthly and that pays the bills, that stops in the bank and pays all the direct debits. I get paid weekly and Emma does the shopping, and we find it works a lot better like that." (Case 13, male)

Thus we found it difficult to allocate many of our couples to a specific system within the typology and instead (as shown below) tried to follow the varied mixes of management and control in different couples' arrangements.

Gendered patterns of managing money

Various studies suggest that in low-income households women are largely responsible for managing the money on a day-to-day basis (Wilson, 1987; Brannen and Wilson, 1987; Pahl, 1989, 1993; Vogler and Pahl, 1994). This has been linked to the female whole wage and housekeeping allowance systems in particular (Vogler, 1998). Some studies find this to be particularly prevalent in couples dependent on income from benefits (Bradshaw and Holmes, 1989; Ritchie, 1990, cited in Molloy and Snape, 1999; Goode et al, 1998a; Molloy and Snape, 1999, p 33). Molloy and Snape (1999) suggested some explanations. One was that 'sole control' is necessary to manage a low income effectively. However, this does not explain why this role tends to fall to the woman. Another explanation is that men may be able to avoid the fact that their income is not sufficient to support the household under this 'female-managed' system (Vogler and Pahl, 1994; Goode et al, 1998a).

According to Snape et al's study (1999), among the couples they researched it was commonly believed that women were more capable of budgeting effectively. Among couples who had traditional ideas about gender roles, in most cases men were responsible for financial management as head of the household, although in some cases this was considered part of women's responsibility for the domestic sphere. Also, in female-managed households, women tended to put others first; they allocated less money to themselves for personal expenditure than to their partners, and prioritised the needs of other household members above their own. Thus it may be seen as more 'efficient' to leave money management to the woman.

However, a number of studies (Goode et al, 1998a; Vogler, 1998; Rake and Jayatilaka, 2002) have emphasised the difference between day-to-day management of money and control over finances, which is a key point in understanding gender differences in financial arrangements in households. Vogler et al (2006) describe this as the 'executive function' versus 'strategic control'. The fact that women manage the money day to day does not necessarily mean that they control household finances. Rake and Jayatilaka (2002, p 19) suggest that, "one way of testing who has control over finances is to inquire as to which partner has the final say in financial decisions". In their own study, one fifth of women in low-income families said that their partners had the final say, while a tenth said they themselves did. Research by Bradshaw and Stimson (1997) also suggested that a decade ago it still tended to be the man who made the big financial decisions in many low-income couples.

Previous research has also found that in general women tend to be in a disadvantaged position when it comes to control of, and access to, financial resources within the household (Millar and Ridge, 2001). In low-income families, women's responsibility for managing the money does not necessarily mean that they have more power, but instead may cause stress and worry because of having to manage on a low income (Goode et al, 1998a; Snape et al, 1999). Vogler (1998) finds that if wives manage money, this can result in greater deprivation for them and higher personal spending for men. Thus, she argues that gender inequalities in access to money result from the allocative system used in the household, rather than just from the relative income of each partner. In some studies, however, women have described a sense of pride and peace of mind in managing the budget successfully, which makes it difficult for them to give this up (for example, Goode et al, 1998a).

Dealing with money as a couple

We asked couples about who managed money on a day-to-day basis, and how money was dealt with overall in their household. This section therefore covers their perceptions of both micro-management of the budget and more generally how they dealt with money[5]. The largest number of couples said that the woman managed money day to day, rather than the man or the man and woman together.

> "She manages it all, I don't do anything, if she asks me to look for the tax credit [form] then I fill it out and we send it off – that's it, I have no idea apart from that." (Case 12, male)

In some couples, the woman retained the debit card for the man's individual account, and/or the man did not know his own PIN number.

> "He just gives me his card and then I just go and draw the money out and pay what needs to be paid, and if he needs money for something I'll just give it to him." (Case 8, female)

Several female respondents said that they used the debit cards from the joint account, but that their husbands did not. In these cases, the women were usually responsible for managing money on a day-to-day basis. One respondent illustrated this well:

> "He's got a bank card, if he wants it it's in the bank … he never does…. No, he never does have money. Mind you, I must admit I keep some back in the house, and if he wants anything he takes it out there." (Case 18, female)

She said that her husband usually tells her if he has taken some money from her stock in the house, but sometimes he forgets. She said that she "tells him off" if money keeps disappearing and she does not know where.

Some couples said that the husband is responsible for managing money on a day-to-day basis. Among these, the wives in a few couples had health problems, thus making it more difficult for them to manage the money, as this one explained:

> "David is ... it's changed since I've finished work. No, it's changed in the last 12 months as I've got worse [ie her health has worsened]." (Case 5, female)

Other couples said that they manage the money 'jointly', which usually meant that they had responsibility for doing different things. In these cases, the husbands were largely responsible for paying bills and rent, while the wives were responsible for household shopping.

> "We do it 50/50 as I say – I'm bills, she's food etc, and then with regards to any other bits and pieces we just discuss it anyway." (Case 17, male)

> "I am mostly responsible for, like, the food shopping and household things, and Tony deals with rent, bills, like electric, gas and that sort of thing." (Case 17, female)

In one couple, although both husband and wife said that they were responsible for managing money jointly, the system they used seemed closer to a housekeeping allowance. The husband managed the joint account and the wife said she rarely used the money in their joint account. The husband gave the wife a certain amount of money to do the household shopping. She also said that her husband often asked her "if she was okay with money". This is another example of difficulties in categorising what couples do in terms of a money management typology[6].

In a number of cases, the partners had different ideas about who actually managed money on a day-to-day basis. In some cases, the men said that it was managed jointly, while their wives said that they managed the money. Two female respondents said that their husbands managed the money, while their husbands said that it was done jointly by "both of us". In addition, one male respondent said that his wife managed the money, but his wife said, "it's both of us". These different views were revealed as a result of doing separate interviews. It makes analysing the data more difficult (and again shows the difficulties of categorising couples into the existing typologies of money management). However, it is important to know that some couples have different ideas on 'who is doing what'.

Changes in dealing with money as a couple

A number of couples said that they had changed the way they managed money over time. One couple said that having income from their grown-up children who had returned to live at home had improved their financial situation, and that the children are now involved in discussions of finances as family members. Having older children living at home was relatively common among our sample. Hitherto, to our knowledge, studies of money management in couples have not investigated the possible implications of the presence of older children on the management of household finances; our findings suggest that this should be a focus of future research.

The second example of changes in money management is closely associated with a change in employment status. One woman said that whereas in the past her husband had been more responsible for managing the finances, since she took a full-time job and her husband retired she had mainly been responsible. When we asked her who she would say was responsible for managing the money on a day-to-day basis, she said:

> "Me. Well, I went back to work in 1991, we sat and talked about [it], obviously I knew how much I was going to be earning ... it was just easier for it to come out of my salary, because I was the one who was earning more money ... before that he used to pay everything, but then he became, he was, well he was made redundant, but when he was of retirement age he then obviously received a pension, but as I said to you that doesn't cover the bills, so it obviously makes sense for the one who's got the most income to sort that out, so that's what we did." (Case 2, female)

In contrast, another female respondent said that after her husband started being seasonally unemployed, she had given him more responsibility for managing the money, in part (it seemed) to make him understand more about money and prices:

> "I think it's since ... I mean, at one time, he didn't — I did everything and I think it's become more now, I suppose, now he's got this job where he does spend a bit more time

at home and he's not travelling so much ... he seems to have taken over that side, which I've let him. [Why?] I think then he realises where the money goes to. I think sometimes men, you know, they haven't got an idea of what things cost for a while...." (Case 9, female)

This is one among various examples of female agency revealed in our findings, which demonstrate how qualitative studies can complement quantitative research in this area.

Influence of previous relationships

There has been some research on remarried couples to investigate whether their management of money differs from that of other couples. Burgoyne and Morison (1997) found a greater degree of separateness in remarried couples' finances[7], but argued that the balance of economic power seemed still to favour men – except for couples who had a similar level of income or assets, or where money was short. It may be that the relatively low/moderate level of income of the couples we interviewed was the reason for their not demonstrating the greater degree of separateness found by Burgoyne and Morison. Our findings certainly suggested that individuals carried forward lessons from their past experiences into their new relationships, but not necessarily in the direction suggested by their study.

A significant proportion of respondents (individuals) had had previous relationships (usually marriages) in which they had lived with another partner. Among these, some felt strongly that the experience of their previous relationship had influenced the way they dealt with money now. These cases sometimes raised the relationship between money management and control, which we examine later. Two women illustrated how their previous husbands were totally in control of money and how they felt about this.

"He was, he had control of everything. I felt worthless really. I didn't have any say in anything whatsoever, anything to do with money, I can't even remember needing a purse ... my place was in the home ... and it was a case of if I needed anything I'd ask." (Case 24, female)

In her current relationship, this woman is the one who mainly manages the money on a day-to-day basis and she much prefers this. Another female respondent also mentioned that her ex-husband used to control the finances and she felt that she had to justify her spending to him.

> "I didn't have access to his wages at all, I had no idea how much his wages were. So for me that was a big ... it upset me greatly, it was very hard and it did cause the divorce, it was very...." (Case 11, female)

She said that in her current relationship the money was managed jointly and she felt happier in this relationship than the previous one.

Several respondents (both female and male) described how their ex-wives/husbands spent too much money and how that had affected them.

> "I had to look after the money because my ex-wife was a spender, if it was in there it had to go, it would burn a hole in her pocket." (Case 11, male)

> "It was always me, and at that time I did have a bank account with money in that my ex-husband quite happily went out and spent ... yes, he cleared my bank account." (Case 15, female)

This female respondent also said that both she and her husband had had bad experiences in their previous relationships, and she thought that this was probably the main reason why they worked so well together now.

> "Because Adam's been married before and his marriage wasn't that great – so I think that's probably why we work so well, because we know what it's like to be sort of stuck in a relationship that's not brilliant." (Case 15, female)

Two men and one woman described how they were happier with the way the money was managed as a couple in their current relationship because they put the money together as joint money. In their previous relationship, finances were more separate.

> "In my first marriage it was a case of 'this is your money, this is mine' ... but my first wife was, I was going to say selfish, but not selfish, no, that's the wrong way to look at it, she always felt that she should be financially independent

and even though she only had a part-time job then, she felt that whatever she earned shouldn't be used for anything else other than herself really." (Case 4, male)

Finally, the experience of independent management between relationships could also be influential, as one man showed in describing his wife's experience of lone motherhood.

"I think the reason I look on myself, shall we say, as the captain, like I said before ... is because before we were married Jodie was on her own for about nine years and she absolutely hated looking after the budget for the family.... There was just herself and the two children and she had the whole burden, if you like, of looking after the financial side of the family." (Case 4, male)

However, in his view, there seemed to be two reasons for his being in charge of the money, which included the fact that he saw himself as the head of the family, or the 'captain'.

Although various interviewees had had bad experiences in their previous relationships, it was only female respondents who said that they had had no control over money at all. In our research, there was an exceptional case of a househusband. His wife used to be the main earner but, now that she could not work, she was getting benefits. She had always been the main earner or income provider and he had been the one who managed the money. In the interview, he did not say that her 'breadwinner' role meant that he felt he had no control over money in the household; he also had a very clear idea of the man as head of the family. When he was asked "how would you say you decide things in general in your family?", he said:

"We decide it basically on the fact that I'm number 1, the wife is number 2, there's a pecking order in the house ... I am the top of the tree." (Case 31, male)

This case suggests, as others have argued, that it is not just who provides what resources that matters in terms of control. We discuss in the conclusions later the implications of findings such as this for our thinking about the relationship of financial management with other factors in couple relationships and wider society.

Control of the finances

Burgoyne and Morison (1997) point out that, while it may be easy to see who has control in male-controlled allowance or whole wage systems, with other systems it is more difficult. The system of organisation is not the whole story. To explore this, therefore, we looked at three areas: big financial decisions, management of the joint bank account (where relevant) and personal spending.

Our respondents were less clear about financial control in terms of decision making than about money management. We asked two main questions: "how are big financial decisions made?" and "who has the final say?". The vast majority of couples said that big financial decisions were made jointly, while the others gave different answers.

> "I would think Jane has the final say, to be honest." (Case 24, male)

> "The big ones it's mainly a joint decision, but I tend to leave the big items for him." (Case 24, female)

A few women said that they followed their husbands' decisions, while one man said that his wife made the decisions. Some respondents of both sexes said that they made the big financial decisions, not their partners. When it came to being asked who had the final say on big financial decisions, more couples perhaps felt forced to pick one individual. More couples had different ideas, than those who said the same. One couple represents this well, in that the husband said that his wife had the final say on big financial decisions, but the wife said that it was her husband.

Vogler (1998) argues that control over decision making is not sufficient as a concept of power. We therefore looked at other possible indicators, including management of joint bank accounts and individuals' position in relation to personal spending.

Joint accounts

Joint accounts tend to be used as a measure of shared financial systems in households, and may sometimes be seen as being synonymous with joint (or partial) pooling. While they are often considered as a 'symbol of togetherness', "this sort of sharing can be driven by necessity rather than ideology" (Rake and Jayatilaka, 2002, p 23). In our research, a strong sense of 'togetherness' was often expressed about joint accounts. The majority of respondents said they had joint accounts and most said that this was important for them. The majority explained this by referring to a sense of trust and sharing within a couple relationship, while some respondents said it was useful to have a joint account for practical reasons. (A small number mentioned both ideological and practical reasons.) This result is slightly different from Burgoyne and Morison's study (1997) on money in remarriage, which found most respondents giving practical rather than ideological reasons. This may be due to differences between the samples in the two pieces of research.

> "If you're a couple, you have to trust each other. If you are committed to each other, it shouldn't be any problem." (Case 10, female)

> "It identifies the source for, yes the source for paying all the necessary household bills that are done regularly, as I say, your basic living things, ... like Council Tax, water, gas, electric etc." (Case 20, male)

Of course, couples may not have equal access to the joint account. Although both members of the couple technically have the right to access it, how access is exercised in practice can be a different matter. This was evident in our study, in that a few women said that they did not draw money from the joint account because they regarded it as their husband's money. In addition, the issue of who managed the joint account was also important – who checked the bank statements, for example.

Individual accounts

Rake and Jayatilaka's study showed that, while with joint accounts it was the practicalities that were stressed, when it came to individual accounts it was different; women said that they wanted them in order to gain some sense of independence. In fact, for some women it was very important to keep their finances separate from their partner's. One focus group participant said that "it [having separate accounts] helps to keep our own identities slightly" (Rake and Jayatilaka, 2002, p 25).

Pahl (1999, p 67) suggested that "the joint account continues to be a powerful symbol of marital togetherness". This was borne out in our interviews, with several people querying how anyone who was married could have individual accounts, as this must indicate a lack of trust.

However, Pahl (1999, p 67) also found a growth of 'partial pooling' (with couples combining joint and individual accounts), which she argued is an indicator of "increasing concern with financial autonomy". It tended to be women who were more likely to have individual accounts.

Among our interviewees, this was also the case: more women than men had individual accounts. Some women emphasised the importance of having an individual account in order to be independent. One said:

> "I think you've got to have a little bit of your own, I wouldn't say security, but I've never been used to being totally hand in hand with somebody with finances." (Case 27, female)

This was evident in Burgoyne and Morison's study (1997), in that independence was one of the main reasons for (remarried) couples to have separate accounts.

One female interviewee said that she preferred to have her own individual account because she did not consider her husband very good with money. This was a recurring theme in our findings overall – that is, relative skill being stated as a reason for certain patterns of money management (and other divisions of labour) between the couple.

This woman also mentioned that she liked to have her own money, so that she did not have to justify what she was spending money on. Having an individual account therefore appeared more important to female than male respondents. No men talked about independence, and hardly any commented on why it was important to have an individual account. Only a few said that it was important, one of whom said that it signified both of them being neither beholden to each other nor in control.

For some women, therefore, having individual accounts was closely related to their sense of freedom and independence, and to not having to ask for money or justify their own spending to their partners. This raises the issue of the relative importance of autonomy when considering gender equality. (The issue of whether personal spending has to be justified is also relevant to who has more control over money – see below.)

Managing the joint account

Some couples said that they managed the joint account jointly, while some couples said the wives managed it, and others said the husbands did. There were also couples who had different ideas. When the answers are analysed by individuals[8], there are clear differences between men and women. For instance, a significant number of men were said by themselves or by partners to be involved in managing the joint account, while fewer women were in the same position, either singly or jointly. Importantly, some female respondents said that their husbands were responsible for managing the joint account, although in some cases their husbands said it was managed jointly. This result is not surprising when we consider that most men are responsible for paying bills and these are often paid through joint accounts. Thus men are more likely to be responsible for checking the bank statement to make sure the bills have been paid.

This means that having a joint account does not always mean sharing power in terms of money management. Another important theme related to managing the joint account was "putting the bills on direct debit", as one person put it. In our research, many couples used direct debit for bills. As most bills are paid from the joint account, and men are often responsible for paying bills, who manages the joint account becomes important.

Justification of personal spending

A difference in the sense of entitlement to personal spending can be one indication of inequalities in relation to money. The evidence from Goode et al (1998a, p 14) suggests that women do not tend to "see themselves as having money of their own", whereas men regard "part of their wages as personal spending money". Women also found it hard to make sense of the concept of money to spend on themselves, while men's pocket money and personal spending were accepted and seen as unproblematic for both partners (Goode et al, 1998a). Both men and women often considered spending for children and the household by women as those women's personal spending, because women's identity was seen as so closely bound up with the family.

In our study, some men had pocket money, or money for leisure, while their partners might not have. This was starkly evident in one couple:

> "Yes I play golf, but that costs me £7.30 every week, that's it, out of my wages, I want £7.30 that's mine, that's rightfully mine." (Case 12, male)

> "I go to my Auntie's up the road. It's a thing I did after I had the third child just so I had that couple of hours to myself really.... And he [her husband] goes to golf on a Saturday, so it's fair, really, you know." (Case 12, female)

Having to justify personal spending to partners may be another indicator of who was in control of the household finances. The majority of our respondents said that they did not feel they had to justify their personal spending to their spouses or partners, while some said that they did. This total was made up of more women than men. (In one couple, both the man and woman said that they felt they had to justify their personal spending to their spouses.)

Among this group, some men said that they felt they had to justify their spending when they bought expensive goods, such as items for a car, a motorbike or a computer. One male respondent said that he felt he had to justify his personal spending because he was not bringing enough money into the household. He was currently on Incapacity Benefit, while his wife was working full time. His wife, on the other hand, said that she did not feel she had to justify her personal spending to her husband.

One woman mentioned that she used to feel she had to justify her personal spending because her husband was the main breadwinner; but she did not feel this any more, because she was now earning her own money:

> "I used to, but I think not now I'm earning my own money. Because he was the main breadwinner, I suppose I felt I had to ask for money if I wanted it for my clothes and things." (Case 18, female)

Several female respondents said that they felt they needed to justify their personal spending when they bought shoes or clothes:

> "Yes, when I got new boots.... Yes because, only, like, clothes and specifically the shoes, because I do know I've got too many, and I know I probably won't wear them, so I do feel that I have to justify those." (Case 16, female)

Crucially, one female respondent said that she often hid the bank statements from her husband:

> "I do dread him looking at his statements, his bank statements, because I think he's going to ask me, well, what did that come out for and why did you get that out ... I hide ... sometimes I think to myself, right, he doesn't often open his bank statements ... because it does cause arguments." (Case 7, female)

This case seems to show that her husband controlled the finances. This was not necessarily clear in other parts of the interview. For instance, when they were asked who had the final say in big financial decisions, the husband said "no one has". When we asked about how big financial decisions were made, both husband and wife said this was done jointly. A range of indicators is needed to establish where control lies.

Another female respondent said that she felt she had to justify her personal spending because there were things she thought she needed, whereas her husband thought she did not. Similarly, one male respondent said that he felt annoyed when his wife spent, because he thought his wife "likes to buy things", although both husband and wife said that they did not feel they had to justify their personal spending. In this couple, his wife was the main earner who brought in the money and he was a househusband. However, he said that he had the final say on big financial decisions and his wife sometimes bought things and did not tell him. This shows that it is not always the main earner who has control over the finances. In this household, it seems that the idea of the man as the head of the family remains strong and is clearly more important than who brings in the money.

Although the gender differences are not very clear, in terms of numbers feeling they have to justify spending to their partners, when we look at what was said more closely it is clear that in general men have stronger influence and control over their wives' personal spending than vice versa. For example, no men said that they have to hide the bank statements from their wives, or do not tell their wives what they bought for themselves. Men tend to say that they feel they have to justify their spending when they buy expensive items. And no men said that their wives made a judgement that they did not need something when they felt they do; this was true only for women.

Continuity of traditional gendered patterns in financial management

Vogler (1998) confirms that the 'female whole wage' system (with the female partner taking the full responsibility for managing finances in the household, apart from the man's personal spending money) was the most commonly used system in low-income families in the 1990s. It was also evident in Goode et al's study (1998a) of low-income couples who had had a baby in the last couple of years. Goode et al divided their interviewees (low-income couples) into three groups: egalitarian, traditional and male dominated. Couples in the 'egalitarian' group had an equal share in financial deprivations and both partners viewed breadwinning as a shared activity. A 'traditional' group viewed breadwinning as men's responsibility and women were responsible for managing the money day to day. In this group, men regularly received pocket money for personal spending. In the 'male-dominated' group, women expected their partners to be breadwinners; both partners were responsible for managing the money, but men always controlled the finances. In all three groups, men had more material advantages than women, particularly in terms of personal spending.

Vogler et al (2006) note that there have been changes in employment, ideology and forms of partnership that might be expected to have an impact on financial management patterns within couples. Pahl (2006) says partial pooling and independent management are now more frequent, with younger and cohabiting couples especially favouring greater independence and access for each to personal spending money. In our sample of low- to moderate-income couples, however, we found some continuity of traditional patterns. One example was that in many couples men were mainly responsible for paying bills, while women had responsibility for household shopping. Although in Pahl's study of gendered spending (2000), payments for the mortgage/rent, utilities etc were omitted[9], she confirms the common responsibility of women for lower-cost items that are usually needed more frequently. Another traditional pattern that was more common in our findings than might be expected was that the woman's management of the household budget included in several cases giving the man a regular (small amount of) pocket money to spend on items such as lunch, cigarettes etc. These findings may be seen as confirming the conclusion of the recent quantitative study by Vogler et al (2006) about the continuing importance of class in relation to the way couples manage money.

Conclusion

This chapter has focused on financial management by couples and its complexities. In many cases, we found it hard to describe the system the interviewees were using to manage their money within a clear typology. It was instead more likely to be 'mix and match', often depending on necessity or the couple's relationship. We found gendered patterns of money management continuing in low- to moderate-income couples who have had children, with women more likely to have day-to-day responsibility for managing the money, and gendered patterns of spending persisting.

Between the lines, we believe that tensions emerge that men and women living in these couples struggle with. Vogler (1998) identified tensions between the ideal of marriage as an equal partnership, breadwinner ideology and individual entitlement to income earned or owned.

In our research, loyalty to 'coupledom' was very evident, although this was more often expressed as jointness and mutuality rather than equality. Both men and women often portrayed all the money coming in as being for the family; for example, the most common description of how money was dealt with was that it all went into "one pot". This was often stated and stoutly held to. As one male respondent typically said:

> "I don't see any of the money as my own. It's all family money and for the family." (Case 4, male)

This could be seen as more a case of describing the ideal type of unitary household than portraying a partnership of equals. Men's income is even more likely to be seen as joint or for the family than women's. But there was certainly some adherence to ideas of marriage as equal partnership.

This competes with adherence to (male) breadwinner ideology. Goode et al (1998b, p 15) concluded that "the female disadvantage which was associated with male financial control derived from men's identity as sole breadwinner". Vogler (1998) notes that the ideology of breadwinning may trump the resource theory of power (that is, earning of money per se giving power and control), as a pound of money earned by one partner may not have the same value as a pound earned by another[10].

However, this may also co-exist with a sense of individual entitlement to earnings or other income. Rake and Jayatilaka's study (2002, p 7) showed that some participants from their focus groups (women of different ages and with different income levels) described how they felt "a great sense of entitlement to the income that they have earned or received directly"[11]. This sense of 'ownership' of money "creates greater control over how that money is spent".

As the sense of entitlement to income is often associated with who earns the money, women are more likely to be disadvantaged. But there was a desire by women in our study for autonomy, and some had managed to achieve a measure of independence. In some cases, this was associated with receiving income from benefits/tax credits. One woman in a couple with two disabled children, for example, said:

> "It probably only changed really in that, with the sort of Disability Living Allowance and things, there's been more money coming, and it's enabled us to do more things ... well, I feel I have more independence with money now, now that I get the money for the children ... so before that, I mean, we've always discussed money anyway, but I have a lot more control over money now."

Some female respondents also mentioned Child Benefit and Child Tax Credit when they were asked what they thought of as 'money in your own right'. We hope to explore the impact of receipt of benefits/tax credits within household relationships in future analysis of the data from this study.

Notes

[1] RES-225-25-2001 (www.genet.ac.uk) – this research is Project 5 in the Gender Equality Network. The other two principal investigators, alongside Fran Bennett, are Professor Holly Sutherland (University of Essex) and Professor Sue Himmelweit (The Open University). Other stages of the project will involve quantitative research and policy simulation.

[2] The research project was conceived before the proposals for change that later became the 2004 Civil Partnership Act. Some issues explored in relation to benefits and tax credits also apply to same-sex couples registered as civil partners; some could apply to registered and unregistered same-sex couples.

[3] A few couples had one partner of pension age.

[4] To maintain anonymity, pseudonyms are used throughout the chapter.

[5] It does not include our findings on borrowing, debt and savings, which will be explored elsewhere.

[6] Note, however, that in many surveys using money management typologies couples are asked to pick the system that is 'closest' to the way they organise things.

[7] 'Remarrieds' in fact included some cohabiting couples.

[8] In some cases both individuals in a couple talked about the management of the joint account in the interviews. These cases are described as couples here. In other cases, only one member of the couple discussed this issue.

[9] This was because they were often paid by direct debit or standing order rather than cash/cheque/card.

[10] It is worth noting, however, that Nyman (1999), in her study of Swedish couples, found that, even when the male breadwinner ideology appeared to have been supplanted by commitment to co-provisioning, this did not remove inequalities in terms of access to income etc within the household.

[11] This could include wages or other forms of income.

Bibliography

Bjornberg, U. and Kollind, A.K. (2005) *Individualism and families: Equality, autonomy, and togetherness*, London and New York, NY: Routledge.

Bradshaw, J. and Holmes, H. (1989) *Living on the edge: A study of the living standards of families on benefit in Tyne and Wear*, Tyneside: Tyneside Child Poverty Action Group.

Bradshaw, J. and Stimson, C. (1997) *Using Child Benefit in the family budget*, London: The Stationery Office.

Bradshaw, J., Finch, N., Kemp, P., Mayhew, E. and Williams, J. (2003) *Gender and poverty in Britain*, Working Paper Series No 6, Manchester: Equal Opportunities Commission.

Brannen, G. and Wilson, G. (eds) (1987) *Give and take in families: Studies in resource distribution*, London: Allen and Unwin.

Burgoyne, C.B. and Lewis, A. (1994) 'Distributive justice in marriage: equality or equity?', *Journal of Community and Applied Social Psychology*, vol 4, pp 101-14.

Burgoyne, C.B. and Morison, V. (1997) 'Money in remarriage: keeping things simple – and separate', *The Sociological Review*, vol 45, no 3, pp 363-95.

Burgoyne, C.B., Clarke, V., Reibstein, J. and Edmunds, A. (2006) '"All my worldly goods I share with you?": managing money at the transition to heterosexual marriage', *The Sociological Review*, vol 54, no 4, pp 619-37.

Cantillon, S., Gannon, B. and Nolan, B. (2004) *Sharing household resources: Learning from non-monetary indicators*, Dublin: Combat Poverty Agency.

Fleming, R. (1997) *The common purse: Income sharing in New Zealand families*, Auckland: Auckland University Press with Bridget Williams Books.

Goode, J., Callender, C. and Lister, R. (1998a) *Purse or wallet? Gender inequalities and income distribution within families on benefits*, London: Policy Studies Institute.

Goode, J., Callender, C. and Lister, R. (1998b) 'Women's work, men's work and welfare', *Poverty*, vol 10, pp 14-17.

Goode, J., Callender, C. and Lister, R. (1998c) 'Whose money is it anyway?', *The New Review*, pp 14-17.

Hills, J., Smithies, R. and McKnight, A. (2006) *Tracking income: How working families' incomes vary through the year*, CASEReport 32, London: Centre for Analysis of Social Exclusion, London School of Economics and Political Science.

Laurie, H. and Rose, D. (1994) 'Divisions and allocations within households', in N. Buck et al (eds) *Changing households: The BHPS 1990 to 1992*, Colchester: ESRC Research Centre on Microsocial Change.

Lister, R. (2005) 'Social justice and gender', *SCRSJ News* (newsletter of the Scottish Centre for Research in Social Justice, University of Glasgow), issue 3, p 8.

Millar, J. and Ridge, T. (2001) *Families, poverty, work and care: A review of the literature on lone parents and low-income couple families with children*, DWP Research Report No 153, Leeds: Corporate Document Services.

Molloy, D. and Snape, D. (1999) *Financial arrangements of couples on benefit: A review of the literature*, In-house Report No 58, London: DSS.

Nyman, C. (1999) 'Gender equality in "the most equal country in the world"? Money and marriage in Sweden', *The Sociological Review*, vol 47, no 4, pp 766-93.

Pahl, J. (1989) *Money and marriage*, London: Macmillan.

Pahl, J. (1993) 'Money, marriage and ideology: holding the purse strings?', *Sociology Review*, vol 3, no 1, pp 7-11.

Pahl, J. (1999) *Invisible money: Family finances in the electronic economy*, Bristol: The Policy Press.

Pahl, J. (2000) 'The gendering of spending within households', *Radical Statistics*, vol 75, pp 38-48.

Pahl, J. (2006) 'Family finances, individualisation, spending patterns and access to credit', Paper presented at the ESRC seminar on 'Beyond Homo Economicus: Emerging Perspectives on Economic Behaviour', Exeter University, 29-30 June.

Rake, K. and Jayatilaka, G. (2002) *Home truths: An analysis of financial decision making within the home*, London: Fawcett Society.

Ritchie, J. (1990) *Thirty families: Their living standards in unemployment*, DSS Research Report No 1, London: HMSO (cited in Molloy and Snape, 1999).

Snape, D., Molloy, D. and Kumar, M. (1999) *Relying on the state, relying on each other*, DSS Research Report No 103, Leeds: DSS.

Vogler, C. (1998) 'Money in the household: some underlying issues of power', *The Sociological Review*, vol 46, no 4, pp 687-713.

Vogler, C. and Pahl, J. (1993) 'Social and economic change and the organisation of money within marriage', *Work, Employment and Society*, vol 7, no 1, pp 71-95.

Vogler, C. and Pahl, J. (1994) 'Money, power and inequality within marriage', *The Sociological Review*, vol 42, no 2, pp 263-88.

Vogler, C., Brockmann, M. and Wiggins, R.D. (2006) 'Intimate relationships and changing patterns of money management at the beginning of the twenty first century', *British Journal of Sociology*, vol 57, no 3, pp 455-82.

Wilson, G. (1987) *Money in the family: Financial organisation and women's responsibility*, Aldershot: Avebury.

NINE

Power and autonomy of older people in long-term care: cross-national comparison and learning

Henglien (Lisa) Chen

Introduction

The current trend in many European countries is shifting caring responsibilities towards the individual and promoting independence among older people. In this chapter it is argued that older people who need long-term care are most likely to be physically/mentally frail and they are more likely to be involved with multiple care actors. It for this reason that the power and autonomy of dependent older people is essential to ensure their quality of care is maintained. However, it also means that securing the autonomy of dependent older people within the complexities of the long-term care system remains a challenge. This chapter seeks to explore some solutions. It focuses on the entire long-term care framework and uses international comparisons to understand the range of policy options in order to learn from the successes (or failures) of foreign care systems. The countries selected – England, the Netherlands and Taiwan – were chosen because each represents a different welfare arrangement. In addition, many eastern countries such as Taiwan share with the West a similar trend of an ageing society (UN, 2001).

The chapter first covers theoretical views on power and autonomy as well as the care systems of older people in the three countries. It is concerned with issues of autonomy, globalisation, welfare typologies, needs, social inclusion and empowerment; the outcomes of autonomy are not purely ethical issues but consist of characteristics among the welfare systems, such as cultural beliefs and practical issues. The chapter then focuses on empirical research to offer an in-depth exploration of the conception of autonomy among the three care systems. It highlights older people's experiences of social and personal barriers that are inhibiting them from becoming more active socially and politically while in care. It also seeks to understand how their experiences of autonomy have affected their care and well-being. The concluding section draws together practical issues and offers signposts for cross-national learning.

Background perspective

Theories and policies in promoting autonomy in the long-term care of older people

In the context of long-term care, autonomy is crucial in determining quality of life and ensuring that older people are to be in control of their care (Österle, 2001; Boyle, 2003). The conventional view of autonomy comes from liberal bioethical thought associated with prioritising self-capability of independence, non-interference, self-determination, self-reliance and choice. This is rather difficult to apply to older people in need of long-term care, many of whom experience physical/mental frailty, despair, social isolation and most of all the loss of functional ability, self-identity and support (Agich, 2003). Specifically, autonomy in the care system links with the concept of right and choice, which is closely related to that of needs. Basic human needs themselves are universal and relatively straightforward to describe. However, the needs element in the relationship between the individual and society is complex and varied (Doyal and Gough, 1991; Langan, 1998). The assessment process, resource rationing, professional power (Walker, 1993) and associated carers (Boyle, 2003) determine the identification of needs and the exercise of choice. It will be demonstrated here that care needs are defined and met differently in different welfare systems.

It is argued that autonomy is not only about the ability to make choices, but about social interaction to make that choice work. It is a multidimensional phenomenon about the 'ins' and 'outs' of society. The dimensions are most likely to be mutually reinforced, resulting in blame, discrimination or segregation of vulnerable/marginal older people (Silver, 1994; Bowring, 2000). Social inclusion and engagement involves strengthening the individual's system of support and participation in social activities that can result in an increased sense of social and personal fulfilment (Mullins and McNicholas, 1986). Empowerment is critical in enabling people to participate openly and directly in making the decisions that govern their lives (Etzioni, 1993). Older people in care want to have choice and control over their daily lives, and need services that support such control (Qureshi and Henwood, 2000). It is also important to build up a support network for older people to be able to address their views on various levels (Percy-Smith, 2000).

In order to achieve this goal, first the individual has a moral responsibility to help themselves as best as they can. The second line of responsibility lies with those close to older people such as family, friends, neighbours and other community members who have personalised knowledge about the individual and are able to tailor the help to what is required. While the first moral responsibility may be a universal basic human need, within specific cultural contexts it requires physical and mental capacity to deliberate (Doyal and Gough, 1991). The latter is affected by the availability of national and local resources. In the Netherlands, there are regulations that safeguard service users' rights, namely the 1995 Medical Treatment Act, which deals with the rights and obligations of patients and care providers; the 1996 Care Institutions Quality Act, which deals with the participation structures in the policy of the institution; and the 1995 Client Right of Complaint Act, which deals with the possibility of appeal through official complaints committees. In England, the 1990 National Health Service (NHS) and Community Care Act emphasises the importance of empowerment in professional practice; the Department of Health has established an official procedure for dealing with complaints relating to health and social care under the 2000 Freedom of Information Act. By contrast, Taiwan is the only country yet to have comprehensive legislation to secure service users' rights, but market provision and family involvement are strong. This study engaged with how far the three care systems widened network support and/or better participation in the decision making of older people to exercise their autonomy.

Why use cross-national research in the long-term care system?

A number of globalisation studies (see, for example, Adams, 2000) focus on the economic debate whether, as trade/finance become more international, countries become more interdependent. This is similar to the debate examining social policy in terms of convergence or divergence (Albert, 1993; Hirst and Thompson, 1996; Mishra, 1999; Bonoli et al, 2000; Kleinman, 2002). This chapter argues that the three countries in this study, England, the Netherlands and Taiwan, show evidence of learning social policy direction from other countries as part of the globalisation phenomenon. English social policy has in particular been influenced by US policy (such as welfare-to-work and the community care model). The Dutch model has proactively learnt from broad cross-national research in developed countries (Jonkers and Troisfontaine, 2004; Merlis and van de Water, 2005; Tjadens et al, 2005). Similarly, Taiwanese welfare development has benefited by learning from the experiences of Europe, Japan, the US and so on (Wu et al, 2001, 2002; Wu, 2003). It suggests that countries are no longer autonomous in terms of their social policy. In addition, there is the global phenomenon of ageing populations. Therefore, there might be a case for learning much more from each other (Doling et al, 2005).

Welfare and long-term care systems

To begin the learning process, it is not possible to understand the long-term care of older people in the three countries without exploring the background against which care takes place, since the policy concerning the long-term care of older people is part of the welfare system as a whole. A country's welfare system is influenced by politico-economic and socio-cultural factors from both external and internal sources. Esping-Andersen's welfare state regimes (Esping-Andersen, 1990) have been adopted in cross-national research, in which he distinguished between 'three worlds of welfare capitalism' by grouping welfare state regimes within the Organisation for Economic Co-operation and Development (OECD) countries into three basic types: social democratic, conservative/corporatist and liberal. The core of his analysis is the notion of 'decommodification', which is an indication of good welfare provision. However, his three welfare regimes have attracted considerable criticism and debate (see Cass, 1990; Shaver, 1992; Lewis, 1993; Orloff, 1993). In his later study that included Japan, Esping-Andersen admitted his ideal type of welfare regime might not apply fully to existing societies (Esping-Andersen, 1997). Similarly, none of the countries in this study has conformed to Esping-Andersen's typologies; instead they seem to constitute hybrids. England has elements of both the universal social democratic and the selective liberal type in "unstable combination" (Taylor-Gooby, 1991). The universal system designed by Beveridge was never put fully into practice and elements of selectivity have been increasingly introduced. Therefore, England can be identified as a 'liberal-social democratic' type of welfare regime. The Netherlands is often compared with Sweden and is regarded as a 'social democratic-conservative' type of welfare regime, based on a general social security system, favoured by Christian democrats, and in turn provides a more comprehensive welfare services model. Taiwan is similar to Japan, offering a 'liberal-conservative' welfare regime with a strong role for non-governmental organisations (NGOs), as well as privileged welfare for state employees, and segmented, corporative social insurance.

The Netherlands' social democratic-conservative type of welfare emerged clearly as a state welfare leader with the English liberal-social democratic type of welfare system a close second, whereas Taiwan's liberal-conservative welfare regime comes third. It may be, however, that Taiwanese private and familial welfare go some way to narrowing the gap between Taiwan and the other two countries. One extremely important emergent fact of population ageing is that eastern societies are now turning to the state (Bengtson and Putney, 2000), while western societies are increasingly recognising the important role of family care. There is little reason to believe that England and the Netherlands are likely to experience further welfare expansion in the near future, but Taiwan will find it necessary to provide more resources to its older population, resulting in a tendency for policy convergence (Chen, 2007: forthcoming).

The macro-welfare system as mentioned has a significant effect on the long-term care policy and framework in the three countries and on the autonomy of older people. The level and range of statutory support to older people in long-term care is higher in the Netherlands than the other two countries (Huijbers and Martin, 1998; DSA, 2004). There are several forms of community and institutional services for the long-term care of older people available in the three countries. NGOs in the Netherlands provide the majority of services; NGOs and some private sector organisations in Taiwan; and local authorities and many profitable private sector organisations in England (Bartlett and Wu, 2000; Brodsky et al, 2000; Cheng, 2000). The characteristics and ideology of the welfare and long-term care systems in the three countries mentioned above result in a range of similarities and differences of autonomy among older people in long-term care, which will be addressed further later in this chapter.

Comparative methodology

There is a long history of nation, state and welfare studies in cross-national research (see, for example, Castles, 1985; Esping-Andersen, 1990; Kennett, 2001; Österle, 2001; Walker and Wong, 2005). Most have done quantitative research; although a few qualitative comparative analyses (see, for example, Ungerson, 1996; 2004; Glendinning, 1998) are available, they were restricted to the micro-contact rather than the welfare system as a whole. Because of the practicalities, cross-national comparison can only be carried out when a full appreciation of culture such as language, values, attitude, care systems and institutions is recognised (van de Vijver and Leung, 1997). Single-person cross-national studies which attempt to cover the full impact of policy are difficult to undertake. While I am fluent in Mandarin and English and am learning Dutch, I also have substantial knowledge and experience of these different cultures from having lived in all three countries; in the context of this study it is important to understand how these differing approaches fit into the wider social welfare systems of the country concerned, and the need for research in a more qualitative manner will certainly persist. This study attempted to do this by centring on the views and experiences of local service users and radiating out to their carers, professionals, local administrators, service providers, civil servants and voluntary agency officials who had held care management/provision responsibilities. As a result, out of a total of 142 participants (46, 45 and 51 in England, the Netherlands and Taiwan respectively), 28 older people (service users) were involved in this study, as Table 9.1 shows.

To maximise the range of service users in this research, five in each country received community care; two in each country received nursing care; and two received residential care in England and Taiwan. Additionally, three (including the one resident in the care hotel) received residential care in the Netherlands. There were a different number of respondents from each group within and across the countries in this

Table 9.1: Interviews conducted

Interviewees	Number of interviews			
	England	The Netherlands	Taiwan	Total
National level	3	6	6	15
Local administrators	4	4	6	14
Service users	9	10	9	28
Informal carers	4	1	2	7
Formal carers	5	9	9	23
Service providers	10	7	8	25
Professionals	11	8	11	30
Total	46	45	51	142

study (see Table 9.1). First, this is because there are different structures to the care system framework in the three countries. Second, each older person had different care needs and required a different level of support. To minimise variation in the comparative research, the service users were female, aged over 60, from the majority ethnic group, and receiving formal care support. Women were chosen partly because of their propensity to live longer than men, and so were more likely to be needing long-term care. Third, the research also chose a specific area (sub-urban) in each country that consisted of urban and rural elements. Finally, identical research methods were used in the three countries, to support a uniform application of practical issues in the field and interpretation of the analysis.

Face-to-face individual semi-structured interviews were carried out on three levels in each country: national, county and municipal. Seven interview schedules were designed to meet each actor's specific experience and knowledge in the care framework. Nonetheless, some questions were asked of all participants to gather views from the top to the bottom of the system. Each interview lasted for an hour on average. While all correspondents answered in such an individual way as to make comparison difficult, they all had something to say and much of the information they provided was relevant. This suggests that it is rather sensible to apply Becker's 'sequential' methodology in the systematic coding and analysis of the interviews, and some thematic characteristics emerged (Becker and Bryman, 2004). Excel and Visual Mind[1] software were adopted through the analysis process to maximise the systematic and consistent results. In addition, photographs were also taken whenever possible to gather some perspective of the daily lives of the 28 older people across the countries, while bearing in mind that they cannot replace words of representation (Pink, 2001).

Vision of autonomy among long-term care for older people

Nearly all (98/114) of the care contributors in the three countries pointed out that people tend not to think about their potential care needs as a consequence of a lack of planning for later life:

> "Nobody wants to think about old age and disease and death and things like that, so, people are not inclined to design their last phase of their life ... the service users find that the

> quality of food is very important and the way and attention of the care." (Senior officials in Arcares, the Netherlands)

For people receiving long-term care, they are concerned about the care they have received at the micro- rather than macro-level:

> "I think they actively address their needs." (Home care manager of Ms Owen[2], England)

> "The older people are more interested and involved in their care rather than the general policy of our agency or government." (Home care manager of Ms Fu and Ms Bai, Taiwan)

This implied the importance and challenge of the systems to empower older people who are more likely to appreciate whatever care they receive. Cultural values and political ideologies have influenced the understanding and expectation of autonomy among older people between the countries. Participants at national, local administration and provider level were asked about what the principal elements were in long-term care provision. The Dutch said they aimed to provide client-centred care and expected their care system to function in terms of 'citizenship' and 'normality', to provide for the basic rights of people:

> "The vision of the Dutch government is that we want elderly people or disabled people to live as normal lives as they can in Dutch society." (Civil servant, Ministry of Health, Welfare and Sport, the Netherlands)

By doing so, the Dutch service provision set a good example by giving more time, flexibility and autonomy to the clients in practice:

> "To meet the individuals' needs.... [Clients] need time to talk. [Helpers should] do the washing, the bed, not quick, quick, quick, but slowly and waiting and resting, and so on...." (Home care manager of Ms Duijts, the Netherlands)

Most English national officials (two out of three) saw their care system as dependent on local resources to provide a safety net of care and to promote older people's independence:

"... the amount of service they get will depend again on their dependency levels, their frailty ... what is available locally and so on...." (Senior official, Commission for Social Care Inspection, England)

Selective care support is further evidenced in care provision at the micro-level in England. Nearly half of the English care providers (four out of ten) visualised the principle of long-term care as primarily a performance of day-to-day basic care tasks with little evidence of empowerment, social and emotional support:

"We're really just there to see to the day-to-day living ... personal care, shopping.... Helping with laundry, ironing, cleaning. That sort of thing...." (Home care manager of Ms Bames and Ms Holmes, England)

However, in Taiwan, all the civil servants, local administrators and service providers identified minimal state intervention coupled with strong market forces by consumers and strong family involvement as important to care. More than half of Taiwanese service providers (five out of eight) supported comprehensive care provision to be compatible in the growing competition in the care market:

"We have not only provided personal care but healthcare, treatment, rehabilitation and social care to the residents. We have our own transport for older people to attend our day hospital for rehabilitation. We provide various types of religious support to our residents." (Nursing home manager of Ms Yen, Taiwan)

Empowerment mechanisms in long-term care systems

The previous section demonstrated different welfare systems shaping different ideologies of autonomy in older people's need for care. This section explores the opportunities whereby dependent older people could address their views of care and participate in the care system. There are a few possibilities for older people to act socially and politically regarding their care. On the macro-level, older people can address their needs indirectly through political voting and by being a member of a pressure group or lobby. At the local or micro-level, older people can exercise their autonomy by direct communication with their carers, service providers and/or families.

Political power of older people at the macro-level

As Table 9.2 shows, most of the older people in the three countries are basically inactive in using their collective autonomy at the macro-level. However, Dutch older people are slightly more active; Taiwan comes second; and England a distant third. None of the English service users had ever joined a pensioner or consumer action group. This may be a result of cultural differences and the historical level of political participation of the informants. Nevertheless, some of the English older respondents emphasised the experience of difficulties of managing their own life that had restricted their motivation for political participation. On the other hand, many of the older participants in all three countries used their power to vote. It was found that older respondents are focused on political parties themselves or social issues in general – pensioners' own interests were not paramount in their minds in any of the countries.

All of the participants at the national level in the Netherlands, nearly all in Taiwan (five out of six) and most in England (two out of three) valued the way in which grey voters had pressurised the state's attention towards ageing issues. Nonetheless, most of the national and local participants across the countries were concerned that increasing grey power was still limited to younger and healthier older people. While ageing issues have been brought to political attention, the awareness of older people in long-term care will continue to depend on support available for those vulnerable older people in order for them to be able to participate openly and directly in making their views heard:

Table 9.2: Macro-political power of older people from older people's perspectives

	Member of a pensioner or consumer group			Voting		
	Yes	No	Total	Yes	No	Total
England	0	9	9	5	4	9
The Netherlands	3	7	10	6	4	10
Taiwan	2	7	9	6	3	9
Total	5	23	28	17	11	28

"... you've always got that big worry that you're talking to the more active older person, because by nature, it's much more difficult to [respond to] people who are house-bound, they're not going to get to meetings and this sort of thing, but, I think it is improving.... I certainly think they should be more involved ... new technology, tele-conferencing, will help considerably." (Senior official, Age Concern England)

Power of older people at the micro-level

Both England and the Netherlands have official channels for clients to address their views regarding their care, but not Taiwan. However, the interviews with the service users across the countries showed most Taiwanese and Dutch respondents felt able to make complaints and have their voices heard. By contrast, English participants felt less able to exercise their power (see Table 9.3).

The Dutch seemed to have a more consistent system in which all the Dutch service users said they had a pressure group (either the consumers federation for people who live in their own home or the client council for people who live in a residential or nursing care home) to help with their care interests and needs. A service user pressure group was established in each institution/organisation where the clients were able to raise various issues regarding their care with support from their families and independent legal professionals.

Ms der Horst, a member of the client council at a nursing home, explained how the council worked:

"We [service users] volunteer or are elected as a member of the client board. There is a meeting once a month of

Table 9.3: Power and autonomy as a service user

	Being listened to				Able to complain			
	Yes	No	No response	Total	Yes	No	Others	Total
England	5	3	1	9	2	6	1	9
The Netherlands	7	2	1	10	8	0	2	10
Taiwan	7	1	1	9	6	0	3	9
Total	19	6	3	28	16	6	6	28

just ourselves [members], before that we have to ask around other residents' views and everything in the meeting has been recorded. We have independent solicitors and administrative support. We would meet our provider manager once every four months to address any issues of care. We also meet other client council members once or twice a year to share information and experiences." (Ms der Horst, the Netherlands)

This confirms Sluijs and Wagner's findings (2003) that care organisations have an obligation to set up a client council. This has improved the involvement of service users in quality management through a non-hierarchical decision-making structure. Indeed, interviews with Dutch service providers found nearly all of them to have valued and taken views from the client council seriously:

"... they can have their say in that and it is certainly taken into account and not just swept [under the carpet]...." (Nursing home manager of Ms Reinaerdts, the Netherlands)

While the National Health Service Complaints Regulations 2004 in England aim to provide opportunities for older people in care to express their views, in comparison with the Netherlands, the English complaints procedure contains hierarchical structures with a strong demand on older people's determination and independence. Accessibility is dependent on the relevant care managers or authority. Most of the English service providers, professionals and carers found that not many service users use the complaints procedure. For those who did use it, most of them were heavily involved with private sources such as family to advocate their rights:

"We have a complaints procedure ... what quite often happens is, the client will say to the carer.... The carer will then pass that on to us for us to look into ... if it's a serious complaint it's done in writing ... more often than not it's come from the family than the actual service user." (Home care manager of Ms Munro, England)

Similarly, Taiwanese older people have been left as solely responsible for their own care with their family and private providers:

"Most of the older people communicate with us through their family whom they feel close with." (Foreign carers agency manager of Ms Chung, Taiwan)

This suggests that the Dutch group supports and channels have empowered older people not only to express individual views but also to participate in improving care services. England and Taiwan, on the other hand, rely on individuals themselves to make their own needs known.

Power and autonomy of family carers

The above showed that the family is significant in the European Union and East Asia in supporting the autonomy of older people. Based on interviews with service providers, professionals, formal and informal carers, the pattern found at local level was that informal carers had more power and autonomy regarding care decisions in Taiwan, followed by the Netherlands and then England. Family members are regularly involved and consulted in the Netherlands and Taiwan. Moreover, the Taiwanese culture of family care and financial responsibility has reinforced family power in the care relationship, whereas in England, most participants stated that informal carers were consulted only when there was a problem. This is especially true when an individual is actually receiving formal care. One emergent finding is that the family carers in all three countries are unlikely to see their power increase. Senior officials at the national level in all three countries explained that family carers have been seen as a micro-relationship and even more secondary in the system.

Care service consultations

Information, consultation, advice and effective expert assistance are fundamental to minimise the gap between legal rights and social reality (Townsend and Gordon, 2002). Those supports should be taken into account in the first instance during intervention and care placement processes as most people have limited knowledge of care options. They are equally important during care provision, because most of the service users have complicated health and social care needs, which may change accordingly.

Interviews with older people suggest that consultation and discussion before providing a service is not uncommon practice in the Netherlands and Taiwan. Much of the consultation was carried out directly between the older people and professionals in the Netherlands, and the service users were well aware of what was happening:

> "Oh yes, I certainly am! Well, I was assessed and got an indication from the RIO [assessment authority] and they asked if they could send my assessment to [service provider], if they could inform other people who come here, and I said yes ... I always think that's the best approach." (Ms Flipsen, the Netherlands)

There is more consultation indirectly through the family in Taiwan (four out of nine). This is probably because Chinese culture assumes that the family has a responsibility for older relatives not dissimilar to those they have for their children:

> "Yes, my daughter did say she heard from her friends that this home is very good and asked me if I wanted to try ... I stayed here one night before the admission." (Ms Pang, Taiwan)

Most (five out of nine) of the English service users were informed but not consulted by their professionals. This confirmed that the culture of professionalism still remains in care practice.

Nonetheless, less face-to-face contact assessment is evidenced in all three countries, in the light of policy desire to improve efficiency. Some professionals in England and the Netherlands argued that this would reduce the ability of frail older people to address their needs and express their views and help professionals to identify appropriate needs:

> "... many older people are hard of hearing, don't understand, and they often don't like to discuss things on the phone. It is often hard enough for them to make themselves clear and it usually works better in a face-to-face conversation ... we are talking about a group of vulnerable people with limitations and I don't think it will work." (assessor social worker of Ms Gramsma, the Netherlands)

During the provision of care services, most (eight out of ten) Dutch and many (five out of nine) Taiwanese service users were consulted and informed about the services they were receiving by their service providers and carers:

> "Yes ... the carers and the nurse always ask how I am and always come to say hello before they change the shift. My sister who lives nearby would also come to visit and ask...." (Ms Wang, Taiwan)

> "Yes, the manager asked what I think of things here, and I said, 'I have no complaints'." (Ms der Horst, the Netherlands)

However, one of the main concerns shared by most actors across the three levels in Taiwan is that most older people do not complain because of a lack of awareness of their rights and entitlements. This may result in a lowering of older people's care expectations and a lack of motivation in making demands:

> "Most of the residents are passive and do not know their rights well...." (Nursing home manager of Ms Yen, Taiwan)

Only a few (three out of nine) of the English service users stated they had been asked about the quality of the care they received. Although some consultation took place, some English service users found they had been excluded from the conversation and their views were not considered.

> Participant: "No, no one asked me about how I think about the care."

> Researcher: "I thought there was a review?"

> Participant: "Well, if there's a review, I wasn't there.... Well, I suppose I was, really, but, I let them get on with it. Normally, they have this meeting, my son's there, and his wife, they're all there. So I just let them get on with it."

> Researcher: "Right. But, don't you prefer to speak for yourself then?"

> Participant: "I do speak for myself. It doesn't go down very well sometimes."

Researcher: "Why not?"

Participant: "Cos they think I'm being funny." (Ms Powell, England)

Boyle (2003) argued that the concept of user involvement in English policy fell short of respecting the right of older people to be, as far as possible, self-determining and autonomous individuals. It has a negative impact on older people's expectation of care and motivation in making demands.

The experiences of older people have been further confirmed by their formal carers; many formal carers in the Netherlands and Taiwan (six out of nine and four out of nine, respectively) but very few in England (two out of five) had regular communication with clients. Many English formal carers responded that the care provisions were in accordance with paper documents or their observation.

Choices of care

When service users were asked whether the care they received was their first choice, all of the Dutch participants said 'yes', but nearly half of the respondents said 'no' in England and Taiwan. Moreover, three out of nine English older people said they had no choice at all:

"What do you mean by choice? I didn't view any other homes if you understand what I'm saying." (Ms Williamson, England)

Indeed, many Dutch professionals and carers indicated that older people had the right to say how much they agreed or disagreed with the decisions and analyses made by the professionals, whereas older people in England and Taiwan mainly had the right to say 'no'.

The limitations of autonomy were found in the restricted nature of other actors' attitudes and abilities in England and Taiwan. In addition, England's social services are overstretched. In all of the interviews with English participants it was evident that resources were a great concern in England. Limited care resources meant restricted choice and support to meet older people's needs and it was not always possible to promote 'empowerment' in practice, which is supposed to be at the top of the agenda:

"Afraid they don't have a lot because there ain't any to be had. We go out and try and commission something, you come back ... to be told, well, we haven't got it. But we haven't got any power what we can put in." (Assessor nurse of Ms Holmes, England)

Measuring the outcome of autonomy across nations?

As autonomy is central to the quality of life in long-term care, happiness and satisfaction – either from a well-being or social justice perspective – it would be an appropriate outcome measurement (Boyle, 2003) for this research to indicate the extent to which an individual's autonomy is supported by intervention, placement and care provision in the three countries.

Living environment and space

For those older participants who received community care, most of them lived in their own home. Many English and Dutch respondents lived alone, but all of the Taiwanese respondents lived in cross-generation households, which may relate to family tradition. Residential care homes in England typically have fewer than 40 residents, by comparison with about 70 residents in Taiwan and 100 in the Netherlands. It is common in Taiwan for two to four people to share the same room. Most of the English residents live in a single room, sometimes with an en suite. The Dutch, on the other hand, have their own bedroom, bathroom, toilet, living room as well as a kitchen unit.

English nursing homes are of a similar size to English residential homes, whereas those in the Netherlands and Taiwan have more than 100 residents. In the Netherlands and Taiwan, nearly all of the nursing care residents share a room with other residents, whereas in England, many single rooms and a few double rooms are available. Dutch and Taiwanese nursing home care is provided by a variety of professionals and carers. By contrast, nursing home care for older people is primarily provided by qualified nurses and carers in England.

The interviews with the services users across the countries indicate that most Dutch older participants, except residents in nursing homes, are satisfied with their accommodation either in the community or in an institution. Dutch accommodation tends to have more living space and privacy for the individual, and the living environments are purpose-built (or appropriately adapted) for people who have disabilities. In contrast, many Taiwanese and some English older participants felt physically restricted in their living environments.

Satisfaction with social life

Social participation is fundamental in exercising citizens' rights, especially older people who normally receive care in a private setting. Enabling older people to remain in regular contact with others meant their views and concerns were less likely to be ignored. Most Dutch, some Taiwanese and a few English older participants were able to visit a wide range of people and places, when and where they liked. Greater family and volunteer support as well as access to public transport made it possible for older participants to go out when they wanted in the Netherlands:

> "Sometimes I visit people for a coffee for instance. I could go out to visit people if I want to. I have to phone the regiotaxi, it is very cheap and I use it a lot, but sometimes you have to wait.... My granddaughter said ... if you want to come again, phone us and we will come and fetch you." (Ms Veltman, the Netherlands)

Strong family and formal care support help the older participants to go out when they want to in Taiwan:

> "Sometimes, I need people to take me out. Sometimes the carer will do and my son will take me out when he has time." (Ms Tsai, Taiwan)

In contrast, the mobility of English service users has been restricted by a lack of support either from their family or services, according to a few of the older English interviewees:

> "I was able before, but not now, because I can't walk on my own. Oh the staffs have got no time, so busy. They always say how busy they are." (Ms Powell, England)

In addition, autonomy can be found in the tiny daily leisure activities such as watching television, which we often take for granted. People can watch television passively in the sense that they are hardly taking anything in, and actively in the sense that their minds are working and they are stimulated. The autonomy of having choice about programmes allows the Dutch and Taiwanese to have interaction with society indirectly:

> "… I watch all the current affairs programmes; I want to know what's going on in the world…." (Ms Duijts, the Netherlands)

By contrast, in England, older people, especially those who are in residential and nursing homes, shared the television in a lounge and were not able to change channel. Although people surrounded them they were not socially included:

> "… I spend [a lot of time] in the lounge; … you just sit in front the television, look out the window and watch the world go by." (Ms Sempik, England)

Satisfaction with the care services received

The service users were asked about their satisfaction with the care services they received, demonstrated by Table 9.4, scoring 4 for very good, 3 for good, 2 for fair, 1 for poor. This produced average scores, with the Netherlands at 3.6 followed by 3 for Taiwan and 2.4 for England. Reliable services, good consultation and carers meeting older people's needs directly led to satisfaction among the Dutch and Taiwanese participants. In addition, older Dutch respondents enjoyed a well-organised and varied choice of social activities. In contrast, unreliable services, and the feeling that they could not always ask for what they needed, led to English older participants' dissatisfaction and had a significant impact on their daily living:

Table 9.4: Service users' satisfaction with the care services

	Very good (4)	Good (3)	Fair (2)	Poor (1)	Total
England	3	2	0	4	9
Taiwan	3	3	3	0	9
The Netherlands	6	4	0	0	10
Total	12	9	3	4	28

"It is, so long as they come in at the time they are supposed to do. I mean [the home care] coming in at ten o'clock and after [to help for preparing breakfast] is no fun ... when you've had nothing to eat or drink. We specified that time when we agreed to have a carer that they would come in round about half past nine." (Ms Becker, England)

Conclusion

Analysing the discussion with these older people shows that they are expected to take more responsibility for their own care. This study was concerned with the difficulties of dependent older people being able to control their lives within a complicated care system. The chapter set out to answer a number of questions about the autonomy of older people who have received long-term care in the countries selected: England, the Netherlands and Taiwan. It explored the evidence that an ageing society and cross-national social policy learning is a global phenomenon that requires documentation through comparative research. It sought to find out if the care systems work to empower the older people in their care; how they work; and why more opportunities come from some systems than others. It was based on the views of various actors who were responsible for older people's care in the three countries.

None of the three countries conform to Esping-Andersen's ideal types for welfare regimes (Esping-Andersen, 1990); instead they seem to constitute hybrids, which espouse the possibility of learning from one another. All three countries emphasised the importance of the independence of older people. However, there are social, cultural, economic and political differences between the three countries as a result of the national ideology of care. More generosity and support of older people in care was found in the Netherlands' social democratic-conservative welfare system, based on their belief in normalisation and citizenship. The liberal-conservative welfare system in Taiwan remains, with strong family support and care market competition, whereas in England's liberal-social democratic welfare regime, the recognition of support for older people is rather modest due to selective and minimal support from the care system. The welfare ideologies are reflected in nations' practice. More consultation is carried out in the Dutch and Taiwanese care systems than in England. Nonetheless, older people in all three countries may have less direct opportunity to express their views when there is a continuing trend for less face-to-face contact between service users and assessors. Dutch older people have more choice regarding their care, followed by the Taiwanese and the English. A lack of care resources is a serious problem in England, which has a significant impact on care quality and the autonomy of the individual as well as the idea of empowerment. The Dutch have more accessible mechanisms and channels for older people to express their views. In contrast, English and Taiwanese older people rely primarily on their families. One extremely important fact to emerge in each of the three countries is that the gap of responsibility between the state, individual and family is closing. However, all three countries tend to overlook the rights of families and they are unlikely to be valued in years to come. This may weaken the empowerment network of older people. Overall, Dutch older people are the most satisfied with their lives based on a better living environment, the extent of access to social participation and fewer feelings of loneliness. Taiwan came second and England a distant third. Based on the above findings, we may conclude that the Netherlands was clearly the lead country in promoting power and normality among older people, Taiwan came second with its strong family support, and England came third.

Points for cross-national learning

While there are further points that could lead to cross-national learning, it should be noted that 142 interviewees is a small number in an ambitious cross-national project. The key findings are therefore indicative and should be treated with caution. Nevertheless, the following suggestions are based on the views from a wide range of actors in the three countries:

- All three countries are heading towards less face-to-face decision making at the local level, which may reduce the service user's perspective from the care assessment outcome.
- The gap in care concerns between micro- and macro-level in England, Taiwan and to some degree in the Netherlands may cause inappropriate policy recommendations. Involving service users and their support network in the policy-making process may be beneficial in ensuring that the care systems adequately set out to meet the needs of long-term care.
- The less hierarchal Dutch model with its channels of communication and consultation may prove beneficial to England's power-imbalanced complaints system. However, policy makers in England

should also consider supporting relevant advocacy and advisory services to assist older people to exercise their autonomy.

- To improve the choice of care services available, England needs investment to increase care resources and may adopt Dutch and Taiwanese imaginative service approaches.
- Improving care resources may increase the autonomy of older people in the English system. However, there is a widespread lack of awareness concerning the rights and needs of older people. Practitioners and carers are likely to need additional training to clarify the issues and help them understand the rationale behind the various approaches.
- The emerging Taiwanese care system has great potential to develop consistent official mechanisms and channels for older people and their families to increase their autonomy, although the impact of these would need to be evaluated.

Acknowledgements

Many thanks to Saul Becker, School of Sociology and Social Policy, University of Nottingham, who helped to initiate the English fieldwork. Thanks to all the participants in the three nations and the valuable criticism of Arthur Gould in the Department of Social Sciences, Loughborough University and Tony Maltby, Centre for Research into the Older Workforce at NIACE.

Notes

[1] The software (www.visual-mind.com) has been used alongside Excel to reinforce/confirm the logical link of participants' views within and across the countries studied.

[2] The names used in this chapter are pseudonyms.

References

Adams, A. (2000) 'Introduction: the challenge of globalisation', in A. Adams, P. Erath and S. Shardlow, *Fundamentals of social work in selected European countries: Historical and political context, present theory, practice, perspectives*, Dorset: Russell House Publishing.
Agich, G.J. (2003) *Dependence and autonomy in old age: An ethical framework for long-term care*, Cambridge: Cambridge University Press.

Albert, M. (1993) *Capitalism against capitalism*, London: Whurr Publishers.

Bartlett, H.P. and Wu, S.C. (2000) 'Ageing and aged care in Taiwan', in D.R. Phillips (ed) *Ageing in the Asia-Pacific region: Issues, policies and future trends*, New York, NY: Routledge, pp 210-22.

Becker, S. and Bryman, A. (2004) *Understanding research for social policy and practice: Themes, methods and approaches*, Bristol: The Policy Press.

Bengtson, V.L. and Putney, N.M. (2000) 'Who will care for tomorrow's elderly? Consequences of population aging East and West', in V.L. Bengtson, K.D. Kim, G.C. Myers and K.S. Eun (eds) *Aging in East and West: Families, states, and the elderly*, New York, NY: Springer Publishing Company, pp 263-86.

Bonoli, G., George, V. and Taylor-Gooby, P. (2000) *European welfare futures: Towards a theory of retrenchment*, Cambridge: Polity Press.

Bowring, F. (2000) 'Social exclusion: limitations of the debate', *Critical Social Policy*, vol 20, no 3, pp 307-30.

Boyle, G. (2003) 'The promotion of quality of life in long-term care policy', ESPAnet Conference Paper, November.

Brodsky, J., Habib, J. and Mizrahi, I. (2000) *Long-term care laws in five developed countries: A review*, Jerusalem: Brookdale Institute of Gerontology and Human Development.

Cass, B. (1990) 'Gender and social citizenship', Annual Social Policy Association Conference Paper, University of Bath.

Castles, F. (1985) *The working class and welfare*, Sydney: Allen & Unwin.

Chen, H.L. (2007: forthcoming) 'Successful ageing in long-term care: cross-national comparison and learning', Doctoral thesis, Loughborough: Loughborough University.

Cheng, S.Y. (2000) 'The relationship between welfare organisations and statutory services: the example of older people in residential care in Taiwan', in S.Y. Chen (ed) *Long-term care*, Taipei: YuChen [in Chinese].

Doling, J., Finer, C.J. and Maltby, T. (2005) *Ageing matters: European policy lessons from the East*, Aldershot: Ashgate.

Doyal, L. and Gough, I. (1991) *A theory of human need*, Hampshire: Macmillan.

DSA (Department of Social Affairs) (2004) *2004 home care supplement project to middle low income disabled older people*, Departmental Memo 0930062794, Taipei: DSA [in Chinese].

Esping-Andersen, G. (1990) *Three worlds of welfare capitalism*, Cambridge: Polity Press.

Esping-Andersen, G. (1997) 'Hybrid or unique?: The Japanese welfare state between Europe and America', *Journal of European Social Policy*, vol 7, no 3, pp 179-89.

Etzioni, A. (1993) *The spirit of community: Rights, responsibilities and the communitarian agenda*, London: Fontana Press.

Glendinning, C. (1998) *Rights and realities: Comparing new developments in long-term care for older people*, Bristol: The Policy Press.

Hirst, P. and Thompson, G. (1996) *Globalisation in question*, Cambridge: Polity.

Huijbers, P. and Martin, A. (1998) *AWBZ: Care insurance in the Netherlands*, Utrecht: Netherlands Institute of Gerontology.

Jonkers, A. and Troisfontaine, N. (2004) 'Policy instruments in the organisation of long-term care and social support', MA thesis, The Hague: Public Administration, Faculty of Social Science, Rotterdam: Erasmus University.

Kennett, P. (2001) *Comparative social policy*, Buckingham: Open University Press.

Kleinman, M. (2002) *A European welfare state? European Union social policy in context*, Basingstoke: Palgrave.

Langan, M. (1998) *Welfare: Needs, rights and risks*, London: Routledge.

Lewis, L. (1993) *Women and social policies in Europe*, Aldershot: Gower.

Merlis, M. and van de Water, P.N. (2005) 'Long-term care financing: models from abroad', *Health and Income Security Brief*, No 9, Washington, DC: National Academy of Social Insurance.

Mishra, R. (1999) *Globalisation and the welfare state*, Cheltenham: Edward Elgar.

Mullins, L.C. and McNicholas, N. (1986) 'Loneliness among the elderly: issues and considerations for professionals in aging', *Gerontology and Geriatrics Education*, vol 7, pp 55-65.

Orloff, A. (1993) 'Gender and the social rights of citizenship: state policies and gender relations in comparative approach', *American Sociological Review*, vol 58, pp 303-28.

Österle, A. (2001) *Equity choices and long-term care policies in Europe: Allocating resources and burdens in Austria, Italy, the Netherlands and the United Kingdom*, Aldershot: Ashgate.

Percy-Smith, J. (2000) *Policy responses to social exclusion: Towards inclusion?*, Philadelphia, PA: Open University Press.

Pink, S. (2001) *Doing visual ethnography*, London: Sage Publications.

Qureshi, H. and Henwood, M. (2000) *Older people's definition of quality services*, York: York Publishing Services.

Shaver, S. (1992) *Body rights, social rights and the liberal welfare state*, SPRC Discussion Paper 38, Sydney: University of New South Wales.

Silver, H. (1994) 'Social exclusion and social solidarity: three paradigms', *International Labour Review*, vol 133, pp 531-78.

Sluijs, E.M. and Wagner, C. (2003) 'Progress in the implementation of quality management in Dutch health care', *International Journal for Quality in Health Care*, vol 15, pp 223-34.

Taylor-Gooby, P. (1991) 'Welfare state regimes and welfare citizenship', *Journal of European Social Policy*, vol 1, no 2, pp 93-105.

Tjadens, F., Goris, A., de Graaf, P., Kraakman, T. and Slijkhuis, B. (2005) *Long-term care in other countries: Lessons for the Netherlands?*, Utrecht: Netherlands Institute for Care and Welfare International Centre.

Townsend, P. and Gordon, D. (2002) *World poverty: New policies to defeat an old enemy*, Bristol: The Policy Press.

UN (United Nations) (2001) *World population prospects*, New York, NY: Statistics Division, UN.

Ungerson, C. (1996) 'Qualitative research methods', in L. Hantrais and S. Mangen (eds) *Cross-national research methods in the social sciences*, London: Pinter, pp 63-5.

Ungerson, C. (2004) 'Whose empowerment and independence? A cross-national perspective on "cash for care" schemes', *Ageing & Society*, vol 24, pp 189-212.

van de Vijver, F. and Leung, K. (1997) *Methods and data analysis for cross-cultural research*, Thousand Oaks, CA: Sage Publications.

Walker, A. (1993) 'Community care policy: from consensus to conflict', in J. Bornat, C. Pereira, D. Pilgrim and F. Williams (eds) *Community care: A reader*, London: Macmillan, pp 204-26.

Walker, A. and Wong, C.-K. (2005) *East Asian welfare regimes in transition: From Confucianism to globalisation*, Bristol: The Policy Press.

Wu, S.-J. (2003) *Project to establish a long-term care system: evaluation report*, Taiwan: Executive Yuan [in Chinese].

Wu S.-J. et al (2001) *Pilot programme for the development of long-term care system*, Taipei: Ministry of the Interior and Department of Health [in Chinese].

Wu S.-J. et al (2002) *Pilot programme for the development of long-term care system: Second year programme plane*, Taipei: Executive Yuan [in Chinese].

TEN

Structural stigma, institutional trust and the risk agenda in mental health policy

Joanne Warner

Introduction

This chapter begins with a brief analysis of the 'changing work paradigm' in globalised economies and the evidence for the impact of this on mental health outcomes, particularly in terms of those who are or may become 'precariously distressed' (Rogers and Pilgrim, 2003). This is followed by an account of structural stigma within mainstream mental health policies and the way in which they continue to reflect a risk agenda. The chapter then identifies the relationship between networks of risk in mental health and the networks of trust that have been negotiated between major constituencies, particularly between the state and relatives of victims of so-called 'community care homicides'. The fourth and final section analyses in more depth the power of the lobby that broadly represents the latter group through the "organising power of grief" (Peay, 1996, p 23, after Rock in the same volume). The chapter concludes by explicating the circular and paradoxical nature of current policies. It is argued that they are liable to fail, not only those citizens who require mainstream mental health services, but also the much larger number of people who, regardless of the reality of the risks, consider their lives and livelihoods as precarious and insecure.

During any single year, more than one in four adults in the European Union (EU) will experience some form of mental ill health[1], the most common forms being anxiety disorders and depression (European Commission, 2005). Suicide accounts for more deaths per annum in the EU than deaths from either homicide, HIV/AIDS or road traffic accidents (European Commission, 2005) and, while suicide statistics are notoriously problematic, the greater likelihood is that this is an under- rather than an over-estimate. In the UK in 2004, 5,906 people aged 15 years or older committed suicide (ONS, 2006). The economic and social costs associated with poor mental health are substantial and are rising throughout Europe, due largely to escalating levels of absenteeism from work (Mental Health Europe, 2002-04). While the severity of more common forms of mental distress such as depression and anxiety is sometimes minimised in comparison with psychotic illnesses such as schizophrenia, there is clear evidence that their impact on social functioning can be major and the economic costs substantial as a result (Glozier, 2002; Layard, 2006). In the UK, the economic cost of depression and chronic anxiety alone has been estimated at £12 billion per annum, the equivalent to 1% of total national income (Centre for Economic Performance, 2006).

The evidence on the social and economic cost of rising rates of mental ill health has led to calls for the issue to be addressed with fresh political impetus, particularly in relation to incapacity for work:

> Mental illness is one of the biggest causes of misery in our society – as I shall show, it is at least as important as poverty. It also imposes heavy costs on the economy (some 2% of GDP) and on the Exchequer (again some 2% of GDP). *There are now more mentally ill people drawing incapacity benefits than there are unemployed people on Jobseeker's Allowance.* (Layard, 2004, p 2; emphasis in original)

However, the exact nature of the relationship between mental ill health and unemployment or incapacity for work is complex (Rogers and Pilgrim, 2003). To begin with, the *direction* of this relationship is by no means clear. While there is evidence for both the detrimental effects of unemployment (and its correlative, poverty) on the mental health of individuals, it is also known that those who experience mental ill health are particularly vulnerable to unemployment, not least because of the stigma and discrimination associated with their condition (ODPM, 2004).

Despite the complexity of the relationship between employment and mental health, a distinction is often made between two broad groups: those that develop mental health problems such as depression in the workplace and those that find it difficult to enter the workplace at all due to severe mental health problems such as psychotic illnesses (Mental Health Europe, 2002-04). This chapter is essentially concerned with the relationship between policies directed at these two groups. It has been argued that a 'conceptual split' exists between policies directed towards:

> ... those who are precariously distressed (to be empathised with) and an alien category of disordered person who poses a serious and unpredictable threat to others living in the community to be distrusted. (Rogers and Pilgrim, 2003, p 62)

Based on the analysis of policy documents and media accounts, this chapter argues that the current orientation of UK 'mainstream' mental health policies, as exemplified by recent successive Mental Health Bills, is likely to undermine strategies that are newly directed at those who develop mental health problems in the workplace. This is chiefly because mainstream mental health policies continue to be aimed at those that are considered to pose an 'unpredictable threat', and thereby reflect a risk agenda that paradoxically reinforces stigmatising and discriminatory responses to mental distress in general (Rogers and Pilgrim, 2003). The major contribution of this chapter is to take this argument further and to demonstrate the role that trust plays in this paradoxical process. Specifically, it is argued that the principal reason for the paradoxical nature of policy in recent years is the concern of successive governments to prove themselves *trustworthy* to particular constituencies in relation to the risk agenda in mental health. The context for this activity is the perceived crisis of trust brought about by the implementation of community care policies in the 1990s.

Mental ill health and the changing work paradigm

There is little doubting the overall benefit conferred on most individuals by working, not least the protection from poverty it can offer, as indicated in the recent welfare reform Green Paper:

> Work is the best route out of poverty. It strengthens independence and dignity. It builds family aspirations, fosters greater social inclusion and can improve an individual's health and well-being. (DWP, 2006, p 2)

This generally positive assumption about the benefits of working underpins many of the policies and indeed welfare practices in relation to people with mental health problems. Current concerns about the numbers of people claiming Incapacity Benefit due to mental ill health have led to a renewed focus on reducing the number of claimants through 'Pathways to Work', as outlined in the 2006 Welfare Reform Bill (House of Commons, 2006). However, this focus on individual claimants is potentially problematic for at least four reasons, first, because the focus on individuals underestimates the impact of deprivation and 'place', in which wider socioeconomic conditions are known to play a significant role (Fone et al, 2006); second, because it ignores the role played by employers in terms of their resistance to recruiting and retaining those with mental health conditions, as discussed later in this chapter; third, because an emphasis on individual claimants and their return to work may actually serve to increase levels of stigma and victimisation felt by those already experiencing mental distress; and fourth, because it underestimates the possible detrimental effects of some forms of employment.

While employment on the whole may be assumed to be good for one's mental health, as understood by the Department for Work and Pensions (DWP, 2006), some forms of occupation do indeed appear to have a detrimental effect. It has long been known that occupations that offer conditions of 'inadequate employment' involving, for example, monotonous tasks with low levels of individual control and high levels of insecurity expose some groups of workers to stressors that are more likely have a detrimental effect on their mental health (Rogers and Pilgrim, 2003; Council of Civil Services Unions/Cabinet Office, 2004). There is growing evidence that these and other more negative experiences of work may be increasing, specifically as a result of globalised economic activity and the 'changing work paradigm'. Indeed, one explanation that has been proposed for the increasing numbers of those who leave work under conditions marked by mental ill health is the risk and uncertainty faced by many workers as a result of rapid organisational and structural change (Mental Health Europe, 2002-04). Under these conditions, workers may increasingly be called on to adapt rapidly to new forms of organisation, increased automation and innovations in information technology. They may also face increased risks associated with specific types of organisational change such as mergers and 'downsizing', and they may be forced to exchange permanent contracts for the short-term ones now characteristic of many sectors (Mental Health Europe, 2002-04; Faragher et al, 2005).

Unsurprisingly, the paradigmatic shifts involved in globalised economic activity appear to be eroding levels of satisfaction and enjoyment at work for large numbers of workers, which in turn appears to have a significant bearing on mental health outcomes. Insecurity at work, low levels of individual control and poorly managed organisational change are all harmful to health, including mental health (Council of Civil Service Unions/Cabinet Office, 2004). In their systematic review of studies relating to mental well-being and job satisfaction, Faragher et al (2005) concluded that dissatisfaction at work was closely linked to high levels of anxiety, depression and low self-esteem. It is significant that many people appear to *perceive* themselves as being vulnerable to these supposed new risks and insecurities regardless of the actual circumstances of their employment or standard of living. As Taylor-Gooby has observed:

> The fear of unemployment has spread more rapidly than unemployment rates have risen. In general, living standards continue to improve for the most people. The solution to the problem of understanding the paradox of insecurity amid affluence is the recognition that awareness of risk permeates society to a much greater extent than do the risks themselves, and that risks traditionally confined to lower social groups have become more prominent in the social world of the middle classes. (2000, p 7)

Increasingly negative experiences in the workplace might be assumed to reflect – and indeed may even be a major *cause* of – a more general condition of 'stalled well-being' across affluent nations; a condition that is contrary to the assumption in microeconomics of the positive relationship between increased wealth and increased self-assessed happiness (Jordan, 2006). The idea that income can be regarded as a proxy measure for subjective well-being is coming under close scrutiny. In simple terms, evidence suggests that the populations of many affluent nations are simply not as happy as they should be, given the level of economic success they are said to enjoy (Layard, 2003). Arguably then, there is more than ever a need for a consistent and coherent set of policies that can address mental health in its widest sense, including these 'felt insecurities'. This is far from what is currently in prospect in the UK. The fundamentally contradictory nature of current UK policies can be illustrated by closer analysis of the concept of stigma as it relates to the risk agenda in mainstream mental health policy.

Structural stigma and mental health policy

In his classic account of the subject, Goffman defines stigma as existing on an interpersonal level when:

> ... an individual who we might have received easily in ordinary social intercourse possesses a trait that can obtrude itself upon attention and turn those of us whom he meets away from him, breaking the claim that his other attributes have on us. He possesses a stigma, an undesired differentness from what we had anticipated.... (Goffman, 1990, pp 11–18)

Thornicroft's detailed and comprehensive report on stigma for the Mental Health Foundation (Thornicroft, 2006) defines the concept in terms of the fears and anxieties projected onto those with a diagnosis of mental illness by others (p 2). Stigma has been identified as a major 'risk factor' in the deterioration in mental state experienced by many mental health service users, a major factor in relapse and as an obstacle to recovery (Thornicroft, 2006). In their survey of over 1,700 adults in the UK, Crisp et al (2000) found negative opinions towards those with mental health problems to be prevalent and, in particular, they found that respondents assumed a strong association between violence, unpredictability and mental illness. Such negative attitudes are also inevitably found among employers, many of whom feel uneasy about employing people with mental health problems with the result that discriminatory employment practices are widespread (Thomas et al, 2002; Thornicroft, 2006). While only 20% of people who have a diagnosis of psychotic illness such as schizophrenia regard themselves as unable to work, 40% of this group remain 'economically inactive' (Glozier, 2002). There is evidence that the position with regard to stigma, schizophrenia and discrimination at work may be worse in the UK than in other European countries (Thornicroft et al, 2004). Among those experiencing depression or anxiety, stigma has been found to take a more internalised form, involving shame, embarrassment and fear of a negative response compared with the stigma arising from types of overt discrimination often experienced by people with a diagnosis of psychotic illness (Dinos et al, 2004).

Policy makers have explicitly sought to reduce the impact of stigma and facilitate the social inclusion of people with mental health problems, primarily by creating the social conditions whereby mental health issues are better understood and responses to them more positive (ODPM, 2004). However, there is evidence that mainstream mental health policies, paradoxically, are themselves partly responsible for the promotion of stigmatising attitudes towards those with mental health problems. The stigma that is promulgated through policies, legislation and also the media can be defined as 'structural stigma' (Corrigan et al, 2005a, 2005b) because it arises from institutional processes rather than the behaviour of individuals. The origins of structural stigma in current mental health policy can be traced to the implementation of the 1990 National Health Service (NHS) and Community Care Act.

Since the implementation of community care policies in the early 1990s there has been a sustained focus in policy and in the media on a *perceived* increase in the risk of violence to others by people with mental health problems. Following the closure of many long-stay psychiatric hospitals and the movement of people with serious and enduring mental illnesses into the community, 'the community' has been regarded as being at increased risk and there has been a *conflation of violence with mental illness* (Pilgrim and Rogers, 1999, p 185). During this period, risk assessment has been regarded as *the* procedure that should safeguard the safety of the public, at the same time as ensuring the well-being of people who were ill and 'dangerous' (Grounds, 1995). The onus has therefore been on professionals to focus on risk reduction and the approach taken by the Department of Health from the early 1990s stressed the importance of the removal of risk altogether:

> ... risk ... must be a prime consideration in discharge decisions. No patient should be discharged from hospital unless and until those taking the decision are satisfied that he [sic] can live safely in the community. (DH, 1994, p 2)

This zero tolerance approach to risk was reflected in many subsequent policy documents, perhaps most powerfully in the Department of Health's 1998 White Paper on mental health policy, *Modernising mental health services*, which had as its subtitle *Safe, sound and supportive*. Underpinning this policy document was the assertion that community care policies had failed and that one of the main indicators of this failure was the presence of people with mental health problems in the community who were "a danger to the public" (DH, 1998, p 24). As well as those people who were now defined as 'high risk', community care policies themselves were thereby also declared unsafe and not to be trusted. This belief received regular apparent confirmation from the frequent occurrence of mental health inquiries into homicides – made mandatory from 1994 by Virginia Bottomley as the then Secretary of State for Health. The impact of inquiries is further magnified by the media accounts that invariably accompany both the homicidal event and the publication of the inquiry report into the circumstances surrounding it (Warner, 2006).

The concerns about risk as expressed through mental health legislation began with the appointment of an Expert Committee in 1998, followed by the publication of a Green Paper in 1999. The 1999 Green Paper was noteworthy for the fact that its overarching principle was the reduction of risk, and the possible perverse impact of this emphasis with regard to stigma was emphasised by Szmukler and Holloway (2000):

> The consequences of further discrimination against persons with mental disorders, as threatened in the Green Paper, will be increased stigma, an avoidance of services by vulnerable individuals who could benefit from them and consequently less public protection, rather than more. (pp 199–200)

The issues continued unresolved through two draft Mental Health Bills published in succession in 2002 and 2004, both of which were abandoned in the face of intense opposition from virtually all major mental health organisations, 78 in total, under the umbrella of the Mental Health Alliance. This consortium of organisations was formed in 1999 and has developed its own policy agenda (Mental Health Alliance, 2005). The main focus of opposition has been on the proposals for supervised community treatment and the widened criteria for detention, particularly under the criterion of 'treatability'. The risk that the proposals for reforming the legislation would lead to increased levels of stigma received particular emphasis. Further, in its review of the proposals for reform of legislation, the Joint Committee Report on the 2004 version (House of Lords/House of Commons, 2005) recommended significant amendments, making explicit reference to stigma and what it considered the proper aims of mental health legislation to be in this regard:

> The primary purpose of mental health legislation must be to improve services and safeguards for patients and to reduce the stigma of mental disorder. (House of Lords/House of Commons, 2005, p 5)

Reforms in mental health legislation may now be made through a third Mental Health Bill, which appeared in the Queen's Speech for new legislation in November 2006. It is effectively formed of proposed amendments to the current 1983 Mental Health Act, including some of the proposals that have been most fiercely opposed.

The popular perception is that mental health policy has failed and that its principal failing has been in its inability to facilitate the containment of 'high-risk' individuals. However, it has been argued that the real failing is that the focus of policy has been on minimising the 'wrong' kinds of risk, including the risk to politicians of being held accountable for adverse events such as homicide (Wolff, 2002). Among the consequences of Labour's modernising, 'risk reduction' agenda in mental health policy, Wolff (2002) lists short-run chaos; a security-centred treatment regime; increased expenditure, particularly on secure options; and uncertainty about implementation. Perhaps most importantly for the purposes of this chapter, another consequence Wolff cites is public disillusionment. This disillusionment arises because violent incidents will inevitably continue to occur and policy makers (along with professionals) will be regarded as *untrustworthy* as a result. The chapter now moves on to analyse in greater depth the nature of the conflict over mental health policy in relation to the twin concepts of risk and trust.

Networks of risk, networks of trust

The current ideological and political struggle within mental health policy can be partly understood in the context of responses to risk involving networks of 'risk objects' (Hilgartner, 1992). Hilgartner (1992) argues that the process of constructing risk objects is in two parts: first, an entity is defined as an object, and second, it is linked to harm. Any entity, including one that is wholly conceptual, can therefore be a risk object. The nature of the processes involved in defining risk is dynamic and conflictual because:

> ... changes in the definition of risk objects can redistribute responsibility for risks, change the locus of decision making, and determine who has the right – and who has the obligation – to 'do something' about hazards. Efforts to construct new risk objects, or redefine old ones, thus often take the form of intense struggles. (Hilgartner, 1992, p 47)

Hilgartner also emphasises the importance of *networks* in which risk objects can be emplaced or displaced. The 'shift to risk' in mental health under community care has involved significant changes in the definition and management of risk within the whole network of mental health policies and practices. It has already been established that within the network of risks constructed out of community care policies, mentally ill people in general have become risk objects in the community (Wilkinson, 1998). The emplacement of mental health service users as risk objects has come about largely because of the *perception* that networks of containment (formerly in the shape of the asylum) under community care have failed (Leff, 2001). This, in turn, can be understood as one of the consequences of the fiscal crisis in welfare more generally:

> Where the mental health field is concerned, however, this fiscal squeeze has come to be associated not with the 'invisible welfare state' of family obligations, but with a newly demonised vision of unchecked madness rampaging in the streets. (Pearson, 1999, p 164)

As Hilgartner (1992) emphasises, the task of constructing risk objects is also a rhetorical one in which *texts* play a key role. The significant role that homicide inquiry reports and media accounts as texts have played in framing the concept of risk in mental health has been emphasised elsewhere (Warner, 2006). This idea is particularly helpful in the context of this chapter because policy documents and proposals for amendments of mental health legislation can also be regarded as key texts in the construction of risk. I will argue here that accompanying the struggle between some of the major social actors in mental health policy to emplace and displace risk objects is a struggle to establish and maintain *networks of trust*.

The concept of trust in relation to policy making has received increasing amounts of attention recently because of the perception that levels of trust in British institutions have declined, particularly over the past two decades (Cabinet Office Strategy Unit, 2002). The wider context for this trend is the increasingly critical attitude towards expert knowledge such as medicine and psychiatry, which has further damaged the extent to which the state and its agents are considered trustworthy in their response to the consequences of new uncertainties (Taylor-Gooby, 2000). Declining institutional trust combined with declining deference for experts and authority has profound implications for how risk can be managed:

> These trends have significant implications for risk
> management because often risks can only be successfully
> managed if there is sufficient trust to ensure government
> can exercise leadership. (Cabinet Office Strategy Unit,
> 2002, p 21)

The Cabinet Office Strategy Unit (2002) includes in its report the need for trust in services in the public sector and the pressure from the media and the public to take action in response to tragedies. In terms of mental health services, asylums were for many the familiar and trusted means through which people felt protected from 'the mad'. Asylums have been replaced by a new locus for care and control in the form of 'community', which is experienced as fragmented, inadequate and largely invisible (Leff, 2001). In a symbolic sense, if not in a 'real' sense, there is ambiguity and uncertainty about the extent to which post-asylum mental healthcare can be trusted to protect 'us' from 'them', and, by extension, if policy makers, as the architects of the changes, are to be trusted.

The rapid changes signalled by community care policies have necessitated rapid realignments of trust on the part of the state and its citizens. Essentially, the tectonic plates on which the old coordinates of risk and trust could be interpreted have now shifted and a continuous process of readjustment is under way. As Barham (1997) emphasises, deinstitutionalisation represents a "drastic reshaping of the ways in which we think about, describe and, in particular, relate to people with a history of mental illness" (p 151). The major players in the new networks of risk and trust can be loosely identified as the state (particularly its welfare systems); mental health service users (newly homogenised as 'risk objects' in post-asylum care), plus organised representations of service users such as Mind; the relatives of those killed by mental health service users (ever-present in the public imagination – especially through media accounts, but also through politically active 'claims makers' such as SANE and The Zito Trust, as discussed in the following section); mental health professionals (including social workers and psychiatrists); and finally, alliances between service users and professionals, predominantly in the form of the Mental Health Alliance, again, discussed in the next section. One of the major battlegrounds on which trust is being forged and broken between these actors is the ongoing struggle over the reform of mental health legislation.

The interaction between the goals of specific interest groups and public prejudice has been proposed as one of the explanations for the distorted focus on risk in mental health (Pilgrim and Rogers, 2003).

I argue here that the principal constituency with which the state has attempted to establish a new alignment of trust has been the interest groups that broadly represent relatives of victims of 'community care tragedies'. This relationship of trust has been mediated through the media and through the creation of an entire genre of investigations into homicides by people with mental disorders in the form of 'the homicide inquiry'. Broadly speaking, trust can be characterised either by non-rational, affective elements or rational, cognitive ones (Taylor-Gooby, 2006). The type of trust that the state has attempted to forge with relatives (and by extension, all of 'us' who perceive ourselves to be at risk from 'them') is the non-rational, affective type. This is because it is ultimately a response to the highly charged and emotional experience of motiveless and random killing. Such trust carries with it the promise that lessons will be learned and that such events will not be repeated; promises that are characteristic of virtually all inquiries into adverse events, including mental health inquiries (Peay, 1996).

The corollary of the state's efforts to forge a trusting relationship with the relatives of victims of 'community care tragedies' is that the state has increasingly shut down channels of trust with at least two other major constituencies: mental health service users and professionals. The response of these two constituencies has been the formation of a new locus of trust, most powerfully represented by the Mental Health Alliance. It is important to note that this alliance is unprecedented and is primarily the product of united opposition to increasingly coercive elements of mental health legislation (Mental Health Alliance, 2005).

In the following section I analyse the response of policy makers to the activities of claims makers and media coverage of their concerns to demonstrate how these have produced the political and social climate within which mental ill health is likely to be increasingly stigmatised.

Claims makers, madness and the media

Public and media disquiet about 'madness' is hardly new, but it warrants closer examination now because of the apparent reconstitution of networks of risk and trust in relation to mental health policy. There have been a number of studies into the effects of media reporting on images of mental illness that testify to the increasingly strong association of mental illness with violence in the media (Philo et al, 1994; Salter, 2003). It has been argued that the media, particularly the press, has set up a "vision of 'the mad'", which associates those who are mentally distressed with waste and danger and identifies them as outsiders (Wilkinson, 1998, p 208). To achieve this, according to Wilkinson, the press deploy certain references, particularly to the notion of a mentally ill person as a menace on the street. This vision of the mad can be understood as reflecting the anxieties that have been provoked by the major cultural and social change that community care policies represent (Pearson, 1999).

The role of the media in the debate about mental health policy and legislation has therefore been central and can be illustrated by a quotation from a recent tabloid article that ran with the headline, "Why don't they EVER put the victims first?":

> Bungling politicians this week axed tough new laws to protect people from dangerous mental patients. The *Mental Health Bill*, which cost millions, aimed to close legal loopholes that let violent psychopaths roam free because they are untreatable. It was scrapped after complaints from mental health groups. Jayne Zito's husband Jonathan was stabbed to death in 1992 by paranoid schizophrenic Christopher Clunis. She set up [T]he Zito Trust to push for changes to mental health laws. Here, Jayne – pictured below right and with her husband, inset – tells Harry Macadam of her anger at the decision to abandon the reforms.
>
> ... But Ministers will now go ahead without further consultation on many things the [Mental Health] Alliance objects to – including community treatment orders and unrestricted treatment for personality disorders. (Macadam, 2006, p 6)

The tone and language in this article typifies the tabloid response to this issue, and the use of the word 'bungling' clearly highlights the perceived failure of politicians to act in trustworthy ways on this issue. In a study of media representations of the 2002 Mental Health Bill, Foster (2006) found that even when newspaper articles were critical of what were regarded as repressive elements in the Bill, they continued to implicitly link mental illness with violence or, alternatively, with passivity and weakness.

In a study of media influences on mental health policy, Hallam (2002) concluded that well-informed individuals such as Jayne Zito (co-founder, with Michael Howlett, of The Zito Trust) and Marjorie Wallace (founder of SANE), both of whom have started successful campaigns on mental health issues, have had a profound influence on the nature of media coverage of community care and, consequently, policy formation. Hallam's research analysed newspaper coverage of the Ben Silcock and the now-iconic Christopher Clunis cases in the 1990s. Contrary to Hallam's expectations, the bulk of the coverage was by broadsheet newspapers such as *The Times*, *The Independent*, *Telegraph* and *The Guardian* rather than by the tabloids. Hallam's study suggests that the nature of claims making in relation to mental health policy is that it is likely to be associated with representations from middle-class and articulate people who are knowledgeable about mental health. There are pressing reasons why successive governments have sought to establish their trustworthiness with groups such as SANE and The Zito Trust, and these relate to the highly emotive nature of their claim to the right to influence policy.

Both Jayne Zito and Marjorie Wallace can be regarded as "claims makers" (Stallings, 1990, p 91) who have succeeded in shaping the coverage of mental health policy in the media. Emotive responses from both SANE and The Zito Trust were widely reported in the press following the announcement in 1998 by Frank Dobson (then Secretary of State for Health) that community care policies had failed and would be ended:

> 'At last someone has listened to my prayer,' Jayne Zito was reported as saying (*Mirror*, 30 July 1998). 'Murders, suicides, broken families ... thank God this obscene system is now being changed,' commented Marjorie Wallace (*Daily Mail*, 29 July 1998). (Hallam, 2002, p 31)

The manifest, literal objectives of the campaign organised by SANE centred on the need to improve services so that service users and carers benefited from changes that were also aimed at reducing risk of harm to others. Despite its emphasis on service users, SANE has been regarded as contributing to the imbalances in policy debate in terms of the emphasis on the risk of harm to others (Hallam, 2002; Pilgrim and Rogers, 2003). The Zito Trust does not have as its focus the interests of mental health service users but instead explicitly describes its primary focus as: "supporting and advising victims of mentally disordered offenders and highlighting gaps and failures in service provision" (www.zitotrustco.uk). The intensely personal experience of Jayne Zito, whose partner Jonathan Zito was killed by Christopher Clunis in 1992, has determined this approach to achieving change in policy in mental health services. The momentum for change that can be generated by such personal experiences as Jayne Zito's has been succinctly defined as "the organising power of grief" (Peay, 1996, p 23, after Rock in the same volume). The Zito Trust has been highlighted as being instrumental in increasing the profile of homicides in the media and shifting government policy towards more coercive models of care that have risk of violence to others as their principal focus (Taylor and Gunn, 1999).

This chapter now concludes by exploring the links between these arguments and those outlined at the beginning of the chapter concerning the increased prevalence of non-psychotic mental health problems such as depression and anxiety and their economic impact.

Conclusion

The chapter began by highlighting the recent interest among economists in mental health policy and their concerns about the economic as well as social costs arising from the increasing prevalence of mental illnesses such as depression and anxiety disorders. It then briefly examined the literature that links this rising prevalence to the changing work paradigm associated with globalisation and, more broadly, to the idea that many people appear to experience modern life as inherently precarious and insecure, regardless of the realities of material security from which many might benefit. It was emphasised that, while these issues highlight the need for coherent and consistent policies that can address 'mental health needs' in the broadest sense, mainstream mental health policy has instead been characterised by an emphasis on risk and dangerousness. This shift in emphasis in policy has contributed to the further stigmatisation of people with mental health problems (Hallam, 2002) and has even been described as a form of 'political appeasement' in relation to a misconceived notion of public safety (Corbett and Westwood, 2005).

Yet challenging the misconceptions about mental illness with alternative 'facts' seems unlikely to resolve the problem. While mental health organisations such as Mind expend a great deal of energy in focusing on the refutation of media distortions, they may underestimate the power of the symbolic dimension of mental illness. Misrepresentations of 'the mad' may well have more to do with the *cultural* concerns associated with such groups and their social function as symbols (Mossman, 1997, p 75). It is clear, in cultural terms, that acts of violence by people with mental health problems are more 'visible' and generally evoke a more emotive response than equivalent acts by those without mental health problems (Barham, 1997). It is worth emphasising that this is even more so when the perpetrator of violence is black (Barham, 1997). The question of what the risks 'really' are may therefore be less relevant for policy-makers than the meaning mental illness carries and the kinds of anxieties and fears it provokes. The focus on risk – its measurement and management – at the expense of meaning has produced policies that cannot fulfil expectations and that will always be deemed to have failed because they excite rather than challenge these cultural anxieties.

Recent mental health policy and attempts to reform legislation therefore appear to have become part of the processes that create and sustain an 'us'/'them' divide as understood by Link (2003). Such policies have enabled and even promoted a form of "dominant misunderstanding" (Link, 2003, p 460) that is comprised of the false belief that deinstitutionalisation has dramatically increased the levels of risk that 'we' are exposed to from 'them'. If stigma can be understood as being, at least in part, the *projection* of fears and anxieties onto the mad 'other' then policies that reflect or actively promote rather than challenge such fears will be bad, not just for the 'them' of the 'us'/'them' divide but also for 'us'. Or, as Wolff puts it, "Paradoxically, policies that play it safe are risky for everyone" (Wolff, 2002, p 827).

It may always have been the case that mental health policy is paradoxical because it:

> ... simultaneously constructs mentally disordered persons as being both 'of' the community, needing and deserving of its care; and as 'outsiders' from whom the community is in need of protection. (Bartlett and Sandland, 2000, pp 296-7)

However, there can be little doubt that this 'dual construction' has become more marked within the past 20 years or so. In simple terms, it can be argued that the right hand of policy has directly fuelled the stigmatising experiences of those who are mentally distressed, while the left hand seeks to ameliorate the effects – both economic and social – of stigma and discrimination in the workplace and elsewhere. The present debate about the reform of mental health legislation represents a fresh opportunity to break down this dual construction and create a more coherent policy framework.

Note

[1] Any discussion of 'mental health and illness' involves potential confusion in relation to terminology and the complex and contested ways in which key concepts can be defined and described. In particular, I recognise that the use of terms such as 'psychosis' and 'depression' begs important

questions about their precise meaning and the degree to which notions of 'mental health and illness' may be considered socially constructed. While a chapter of this scope cannot, for practical purposes, address the complexity of such issues as well as its central themes of risk and trust in relation to policy, it is important to be clear about the choice of terminology adopted here. Where a specific diagnostic category such as depression is under discussion, the precise term is used; otherwise, broad terms such as 'mental ill health' or 'mental health problems', which can encompass a wide range of experiences and conditions, are used. The terminology used in this chapter therefore reflects the wide range of language used by the commentators whose work it draws on.

References

Barham, P. (1997) *Closing the asylum: The mental patient in modern society* (2nd edn), London: Penguin.

Bartlett, P. and Sandland, R. (2000) *Mental health law: Policy and practice*, London: Blackstone Press.

Cabinet Office Strategy Unit (2002) *Risk: Improving government's capability to handle risk and uncertainty*, London: Cabinet Office Strategy Unit.

Centre for Economic Performance (2006) *The depression report: A New Deal for depression and anxiety disorders*, London: Mental Health Policy Group, Centre for Economic Performance, London School of Economics and Political Science.

Corbett, K. and Westwood, T. (2005) '"Dangerous and severe personality disorder": a psychiatric manifestation of the risk society', *Critical Public Health*, vol 15, no 2, pp 121-33.

Corrigan, P.W., Watson, A.C., Gracia, G., Slopen, N., Rasinski, K. and Hall, L.L. (2005a) 'Newspaper stories as measures of structural stigma', *Psychiatric Services*, vol 56, no 5, pp 551-56.

Corrigan, P.W., Watson, A.C., Heyrman, M.L., Warpinski, A., Gracia, G., Slopen, N. and Hall, L.L. (2005b) 'Structural stigma in state legislation', *Psychiatric Services*, vol 56, no 5, pp 557-63.

Council of Civil Services Unions/Cabinet Office (2004) *Work stress and health: The Whitehall II Study*, London: Public and Commercial Services Union.

Crisp, A., Gelder, M., Rix, S., Meltzer, H. and Rowlands, O. (2000) 'Stigmatisation of people with mental illness', *British Journal of Psychiatry*, vol 177, pp 4-7.

DH (Department of Health) (1994) *Guidance on the discharge of mentally disordered people and their continuing care in the community*, NHS Executive Health Service Guidelines HSG(94)27, London: DH.

DH (1998) *Modernising mental health services: Safe, sound and supportive*, London: DH.

Dinos, S., Stevens, S., Serfaty, M., Weich, S. and King, M. (2004) 'Stigma: the feelings and experiences of 46 people with mental illness', *British Journal of Psychiatry*, vol 184, pp 176-81.

DWP (Department for Work and Pensions) (2006) *A New Deal for welfare: Empowering people to work*, London: The Stationery Office.

European Commission (2005) *Improving the mental health of the population: Towards a strategy on mental health for the European Union*, Green Paper, Brussels: European Commission.

Faragher, E.B., Cass, M. and Cooper, C.L. (2005) 'The relationship between job satisfaction and health: a meta-analysis', *Occupational and Environmental Medicine*, vol 62, pp 105-12.

Fone, D., Dunstan, F., Williams, G., Lloyd, K. and Palmer, S. (2006) 'Places, people and mental health: a multilevel analysis of economic inactivity', *Social Science and Medicine*, doi: 10.1016/j.socscimed.2006.09.020.

Foster, J. (2006) 'Media presentation of the Mental Health Bill and representations of mental health problems', *Journal of Community and Applied Social Psychology*, vol 16, no 4, pp 285-300.

Glozier, N. (2002) 'Mental ill-health and fitness for work', *Occupational and Environmental Medicine*, vol 59, pp 714-20.

Goffman, E. (1990) *Stigma: Notes on the management of spoiled identity*, London: Penguin.

Grounds, A. (1995) 'Risk assessment and management in clinical context', in J. Crichton (ed) *Psychiatric patient violence: Risk and response*, London: Duckworth, pp 43-59.

Hallam, A. (2002) 'Media influences on mental health policy: long-term effects of the Clunis and Silcock cases', *International Review of Psychiatry*, vol 14, pp 26-33.

Hilgartner, S. (1992) 'The social construction of risk objects: or, how to pry open networks of risk', in J.F. Short and L. Clarke (eds) *Organizations, uncertainties and risk*, Boulder, CO: Westview Press, pp 39-53.

House of Commons (2006) *Welfare Reform Bill*, Bill 208, London: The Stationery Office.

House of Lords/House of Commons (2005) *Joint Committee on the Draft Mental Health Bill, Volume I*, London: The Stationery Office.

Jordan, B. (2006) 'Public services and the service economy: individualism and the choice agenda', *Journal of Social Policy*, vol 35, pp 143-62.

Layard, R. (2003) 'Happiness: has social science a clue?', Lionel Robbins Memorial Lectures delivered at London School of Economics and Political Science, 3-5 March (http://cep.lse.ac.uk/events/lectures/layard/RL030303.pdf).

Layard, R. (2004) 'Mental health: Britain's biggest social problem?' (www.strategy.gov.uk/downloads/files/mh_layard.pdf).

Layard, R. (2006) 'The case for psychological treatment centres' (http://cep.lse.ac.uk/layard/psych_treatment_centres.pdf).

Leff, J. (2001) *Care in the community: Illusion or reality?*, Chichester: Wiley.

Link, B. (2003) 'The production of understanding', *Journal of Health and Social Behaviour*, vol 44, pp 457-69.

Macadam, H. (2006) 'Why don't they ever put the victims first?', *The Sun*, 25 March, p 6.

Mental Health Alliance (2005) *Towards a better Mental Health Act: The Mental Health Alliance Policy Agenda* (www.mentalhealthalliance.org.uk/resources/documents/AGENDA2.pdf).

Mental Health Europe (November 2002-November 2004) Mental Health Economics European Network I, Paper C: 'Mental health and unemployment' (www.mhe-sme.org/en/documents/Employment%20and%20Mental%20H.doc: Mental Health Europe).

Mossman, D. (1997) 'Deinstitutionalization, homelessness, and the myth of psychiatric abandonment: a structural anthropology perspective', *Social Science and Medicine*, vol 44, no 1, pp 71-84.

ODPM (Office of the Deputy Prime Minister) (2004) *Mental health and social exclusion*, London: Social Exclusion Unit.

ONS (Office for National Statistics) (2006) (www.statistics.gov.uk).

Pearson, G. (1999) 'Madness and moral panics', in J. Peay and N. Eastman (eds) *Law without enforcement: Integrating mental health and justice*, Oxford: Hart, pp 159-71.

Peay, J. (ed) (1996) *Inquiries after homicide*, London: Duckworth.

Philo, G., Secker, J., Platt, S., Henderson, L., McLaughlin, G. and Burnside, J. (1994) 'The impact of the mass media on public images of mental illness: media content and audience belief', *Health Education Journal*, vol 53, pp 271-81.

Pilgrim, D. and Rogers, A. (1999) *A sociology of mental health and illness* (2nd edn), Buckingham: Open University Press.

Pilgrim, D. and Rogers, A. (2003) 'Mental disorder and violence: an empirical picture in context', *Journal of Mental Health*, vol 12, pp 7-18.

Rogers, A. and Pilgrim, D. (2003) *Mental health and inequality*, Basingstoke: Palgrave Macmillan.

Salter, M. (2003) 'Psychiatry and the media: from pitfalls to possibilities', *Psychiatric Bulletin*, vol 27, pp 123-5.

Stallings, R.A. (1990) 'Media discourse and the social construction of risk', *Social Problems*, vol 37, no 1, pp 80-95.

Szmukler, G. and Holloway, F. (2000) 'Reform of the Mental Health Act: health or safety?', *British Journal of Psychiatry*, vol 177, pp 196-200.

Taylor, P.J. and Gunn, J. (1999) 'Homicides by people with mental illness: myth and reality', *British Journal of Psychiatry*, vol 174, pp 9-14.

Taylor-Gooby, P. (ed) (2000) *Risk, trust and welfare*, Basingstoke: Macmillan.

Taylor-Gooby, P. (2006) 'Trust, risk and health care reform', *Health, Risk and Society*, vol 8, no 2, pp 97-103.

Thomas, T., Secker, J. and Grove, B. (2002) 'Job retention and mental health: a review of the literature', Unpublished, London: Institute for Applied Health and Social Policy, King's College London.

Thornicroft, G. (2006) *Ignorance + Prejudice + Discrimination = Stigma*, London: Mental Health Foundation.

Thornicroft, G., Tansella, M., Becker, T., Knapp, M., Leese, M., Schene, A. and Vazquez-Barquero, J.L. (2004) 'The personal impact of schizophrenia in Europe', *Schizophrenia Research*, vol 69, pp 125-32.

Warner, J. (2006) 'Inquiry reports as active texts and their function in relation to professional practice in mental health', *Health, Risk and Society*, vol 8, no 3, pp 223-37.

Wilkinson, J. (1998) 'Danger on the streets: mental illness, community care and ingratitude', in A. Symonds and A. Kelly (eds) *The social construction of community care*, Basingstoke: Macmillan, pp 208-19.

Wolff, N. (2002) 'Risk, response, and mental health policy: learning from the experience of the United Kingdom', *Journal of Health Politics, Policy and Law*, vol 27, no 5, pp 801-32.

ELEVEN

Rising or falling to the challenges of diversity in Europe? Social justice and differentiated citizenship

Eithne McLaughlin and Gerry Boucher

Introduction

In *Wasted lives*, Bauman (2004a, p 7) argues that a consequence of late modernity is that "the problems of human waste and human waste disposal weigh ever more heavily on the liquid modern consumerist culture of individualisation". This results in the absence of outlets for 'safe disposal' of surplus and redundant populations, including 'unwanted' immigrants, and specifically asylum seekers, who are not specifically 'invited' by national immigration policies. It also includes minority ethnic groups who do not sufficiently assimilate their cultural differences into harmlessness, or preferably out of existence, leaving intact the idealised homogeneous national culture. This problem of 'human waste disposal' fuels alarm about global over-population involving mass movements of people, playing a key part in the diffuse 'security fears' in emergent global strategies and, consequently, the logic of power struggles (Bauman, 2004a, p 7).

The main objective of this chapter is to share reflections and analysis prompted by these observations on diffuse security fears. In particular, we examine the contribution of social policy to the presence of harmonious intergroup relations in terms of both equality and diversity through consideration of the 'family' of related ethnic, equality, immigration and integration policies. Socially just citizenship at both the level of the individual and the cultural group is, we contend, a necessary condition for democratic sustainability and 'perpetual peace' (Kant, 1795). The chapter builds on the work of the Equality and Social Inclusion in Ireland Project, funded under Strand 2 of the Peace II/SEUPB North–South

Programme, carried out in Belfast and Dublin Ireland over the period 2004-06 (see www.qub.ac.uk/sites/EqualitySocialInclusionInIreland-HomePage).

Arguably, one of the most significant legacies of the Enlightenment for modern social and political thought has been the Kantian belief that the universal community of human kind is "... the end or object of the highest moral endeavour" (Bull, 1977, p 27). This view is rooted in the belief that all human beings are fundamentally the same – or at least have the same moral standing in terms of the idea of the universal brotherhood of humanity. This view is shared by both the political right and the political left. It is not, however, without its dissenters (see, for example, Nussbaum, 2005, on recognition of other species).

Despite commitment to and compliance with the liberal normative value system of international human rights to an extent unparalleled on other continents, European nation states have nonetheless found themselves ill prepared to deal with expressions of popular racism, fascistic political tendencies, resistance to multiculturalism, and fear of visibly different minority ethnic groups. The stalling of the Hague Programme and negativity towards enlargement and Turkish membership in particular indicate that European political cultures and institutions have discourses and policy toolkits that are insufficient to the challenges of the management of equality and diversity within and between late modern 'nation' states (Kukathas, 2003; Cooper, 2004; Eisenberg and Spinner-Halev, 2005).

The movement of people across national boundaries challenges one of the main functions of the nation state, specifically the creation and maintenance of national borders and boundaries – physical/spatial and social (Weber, 1947, p 156; Poggi, 1978, pp 92-3; Giddens, 1981, p 90, 1985, p 20). The security and well-being of the polity created by these boundaries has been and continues to be the raison d'être of and for the nation state. Despite the much vaunted 'hollowing out' of the nation state, national governments largely retain these traditional functions. This chapter argues that the protection and promotion of the well-being of 'home' populations has to be understood not only in traditional social welfare policy terms, but also the politics and management of intergroup relations (referred to hereafter as community relations). We recognise, however, that the term 'community relations' is problematic. It is problematic politically because it implies a homogeneity and unity within a social category that probably does not exist; it is also problematic scientifically because it converts social categories into social groups.

Yet community relations increasingly constitute one of the main activities of democratic national government in the 21st century. This is evidenced by the increase in equality legislation and the rise in political importance of ethnic, immigration and integration policies across European countries. The organisation and management of internal difference is effected directly through equality, ethnic, immigration (including asylum) policies; integration policies such as naturalisation and citizenship rules; and indirectly through residency criteria governing access to social welfare and public services. This chapter applies to these policy fields a critical social theory approach to the nation state and social welfare systems within these, placing issues of equality and diversity in the context of socio-cultural insecurities and social justice.

Within this context, we claim that the development of negative forms of differentiated citizenship (Young, 1989) is part of the problem, not the solution. These distinguish between categories of 'unwanted' immigrants and 'unassimilable' minority ethnic groups within Europe, creating hierarchies of citizenship rights. We further propose that understanding the role of social justice in community relations is central to the nation state's responses to people movements across national boundaries in the 21st century. To understand this also means appreciating the way security of the polity and the individual is achieved through social means rather than through criminal justice or military means. This is what we term the 'new social security'.

The second part of the chapter examines the nation state with respect to processes of globalisation; the third looks at the family of social justice policies involving equality, ethnic and immigration, and integration policies, and negative differentiated citizenship at the European Union (EU) level; while the concluding section begins to theorise the significance of socially just policies for peaceful community relations between social groups in contemporary societies. We argue here that the development of negative forms of differentiated citizenship poses a threat to the peace, security and the long-run sustainability of western European liberal democracies. The chapter does not seek to provide a review of the literatures on citizenship – which would require a great deal more space than we have at our disposal (for reviews, see van Steenbergen, 1994; Walby, 1994; Turner, 1996; Shafir, 1998; Lewis, 2004).

Entrenching the nation state, retrenching the welfare state

Contemporary debates in the post–Cold War period have oscillated between those who argue that the nation state is being superseded by the forces of globalisation, and those who argue that the basic features of the nation state and the international system based on nation states remain largely intact (see, for example, Ohmae, 1995; Strange, 1996; Mann, 1997; Sassen, 1998; Held et al, 1999; Hirst and Thompson, 1999; Castells, 2000; Saul, 2005).

In empirical terms, the post–Cold War era can be currently divided into two periods within these debates. In the first period from 1989 to 11 September 2001, the primacy of 'globalisation' was arguably dominant; while, in the second, from 11 September 2001 to the present, there has been a noticeable return of the state, initially in terms of national security. Lately, issues of national economic sovereignty have become more important. This is evidenced in the apparent collapse of the Doha round of World Trade negotiations; the increasing role of the Chinese state in the global economy; French and Dutch rejections of the Nice Treaty; and significant modifications to the European Services Directive.

While moving to different policy rhythms, there have been parallel debates about the role and significance of globalisation and nation states in welfare state restructuring and retrenchment in Organisation for Economic Co-operation and Development (OECD) countries; and about an apparent return to traditional homogeneous notions of the 'nation', 'national culture' and 'national identity' (see Smith, 1991). The latter is largely in response to higher rates of immigration and a rise in national cultural diversity in the economically globalising post–Cold War era in OECD nation states. Arguably, the former has generated public 'social insecurity' and the latter, sadly, public fears of 'cultural insecurity'. In these senses, one can talk about an entrenchment of the nation state and a retrenchment of the welfare state.

Yet there is much continuity between the contemporary era and historical eras of the past. Continuity arises from the fact that interdependencies between territories have always existed. Depiction of the past as 'not global' has been part of the social construction of world history by the powerful former colonial powers, whose exploitation of the resources of other lands has been submerged under a Eurocentric account of human historical progress and development. At the same time, 'globalisation' in the restricted sense of an increased number of interactions between people and institutions in different parts of the globe poses a challenge to the nation state. This highlights a tension in liberal theory in which the nation state has been a vehicle of liberalism, but also a contradictory universal or 'globalising' element within it (Kymlicka, 1995). In this sense, nation states like Europe as a whole are unfinished adventures (Bauman, 2004b).

One of these unfinished adventures involves the changing role of social citizenship rights and entitlements embedded in national welfare states, and the relationship between formal and substantive social rights within these. The latter relationship is of particular importance in debates about increases in national inequalities. Although it is agreed that inequality rose throughout Europe in the last 25 years of the 20th century, the causes of the rise are not agreed. More specifically, substantial disagreement continues as to whether systems of social protection in capitalist democracies did or did not retrench and roll back after 1970 and how much or how little this contributed to the rise in inequality on social class and other grounds (Giddens and Diamond, 2005).

On the one hand, retrenchment was the declared aim of the 'small government' neoliberal leaders such as Thatcher and Reagan. On the other hand, their success in achieving their goal was much more limited – whether by path dependency or other factors – than they admitted publicly. As Swank (2005) notes, early aggregate public expenditure studies indicated little retrenchment (Pierson, 1996). Other studies that used data on social services programmes and welfare state employment, like Clayton and Pontusson (1998), and detailed surveys of programmatic change across time in large numbers of democracies (Huber and Stephens, 2001; Swank, 2002), concluded that roll-back had been more widespread than aggregate analyses had revealed.

A further possibility is that analytic disaggregation by 'target' population subgroup, rather than service activity domain and a total quantum of service activity, shows higher levels of retrenchment. This possibility has not, to our knowledge, been systemically tested as yet. The retrenchment of social protection and social rights for some population subgroups compared to others would reflect development of negative differentiated forms of citizenship (see Clavero and Daly, 2002). Korpi and Palme's Social Citizenship and Rights Project (2003) and their comparative welfare state entitlements data set should make more fine-grained assessment such as this viable in the future.

Overall, Swank concluded that "welfare state decommodification has on average modestly declined in both large social democratic and predominantly liberal welfare states; some more notable changes in decommodification have occurred in individual welfare states such as the Netherlands; Sweden and New Zealand" (Swank, 2005, p 184). Arguably, these notable changes and more modest declines in social rights and entitlements have led to the public perception – and for many the reality – of material social insecurity.

Similarly, the recent entrenchment of the nation state vis-à-vis globalisation is in many ways a political response to the reality of declining substantive national sovereignty, and the public perception of this. In this sense, recognition that the nation is a state of mind as much as a material entity has grown over the past decade, under the influence of global trends. Or, as Bauman argues, "with the sovereignty of nation states vividly displaying its limitations ... the traditional model of society loses its credence as a reliable frame of reference" (1998, p 57). Of course this does not mean that either 'national' cultures or national political institutions are about to disappear; their loss of legitimacy in analytical terms may or may not be matched by this historical diminishment.

Despite the perceived policy dilemma of increased national cultural diversity caused by people movements and other globalising forces, the nation state has had considerable success in resisting domination by global forces and institutions. Culturally, the extension of the boundaries of the EU has contributed, on the one hand, to the erosion of borders within the Union's area and, on the other hand, to more rigid external borders between the EU and the world beyond. Likewise, globalisation has been argued to have increased localism and particularism on the one hand, and cosmopolitanism on the other (Bauman, 1998).

Further, nationalism has changed – rather than ended – as a political and social force with 'mental borders' gaining importance within national populations, stimulating greater expressions of anxiety about 'the nation'. Consequently borders today are studied as discursive practices and narratives of the visible and invisible boundaries constructed between a variety of 'Us', 'Them' and 'Others', not as the physical apparatus of spatial boundary management. Borders are not simply physical security lines and the apparatus of 'security' but rather elements in the historical and contemporary construction of social inclusion, social exclusion, community, citizenship and the nation (Paasi, 2001; Newman, 2006; Rumford, 2006).

The relationship between 'real' primary communities, characterised by direct interpersonal contact, and 'imagined' virtual communities, is at the heart of contemporary critical social and political theory, and should be at the heart of the analysis of social policy. At the level of the state, however, 'race' and nation have been just as important axes of welfare state construction as the family and the market. The connections between the issues posed by ethno-national diversity and the traditional concerns of 'social policy' such as material redistribution and well-being may at first sight be obscure, but the connection lies in the hierarchies of power, resources and respect created and recreated by capitalist liberal welfare states.

Where these hierarchies are blatantly unjust they erode democracy itself by turning it into a crude form of majoritarianism. These hierarchies have traditionally been studied in the social justice literature in terms of individuals and social class; abandoning methodological individualism and embracing intersubjectivity necessitates study of these hierarchies in terms of the duality of human nature, that is, as both individuals and as social groups. Social groups today may have an ascribed or assumed relation to the individual involving a wide range of social traits such as social class, ethnicity, religion, gender, sexual orientation and impairment.

Regrettably, it appears that public perceptions of decline in national sovereignty increase with ethno-cultural diversity, leading to a sense of 'cultural insecurity'. This in turn has underpinned a return to official nationalisms and traditional national cultures and identities. When combined with public perceptions of material social insecurity, this is a powerful, if retrograde, political tonic. Unfortunately, it is a tonic that has often been used as a policy resource by national governments to justify and implement policies of negative differentiated citizenship against certain groups of socio-cultural 'outsiders' such as asylum seekers, 'illegal' immigrants and specific minority ethnic groups. In doing so, national governments seek to re-legitimise their governance of nation states in the face of real or perceived losses of national sovereignty to transnational forces like globalisation.

In the next part of this chapter we focus on policies that rest on distinctions of ethno-national traits. We explore the links between immigration and integration, ethnic and equality policies against this theoretical context of change and continuity in the role and theorisations of the nation state and its management of cultural and political difference.

Social justice policies and negative differentiated citizenship

The 18th- and 19th-century nation state projects across Europe involved foundation myths of cultural homogeneity to create a high level of consanguinity between political and cultural institutions, borders and boundaries (Breuilly, 1982). Within these myths the normality of spontaneous people movements, cultural diversity, political identities and belongings were all sacrificed to the altar of the nation state. The legacy of national foundation myths for contemporary welfare democracies is the perception that migration across national boundaries, and the presence of minority ethnic groups, are social problems (Clarke, 2005) threatening to destabilise liberal democratic nation states. This is in spite of the clear demographic need and continuing economic demand for immigrants in most EU countries.

The security responses of 'Fortress Europe' during the 1990s (Geddes, 2000), and to the urban unrest in autumn 2005 in France, have been insufficient and damaging because of their adverse impact on the basic principle of moral equality between individuals and groups. The equality 'regimes' in force at the national level in Europe, and the federal levels in North America, are marked by a separation between the discourses of international human rights and that of equality, equity and non-discrimination of 'domestic' social policy. This separation is unhelpful, replicating international political structures of governance and impeding the development of cross-national social movements of resistance (Bourdieu, 1998).

Drawing on Wittgenstein's concept of 'family resemblances' (1953), we suggest there are 'family resemblances' of formal and substantive equality between social and cultural groups in national societies 'housed' under equality, ethnic and immigration (including asylum and refugee) and integration policies. We refer to these as the 'family' of social justice policies. The equality and social justice 'regime' of a country is formed by the content of this family of social justice policies and the policies' articulation with each other, combined with the equality impact of the state's social welfare and fiscal systems. Further, we suggest that the family of social justice policies, alongside the more diffuse activities of the state, constitutes the nation state's management of community relations between social and cultural groups in the national society.

The discussion of negative differentiated citizenship draws on Young's concept of differentiated citizenship in which the national accommodation of cultural diversity is addressed through legal or constitutional group-specific rights above normal civil, political, social and economic citizenship rights (1989, p 258, in Kymlicka, 1995, p 26). We may call this positive differentiated citizenship to distinguish it from the development of negative forms of differentiated citizenship. This uses cultural diversity from the national 'norm' to differentiate between categories of 'unwanted' immigrants and 'unassimilable' minority ethnic groups within Europe, creating hierarchies of citizenship rights (see also Morris, 2002; Lewis and Neal, 2005; Morrisens and Sainsbury, 2005; Sainsbury, 2006).

It would be wrong to suggest that differentiated citizenships are a new development historically. For example, the idea that everyone in the UK has had the same rights as their peers is part of the construction of the UK as a fair and just society, but in fact citizenship rights were absent or lesser for peoples of the Celtic fringe, married women, disabled people, children and those 'born elsewhere'. As such, complete citizenship in a T.H. Marshall sense was available only for non-disabled adult white men (Lewis, 2004).

In this sense, citizenship and membership of the polity is not a static status; rather it is constituted by the processes, practices and orientations of everyday life. The nation's construction of itself and the other is permanently active; and just as capitalism 'works' by creating needs and then filling those needs with market products and services, nation states often create perceived insecurities that they then remove or reduce, justifying their existence.

Further, citizenship itself is a status with growing intranational as well as international variability. Inter- and multi-culturalism are under attack as some liberal commentators argue there must be a single national culture, referred to in the UK as the 'cricket test'. This is not a new idea as Titmuss (1963) believed that a strong welfare state depended on a high level of cultural homogeneity. His argument was more sophisticated than the 'cricket test' in that he claimed that cultural homogeneity was necessary in order to generate sufficient solidarity to legitimate a generous social welfare system. His premise that solidarity is not 'naturally' extended to those who are different from 'us' is, however, a depressing one.

More recently, Jessop's otherwise comprehensive theory of the capitalist state (2002) noticeably lacks a theorisation of the state's role in the management of difference and inequality between social groups within its boundaries. The few times that issues of socio-cultural diversity and equality are mentioned with respect to gender, ethnicity and 'race', they are considered as 'secondary variations' that "are not themselves central topics of enquiry in this work" (2002, pp 3-4, 65, 150). By applying Young's concept of differentiated citizenship in a new way, we hope to create a discourse about these issues and thus improve on existing theorisations of the welfare state under capitalism.

However, due to considerations of space, we will focus on the relationship between the family of social justice policies and negative differentiated citizenship at the EU level, as in EU member states, there has been a rise in formal equality and ethnic policies, improving positive citizenship rights, along with a fall in equality and rights covered by immigration and integration policies towards non-national and minority ethnic groups. This has resulted in practices of negative differentiated citizenship. The EU is treated here as a distilled reflection of national-level policy making and, particularly in terms of immigration policy, "as an attempt by the member states to resolve problems of international regulatory failure in new external venues at European level" (Geddes, 2003, p 127; see also pp 143-6).

The clearest example in terms of the range of countries involved and the extension of formal equality policies involves the two EU 'race' directives of 2000 (EC, 2000a, 2000b). These drew on the EU's increased competence in this policy area based on Article 6a (the new Article 13) in the Treaty of Amsterdam, mandating "appropriate action to combat discrimination based on sex, racial or ethnic origin, religion or belief, age or sexual orientation" (European Communities, 1997, p 26). The first directive is intended to implement "the principle of equal treatment between persons irrespective of racial or ethnic origin" (EC, 2000a); and the second extends this "framework for equal treatment in employment and occupation" to social groups based on "religion or belief, age or sexual orientation" (EC, 2000b, pp 11, 16). Yet, both directives explicitly exclude 'non-nationals' from their protection, constructing a category of negative differentiated citizenship with respect to equal treatment.

In terms of ethnic policies, the best EU example is the implementation of the political 'Copehagen Criteria' of 1993 to the 10 new member states prior to May 2004, and to Bulgaria and Romania before January 2007. Specifically, one of the political criteria states that a candidate for new member state must demonstrate 'respect for and protection of minorities'. In practice, this involved a combination of European Commission monitoring, issuing of regular reports, negotiations in the Accession Partnerships of 1998, and the adoption of programmes to improve minority rights and protections in each candidate state (Eumap, 2002, pp 17-20).

However, unlike the 'race' equality directives of 2000, the implementation of the Copenhagen criterion with regards to minority protection is non-binding legally; this was also the only criterion explicitly excluded from transposition into the Amsterdam Treaty (Toggenburg, 2000, pp 11-14). As such, it does not legally enforce positive differentiated citizenship rights to minority ethnic groups, and leaves scope for practices of negative differentiated citizenship against national minority ethnic groups like the Roma in Bulgaria, the Czech Republic, Hungary, Romania and Slovenia, and against Russian speakers in Estonia and Latvia (see Eumap, 2002).

This expansion of formal equality and ethnic policies in the EU has been offset by the EU's and member states' restrictive immigration policies, and a "reassertion of policies that emphasise socio-economic integration ... plac[ing] more onus on immigrants to adapt" (Geddes, 2003, pp 4-5). Overall, EU policy responses to migration and ethnic diversity have been placed in terms of economic and security paradigms. This has meant the dominance of issues of national security, the control of people movements and assumptions that cultural diversity is inherently problematic expressed in public discourse and policy development (Schierup et al, 2006, p 67). This has been institutionally expressed by placing immigration and integration policy under the remit of national justice and interior ministers in the Council of Ministers, and the Directorate-General responsible for policy fields of 'justice, freedom and security'.

The EU's securitised approach to immigration and integration has led to contradictions between anti-discrimination equality policies and the appalling treatment of asylum seekers and 'illegals'. Thus, Schierup et al contend that the "already diluted right to asylum appears to be on the verge of being debased to the level of a merely formal commitment", while the "EU is exploiting, as a pariah and a scapegoat ... the 'illegals' that simultaneously serve as indispensable cogs in the Union's much desired flexible economy" (Schierup et al, 2006, pp 78-9). There is a second "contradiction between integration and flexibility" in which the EU's aim of a long-term approach to integration is in practice subordinated to "the requirements of flexibility" in the economy and labour market (2006, p 72). In both cases, the contradiction favours practices of negative differentiated citizenship against asylum seekers, 'illegal' and legal immigrants. As such, the family resemblance between social justice and other social policies is obscured, and the discourses and practices of negative differentiated citizenship justified.

The EU's policies of negative differentiated citizenship have been part of a broader shift in EU social policy away from substantive citizenship and social welfare to a narrower focus on "exclusion from or inclusion in paid work or self-employment" (2006, p 17). This shift in policy emphasis is an indication of the EU's support for a neoliberal policy agenda to "dismantle social rights of citizenship" and to remove "barriers to the establishment of 'the market' as the dominant form of regulating economy and society" (2006, pp 16-17). This represents a third contradiction between formal equality and minority ethnic policies and the undermining of substantive social citizenship rights and material social security. This is similar to the effects of welfare state retrenchment mentioned above in terms of European nation states.

These contradictory trends mean that increases in formal equality such as prohibitions on discrimination against specified socio-cultural groups may be offset by increases in socioeconomic inequality, and decreases in formal equality for some 'non-national' and minority ethnic groups. In many EU countries too, internal hierarchies of treatment and resourcing between indigenous and non-indigenous minority ethnic groups have been introduced. For instance, in countries like the Netherlands, Sweden and the UK, policies of deterrence, dispersal, detention and material degradation are applied to asylum seekers; these individuals are denied basic social rights and entitlements in the hope they will 'voluntarily' leave or agree to be 'repatriated', and stop being a 'burden' on the state and a 'threat' to the indigenous 'national' people (Robinson et al, 2003; Fekete, 2005).

Castles and Miller call this policy shift to restrictive European and national immigration policies, "a quest for control, [and] a sustained effort to prevent illegal migration and abuse or circumvention of immigration regulations" (2003, p 94). More broadly, Castles and Miller discuss this state quest for control in terms of policies relating to employer sanctions; legalisation programmes; temporary foreign worker admissions programmes; refugees and asylum; the migration industry; and human smuggling and trafficking (2003, pp 95-117).

These policies are often politically justified in terms of the increasing rates of immigration. The International Organization for Migration (IOM) indicates that the number of migrants rose from 75 to 150 million people in the world from 1965 to 2000, and to 175 million migrants across the world by 2004 (IOM, 2005, p 13). The IOM also reports that "international migrants are increasingly concentrated in developed countries", with almost all of "the entire growth in international migrants stocks during the 1990s [being] absorbed by developed countries, in particular the US, Europe and Australia" (2005, pp 383-9).

Looking at Europe as a whole, the IOM claims that "the number of international migrants also increased significantly, particularly in the 1990s", rising "from 19 to 33 million from 1970 to 2000" with "their share of the total population" increasing from "4.1 per cent to 6.4 per cent" (2005, p 381). While the vast majority of these immigrants are economically active and meet existing employer demands, whether legal or not, the demographic effects of immigration in terms of stabilising ageing populations in Europe is striking. Specifically, the IOM argues that, "Europe ... would have experienced a population decline of 4.4 million during 1995-2000 had it not been for migrant inflows" (2005, p 383).

However, even with these increases, the share of migrants as a percentage of global population is only 2.9% (IOM, 2005, p 13; see also Wheen, 2004). Looked at from a different perspective, this means that roughly 97% of the world's population 'stays at home' in the sense that they do not migrate across international borders to live in a different country for more than three months at a time. Further, by focusing only on the aggregate increase in immigration or specific increases in state-imposed policy categories, national governments often ignore the multiple causes of this international migration (Castles and Miller 2003, p 4; IOM, 2005, p 380). These include the EU's and member state governments' support for neoliberal economic and financial policies that foster global inequalities and create 'free trade' in the movements of people as labour.

This leads to three more contradictions that the EU and its member state governments have largely created for themselves. First, the EU and its national governments have contributed to shaping neoliberal economic globalisation and neoliberal European integration, yet these governments deny their role in fostering immigration to Europe that is partly a consequence of these policies. Second, the EU and the member states have decreased social citizenship rights and increased material social insecurity through these neoliberal economic policies and welfare state restructuring; yet European and national politicians often blame the forces of 'globalisation', or scapegoat immigrants and minority ethnic groups, for the socioeconomic effects of their policies. Third, the EU and national governments have 'cut off' immigration and integration policies from the family of social justice policies, constructing categories of 'unwanted' and 'threatening' 'Others' that generate 'cultural insecurity' in their 'indigenous' populations; yet European and national leaders claim that they are only responding to 'public' concerns about immigrant numbers and 'fears' of national cultural dilution.

Is there no alternative to these contradictory European discourses, policies and largely negative effects? In particular, is there no alternative to the relationship between globalisation and ethnic nationalism that European and national governments use to justify neoliberal economic and state policies, and to re-legitimise continuing governmental authority over nation states? The concluding section of this chapter hopes to begin a discussion of this by briefly examining the significance of socially just policies for peaceful community relations between social and cultural groups in contemporary European societies.

Conclusion

Let us first address the issue of the return to ethnic nationalism in Europe. The first point is to re-open the public and political debate on integration, arguing that it is not necessarily the same thing as cultural uniformity or assimilation. The 'national project' does not have to be one of cultural uniformity; it can be one of economics and other forms of politics. For example, the 'American dream', particularly in its post-civil rights version, is not about cultural uniformity but the aspiration of an open society with high levels of social mobility and opportunity. Similarly, Pierre Trudeau's dream for Canada was the creation of a society with high social solidarity and decency, an ethically informed country in which individuals mattered, but individualism did not run amok and diversity was embraced within all public spaces.

Drawing on the historical experiences of immigration of these countries, Kymlicka argues for liberal nation building and a liberal nationalism; these are based on "thin" forms of socio-cultural integration and full citizenship rights for all immigrants and national minority ethnic groups, combining "institutional and linguistic integration" without the "adoption of any particular set of customs, religious beliefs or lifestyles" (2000, pp 195, 197-8). According to Kymlicka, this form of liberal nationalist integration allows "maximal room for the expression of individual and collective differences, both in public and private", while public institutions adapt "to accommodate the identity and practices of ethnocultural minorities" including new immigrant groups (2000, p 195).

In this liberal form of nationalism, social cohesion and equality between diverse socio-cultural groups is built not on uniformity but what in Northern Ireland is called parity of esteem (McLauglin and Monteith, 2005; McLaughlin et al, 2006). This requires a triumvirate of socially just policies, public institutions and structures that express hopes for and obligations to each other. Social cohesion and equality are built on a "more open definition of national community" in which "anyone can join the nation if they want to do so" (Kymlicka, 2000, p 197). In this re-defined national community, peaceful community relations between socio-cultural groups, and individuals therein, are based on the implementation of formal and substantive social justice policies. In this scenario, immigration and integration policy is returned to the 'family' of equality and ethnic policies. These policies are also expanded accordingly to fulfil the conditions of liberal nationalism, transforming practices of negative to positive differentiated citizenship.

To address the issue of globalisation and the nation state requires parallel and complementary re-definitions of national and social security. The point is to overcome the social differentiation, which, together with inequality of opportunity and weak social rights, (re)produces systems of disadvantage between indigenous citizens and those born elsewhere. At a broader level, it is also about redressing the growing fragility of basic moral equality that is a threat to peace and democracy in contemporary European nation states and in the EU as a whole.

The assumption has been that national security is produced by security policy and provision, that is, by people and armament controls and the maintenance of military forces. However, both nationally and internationally, it is now being recognised that insecurity and therefore security are also produced by social policies. In particular, security is generated by the presence or absence of justice in relationships between subgroups within countries and in relations between countries. Similarly, social security has been used as a technical form to refer to systems and structures of income replacement. The re-definition of the term by the Netherlands in its development of the 'flexi-curity state' (Visser and Hemerijck, 1997) arguably reflects the way the European nation state is re-inventing a role for itself as the manager of risk and the provider of personal security through social means. This broadens the traditional primary function of the liberal democratic state – the provision of personal security through law and order and defence functions.

Arguably, injustice creates insecurity through its corrosive effects on democracy and on the ontological security of individuals and social groups. Injustice generates a lack of trust and socially conflictual relations, with the converse being true for justice. Security generated through national social policies and non-majoritarian political institutions is the key to understanding the long-run sustainability of democratic systems. This fact was recognised by Kant in his stipulation of the necessity of a republican constitution as a necessary condition of Perpetual Peace (Kant, 1795). We use the term the 'new social security' as shorthand to refer to the idea that it is possible to produce intra- as well as international security and peace through social means.

The recognition that a traditional national security response is insufficient to the task of security of the polity is contained in the European Council's strategy document *A secure Europe in a better world* (EC, 2003). However, the discourses of social justice, liberal nationalism and a new social security as converging paths to peaceful intra- and international community relations, co-existing with those of traditional national security, in European policy is an uneasy and ill-developed one. As such, the mechanisms by which these discourses can overlap in practice remain obscure. It is hoped that in this chapter we have begun to show how a debate on the relationship between the family of social justice policies and differentiated citizenship can be fruitful and productive in rising to the challenge of diversity in Europe.

References

Bauman, Z. (1998) *Globalisation and its human consequences*, Cambridge: Polity Press.

Bauman, Z. (2004a) *Wasted lives, modernity and its outcasts*, Cambridge: Polity Press.

Bauman, Z. (2004b) *Europe: An unfinished adventure*, Cambridge: Polity Press.

Bourdieu, P. (1998) *Acts of resistance* (translated by Richard Nice), Cambridge: Polity Press.

Breuilly, J. (1982) *Nationalism and the state*, Chicago, IL: Chicago University Press.

Bull, H. (1977) *The anarchical society*, London: Macmillan.

Castells, M. (2000) *The rise of the network society* (2nd edn), Oxford: Blackwell.

Castles, S. and Miller, M. (2003) *The age of migration* (3rd edn), Basingstoke: Palgrave Macmillan.

Clarke, J. (2005) 'Welfare states as nation-states: some conceptual reflections', *Social Policy and Society*, vol 4, no 4, pp 407-17.

Clavero, S. and Daly, M. (2002) *Access to social rights in Europe*, Strasbourg: Council of Europe Publishing.

Clayton, R. and Pontusson, J. (1998) 'Welfare state restructuring revisited: entitlement cuts, public sector restructuring and inegalitarian trends in advanced capitalist democracies', *World Politics*, vol 51, no 1, pp 67-98.

Cooper, D. (2004) *Challenging diversity: Rethinking equality and the value of difference*, Cambridge: Cambridge University Press.

EC (European Council) (2000a) *Council Directive 2000/43/EC of 29 June 2000: Implementing the principle of equal treatment between persons irrespective of racial or ethnic origin*, Luxembourg: Official Journal of the European Communities.

EC (2000b) *Council Directive 2000/78/EC of 27 November 2000: Establishing a general framework for equal treatment in employment and occupation*, Luxembourg: Official Journal of the European Communities.

EC (2003) *A secure Europe in a better world*, Strasbourg: EC.

Eisenberg, A. and Spinner-Halev, J. (eds) (2005) *Minorities within minorities: Equality, rights and diversity*, Cambridge: Cambridge University Press.

Eumap (2002) *Monitoring the EU accession process: Minority protection* (www.eumap.org/topics/minority/reports/minority02).

European Communities (1997) *Treaty of Amsterdam: Amending the Treaty of the European Union, the Treaties establishing the European Communities and certain related Acts*, Luxembourg: Official Publications of the European Communities.

Fekete, L. (2005) 'The deportation machine: Europe, asylum and human rights', *Race & Class*, vol 43, no 2, pp 23-40.

Geddes, A. (2000) *Immigration and European integration: Towards Fortress Europe?*, Manchester: Manchester University Press.

Geddes, A. (2003) *The politics of migration and immigration in Europe*, London: Sage.

Giddens, A. (1981) *A contemporary critique of historical materialism, Vol 1: Power, property and the state*, London: Macmillan.

Giddens, A. (1985) *A contemporary critique of historical materialism, Vol 2: The nation-state and violence*, Cambridge: Polity Press.

Giddens, A. and Diamond, P. (eds) (2005) *The new egalitarianism*, Cambridge: Polity Press.

Held, D., McGrew, A., Goldblatt, D. and Perraton, J. (1999) *Global transformations*, Cambridge: Polity Press.

Hirst, P. and Thompson, G. (1999) *Globalization in question* (2nd edn), Cambridge: Polity Press.

Huber, E. and Stephens, J.D. (2001) *Partisan choice in global markets: Development and crisis of advanced welfare states*, Chicago, IL: University of Chicago Press.

IOM (International Organization for Migration) (2005) *World migration 2005*, Geneva: IOM.

Jessop, B. (2002) *The future of the capitalist state*, Cambridge: Polity Press.

Kant, I. (1795) *Perpetual peace: A philosophical sketch* (www.constitution.org/kant/perpeace.htm).

Korpi, W. and Palme, J. (2003) 'New politics and class politics in the context of austerity and globalization', *American Political Science Review*, vol 95, no 3, pp 425-46.

Kukathas, C. (2003) *The liberal archipelago: A theory of diversity and freedom*, Oxford: Oxford University Press.

Kymlicka, W. (1995) *Multicultural citizenship*, Oxford: Oxford University Press.

Kymlicka, W. (2000) 'Nation-building and minority rights: comparing West and East', *Journal of Ethnic and Migration Studies*, vol 26, no 2, pp 183-212.

Lewis, G. (ed) (2004) *Citizenship: Personal lives and social policy*, Bristol: The Policy Press and The Open University.

Lewis, G. and Neal, S. (2005) 'Introduction: contemporary political contexts, changing terrains and revisited discourses', *Ethnic and Racial Studies* (Special Issue on Migration and Citizenship), vol 28, no 3, pp 423-44.

McLaughlin, E. and Monteith, M. (2005) 'Ten best practices and eight social rights', *The Journal of Poverty and Social Justice*, vol 14, no 2, pp 115-38.

McLaughlin, E., Khaoury, R. and Cassin, M. (2006) 'Complex forms of discrimination: should institutional and systemic discrimination be prohibited?', Paper presented at the 'Developing Alternatives: Equality and Social Inclusion in the 21st Century' Conference, Belfast, 1-3 February 2006.

Mann, M. (1997) 'Has globalization ended the rise and rise of the nation-state?', *Review of International Political Economy*, vol 4, no 3, pp 472-96.

Morris, L. (2002) 'Britain's asylum and migration regime: the shifting contour of rights', *Journal of Ethnic and Migration Studies*, vol 28, no 3, pp 409-25.

Morissens, A. and Sainsbury, D. (2005) 'Migrants' social rights, ethnicity and welfare regimes', *Journal of Social Policy*, vol 34, no 4, pp 600-37.

Newman, D. (2006) 'The lines that continue to separate us: borders in our "borderless" world', *Progress in Human Geography*, vol 30, no 2, pp 1-19.

Nussbaum, M. (2005) *Frontiers of justice: Disability, nationality and species membership*, Cambridge, MA: Harvard University Press.

Ohmae, K. (1995) *The end of the nation-state: The rise of regional economies*, New York, NY: The Free Press.

Paasi, A. (2001) 'Europe as a social process and discourse: considerations of place, boundaries and identities', *European Urban and Regional Studies*, vol 8, no 1, pp 7-28.

Pierson, P. (1996) 'The new politics of the welfare state', *World Politics*, vol 48, no 2, pp 143-79.

Poggi, G. (1978) *The development of the modern state*, Stanford, CA: Stanford University Press.

Robinson, V., Andersson, R. and Musterd, S. (2003) *Spreading the 'burden'? A review of policies to disperse asylum seekers and refugees*, Bristol: The Policy Press.

Rumford, C. (2006) 'Theorizing the borders', *European Journal of Social Theory*, vol 9, no 2, pp 155-69.

Sainsbury, D. (2006) 'Immigrants' social rights in comparative perspective: welfare regimes, forms of immigration and immigration policy regimes', *Journal of European Social Policy*, vol 16, no 3, pp 229-44.

Sassen, S. (1998) *Globalization and its discontents*, New York, NY: The New Press.

Saul, J.R. (2005) *The collapse of globalism*, London: Atlantic Books.

Schierup, C.-U., Hansen, P. and Castles, S. (2006) *Migration, citizenship, and the European welfare state*, Oxford: Oxford University Press.

Shafir, G. (ed) (1998) *The citizenship debates*, Minneapolis, MN: University of Minnesota Press.

Smith, A.D. (1991) *National identity*, London: Penguin.

Strange, S. (1996) *The retreat of the state: The diffusion of power in the world economy*, Cambridge: Cambridge University Press.

Swank, D. (2002) *Global capital, political institutions, and policy change in developed welfare states*, Cambridge: Cambridge University Press.

Swank, D. (2005) 'Globalisation, domestic politics, and welfare state retrenchment in capitalist democracies', *Social Policy and Society*, vol 4, no 2, pp 183-96.

Titmuss, R. (1963) *Essays on the welfare state* (2nd edn), London: Unwin University Press.

Toggenburg, G. (2000) 'A rough orientation through a delicate relationship: the European Union's endeavours for (its) minorities', *European Integration Online Papers*, vol 4, no 16 (http://eiop.or.at/eiop/texte/2000-016.htm).

Turner, B. (1996) *Citizenship*, London: Penguin.

van Steenbergen, B. (ed) (1994) *The condition of citizenship*, London: Sage Publications.

Visser, J. and Hemerijck, A. (1997) *A 'Dutch miracle': Job growth, welfare reform and corporatism in the Netherlands*, Amsterdam: Amsterdam University Press.

Walby, S. (1994) 'Is citizenship gendered?', *Sociology*, vol 28, no 2, pp 379-95.

Weber, M. (1947) *The theory of social and economic organisation* (edited by Talcott Parsons), New York, NY: The Free Press.

Wheen, F. (2004) *How mumbo jumbo conquered the world*, London: Harper Perennial.

Wittgenstein, L. (1953) *Philosophical investigations* (translated by G.E.M. Anscombe) (3rd edn), New York, NY: Macmillan.

Young, I.M. (1989) 'Polity and group difference: a critique of the ideal of universal citizenship', *Ethics*, vol 99, no 2, pp 250-74.

Part Three
Migration and social policy

TWELVE

Enlarging concerns: migration to the UK from new European Union member states

Dhananjayan Sriskandarajah

Introduction

In the UK, as in many other European Union (EU) member states, discussions about the merits of EU enlargement have been dominated by concerns about the scale and impacts of migration from new member states to older ones. Relatively little is said about the economic and political advantages that EU enlargement can bring to existing and new member states. In contrast, public debates on enlargement seem to be dominated, almost fixated, by fears about immigrants from new member states and the impacts they will have on UK labour markets, public services, welfare provision and crime.

In the lead up to the accession of 10 new member states on 1 May 2004, the UK government came under public pressure to limit the right of free movement for workers to protect the UK. In the event, the government resisted these pressures and was one of three existing member states that did not impose restrictions. Two years later, faced with similar pressures to restrict the access of Romanian and Bulgarian workers when their countries joined the EU, the UK government changed its stance and decided to introduce restrictions.

This chapter examines the context in which these two different policy decisions were taken as a way of drawing out some of the complexities and contradictions of migration policy making in the UK. It begins by looking at the environment in which the 2004 decision was made and then reviews the empirical evidence on the scale and impacts of migration from the new member states. It then asks why, in the face of the apparent benefits of a liberal approach, policy makers changed their minds on Romanian and Bulgarian workers. The chapter concludes by considering some of the broader political challenges around migration.

May Day panic

Under the treaties governing the accession of the 10 new member states joining the EU in 2004, existing member states had the option of restricting the access of workers from new member states to their labour markets. This 'transitional' period of up to seven years was meant to ease any potential problems associated with the movement of large numbers of people from poorer new members to richer existing members. In December 2002, the UK government announced its intention to allow workers of the eight Central and Eastern European accession states (A8) unrestricted access to its labour market as soon as they joined the EU[1].

This decision, largely unnoticed at the time, was ostensibly built on the UK's commitment to one of the founding principles of the EU, namely the freedom of movement. The relatively liberal approach was reinforced by expert predictions that migratory flows from the new member states to the UK would be relatively small (Boeri and Brücker, 2000; Brücker et al, 2003; Dustmann et al, 2003). Based on the evidence of relatively small past flows from Eastern Europe to the UK (around 15,000 people are estimated to have migrated to the UK annually from the whole of Eastern Europe including the former USSR) and the assumption that all existing member states would take a liberal approach, one study (Dustmann et al, 2003) predicted net annual flows of A8 migrants of between 5,000 and 13,000.

Yet, as May Day 2004 drew closer, panic seemed to set in among UK policy makers. During late 2003 and early 2004 several other existing EU member states that had promised free labour market access began reneging on their promises because of concerns about the damage that new migrants would do to their struggling labour markets. This put the spotlight firmly on whether or not the UK should reverse its liberal stance. Sections of the UK media, particularly those sceptical about both EU enlargement and further immigration, had a veritable field day with stories about the government's unwillingness to stem the impending 'flood' of Eastern Europeans apparently heading to the UK. Headlines such as "See you in May. Thousands of travellers are on their way" (*The Sun*, 19 January 2004) and "Stop the invaders" (*Daily Star*, 12 February 2004) are indicative of the anxiety that the media both reflected and exacerbated.

Indeed, anxieties about immigration had already emerged as one of the top concerns among the UK electorate. According to one regular survey (MORI, 2006), those identifying race and immigration as being of concern rose from around 5%-10% during the 1970s and 1980s to range between 35% and 40% in the past couple of years. Another poll conducted in 2003 suggested that 85% of people did not think that the government was is in control of immigration (MORI, 2003). Eastern Europeans in particular have been central in the creation of public myths and fear around migration. In 2000, around a quarter of all asylum applicants came from Eastern Europe (including war-torn Serbia and Kosovo) (Home Office, 2004a). In 2003, Romanians and Bulgarians were at the centre of a scandal over fraudulent visa applications that eventually led to the resignation of the Immigration Minister a month before the 2004 round of enlargement.

Amidst this media 'frenzy', public concern and political crisis the Prime Minister convened several special Cabinet meetings to discuss options. The outcome was that the UK government stood firm and granted accession workers unrestricted access to its labour market for several reasons. While the principle of free movement may well have been important, more pragmatic reasons to do with labour demand may have been at play. The UK had one of the lowest unemployment rates in the EU and was experiencing critical skill shortages in certain areas, particularly the low-skilled sectors. By welcoming accession migrants, the UK also stood to gain an advantage in attracting the best highly skilled and entrepreneurial migrants from these countries. The government was also explicit about the role that the policy of free movement would play in reducing the demand for illegal workers. The then Immigration Minister said of the decision, "these measures will enable the workers we need to work here legally rather than fuelling the sub-economy – a modern day slave trade, exploiting migrant workers and undercutting employees" (Home Office, 2004b). Some sections of the UK government also pushed strongly for free movement by emphasising the diplomatic gains that could be won through fully engaging with the spirit of EU enlargement. Finally, and perhaps most importantly, the UK government based its decision on the relatively small numbers predicted by experts rather than the larger flows envisaged by the press.

The UK government did, however, make minor political concessions to quell public fears. It inserted a last-minute clause into the 2003 European Union (Accessions) Act that allowed free movement of workers provided that newly arrived accession nationals (and those who had been working in the UK for less than 12 months) register under a newly created worker registration scheme (WRS) for a £50 fee (which has since increased to £70). In order to calm worries about 'benefit tourism', the government also required that A8 migrants prove their 'right to reside' in the UK before they could access UK state benefits. This required workers to have been in continuous employment for over a year (with breaks of fewer than 30 days) before they could claim income-related benefits, although they could have access to in-work benefits such as tax credits and child benefits.

Flood or trickle?

Estimating the exact scale of migration from the A8 since 2004 is made difficult because existing data sources do not capture total flows. According to the government's *Accession monitoring reports* (Home Office et al) there were 427,000 approved applications to the WRS between May 2004 and June 2006, running at between 40,000 and 60,000 a quarter since enlargement (see Figure 12.1). It is important to note what these figures count and do not count. The figures are gross application numbers and do not count workers who have stopped working and returned to their home country. However, the figures exclude a further 150,000 A8 nationals who may be in the UK as self-employed[2]. Nor do they include 36,000 dependants of A8 migrants (just under half were aged under 17 years old) (*Accession monitoring reports*, Home Office et al). Of course the figures also do not include those who do not register at all, through ignorance, cost (both to employee and employer) or the perception that they would not be in the UK long enough to 'make it worthwhile' (Anderson et al, 2006).

Figure 12.1: Approved applications to the WRS by quarter

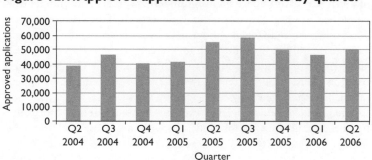

Source: Home Office et al, *Accession monitoring reports*

According to the UK's International Passenger Survey (IPS), which provides estimates of gross and net flows of long-term migrants (people intending to stay in the UK for a year or longer), the net immigration from an enlarged EU has risen since 2004. During 2004 and 2005, net immigration of accession nationals was 133,000 (ONS, 2006a) – or under half of WRS registrations during that time. In comparative terms net immigration from an enlarged EU has gone from around 20,000 per annum to around 80,000 in 2004 and 2005, suggesting that the enlarged EU is on its way to becoming the most important region of origin of immigrants to the UK. Poles, who account for some 62% of WRS applicants, were the single largest nationality of immigrants to the UK in 2005 (ONS, 2006a). Yet these figures are based on a relatively small sample and refer only to those people who come for long periods. There is much evidence to suggest that migration from A8 is seasonal and temporary in nature. For example, when IPS data is broken down by inflows and outflows and by half-year, it is clear that outflows have started to increase (Figure 12.2).

There is also considerable evidence to suggest that most A8 migrants will not even appear in the IPS migrant data. For example, IPS visitor data shows that between June and August 2006, 92% of A8 visits were planned for less than three months (ONS, 2006b). Around 49% of WRS registrations were for temporary employment (*Accession monitoring*

Figure 12.2: Net inflows of A8 nationals to the UK (2004-05)

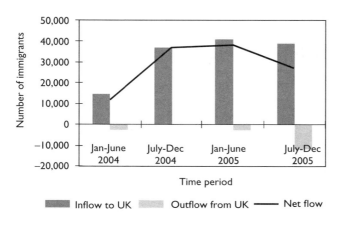

Source: ONS (2006a)

reports, Home Office et al). It is also likely that many A8 workers are engaged by employment agencies to work in temporary jobs (34% of WRS registrants fall into the 'administration, business and management' category in which employment agencies sit and, within this category, the proportion of temporary workers rises to 89%). Some 22% of Poles surveyed said they were seasonal workers (CRONEM, 2006). Figure 12.1 above suggests that a slight increase occurs annually over the summer, suggesting seasonal employment.

The estimated changes in the *stock* of A8 migrants aged over 16 and in employment collected from the quarterly Labour Force Survey (LFS) are relatively small[3]. Between spring 2003 and spring 2006, the stock of A8 migrants aged over 16 increased by 212,500 (Ruhs, 2006) (Table 12.1).

In summary, while it is clear that migration from the A8 to the UK since 2004 has been at an unprecedented scale, it is difficult to estimate accurately the increase in A8 nationals living and working in the UK at any one time. As the LFS suggests, the likely figure is probably in the order of 200,000. This would mean an annual net increase of about 100,000, certainly larger than official estimates but smaller than what many newspaper headlines report.

Table 12.1: Increase in the stock of migrants from A8 countries (2003-06)

	A8 migrants aged 16+	A8 migrants in employment	A8 migrants' share in total migrant employment	A8 migrants' share in total employment
April-June 2003	118,400	43,200	1.7%	0.15%
April-June 2004	133,700	75,100	2.9%	0.27%
April-June 2005	222,300	150,300	5.4%	0.53%
April-June 2006	330,900	246,900	7.9%	0.87%

Source: Ruhs (2006), Table 3.

Boon or burden?

While there has been controversy over the numbers of A8 migrants in the UK, the impacts of A8 migration on the UK have also been the subject of much scrutiny. Here too there seems to be divergence between research evidence (which suggests that the experience has been largely positive) and public discussion (which has been dominated by concerns over the impacts of A8 immigration). For example, the likes of the Bank of England (2006) and the Ernst and Young ITEM club (2006) have found that recent A8 immigration has reduced upward wage pressure in a labour market that risked overheating, thereby easing inflation rates and leading to lower-than-expected interest rates (by half a point). In contrast, sections of the British press continue to run stories about the adverse impacts of A8 immigration. Stories such as "Slough torture" (*Sunday People*, 26 November 2006) about the "nightmare" of Eastern European migration into the town of Slough and "Sacked because we are British" (*Daily Express*, 11 December 2006) about a group of British workers apparently replaced by cheaper Polish workers are commonplace.

There are also divergent views about how well A8 migrants have been received into local communities. At one level, it is clear that being predominantly white, Christian and in work has meant that A8 migrants have received a more positive reception than previous waves of immigrants (IPPR, 2007). Most members of host communities recognise the economic benefits that A8 migrants bring. However, there are also notable undercurrents of tension around competition for resources, especially among economically vulnerable sections of the host community and in small, rural communities where changes in population were most apparent. Sections of established communities were concerned about migrants' access to welfare entitlements and social housing as well as the effects on wages, unemployment, house prices and public services.

A trawl of the available evidence suggests that, while there may have been stresses and strains associated with A8 migration since 2004, the experience at least in economic terms has been largely positive.

Employment and wages

In terms of the labour markets, the injection of predominantly young A8 migrants (82% of WRS registrants are aged between 18 and 34; see *Accession monitoring reports*, Home Office et al) has boosted the employment rate of A8 nationals living in the UK from 57% in 2003 to 80% in 2005. This means that A8 nationals have one of the highest employment rates of any nationality, including UK born (Gilpin et al, 2006). Their arrival has already swelled the pool of labour (Figure 12.3), allowing some sectors to increase output (Portes and French, 2005; Ruhs, 2006; see also Dustmann et al, 2005). There seems to be no statistical link between the rise in the unemployment benefit claimant count and A8 migration (Gilpin et al, 2006).

When it comes to wages, while there has been anecdotal evidence to suggest that wages in some sectors in some parts of the UK have fallen, there is little robust evidence that A8 migration has led to falling wages across the economy. Wage growth (the line in Figure 12.3) has actually been steady since 2004 and in fact slightly higher than in the years immediately preceding EU enlargement. Indeed, Manacorda et al (2006) and Dustmann et al (2005) find no discernable impact of all immigration (not just A8 immigration) on the wages of UK workers, although they do suggest that the earnings of previous waves of immigrants may be affected.

There is also evidence to suggest that A8 workers are complementing UK workers in important ways. The 2003 National Employer Skills Shortage Survey identified that there were 271,000 hard-to-fill vacancies, mostly in elementary occupations, health and social work, hotels and catering, construction and retail (LSC, 2004). Data on employment type for WRS workers, shown in Table 12.2, suggest that accession workers were filling these service sector or low-skilled vacancies.

Figure 12.3: Economically active people and wage growth in the UK (1992-2006)

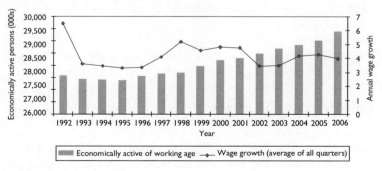

Source: ONS *Labour Market Statistics*

Table 12.2: Registered A8 migrants, by selected occupation (July 2004-June 2006)

	Registered workers (July 2004-June 2006)	% of total registered workers
Process/warehouse operative	121,080	28.3
Cleaner/domestic staff/maid	34,265	8.0
Packer	24,130	5.6
Kitchen and catering assistant	24,090	5.6
Farm worker/farm hand	18,105	4.2
Care assistant and home carer	12,610	2.8
Sales/retail assistant	10,535	2.3
Labourer	10,525	2.3
Bus, lorry, van driver	5,065	1.2
Dental practitioner/nurse/hygienist	610	0.1

Source: *Accession monitoring reports* (Home Office et al)

Research with employers who have hired A8 workers suggests that the experience has generally been positive, especially where hiring local workers to do the same jobs was proving difficult prior to 2004. Many businesses, particularly small enterprises, report substantial growth as a result of A8 workers, and A8 migrants were praised for their work ethic and reliability (Anderson et al, 2006; Dench et al, 2006).

While employment rates among A8 nationals may be high, there is evidence that many new arrivals are under-employed in low-skilled occupations. A higher proportion of A8 migrants than the EU15 national average have medium-level qualifications and there are similar proportions of highly qualified people (EC, 2006a) yet they are concentrated at the lower end of the employment spectrum. Drinkwater et al (2006) find that although Poles who entered the UK after May 2004 have a higher average age of leaving education than most other recent immigrant groups, they are employed in low-skilled work for low wages. Many migrants are prepared to accept this trade-off as they see low-skilled work as a 'stepping stone' to more professional employment (Anderson et al, 2006). However, this brain waste may mean that the UK may be missing out on the additional skills of these migrants (IPPR, 2006a).

Public services and benefits

Another area of much concern has been the access that A8 migrants can and do enjoy to UK public services and benefits. Headlines such as "55,000 migrants claiming benefits" (*Daily Express*, 21 November 2006) are a reminder that worries about 'benefit tourism' remain important public discussions, despite the measures taken by the government to restrict income-related benefits. Indeed, as a result of these restrictions, only 1% of WRS registrants applied for income-related benefits and of those only 13% were allowed them.

There is also good reason to think that, at least for the time being, A8 migrants are not placing great demands on the UK benefits system or on UK public services more generally. For a start, only 6.6% of those registered with the WRS have dependants (*Accession monitoring reports*, Home Office et al). Given that most A8 workers are here for short periods, they are also unlikely to be eligible for or interested in accessing UK benefits. In fact, these predominantly young, single, temporary workers may be making important contributions to the UK public purse. Although A8 workers may be low earners (over three quarters are paid the minimum wage), they do nevertheless make important fiscal contributions, especially as they work longer hours than their respective occupational averages (Anderson et al, 2006). And A8 migrants are also filling important public service roles. Between May 2004 and June 2006, 610 registered to work in dentistry, 720 in teaching, 870 in nursing, and 240 as social workers (*Accession monitoring reports*, Home Office et al).

There have, however, been complaints about A8 migration putting a strain on public services in some parts of the UK. This appears to have primarily been in places that have not historically experienced large flows of immigration and do not have the resources or institutional knowledge to cope with relatively large inflows of people. Indeed, given that WRS data suggests that only 10% of A8 workers are based in London with the rest spread across the UK, it is almost certain that A8 workers are arriving in parts of the UK that are not used to or prepared for receiving immigrant groups. Several local authorities, most notably Slough Borough Council, have been quick to point out that their centrally allocated funding base is not sufficient to provide adequate services to a growing population. The chair of the Local Government Association suggested in August 2006 that local authority taxes might have to rise by 6% to cover the costs of coping with rising migration in some places (BBC News, 2006b). The UK national statistician and the chair of the government's Statistics Commission have also called for a more robust system of measuring internal and external migration (Wintour, 2006). What is clear in this case, however, is that the 'problem' is not so much to do with immigrants themselves but with inadequate mechanisms for calculating local population changes and for allocating local authority funding.

There have also been some concerns over the rise in homelessness among A8 nationals. In March 2006, 15% of people using homeless services in London were accession nationals (Homeless Link, 2006). Their exclusion from out-of-work benefits means that homeless hostels cannot officially house unemployed A8 nationals and there has been an increase in Eastern Europeans sleeping rough, particularly in Central London. Inability to access social care services may also mean that some A8 nationals are ending up spending longer in hospitals than is ideal.

Romania and Bulgaria

It is in the post-2004 enlargement context that discussions about what to do about free movement of Romanian and Bulgarian workers after their countries joined the EU took place. On the face of it, the decision should have been relatively simple. The impacts of the previous enlargement were not as bad as many had claimed and the UK gained in important ways. In any case, this time round the acceding countries had a smaller population than those that joined in 2004. And allowing free movement would also make sense so that already overstretched immigration control resources would not be directed at regulating the movement of EU citizens who have the right to travel to the UK and who would have full EU rights within a few years. Since the same principles, promises and pragmatic considerations that led to a relatively liberal approach applied last time round should still apply, a similarly liberal approach may have been expected.

Yet there was a dramatic policy reversal in the UK government's approach to the free movement of workers from Romania and Bulgaria. On 24 October 2006 the government announced that it would make use of the 'transitional' arrangements in the Accession Treaties to impose restrictions on the numbers of Romanians and Bulgarians allowed to work in the UK (Home Office, 2006). While highly skilled Romanians and Bulgarians and the self-employed would still be able to work in the UK, lower-skilled Romanian and Bulgarian workers would only be able to access a limited number of 20,000 positions per year in the food processing and agricultural sectors. While the government said that it would review this policy annually and that it would consider extending the low-skilled quota to other sectors if there was sufficient evidence of emerging skills gaps, its intention to be more restrictive on the free movement of workers was made clear.

There are of course several straightforward reasons for the policy reversal. First, it was argued that UK labour market conditions were not as tight in 2006 as they were in 2004 and that A8 workers would be able to fill any vacancies that arose so that Romanian and Bulgarian workers were not as critical this time around. Second, voices calling for free movement were few and far between. Even the Confederation of British Industries (CBI), the leading business group in the UK, called for a 'pause' in migration from the expanded EU (Elliot, 2006). Third, public perceptions of Romanians and Bulgarians seem to be less favourable than they are of other Eastern European nationals. Associations with criminality and corruption are emphasised not only by the media but also by the government. For example, a leaked Home Office document of July 2006 warned of '45,000 undesirable' criminal migrants expected to arrive in the UK from Romania and Bulgaria after accession (Wooding, 2006). Another leaked government memo states that "there is a concern that free movement will encourage people from Romania and Bulgaria to come to the UK, drawn towards organised criminal activities already well established in the UK", and cites figures suggesting that Romanians are responsible for 80% to 85% of UK cashpoint crime (Hickley, 2006). Fourth, with two, not eight, new members in question, the diplomatic benefit of allowing free movement was not as large this time around. Finally, since other existing member states were unlikely to allow free movement of workers the UK did not again want to be one of a few states to take a liberal approach and thereby attract larger-than-expected flows.

Whether the announced measures will actually be effective in controlling the flows of workers from Romania and Bulgaria is doubtful. For a start, data from other EU member states indicates that restrictive policies do not automatically curb labour migration flows. For example, despite imposing transitional restrictions in 2004, Austria and Germany continue to attract large numbers of A8 workers. Indeed, they make up a greater proportion of the Austrian labour market (1.4%) and German labour market (0.7%) than of the UK labour market (0.4%) (EC, 2006). While many of the migrants to countries like Austria and Germany are legal guest workers, there have been reports of undocumented work, bogus 'self-employed work' or subcontracting to get around restrictions. By restricting labour market access to people who can freely enter the UK as EU citizens, the UK government could be simply creating more scope for illegal working. From 2007, Romanians and Bulgarians will be able to travel without a visa to the UK for a period of up to three months. Once they are there, it is likely that those who do not have a legal right to work will slip into the illegal workforce. There are also greater possibilities for semi-compliance or 'disguised working'. For example, Romanians and Bulgarians may enter the UK as self-employed workers but become in effect subcontracted employees.

An increase in illegal migration will do little to allay the public's fears about large numbers of arrivals. Previously, we argued that awareness of statistics out of context had done more harm than good but at least the public knew that immigrants were being counted. This time, it will not be possible to put numbers of illegal workers into any context. All this will occur in the context of rising numbers of A8 WRS registrations, perhaps fuelling perception that, despite the tough approach, immigration is still climbing. Similarly, the current policy will not necessarily address concerns about wages being undercut. By not having access to the protection of the minimum wage and labour rights, irregular migrants from Romania and Bulgaria may actually end up doing more damage than legal flows would have done. Illegal workers do not have any legal entitlements to welfare or public services. This means that they may often be living in inadequate conditions and in poor health. If the restrictions placed on Romanians and Bulgarians increase irregular migration, there could be more cases of Eastern European homelessness and not less. But if this is the case, the fear of being caught would prevent illegal migrants from seeking help at homeless shelters.

Managing migration?

Taken together, the UK's experience of policy making on free movement of workers from new EU member states joining in 2004 and 2007 illustrates some of the complexities and contradictions of managing migration. On the face of it, allowing free movement of workers from countries that join the EU, a regional entity created on the very principle of free movement, seems fairly uncontroversial. These are countries that will become long-term economic and political partners and allowing free movement of workers between them and the other member states would be a natural complement to the free movement of goods, services, capital, visitors, students and business people that exists between them. Yet it is clear that fears about migration can and do overshadow the many other benefits that EU enlargement can deliver for all member states. It is also clear that domestic concerns about the scale and impacts of likely migratory flows can and do overshadow the commitment to free movement. In the UK, discussions about what to do about EU enlargement must be seen in the context of wider political challenges around managing migration.

The post-enlargement experience is a firm reminder that numbers matter when discussing migration. Popular hostility to immigration seems to stem in a large part from the perceived scale of immigration apparently taking place. In the particular case of A8 migration, the divergence between low official estimates of the likely flows and the high actual flows has also been central.

Data from WRS registrations, a system instituted in part to reassure the public that post-enlargement flows would be beneficial, have ended up having the opposite effect. With every quarterly publication of data on total WRS registrations comes a renewed frenzy about the numbers of A8 nationals arriving in the UK. While the factor by which the 'official' estimates apparently got it wrong increases each time (for example, "The Government underestimated the migration from the former Soviet bloc countries that joined in May 2004 by a factor of more than 40" by late 2006: see Johnston, 2006), the recurring theme is that the decision to allow free movement was wrong because the numbers involved are too large.

It is of course true that the scale of migration from A8 countries is large, perhaps of a scale unprecedented in the UK's history and certainly more than expected by anyone. However, it is also true that there has been inadvertent and, in some cases, deliberate confusion of data. The most obvious confusion has been between gross numbers of applications for the WRS and net migration numbers. While the former have run into hundreds of thousands, because many A8 workers leave after a short period of work, the latter are estimated to be much smaller. Headlines such as "'Nearly 600,000' new EU migrants" (BBC News, 2006a) suggest that these people all currently reside in the UK, which is clearly not the case. Public figures have sometimes misconstrued or exaggerated the figures. Frank Field, a Labour MP and ex-minister, stated, "We foolishly went ahead and had an open-door policy and instead of between 5,000 and 13,000 people arriving, in the first year something like half a million did" (BBC News, 2006c). The actual figure of registered workers was 250,000, and even this was a gross figure. In other cases, the confusion seems more deliberate. For example, *The Sun* newspaper ran a story headlined "One million flood in" (9 February 2005), opening with the claim "A MILLION Eastern Europeans have come to Britain since EU enlargement in May last year, official new figures will reveal today".

However, this figure actually refers to the estimated 923,000 *visitors* and not *migrants* who came to the UK from A8 countries.

Regardless of what the exact figure is, the experience of A8 migration has reinforced the centrality of numbers in discussions about migration. Workers from A8 are just the latest group at the centre of attention to arrive on a seemingly unprecedented scale, joining previous waves of asylum seekers, spouses and family members, labour migrants and irregular migrants. Public discussions are rarely about what drives these flows (for example, unmet labour market demand in the UK or political turmoil in countries of origin of asylum seekers) but seem almost fixated on their size. What seems to matter is that a city the size of Birmingham worth of immigrants will apparently arrive in the next few years. The fact that they will arrive because they are citizens of the EU or that they come to fill vacancies that British workers are unwilling or unable to fill does not feature in public discourse. This focus on numbers has in turn reinforced the belief that immigration is out of control, that rising immigration is necessarily a bad thing for the UK. The implications of this view for policy makers of course are that the best way to regain 'control' will be to bring numbers down.

Given that the overwhelming majority of the British public think that the government does not have control over immigration and given how central a political issue immigration has been in recent years, the importance of regaining control cannot be underestimated. Allowing A8 nationals unfettered access to the UK in 2004 did little to alter these views. On the contrary, that more people than expected came reinforced the belief that the system was totally out of control. Seen in this context, allowing similarly free access to Romanian and Bulgarian workers would have been even worse. The challenge to regain 'control' was made all the more important because of several incidents during 2006 that further diminished public confidence in the Home Office. These included the apparent release of around 1,000 foreign national prisoners from UK jails without their being considered for deportation, a scandal in which a Home Office official was alleged to have offered UK visas in exchange for sex and the discovery that the Home Office itself had been employing illegal immigrants to clean some of its buildings.

These and other events led to the departure of one Home Secretary and to his successor, John Reid, declaring that the Department he had inherited was not 'fit for purpose'. Much of what Reid has been doing seems to be aimed at rebuilding public confidence, especially in terms of being 'in control' of immigration. This was made clear in August 2006 when he broke with the government's usually flexible approach to economic migration by talking of wanting only an 'optimum number of migrants' (Travis, 2006). Greater importance was put on enforcement and removals, the Immigration and Nationality Directorate is in the process of being given greater management powers through agency status, the idea of a uniformed border guard was floated, and the enforcement budget was doubled.

The principle of 'free' movement of Romanians and Bulgarians stood in sharp contrast to this renewed emphasis on 'controlling' or at best 'managing' migration flows. Perhaps not surprisingly, the government took the decision to restrict the free movement of workers from these countries and, given the focus on numbers, introduce a numerical cap on the number of low-skilled Romanian and Bulgarian workers permitted to work in the UK. In addition to this move, the government has also made clear that it expects to reduce the scale of immigration from outside the EU because it believes most immediate UK labour market needs can be met by EU workers. Many expect that numerical caps on non-EU inflows will also soon be introduced. Whether these measures will be workable or not is unclear but, at least for the time being, the political priority is one of being, or seeming to be, in greater 'control' of immigration into the UK.

Conclusion

The UK experience before and since the 2004 EU enlargement demonstrates some of the fundamental challenges facing migration policy makers. On paper, allowing free movement of workers within an enlarged EU seems straightforward. The movement of relatively small numbers (compared to total EU population) of workers across largely uncontrolled borders seems true to the principle of free movement on which the EU was built and true to the promise of EU integration given to acceding members. Yet, in practice, the political context in which domestic decisions are taken has meant that what was a bold and beneficial decision in 2004 has become an almost impossible option in 2006.

In the two years or so between the two decisions being taken, there has been a curious interplay between evidence and public opinion. The government may have taken the bold decision of allowing free movement of workers but, driven by the need to reassure people that the situation would be kept under control, it created the WRS in 2004. But the larger-than-expected (gross) flows revealed in WRS data then undermined confidence even further. This seems to have made the UK government even keener to ensure that public concerns were addressed when it came to the decision on Romania and Bulgaria. In the event, the approach to workers from these countries has been more restrictive but, curiously, there will not be a data source that will measure how many Romanians and Bulgarians arrive in the UK and therefore measure how successful the government has been. This begs at least one intriguing question: would the decision on Romania and Bulgaria have been different if the government had decided not to collect data on A8 workers arriving in the UK?

As discussed above, in the short term, restrictions on Romanian and Bulgarian workers may actually lead to the unpalatable situation of promoting irregularity. Although the move to restrict free movement of workers from these countries may have allowed the UK government to reassure the British public that it had immigration under control, there is a risk that public confidence may be further undermined if irregular flows increase. On the other hand, the absence of official records of irregular flows may mean that the government will not come under such scrutiny this time round, despite the fact that large flows may be taking place.

Whatever the case, the experience of EU enlargement serves as an important reminder of how difficult managing the politics of migration can be, even where the economic and strategic drivers behind migratory flows are fairly straightforward. Perhaps more worrying is that in their eagerness to address public concerns around immigration, policy makers do not address the longer-term substantial challenges in this area. For example, the fact that A8 workers are highly mobile and stay in the UK for a short period raises some intriguing questions about what sort of reception and integration services should be provided for them. For example, should a local authority be providing the same level and type of service provision to a Polish worker who plans to be in the UK for three months, as it would for a refugee? How can resource allocation to local authorities and other service providers be designed to respond quickly and effectively to highly mobile populations? Some of these migrants will inevitably stay and, in the long term, policy makers will have to devise better ways of promoting integration and social cohesion among an increasingly diverse population. Unfortunately, policy makers seem to have their hands full dealing with the immediate challenge of the politics of migration.

Notes

[1] Under accession treaties, existing EU member states have the right to restrict labour market access to workers from the so-called A8 countries that joined the EU in 2004 (Czech Republic, Estonia, Hungary, Latvia, Lithuania, Poland, Slovakia and Slovenia) for up to seven years. Workers from Cyprus and Malta, which also joined at the same time, enjoy unrestricted access.

[2] Home Office Minister Tony McNulty estimated that if self-employed workers were included the number of A8 migrants who entered the UK between May 2004 and September 2006 could be nearer 600,000 (BBC News, 2006a).

[3] In his analysis, Ruhs (2006) points out that, even though a large proportion of A8 migration is likely to be temporary, changes in the stock of A8 migrants may still be underestimates as there are issues with capturing minority group data in the Labour Force Survey.

Acknowledgement
I would like to thank Catherine Drew for her research assistance.

References
Anderson, B., Ruhs, M., Rogaly, B. and Spencer, S. (2006) *Fair enough? Central and East European migrants in low-wage employment in the UK*, Oxford: COMPAS (www.compas.ox.ac.uk/changingstatus/Downloads/Fair%20enough%20paper%20-%201%20May%202006.pdf).

Bank of England (2006) *Inflation report: August 2006*, London: Bank of England (www.bankofengland.co.uk/publications/inflationreport/ir06aug.pdf).

BBC News (2006a) '"Nearly 600,000" new EU migrants', *BBC Online*, 22 August (http://news.bbc.co.uk/1/hi/uk_politics/5273356.stm).

BBC News (2006b) 'Council tax "rises for migrants"', *BBC Online*, 8 August (http://news.bbc.co.uk/1/hi/uk_politics/5255038.stm).

BBC News (2006c) 'Warning over new EU immigration', *BBC Online*, 31 July (http://news.bbc.co.uk/1/hi/uk_politics/5231768.stm).

Boeri, T. and Brücker, H. (2000) *The impact of eastern enlargement on employment and labour markets in the EU member states*, Berlin and Milan: Employment and Social Affairs Directorate General of the European Commission.

Brücker, H., Alvarez-Plata, P. and Siliverstovs, B. (2003) *Potential migration from Central and Eastern Europe into the EU-15 – An update*, Berlin: DIW for the European Commission (www.diw.de/deutsch/produkte/publikationen/gutachten/docs/report_european_commission_20040218.pdf).

CRONEM (Centre for Research on Nationalism, Ethnicity and Multiculturalism) (2006) 'Polish migrants survey results' (commissioned by BBC *Newsnight*), University of Surrey: CRONEM (www.surrey.ac.uk/Arts/CRONEM/CRONEM_BBC_Polish_survey%20_results.pdf).

Dench, S., Hurstfield, J., Hill, D. and Akroyd, K. (2006) *Employers' use of migrant labour*, London: Home Office, June (www.homeoffice.gov.uk/rds/pdfs06/rdsolr0406.pdf).

Drinkwater, S., Eade, J. and Garapich, M. (2006) *Poles apart? EU enlargement and the labour market outcomes of immigrants in the UK*, IZA Discussion Paper No 2410, Bonn: IZA (www.iza.org/).

Dustmann, C., Fabbri, F. and Preston, I. (2005) 'The impact of immigration in the British labour market', *The Economic Journal*, vol 115, pp F324–F341.

Dustmann, C., Casanova, I., Preston, M. and Schmidt, C. (2003) *The impact of EU enlargement on migration flows*, Home Office Online Report 25/03, London: The Stationery Office (www.homeoffice.gov.uk/rds/pdfs2/rdsolr2503.pdf).

EC (European Commission) (2006) *Report on the transitional arrangements set out in the 2003 Accession Treaty (period 1 May 2004–30 April 2006)*, Brussels: COM (2006) 48 Final (http://europa.eu.int/eur-lex/lex/LexUriServ/site/en/com/2006/com2006_0048en01.pdf).

Elliot, L. (2006) 'Migration threatens social fabric, says CBI chief', *The Guardian*, 6 September.

Ernst and Young ITEM Club (2006) *Economic outlook for business: Spring 2006*, Issue Number 35, London: Ernst and Young (www.ey.com/global/download.nsf/UK/Economic_Outlook_for_Business_04-06/$file/EY_ITEM_Economic_Outlook_Spring_Apr_06.pdf).

Gilpin, N., Henty, M., Lemos, S., Portes, J. and Bullen, C. (2006) *The impact of free movement of workers from Central and Eastern Europe on the UK labour market*, DWP Working Paper No 29, London: DWP (www.dwp.gov.uk/asd/asd5/wp29.pdf).

Hickley, M. (2006) 'Eastern European immigrants carry out tenth of crime', *Mail on Sunday*, 2 November (www.mailonsunday.co.uk/pages/live/articles/news/news.html?in_article_id=413985&in_page_id=1770).

Home Office (2004a) *Control of immigration: Statistics United Kingdom 2004*, London: The Stationery Office (wV).

Home Office (2004b) *No UK benefits for EU accession countries*, Home Office Press Notice 069, 23 February (http://press.homeoffice.gov.uk/press-releases/No_Uk_Benefits_For_Eu_Accession_).

Home Office (2006) *Controlled access for accession states*, London: Home Office (www.homeoffice.gov.uk/about-us/news/accession-states-limits).

Home Office, Department for Work and Pensions, Inland Revenue and Office of the Deputy Prime Minister (various years) *Accession monitoring report*, London: The Stationery Office (www.ind.homeoffice.gov.uk/aboutus/reports/accession_monitoring_report).

Homeless Link (2006) *A8 nationals in London homelessness services*, London: Homeless Link (www.homeless.org.uk/policyandinfo/research/archive/A8%20nationals%20Executive%20Summary%20low%20res.pdf).

IPPR (Institute for Public Policy Research) (2006) *EU enlargement: Bulgaria and Romania – Migration implications for the UK*, London: IPPR (www.ippr.org/publicationsandreports/publication.asp?id=457).

IPPR (2007) *The reception and integration of new migrant communities*, London: Commission for Racial Equality.

Johnston, P. (2006) 'Labour refuses to estimate migrant influx', *Daily Telegraph*, 8 December (www.telegraph.co.uk/news/main.jhtml?xml=/news/2006/12/08/nmigrant08.xml).

LSC (Learning and Skills Council) (2004) *National Employers Skills Survey 2003: Main report*, Coventry: LSC.

Manacorda, M., Manning, A. and Wadsworth, J. (2006) *The impact of immigration on the structure of male wages: Theory and evidence from Britain*, IZA Discussion Paper No 2352, Bonn: IZA (www.iza.org/).

MORI (2003) *British views on immigration* (www.mori.com/polls/2003/migration.shtml).

MORI (2006) *Political trends monitor* (www.mori.com/polls/trends/issues.shtml).

ONS (Office for National Statistics) (2006a) *International migration*, News Release, November, London: ONS (www.statistics.gov.uk/pdfdir/intmigrat1106.pdf).

ONS (2006b) *Visits to the UK from the enlarged EU*, London: ONS (www. statistics.gov.uk/downloads/theme_transport/Visits_to_UK_Aug06. pdf).

Portes, J. and French, S. (2005) *The impact of free movement of workers from Central and Eastern Europe on the UK labour market: Early evidence*, DWP Working Paper No 18, London: Department for Work and Pensions (www.dwp.gov.uk/asd/asd5/WP18.pdf).

Ruhs, M. (2006) *Greasing the wheels of the flexible labour market: East European labour immigration in the UK*, Working Paper No 38, Oxford: COMPAS.

Travis, A. (2006) 'Home secretary wants to set "optimum" level of immigration', *The Guardian*, 7 August (http://society.guardian.co.uk/ asylumseekers/story/0,,1838930,00.html).

Wintour, P. (2006) 'Inaccurate migrant numbers may lead to rise in Council Tax', *The Guardian*, 8 August.

Wooding, D. (2006) '45,000 crims to come here', *The Sun*, 24 July (www. thesun.co.uk/article/0,,2-2006340084,,00.html).

THIRTEEN

Gendered immigrations, policies and rights in the UK

Eleonore Kofman

In the past decade, immigration and net migration into the UK have increased substantially. At the same time it has become more diversified, not only in terms of countries of origin but also the different forms of entry, statuses and rights conferred by the state. There are also large variations in the proportion of female nationals among the many nationalities present in the UK, with an average of 48.6% in 2006 (Salt, 2006), rising to over 60% for the Philippines and a number of European states, but falling to below 40% for those from Bangladesh and Iran. In the most recent flows, the largest nationalities, such as Polish, Indian, Lithuanian and Slovakian, currently dominating labour migration, have relatively low proportions of women[1].

Although women are present in all flows, each form of entry reveals very different proportions of females. Asylum seekers are the least feminised group of entrants (30% of principal applicants and 53% of dependants in 2004) in contrast to family migration, which is around two thirds female. The third major route is labour migration where the proportion of females varies considerably by nationality and sector of employment. However, the UK's global position and relatively open labour markets, due in part to its colonial links, have meant that, unlike many other European states, female migrants are to be found across a range of employment sectors and sites, both skilled and less skilled (Kofman et al, 2005).

Immigration policies contribute to shaping the gendered nature of these flows. The intersection of gender with other social divisions such as nationality, education, and economic, social and cultural resources in conjunction with immigration policies also create a complex matrix of stratification. The gendered outcomes and stratified rights and access to settlement and citizenship are not necessarily overtly enunciated but result from the ways in which the criteria relating to different forms of immigration are applied. So too do gendered representations of particular forms of migration impact on the development of policies. Asylum seekers are largely seen as young mobile men while family migrants are primarily women, less interested in joining the workforce than men (Kofman, 2004).

There has, however, been no comprehensive study of how policies influence the arrival and settlement of women migrants even though (often outmoded) gendered assumptions underlie policy. Thus, although there is increasing research on the gendered aspects of different channels of entry to the UK (Kofman et al, 2000; Morris, 2002; Yuval–Davis et al, 2005) there has been little overall analysis of the gendered implications of managed migration or of its specific policies (Kofman et al, 2005).

In this chapter, I first outline the gendered dimension of different migratory flows, starting with different sectors of migrant labour. One of the recent areas of expansion has been that of social care in diverse sites, skills and sectors. I then examine specific issues arising from family and asylum flows. As noted above, the different channels of entry and social divisions give rise to differentiated and stratified economic and welfare rights that have increasingly been codified in immigration regulations. Thus, in the second section of the chapter, I examine the gendered aspects of immigration policies, especially in relation to some of the changes currently being implemented within a framework of managed migration.

Channels of immigration

Labour migration and female employment

The UK has a history of female labour migration from neighbouring countries, such as Ireland (Walter, 2000), its former colonies, particularly in the Caribbean, and post-war Eastern European voluntary workers (McDowell, 2005). Much of the earliest writing on female immigration was concerned with employment in manufacturing and low-level services (Phizacklea, 1983). By the late 1970s, female routes for Commonwealth and other less skilled migrants were closed down as the UK began to turn to the European Community. Family migration and its input into the labour market continued.

However, by the late 1990s labour market shortages in many sectors of the UK economy led to higher inflows of labour migrants. Women have formed an increasingly important part of such migration as a number of the sectors with severe shortages – education and health – are female dominated. Although migrant women's participation in male-dominated sectors such as Information and Communication Technology (ICT), finance and business has increased, on the whole, migration has reinforced extant gender divisions in the workplace with migrant women participating in a wide range of sectors similar to those in which white British-born women participate, including hospitality, industrial cleaning and retailing (see Table 13.1).

Within the European context, the UK displays a distinctive distribution of migrant women's employment. Most European research has, however, focused on selected sectors or groups of female migrants, especially those in domestic labour and sex work, which is not necessarily appropriate to the British context. Numerous gaps have been left in our knowledge of female migrants in employment sectors and occupations, such as hospitality and social care, that are only now becoming the object of study in the UK (ongoing studies by the Working Lives Institute, London and COMPAS, Oxford). In some cases the gender dimension awaits analysis (Anderson et al, 2006). So too have skilled sectors received relatively little attention (Raghuram and Kofman, 2002; Raghuram, 2004; Kofman and Raghuram, 2006; Winkelman-Gleed, 2006).

As Table 13.2 shows, 'foreigners' are especially prominent in the health, social services and education sectors that provide employment for many

Table 13.1: Employment patterns of female immigrants and UK-born white, black and minority ethnic women (1979 and 2000)

	UK-born white		UK-born black and minority ethnic		Immigrants	
	1979	2000	1979	2000	1979	2000
% manufacturing	15	10	16	9	16	10
% retail	11	13	11	11	6	10
% hotel/restaurant	3	5	5	4	4	5
% finance	4	16	3	24	3	18
% education	8	14	3	9	5	12
% health	6	20	3	17	10	23
% public	n/a	33	n/a	31	n/a	31

Note: All figures are population weighted, excluding those in full-time education. Figures are the percentage of all employees in each origin category.

Source: Dustmann et al (2003)

Table 13.2: Employment of women by nationality in selected countries, by percentage (1994 and 2004)

	1994		2004	
	Foreigners	Nationals	Foreigners	Nationals
Household services				
Spain	27.1	6.9	36.0	4.6
France	14.7	3.5	21.1	3.8
Greece	35.0	1.5	42.4	1.3
Italy	10.3	27.9	1.6	2.3
UK	3.7	1.1	3.1	0.8
Hotel and restaurants				
Germany	10.8	3.2	11.5	3.8
Spain	24.4	7.1	19.0	7.5
France	8.5	3.8	6.0	3.4
Greece	12.2	6.4	16.3	7.4
UK	6.5	5.7	7.6	5.2
Health and social services				
Belgium	14.5	19.3	15.9	22.4
Germany	11.9	11.7	15.7	19.6
Denmark	37.6	26.9	27.4	32.6
France	10.5	16.9	12.1	20.3
UK	21.0	18.8	25.0	20.6
Education				
Belgium	6.8	15.3	7.5	14.8
Germany	3.4	7.9	5.7	8.8
Spain	9.5	9.8	3.8	10.2
France	4.8	11.3	6.8	10.5
Italy	16.1	14.8	4.2	14.0
UK	12.5	11.4	11.4	14.4
Information technology				
UK	n/a	n/a	1.5	0.8

Source: European Community Labour Force Survey 2004

skilled migrants. This is reflected in the relatively high percentages of foreign-born women, including those from non-OECD (Organisation for Economic Co-operation and Development) countries, who are employed in highly skilled professions (SOPEMI, 2006, p 64), and the relatively low proportion of migrant women who are over-qualified in the work they are doing compared to most other European Union (EU) states, especially the southern European ones. The single largest shortage occupation of formal employment has been that of nursing where the numbers registering from overseas with the Nursing and Midwifery Council rose sharply from 1998/99 to 2003/04. Since then, the numbers of overseas nurses have declined in response to financial crises in the National Health Service.

Table 13.3 does not give a comprehensive picture of non-British nurses as it does not include those trained within the EU and whose qualifications are recognised by an intergovernmental agreement. All nurses have to submit evidence of their training and professional experience but non-EU nurses also have to pass an International English Language Testing System. An additional difference among overseas nurses and their incorporation into the labour market is between those who are directly recruited and whose registration is undertaken

Table 13.3: Initial Nursing and Midwifery Council overseas admissions to the register, by country

Country	1998/99	2001/02	2004/05
Philippines	52	7,235	2,521
India	30	994	3,690
South Africa	599	2,114	933
Australia	1,335	1,342	981
Nigeria	179	432	466
Zimbabwe	52	473	311
New Zealand	527	443	289
Ghana	40	195	272
Pakistan	3	207	205
Kenya	19	155	99
Total	3,568	15,062	11,416

Note: Individual figures are given for the ten most significant countries of origin, therefore columns do not sum to totals shown.
Source: Winkelman-Gleed (2006, p 27)

by recruitment agencies and those who arrive independently and need to sort out their registration and employment. Most nurses from third world countries start at the bottom of the pay scale after they become registered, regardless of their previous experience, and confront obstacles in career progression. Few are to be found in senior positions (Winkelman–Gleed, 2006, p 27).

At the same time the boundaries between care work and nursing are blurring as experience gained in care homes is being recognised as a form of adaptation course for migrant nurses. Nurses can therefore use caring as a route into a nursing career although the extent to which the aspirations of such nurses to move into nursing are being fulfilled is not yet known. It is likely that while labour shortages in the care sector may help nurses find employment, this may eventually become a labour market trap. Recent reports have highlighted the deskilling of third world nurses brought in under work permits for nurses but working in care homes as part of the 'adaptation' programme. This programme usually requires work experience in a recognised care centre (care home, hospital, etc) for between three and six months (CAB, 2004; Anderson and Rogaly, 2005) and is a prerequisite for nurses to obtain registration to work in the UK. Once they have passed this phase, they can register with the Nursing and Midwifery Council and receive pay at the nursing scale. Some homes have employed these staff to undertake menial tasks, paid them at lower rates than cited on their work permit (CAB, 2004, p 8) and delayed their registration in order to continue paying them at lower rates.

The care sector in the UK employs over one million workers, with 860,000 employed as social care workers and 317,000 as childcare workers in the period 2001-04 (Simon and Owen, 2005). About 84% of all social care employees are women (Roche and Rankin, 2004), while 98% of childcare workers are women (EOC, 2004). Direct recruitment into the care labour market has also increased. The General Social Care Council (GSCC) opened up registration to social workers who had trained overseas in April 2004. This forms one part of the overall regulation process of social work and care work. In 1999-2000 the GSCC issued 482 letters of verification to overseas social workers confirming their qualifications. In 2003-04 a total of 2,534 letters were issued to applicants from 58 countries wishing to practise in the UK. Those from Australia (424), South Africa (342) and the US (315) headed the list, followed by Canada and India with over 250 applicants each. Furthermore a number of countries that had only a few applicants in 2001-01, such as the Philippines and Romania, had increased substantially by 2003-04. Although figures for verification of overseas social work qualifications are still small, active recruitment is being recognised as a possible way of addressing the shortage of workers in this sector (Eborrall, 2005).

Future demand for female migrant labour will be influenced by a number of developments that will change the participation of women in the labour market and alter the contours of welfare. These include the shift to an adult worker model where both partners work, the expansion in the provision of childcare, both at home and increasingly in schools, and the impact of new legislation such as the Care Standards Act (2000), which has raised standards and costs but driven down wages. The reclassification of tasks and use of assistants rather than fully qualified professionals in a number of welfare sectors (for example, care, education and health) and the attendant deskilling of these jobs will also affect the desirability of such work.

Government policy is also increasingly transferring care work from the public sector into the home. For instance, the shift to direct payments rather than the use of community care services is likely to create new household markets for care. The expansion of childcare provision within a social investment perspective (Dobrowolsky and Jenson, 2005) is extending subsidised provision to the home. These shifts serve to increase the demand for care workers, on the one hand, and to make it a less desirable occupation on the other, so that labour market shortages in this sector are likely to continue. The transfer of migrant labour from South to North has been conceptualised as a global care chain (Hochschild, 2000, p 131), defined as "a series of personal links between people across the globe based on the paid or unpaid work of caring". The chains may vary in their number and connective strength, combining internal and international caring links. Others such as Sassen (2000) have drawn attention to the counter-geographies of globalisation in which the wealthy North relies on the poorer South for its low-paid and flexible service provision.

The above analyses tend to be very general and do not take into account the ways in which migrant labour is incorporated into different welfare regimes, the effect of immigration regulations, the changing backgrounds of migrants and new care policies (Kofman, 2006). Thus in the UK it is likely that the new policies will lead to new divisions between care workers based on their site of work (private homes, public sector) and migrant status. At the moment, the workforce in nurseries tends to be young, female and white (Pandya, 2005), and it is unclear whether the new forms of migration will also exacerbate differences based on age and 'race'. For the more skilled end of the care sector, the government has recognised the category of senior carer (NVQ Level 2/3) for which work permits may be issued but for the less skilled, it envisages Eastern European workers as making up the necessary shortfalls in labour. In the two years from July 2004, 12,610 (5%) Eastern Europeans registered as care workers (Home Office, 2006). The gender differences in conditions of work and wages among Eastern Europeans who have registered under the worker registration scheme have not yet been analysed (ongoing COMPAS study). However, the Trades Union Congress (Hardy and Clark, 2005) noted that those working in care homes, which are often small, poorly unionised and isolated, may face particular problems and, although legally employed, are often not aware of their employment rights and recourse against sexual harassment. Those in the residential care sector often face highly exploitative conditions (Anderson and Rogaly, 2005); they may have temporary or part-time jobs and are not always integrated into the social security system (Lethbridge, 2005, p 12). Although there are moves to upgrade the qualifications of care workers, such upgrading may be less accessible for migrant workers (Lethbridge, 2005, p 14).

Thus the role of migrant labour in changing and supporting welfare regimes needs to be explored (Williams, 2003; Kofman, 2006). Yet there is little knowledge of migrant involvement in diverse care sectors. General studies often mask differences between subsectors and/or refer to minority ethnic categories that, in the light of recent immigration, fail to identify the use of white Eastern Europeans. The real extent of migrant presence, especially in London, is picked up in smaller-scale studies of particular nationalities such as the Zimbabweans (McGregor, 2006) or of the low paid (Evans et al, 2005). In the latter study, it was estimated that 90% of London's low-paid workforce were migrants and that the various labour markets were gender segregated. Men tended to work in the semi-public spaces of office cleaning or the Underground and women in semi-private spaces such as hotels and care work in the home.

Some of the tasks undertaken within the care sector are also undertaken in hospitality jobs such as cleaning, waitressing, housekeeping and reception work. Hence, they too are highly feminised but there has been little analysis of the gendered aspects of such temporary work so far (DRC, 2004; Anderson and Rogaly, 2005), although we do know that the gender breakdown varies considerably according to nationality, age and sector. For instance, there appear to be differences among migrant women from the different Eastern European countries in terms of the industries in which they seek employment and the level of skills they bring. Also, younger women may find it easier to find employment in the hospitality sector than older women, who find themselves choosing self-employment or home working.

Domestic labour, which has received considerable attention internationally, has been under-researched in the UK (but see Anderson, 2000, 2006; Cox, 2006). It should also be noted that this category may be used in a very general sense and in reality often includes care work performed in the home. Domestic work, which has attracted large numbers of female labour migrants in many European countries except for Scandinavia, is less well developed here (see Table 13.2) but growing. Unlike in Southern European countries, there is no labour route for household work in the UK except for the migrant domestic worker scheme, which is limited to those accompanying an employer coming from abroad. Numbers have stayed fairly stable at just over 10,000 per annum (Home Office, 2005b). Nevertheless, migrants may be working in this sector with varied immigration statuses (Anderson, 2006), including au pairs (Newcombe, 2004; Cox, 2006), asylum seekers (who do not have the right to work), students earning additional money, Eastern Europeans who may have registered as workers, and lastly, those who originally entered through the migrant domestic worker scheme. Migrant workers may be employed directly by the household or by agencies, and if the former, are not covered by the 2003 Race Relations Amendment Act. At the same time, changing ways of funding social care and its commodification, especially through direct payments for disabled people, and more recently, older people, are also likely to increase the number of workers employed directly by the household (Ungerson, 2003, 2005), although the distribution across categories may fluctuate. For example, the numbers of au pairs entering have sharply declined from 15,300 in 2003 to 5,640 in 2004 (1,720 not including the accession states) and 2,360 in 2005 (Home Office, 2005b). Obviously nationals of accession states now have possibilities other than being au pairs.

Self-employment has also been on the increase, especially among migrant South Asian, Chinese and Turkish women (Struder, 2002). Women enter self-employment both in order to achieve flexibility in combining work and familial responsibilities, and due to labour market disadvantages. Activities such as advocacy, mediation, interpreting and general community work are also increasingly offering employment opportunities for migrant women enabling them to break out of manufacturing and low-level service employment and to deploy other skills. Women, who are unable to work in the area of their qualification, may initially take up these jobs on a voluntary basis (Erel et al, 2004). However, although these activities can provide rewarding employment opportunities, they may at the same time leave migrants trapped in services for other migrants, as has been noted in social work and teaching in Germany and the Netherlands (Lutz, 1993). The likely expansion of integration programmes in the future may further improve job opportunities in this sector but there is a substantial risk that these jobs may only generate fixed-term and insecure employment.

Family migration

Since a raft of regulations controlling labour migration was introduced in 1962, family migration has emerged as the single most enduring, although also restricted, basis for entry of migrants to the UK. Family migration is even more important when it comes to grants of settlement, with just under half of all those permitted to settle falling into this category. However, since 1997 the number of family members settling has not grown at the same pace as the other two major categories of employment and asylum grants (Table 13.4). However, within this category the number of children entering has grown substantially.

Table 13.4: Grants of settlement, by category (1995 and 2005)

Category	1995	% of total	2005	% of total
Completion four years (work, permit free, business)	4,310	7.8	27,415	15.3
UK ancestry seeking to work	1,080	1.9	4,795	2.7
Refugees, of whom:	1,600	2.9	33,850	18.9
Family ILR exercise			10,780	6.0
Other discretionary leave	2,720	4.9	4,050	2.3
Husbands	12,680	22.9	15,780	8.8
Wives	19,940	35.9	30,210	16.7
Children	8,630	15.6	45,445	25.4
Parents, grandparents	2,010	3.6	1,465	0.8
Other dependants	1,660	3.0	11,520	6.4
Other or unknown categories	850	1.5	4,635	2.6
Total	55,480	100.0	179,120	100.0

Note: ILR = indefinite leave to remain
Source: Immigration and Borders Agency (2006)

Although the dominant category of settlement (Immigration and Borders Agency, 2006), family migration has hardly received any attention or research (Kofman, 2004; Raghuram, 2004). It has, however, some distinctive aspects and is the most feminised of the three major channels of entry and settlement in the country. In 2005, 27,300 women were admitted for purposes of marriage or cohabitation compared with 14,300 men (Home Office, 2005b). In terms of settlement 30,210 women were granted settlement compared to 15,760 men. However, gender divisions vary markedly based on regions of entry. There are also increasing numbers of men in family migration. The predominance of women in the family category led to a conceptual collapse of female migration into family migration in much policy discussion so that male family migrants have received little or no attention (Raghuram, 2004).

We can distinguish between different kinds of family migration on the basis of how family formation intersects with migration, for example whether the family formed before migration or as a result of migration. Moreover, the nature of the family (presence of children in particular, as rights to bring in parents and other relatives is very limited) also affects migration. The following typology of family migration (Kofman, 2004) offers one route into unpacking this complexity:

- *family reunification migration*, where primary migrants bring in members of the immediate family (children, spouses and parents and others where permitted);
- *family formation migration*, where migrants with settled status or British-born children of migrants bring in marriage partners, often from their parents' countries of origin;
- *marriage migration*, where permanent residents or citizens bring in a partner they have met while abroad for purposes of work, study or holiday;
- *whole family migration*, where the entire family migrates together.

As family migration has a derivative status, both entry and right to work are dependent on the immigration category under which the primary migrant enters. For instance, spouses of skilled migrants and students have both right of entry and the right to work, while many lesser skilled workers have no right to bring in family members. Among the less skilled, domestic workers are one exception as they are permitted to bring in family although the conditions of work, including the nature of live-in work, means that they are rarely able to avail themselves of this right. Nonetheless all spouses are subject to the two-year probationary period, although for spouses of UK nationals or permanent residents proof of domestic violence may enable them to be given permanent status before the probationary period has ended.

Asylum and refugees

Asylum statistics by gender have only been published since 2001. In 2004 30% of asylum applicants, excluding dependants, were women. Although relatively low, this has been increasing (ICAR, 2006). The proportion of women is highest among applicants from Somalia, Zimbabwe, China and Congo; it is higher for countries where there is civil unrest and war and lower in countries where women's rights are repressed and where the primary focus of human rights violations is political and civil rights abuses. Eighty per cent of female asylum seekers are under 35 years of age. Women frequently have specific grounds on which they seek asylum. For instance, female principal applicants may apply for asylum on the basis of indirect persecution, such as where women are persecuted due to their link to a family member. Thus in Ceneda's study (2003) abuse due to political association was a common reason for women seeking asylum as abuse of the female relative is often used as a tool for controlling other (male) family members' involvement in political activity. These cases are often difficult because women may have little or no knowledge about why their family members are being persecuted, and therefore why they are being persecuted themselves.

Another category that primarily applies to women asylum seekers is that of gender-specific persecution. This involves persecution that women face because of their sex (such as female genital mutilation) and usually includes gender-specific forms of harm. It also covers violence or fear based on failure to comply with social norms that govern women's behaviour. The violence that women may face if they refuse to wear the veil may be included in this category. Finally, women may seek asylum after suffering gender-based violence because of their wider political activity. Here the activities that women engage in may be the same as men, but the form of retribution may be gender specific – usually including rape. This is a common cause for women claiming asylum with one study reporting that 50% of women claiming asylum, in the UK have been raped (Refugee Council, 1996). The incidence of severe harm is also very high among those having received exceptional leave to remain (ELR) or refugee status (Ceneda, 2003)[2].

Historically the gender composition of refugees and public

representations of them as almost always male have also led to masculine bias in the provision of support for asylum seekers and refugees. The Home Office policy of dispersal introduced in 1999 and delivered by the National Asylum Support Service (NASS) since 2000 is one such example. It presumes a highly mobile male individual who has no dependants so that the difficulties that women face through dispersal are not adequately considered. For instance, one study found that women's access to appropriate housing, health, interpreters and legal firms or similar minority ethnic groups to which an asylum seeker could turn for help were particularly affected through the dispersal policies (Dumper, 2002). A high proportion (43%) of those receiving NASS support for accommodation were female. Men's greater public presence within their communities has meant that they also appear to find it easier to access support systems from networks within the community (Dumper, 2002, p 19).

Managed migration and stratified rights

Barbara Roche's keynote speech at the conference on 'UK Migration in the Global Economy' in September 2000 marked the beginning of the UK's new approach of 'managing migration'. This approach brings together different forms of migration, including those associated in theory with normative principles – asylum and family reunification – under an overarching framework (Morris, 2004). Migration is managed in order to deliver the UK's economic interests within the context of a competitive global economy, while at the same time 'maintaining social cohesion'.

The links between immigration and employment become a central feature of such a policy (Duvell and Jordan, 2003). The UK's successful positioning within a global economy is seen in part as being able to fill its labour market shortages so that the acknowledged corollary of the pursuit of the national economic interest is the closure of other possible reasons and routes of entry, notably for undocumented migrants and asylum seekers. This requires tighter control and deterrence, externally and internally (Morris, 2004, p 3). Over the past few years the emphasis on migration working to Britain's benefit has been affirmed ever more forcefully (Home Office, 2005a).

Managed migration offers a new emphasis on a regulated opening up of migration but within the context of differential contractual obligations and rights for different categories of migrants (with highly skilled at one end and low skilled at the other). This leads to a more pronounced stratification, or system of inclusion and exclusion, through migrant statuses and rights to settlement (Kofman, 2002; Morris, 2002). So while some groups, namely the skilled, have seen their rights expand, others, particularly asylum seekers and the less skilled, have experienced a contraction in their rights (Morris, 2004). The Highly Skilled Migrant Programme (HSMP), introduced in January 2002, allowed migrants meeting a high standard of qualifications and work experience in their homeland to enter the UK without a firm job offer. Applicants can bring in family members, including cohabiting partners, who in turn also have the right to work. On the other hand, there is the increasing problematisation of those who are unlawfully present, for example those who have entered clandestinely or who are overstaying (DRC, 2004; Pinkerton et al, 2004).

The latest revision (Home Office, 2005a) to policy has introduced a new five-tiered scheme that brings all the current work schemes and students into a single points-based system. The HSMP (7 November 2006)[3] has been the first to be incorporated into the new points-based system where it constitutes the first and highest tier. The old work permit system will become the second tier, allowing migrants to proceed to long-term settlement and eventual citizenship. The highly skilled will not require a sponsor but the second tier will be tied to a sponsor. The low skilled (proposed third tier), for whom official channels had been expanded through sector-based schemes since 2003, are to be phased out over time in the light of the supply of labour from new EU members. In future, this route will be very limited, treating low-skilled non-EU labour as flexible guest workers whose rights to settlement are severely circumscribed.

Family migration has also been integrated into the system of managed migration. In family migration (reunification, formation and accompanying), the skilled may bring in partners while the less skilled may not. Switching from a temporary status to a settlement status through the marriage route has been disallowed since July 2003 on the basis that this would thwart the government's ability to manage numbers and control entry. On the other hand, much immigration policy enforces dependency on spouses, at least temporarily. In 2003 the refrain of bogus or sham marriages led to the extension of the probationary period from one to two years and in February 2005 tougher rules were imposed on the marriage of spouses of British citizens and of permanent residents from outside the EU who had only short-term visas. However, in April 2006 the High Court judged the restrictions unreasonable and in breach of the 1998 Human Rights Act (BBC, 10 April 2006).

The life chances of refugees are also significantly and lastingly influenced by the economic and legislative climate at time of entry and the process of 'managing migration' from an economic perspective appears to significantly influence the experiences of those seeking asylum today (Bloch, 2004b). As a result, as in much of the migration debate an increasingly important vector of difference is the possession of skills. The Home Office's decision to flag up the applications for asylum based on skills means that those with skills (especially professional skills in occupations that are facing shortages) are likely to be offered specific packages for integration into the workforce, something that is simply not on offer for less-skilled refugees.

The government has also been active in policy making regarding irregular migration and sex trafficking. In effect there have been several regularisations such as that of overseas domestic workers from July 1998 to October 1999, a one-off amnesty for asylum seekers and their families who had been in the UK for more than three years in 2003, amnesty for undeclared family members of refugees (closed in December 2004) as well as de facto regularisation of Central and Eastern European workers when their countries entered into the EU. The extent of trafficking is hard to assess and occurs across a wide range of sectors, such as domestic work, care and hospitality, and not just for purposes of sex work. This arises from the demand for both cheap services, encouraged by widespread subcontracting, and sex.

Sex trafficking has been addressed through the 2003 Sexual Offences Act and the inclusion of a separate offence for all forms of labour exploitation (agricultural, domestic, sexual) in the Asylum and Immigration (Treatment of Claimants, etc) Act in 2004 (Skrivankova, 2006). Those arranging or facilitating the movement into, within, or out of, the UK in order to sexually exploit may receive prison sentences of up to 14 years. These recent initiatives have been prompted by a spate of international and European measures such as the UN Trafficking Protocol (2000) and the EU Council Framework Decision on Combating Trafficking in Human Beings (July 2002). Non-governmental organisations (NGOs) have been especially active in lobbying governments, the EU and international organisations in seeking a rights-based approach that does not lead to the victimisation of the person being trafficked, allows them to stay in the country for a three-month period of reflection, and to have access to employment and support services (van den Anker, 2003). Some have argued that, as a victim of gender-based persecution, a trafficked woman should be entitled to entry into the refugee-determination process to ascertain whether she has a well-founded fear of persecution; some have argued for the recognition of trafficking as a form of gender-based persecution under the refugee convention (Shearer Demir, 2003).

Stratified rights and access to welfare

The key axes of stratified rights are nationality, channel of entry (labour, family, asylum), skills and education. These intersect to produce a complex and differentiated series of rights such as labour market restrictions, the right to switch from one category to another, settlement, family reunification and formation, and access to welfare. A major factor of differential rights is nationality – EU16, A8 accession and non-EU – that determines both rights and conditions of work. The level of education and skills do not matter for EU nationals but regulate entry and rights for non-EU nationals. The rights of the latter, such as duration of stay, labour market restrictions, family formation and eventual settlement and citizenship strongly depend on their human capital (education, earnings). The rights of spouses also vary according to the nationality of the applicant. EU migrant workers may use their mobility rights to bring in a non-EU partner without the imposition of material conditions, such as adequate housing and economic resources, which are required for British citizens and other permanent residents. The spouse's right to remain depends on the relationship persisting for the two-year probationary period except where domestic violence can be demonstrated. Table 13.5 outlines very generally some of these key differences[4].

Gendered implications

The gendered outcomes of managed migration result primarily from the differential valuation of (gendered) skills, related in part to prevailing labour market shortages and the sites in which work takes place, for example public or private spaces. The proposed five-tier system makes a number of gendered distinctions. Women form less than a quarter of HSMP applicants and figures on acceptances of HSMP by occupational groups are dominated by finance, ICT, business and management[5] and the medical professions. Most of these occupations are skewed towards the private sector. Selection criteria, such as qualifications, income level and work experience, are all likely to be higher barriers for women than men. The more feminised welfare sectors, such as health and education, are, on the other hand, some of the leading occupations among the ordinary work permit system, or the new second tier. The second tier (which

Table 13.5: Immigration status and labour market, family and welfare rights

Nationality/ Channel of entry	Skills and education	Labour market restrictions	Switching/ settlement	Family	Welfare rights
European Economic Area (EEA) (excluding A8)*	No	Open	ILR after five years	May bring in non-EU spouse, children up to 21 and ascendants	If never economically active no access to social assistance
A8	No	Open but must register or be self-employed	ILR after five years	Yes but not ascending or descending family	Same as above for worker and self-sufficient
Business – non-EU	One year initially, may be extended	Must have £200,000 and create employment for two UK residents	ILR after five years	Yes	NRPF
Spouse of British citizen or long-term resident	No skills or education but spouse partner to have resources	Immediate access to labour market	ILR after probationary period of two years	Yes	NRPF for two years

*EEA consists of EU, plus Liechtenstein and Norway

continued ...

Table 13.5 (continued)

Nationality/ Channel of entry	Skills and education	Labour market restrictions	Switching/ settlement	Family	Welfare rights
Non-EU	First tier (HSMP)	Does not need job offer or sponsor Two years initially	Must demonstrate desire to settle; ILR after five years	Yes may bring in spouse and dependent children to 18	NRPF for five years
	Second tier (work permit)	Requires sponsor and job and normally with NVQ Level 3	Yes, to first tier if conditions fulfilled ILR after five years	Yes, spouse and dependent children to 18	NRPF for five years
	Third tier (low skilled)	No skill demanded Restricted to employer and for one year maximum	No	No	NRPF
	Fourth-tier student	Appropriate qualification and English	For Masters may stay one year after course ends	Yes, spouse and dependent children to 18	NRPF
Au pair		No skills Only in private homes but can switch family	24 months maximum and no settlement	No	NRPF

continued ...

Table 13.5 (continued)

Nationality/ Channel of entry	Skills and education	Labour market restrictions	Switching/ settlement	Family	Welfare rights
Asylum	Skills and education not relevant	No right to work	No right to settle unless refugee or humanitarian status granted	No	Outside welfare system Benefits from Home Office
Refugee Humanitarian		Work in any occupation	ILR after five years	Yes – no proof of resources required	Can access public funds
Migrant domestic worker	No skills	With employer on entry	ILR after five years	Yes	NRPF

Notes: ILR = indefinite leave to remain, that is, the right to remain without a time limit; NRPF = no recourse to public funds, which are income-related benefits such as Income Support, income-based Jobseeker's Allowance, State Pension Credit, Housing Benefit or Council Tax Benefit or a full housing duty as a homeless person.

Source: Adapted from Seddon (2006)

requires applicants to have skills equivalent to NVQ Level 3 and above) is envisaged to meet labour requirements at the less-qualified and lower-income end of skilled work. Unlike the first tier, second-tier migrants will require a sponsor (employer, faith community or local authority) who will ensure they comply with the regulations of employment and residence. Like the first tier, this route has rights of family reunification, and the possibility of settlement. Although professionals, such as nurses and teachers cited in the White Paper (Home Office, 2005a) as examples of the second tier, are not barred from applying through the first tier, the lower wage levels in these heavily feminised sectors will often mean that women may not have the income levels to apply through the first. Much more severe is the proposed plan to heavily restrict the migration of the lesser skilled (under tier three) on grounds that the demand for lesser-skilled jobs will be largely met by migrants from the new EU member countries. However, this does not take into account that over time EU migrants may also be unwilling to engage in lesser-paid jobs. In particular, the regulations fail to recognise the significance of continuing labour shortages in sectors such as care and domestic work that depend on migrant female labour.

Women, many of whom are family migrants, are also more likely to be affected by the emphasis on labour migration, which is becoming the only socially acceptable route of entry to the UK. The restrictions on marriage migration and the language of 'sham marriages' is likely to make the entry and marriage of female migrants increasingly difficult. At the same time cultural perceptions of gendered familial relations have shaped family migration policy largely based on the assumption that spouses are female and dependent. In an initial period, family migrants are sponsored and on probation, and thereby barred from access to public funds.

The gendered assumptions that underlie family reunification policy also form the basis for the community cohesion and citizenship initiatives that followed the disturbances in northern cities in summer 2001. In this instance stereotypical images of 'traditional' patriarchal gender relations (South Asian communities and generally Muslim) and women isolated from the external world drive both immigration and settlement policies (Yuval-Davis et al, 2005) and fail to adequately recognise the diversity of women's experiences and situations.

Public representations of refugees as young and single males marginalise women refugees. Even more significant has been the difficulty of getting gender persecution to be taken seriously in the determination of asylum claims, thereby denying women political agency.

How might we develop a gendered analysis of the implications of immigration and settlement policies? *Citizenship and Immigration Canada* applied gender-based analysis to various aspects of the Immigration and Refugee Protection Act, which was implemented in 2002. Status of Women Canada (2003) defines gender-based analysis as:

> ... a process that assesses the differential impact of proposed and/or existing policies, programs and legislation on women and men. It makes it possible for policy to be undertaken with an appreciation of gender differences, of the nature of relationships between women and men and of their different social realities, life expectations and economic circumstances. It is a tool for understanding social processes and for responding with informed and equitable options.
>
> It compares how and why women and men are affected by policy issues. Gender-based analysis challenges the assumption that everyone is affected by policies, programs and legislation in the same way regardless of gender, a notion often referred to as 'gender-neutral policy'.

Applying gender-based analysis does not necessarily resolve the different impact of immigration policies on women and men; it does, however, clarify how the criteria operate and their potential outcome.

Conclusion

The introduction of a managed migration scheme in the UK has codified the increasing utilitarian rationale into which all forms of immigration must fit. The rights and routes to settlement are therefore determined in relation to an economic calculus. In this chapter I have highlighted the ways in which routes of entry and immigration policies, and therefore rights, are not gender neutral. Each of the routes of entry has different gender compositions and representations. What this means is that policies have different implications and outcomes for women and men. In some cases the criteria laid down for a form of entry are likely to favour men rather than women; in other cases it is assumed that a particular flow is largely or entirely filled by women or men.

The gender basis of managed migration is most clearly demonstrated in the new five-tier system. Thus the privileged conditions attached to the HSMP, based on a notion of human capital and measured by educational levels and prior earnings, tends to favour men. It is likely that the further emphasis on youth may also prove more difficult for women at a time in the life cycle when they are getting married and having children. It is by the late twenties when one is most likely to be able to earn the highest number of points from education and age and when high earnings may be achieved in the largely male finance sector. At the lower end, the devaluation of female sectors and their skills, in care in the home and residential home care, means that women may enter only on very restrictive conditions. The introduction of a guest worker policy results in highly stratified rights to welfare, settlement, family formation and eventual citizenship.

Here too the role of nationality (division between EU/non-EU and first world/third world) determines the conditions of entry, access to welfare and options on offer. As we have seen, UK immigration policy has increasingly been constructed on the assumption that the enlarged EU, now including Bulgaria and Romania, will be sufficient to supply all its less-skilled labour needs. Only the skilled from the third world need apply.

Notes

[1] The average percentage of females among foreign nationals (662,390) allocated National Insurance numbers in 2005-06 was 45.8% but for Polish people (171,380) it was 40.9% and for Indian people (45,980) 36.9% (figures supplied to author by DWP).

[2] Since 1 April 2003, the Home Office has replaced ELR by two new forms of leave: humanitarian protection and discretionary leave. Humanitarian protection is granted to anyone who would, if removed, face in the country of return a serious risk to life or person arising from the death penalty or unlawful killing or torture, inhuman or degrading treatment or punishment. Discretionary leave may be granted to asylum applicants who are considered not to be in need of international protection or who are excluded from such protection but are allowed to remain for other reasons, for example because they have children or relationships in the UK.

[3] One of the main changes in the new rules is the introduction of a points system similar to that on entry to determine extension of the status after the initial two-year period. Previously it had only been stipulated that applicants had to show that they had made reasonable efforts to be economically active. There is some evidence that HSMP holders from

third world countries were experiencing difficulties in finding work commensurate to their qualifications due to racial discrimination.

[4] Thanks to Sue Lukes for guiding me through the complex maze of regulations about access to welfare.

[5] The emphasis on business and management was reinforced in April 2005 when the Masters of Business Administration (MBA) route was added. Having an MBA from one of the top 50 schools in the world automatically gives the applicant all the necessary points.

References

Anderson, B. (2000) *Doing the dirty work? The global politics of domestic labour*, London: Zed Press.

Anderson, B. (2006) *A very private business: Migration and domestic work*, COMPAS Working Paper 28, Oxford: University of Oxford.

Anderson, B. and Rogaly, B. (2005) *Forced labour and migration to the UK*, Oxford: COMPAS, University of Oxford, in collaboration with the Trades Union Congress.

Anderson, B., Ruhs, M., Rogaly, B. and Spencer, S. (2006) *Fair enough? Central and East European migrants in low-wage employment in the UK*, Oxford: COMPAS, University of Oxford.

BBC (2006) 'Sham marriages law breaches rights' http://news.bbc.co.uk/1/hi/uk/4894544.stm

Bloch, A. (2004) *Making it work. Refugee employment in the UK*, Working Paper 2, London: IPPR.

CAB (Citizens' Advice Bureaux) (2004) *Nowhere to turn – Cab evidence on the exploitation of migrant workers*, London: CAB.

Ceneda, S. (2003) *Women asylum seekers in the UK: A gender perspective*, London: Asylum Aid.

Cox, R. (2006) *The servant problem: Domestic employment in a global economy*, London: IB Tauris.

DRC (Development Research Centre) (2004) *Migration, globalisation and poverty: Temporary worker schemes in the UK: Impacts on pro-poor policy*, Workshop report (www.migrationdrc.org/news/reports/TWSworkshopreport1.pdf).

Dobrowolsky, A. and Jenson, J. (2005) 'Social investment perspectives and practices: a decade in British politics', in M. Powell, L. Bauld and K. Clarke (eds) *Social Policy Review 17*, Bristol: The Policy Press/Social Policy Association, pp 203-30.

Dumper, H. (2002) *Is it safe here? Refugee women's experience in the UK*, London: Refugee Action.

Dustmann, C., Fabri, F., Preston, I. and Wadsworth, J. (2003) *Labour market performance of immigrants in the UK labour market*, Online report 05/03, London: Home Office.

Duvell, F. and Jordan, B. (2003) 'Immigration control and the management of economic migration in the United Kingdom: organisational culture, implementation, enforcement and identity processes in public services', *Journal of Ethnic and Migration Studies*, vol 29, no 2, pp 299-336.

Eborrall, C. (2005) *The state of the social care workforce in England: Second annual report of the Topss England Workforce Intelligence Unit*, Leeds: Topss.

EOC (Equal Opportunities Commission) (2004) *Supporting parents and carers*, London: EOC.

Erel, U., Tomlinson, F., Sheibani, A., Kowarzik, U. and Jeffreys, S. (2004) *Women refugees: From volunteers to employers*, London: Institute of Working Lives.

Evans, Y., Herbert, J., Data, K., May, J., McIlwaine, C. and Wills, J. (2005) *Making the city work: Low paid employment in London*, London: Queen Mary, University of London.

Hardy, J. and Clark, N. (2005) 'EU enlargement, workers and migration: implications for trade unions in the UK and Poland', Global Unions Research Network International Workshop 'Trade Unions, Globalization and Development: Strengthening Rights and Capabilities of Workers', New Hamboro, Brazil, January.

Hochschild, A. (2000) 'Global care chains and emotional surplus value', in W. Hutton and A. Giddens (eds) *On the edge: Living with global capitalism*, London: Jonathan Cape, pp 130-46.

Home Office (2004) *Gender issues in the asylum claim*, London: Home Office.

Home Office (2005a) *Controlling our borders: How Britain can make migration work*, London: Home Office.

Home Office (2005b) *Control of immigration: Statistics United Kingdom 2005*, London: Home Office.

ICAR (Information Centre about Asylum and Refugees) (2006) *Women refugees and asylum seekers in the UK* (http://icar.org.uk/?lid=6395, 17/08/06).

Immigration and Borders Agency (2006) *Accession monitoring report May-June 2006*, London: Home Office (www.ind.homeoffice.gov.uk/aboutus/reports/accession_monitoring.html).

Kofman, E. (2002) 'Contemporary European migrations, civic stratification and citizenship', *Political Geography*, vol 21, no 8, pp 1035-54.

Kofman, E. (2004) 'Family-related migration: a critical review of European studies', *Journal of Ethnic and Migration Studies*, vol 30, no 2, pp 243-62.

Kofman, E. (2006) 'Migration, ethnicity and entitlements in European welfare regimes', in A. Guichon, I. Novikova and C. van den Anker (eds) *Women's social rights and entitlements*, London: Palgrave, pp 130-54.

Kofman, E. and Raghuram, P. (2006) 'Women and global labour market trends: incorporating the skilled', *Antipode*, vol 38, no 2, pp 282-303.

Kofman, E., Phizacklea, A., Raghuram, P. and Sales, R. (2000) *Gender and international migration in Europe: Employment, welfare and politics*, London: Routledge.

Kofman, E., Raghuram, P. and Merefield, M. (2005) *Gendered migrations: Towards gender sensitive policies in the UK*, Asylum and Migration Working Paper 6, London: Institute of Public Policy Research.

Lethbridge, J. (2005) *Care services in Europe*, London: International Public Services Research Unit.

Lutz, H. (1993) 'In between or bridging cultural gaps? Migrant women from Turkey as mediators', *New Community*, vol 19, no 3, pp 485-94.

McDowell, L. (2005) *Hard labour: The forgotten voices of Latvian migrant 'volunteer' workers*, London: UCL Press.

McGregor, J. (2006) '"Joining the BBC (British bottom cleaners)": Zimbabwean migrants and the UK care industry', Paper presented at RGS-IBG Conference, London, August/September.

Morris, L. (2002) *Managed migration: Civic stratification and rights*, London: Routledge.

Morris, L. (2004) *The control of rights: The rights of workers and asylum seekers under managed migration*, London: Joint Council for the Welfare of Immigrants.

Newcombe, E. (2004) *Temporary migration to the UK as an au pair: Cultural exchange or reproductive labour?*, Sussex Migration Working Paper 21, Falmer: University of Sussex.

Pandya, N. (2005) 'Where are the child carers?', *The Guardian*, 5 March, p 25.

Phizacklea, A. (ed) (1983) *One way ticket: Migration and female labour*, London: Routledge.

Pinkerton, C., MacLaughlan, G. and Salt, J. (2004) *Sizing the illegally resident population in the UK*, RDS 58/04, London: Home Office.

Raghuram, P. (2004) 'The difference that skills make: gender, family, migration and regulated labour markets', *Journal of Ethnic and Migration Studies*, vol 30, no 2, pp 303-22.

Raghuram, P. and Kofman, E. (2002) 'State labour markets and immigration: overseas doctors in the UK', *Environment and Planning A*, vol 34, pp 2071-89.

Refugee Council (1996) *Women refugees*, London: Refugee Council.

Roche, D. and Rankin, J. (2004) *Who cares? Building the social care workforce*, London: IPPR.

Salt, J. (2006) *International migration and the United Kingdom: Report of the United Kingdom SOPEMI correspondent to the OECD 2006*, London: Migration Research Unit (www.geog.ucl.ac.uk/mru/publications. htm).

Sassen, S. (2000) 'Women's burden: counter-geographies of globalization and the feminization of survival', *Journal of International Affairs*, vol 53, no 2, pp 503-24.

Seddon, D. (2006) *Immigration, nationality and refugee law handbook*, London: Joint Council for the Welfare of Immigrants.

Shearer Demir, J. (2003) *The trafficking of women for sexual exploitation: A gender-based and well-founded fear of persecution?*, New Issues in Refugee Research Working Paper No 80, Geneva: UNHCR.

Simon, A. and Owen, C. (2005) 'Using the Labour Force Survey to map the care workforce', *Labour Market Trends*, May, pp 201-8.

Skrivankova, K. (2006) *Trafficking for forced labour: UK country report*, London: Anti-Slavery International.

SOPEMI (2006) *International migration outlook*, Paris: OECD.

Status of Women Canada (2003) 'Gender-based analysis: a guide for policy-making', (revised edition, 1998) Ottawa (www.swc-cfc.gc.ca/pubs/gbaguide/index_e.html).

Struder, I. (2002) *Migrant self-employment in a European global city: The importance of gendered power relations and performance of belonging of Turkish women in London*, Research Paper 74, London: Department of Geography, London School of Economics and Political Science.

Ungerson, C. (2003) 'Commodified care work in European labour markets', *European Societies*, vol 5, no 4, pp 377-96.

Ungerson, C. (2005) 'Gender, labour markets and care work in the five European funding regimes', in B. Pfau-Effinger and B. Geissler (eds) *Care and social integration in European societies*, Bristol: The Policy Press, pp 49-72.

van den Anker, C. (2003) 'Trafficking in the UK: A country report for the NEWR workshop', Amsterdam, April.

Walter, B. (2000) *Outsiders insiders: Whiteness, place and Irish women*, London: Routledge.

Williams, F. (2003) 'Rethinking care in social policy', Paper presented at the annual conference of the Finnish Social Policy Association, 24 October, Joennsu.

Winkelman-Gleed, A. (2006) *Migrant nurses: Motivation, integration and contribution*, Oxford: Radcliffe Publishing.

Yuval-Davis, N., Anthias, F. and Kofman, E. (2005) 'Secure borders and safe haven: the gendered politics of belonging beyond social cohesion', *Ethnic and Racial Studies*, vol 28, no 3, pp 313-35.

FOURTEEN

Migration, older people and social policy

Anthony M. Warnes

This chapter focuses on the challenges that older migrants present to established principles and systems of social welfare. It features the elaboration of policies for the welfare of foreign migrants since the mid-20th century in Europe, and more specifically the UK. The particular focus is on the circumstances of older people. Migration policy (or more precisely immigration policy) is very often seen as separate from social policy, while several important welfare measures, particularly those founded on social insurance and 'intergenerational solidarity' principles, implicitly presume a 'closed' or isolated national population and are confused by arrivals and departures. The disjunction creates a systemic tension between migration and social policies, which for half a century has been tackled by intricate special arrangements, as it were, to bridge the gaps: this chapter discusses whether this piecemeal, reactive approach is sustainable or needs to be replaced with more fundamental reform.

The chapter has five sections. It begins with further discussion of the challenges that large numbers of immigrants *and emigrants* raise for the established systems of state-supported and managed welfare in Western European countries. The second section describes the major types of 'older foreign migrants', showing that they are more diverse than is popularly understood, and specifies the kinds of challenges that they raise for established social policy. The third section is a selective guide to recent research about older migrants, and summarises the latest evidence about the number of UK state pensioners who are resident in foreign countries. The fourth section turns to the processes by which healthcare and welfare policies are 'harmonised' among the member nations of the European Union (EU), and evaluates the potential of current policies for achieving the required radical reform. The final section argues that the pressures for reform in certain underlying principles of 'social insurance' and the bases of entitlement will continue to grow, and require new kinds of 'welfare contract' for migrants of different ages.

Social welfare policies for migrants: the special influences

In states with popularly-elected democratic governments, social welfare policies in their broadest guise are generally a compromise between materialist and humanitarian ambitions. The parallel influences have been most evident in the elaboration of state educational policies since the last quarter of the 19th century. The enormous expansion of compulsory educational provision for each young person has been driven by both 'economic competitiveness' and 'individual welfare' concerns, but inculcating job skills (and in recent years civil behaviour) have probably carried more weight than transmitting the values and benefits of a 'liberal education'. Similarly, among the many forces that led to the elaboration of state-subsidised health and personal social services, the concern to nurture stronger and more productive workers and soldiers has been enduring (it was explicit during and after the First World War). The 'generative' instinct to be concerned for the health and welfare of the population, particularly children, has timelessly jostled for influence with dispassionate calculations of the population's capacity as a factor of production. Similar considerations partly explain why child social work and paediatrics attract far more support and prestige than the care and treatment of sick and frail older people.

Sometimes the interests of capital are dominant, at other times welfare concerns prevail, and occasionally policy has switched abruptly between the two, as in the US during the deep 1930s depression, when around 14 million workers lost their jobs, and "huddled figures shuffling despondently in breadlines or at soup kitchens testified to destitution and suffering to an extent unknown in American history" (Trattner, 1974, p 228). President Hoover's attitude was caricatured in December 1930, when he approved a congressional appropriation of $45 million to feed stricken livestock in Arkansas, but opposed $25 million to feed starving farmers and their families (Nye and Morpugo, 1955, p 660; Trattner, 1974, p 231). A radical turnaround was required and came with the New Deal programmes. The large waves of foreign immigrants that entered the richest countries of the world during the second half of the last century and that continue today present equally serious challenges, if not from the scale of destitution and family disruption, but in exposing the obsolescence of hallowed welfare principles and delivery mechanisms. The challenges arise not only from the generally disadvantaged circumstances of immigrants, and the insults many experience through ignorance and prejudice, but also, if less obviously, from the welfare expectations of those who leave the country.

The most general difficulty that migrants raise for social policy is that their biographies are inconsistent with several assumptions of social insurance schemes and welfare programmes, particularly so with older migrants. The explicit or implicit logic of collective insurance is 'solidarity', that support for above-average spending on those who are temporarily sick, disadvantaged, or old and frail, is acceptable if the same support is certain when those making the insurance contributions are in need. The schemes also generally depend on the transfer through time of risks and responsibility, or in other words on an intergenerational contract. Heavy pensions and healthcare spending on older people are supported, even in the US, not only because of a widely shared humanitarian sympathy ('it is the right thing to do'), but also as insurance for one's own old age.

Two very different groups of migrants affront the logic and the underlying social and political contracts. The most evident, as frequently sensationalised by those sections of the mass media that happily fan xenophobia, is when young working-age 'foreigners' migrate to a country but do not support themselves or their dependants, and seek income, housing, educational and healthcare benefits. The new migrant has not contributed to general taxation or to a 'social insurance fund', and can be a heavy charge. The grossest offenders to the territorial bounds of state welfare are disparaged as 'welfare or benefits tourists'. While we applaud people who intelligently and energetically manage their own and their family's financial affairs and welfare, when newcomers maximise their 'take' of benefits funded from general taxation, admiration turns to scorn.

When European social insurance schemes were designed and established during the late 19th and early 20th centuries, the assumption was of a captured national population or a 'closed system'. As most evident in Germany, many were funded and organised through full-time employed male 'breadwinners' – support for spouses and children, and for the couple in retirement, was channelled through the male subscriber. Such arrangements partly explain the incompatibility of continental European welfare systems with social protection for immigrant labourers, who consequently were designated as guest workers, expected to stay only temporarily, and *not* brought into the mainstream welfare system (Bolzman et al, 2004).

In comparison to the continental models, British social welfare has been less structured around insurances for specific purposes with clearly specified beneficiaries. The National Insurance scheme relies on pay-as-you-go funding (effectively through a payroll tax) for unemployment, maternity, sickness, dependants' and old-age benefits, while a wide range of housing-related benefits derive from a 'local resident' criterion, as for entitlement to social (state-subsidised) housing and specialist accommodation for older people. Until recently, indeed, being a resident of the UK has been sufficient in practice (if not *de jure*) to be accepted on the electoral register, and to access state educational provision and most National Health Services. As the 'value' of state welfare has increased, so the eligibility rules have tightened. Little more than half a century ago in the UK, every native of a Commonwealth country could hold a British passport and had full citizenship rights; now the presumption is that any non-EU citizen is subject to immigration restrictions and welfare exclusion.

The recent expansion of the EU has led to an increase in migration from the new Eastern European member states to Britain. The entitlements of citizens from the eight accession states (A8 nationals) in 2004 are restricted, and citizens of the two states that joined in 2007 (A2 nationals) have limited working rights. While the majority of Eastern European migrants obtain employment and accommodation, a minority become homeless. Many homelessness organisations, especially in London, have reported an increase in clients from A8 countries, and find it difficult to support them for language reasons and because they are not entitled to Housing Benefit. Because Housing Benefit will not pay the fees, A8 rough sleepers cannot be taken into hostels (Homeless Link, 2007). The result is that the immense work that has been done since the early 1990s to reduce rough sleeping in London (since 1997 to meet Tony Blair's target of a two-thirds reduction) has been put aside, one hopes temporarily. Certain London boroughs, which administer Housing Benefit, have argued that the A8 nationals should not be included in their rough-sleeper counts. The Department for Communities and Local Government has responded: "Following representation from some London Boroughs that inclusion in the national estimate of rough sleepers who do not have recourse to funds (mainly A8 nationals) and therefore cannot be supported and moved off the streets is misleading, we would like to monitor the numbers in this group separately" (Hilditch, 2007; Wearn, 2007). Although parochial and probably a temporary absurdity, the episode illustrates the harm that arises when migration and social policies and procedures are not mutually informed.

The second non-compliant group are older people who emigrate in and for retirement, especially to less rich countries. Consider the situation of Spain. Clearly it is not reasonable to expect the Spanish government and people to fund the same income, healthcare and personal social services entitlements that Northern European retired migrants have in their own countries. Formulating appropriate welfare policies and social protection for retirement migrants is frustrated by the equivocal residential status of many cross-border movers within the EU. There are fine gradations between the long-stay (or residential) tourist, the seasonal migrant and the 'totally displaced' migrant. Some movers change their residential behaviour every year. As has been shown of Canadian 'snowbirds', who spend the winter in Florida or Arizona, their seasonal migrations are explicitly timed to retain eligibility for Canadian health and welfare benefits (Longino et al, 1991). By choreographing their entitlements, resources and insurances in different countries, most retirement migrants manage their affairs well and achieve their overall objective, to raise the quality of their life, but some are casualties of income loss, financial abuse, bereavement or the onset of severe ill health (Betty and Cahill, 1999; Hardill et al, 2005). Well-established associations of British pensioners in Australia, Canada, New Zealand and South Africa, all associated in the World Alliance of British Expatriate Pensioners, lobby hard for the same benefits as received by those resident in the UK, such as inflation adjustments to their payments (see http://wabep0.tripod.com/).

Another special factor that disturbs the normal relationship between the resident and state welfare is that most international migrants have cultural, religious and language differences from the host population, and these readily excite prejudice and xenophobia. In its coarsest manifestations, as in sensationalist newspapers, the material *and* welfare interests of the majority, the indigenous population, are couched as directly opposed to those of migrants. Policies towards immigrants can quickly switch, from encouragement to exclusion and even repatriation (as with those of Chinese and Pacific Islands origins from Australia between 1900 and 1950). It is clear that in the range of possible social policies for migrants, at one extreme governments decide that their welfare is of no account, and they either repatriate and exclude or ignore them (a recent instance being the *de facto* expulsion of white farmers from Zimbabwe). No government has ever enacted the other extreme, that a newly arrived migrant is entitled to all the benefits and subsidised services available to the host population.

Principal groups of older migrants and their migrations

There are in essence two categories of older migrants, those who migrated in early adulthood and have reached old age at their destinations, and those who move to another country in old age. The former, the labour migrants who formed the first mass flows into Northern Europe from the 1950s, whatever their and their employers' original intentions, stayed and aged in the destination countries. Many came from depressed rural areas and had relatively little education and few formal or technical job skills. They include some of the most disadvantaged and socially excluded of Western Europe's older people (Chau and Yu, 2000; Yu, 2000; Brockmann and Fisher, 2001; Silveira and Allebeck, 2001; Burholt, 2004a, 2004b). They are markedly heterogeneous, not just by origin and cultural and ethnic characteristics, but also in the extent to which they have raised children and formed social networks in the adopted country; both condition their ability to develop satisfying roles when no longer in work and, should their abilities decline, to turn to informal family and community support (Silveira and Allebeck, 2001). There is also considerable diversity in their knowledge of, entitlements to, and utilisation of, state income, social housing, social service and healthcare benefits and services.

The second broad category, retirement migrants, are also diverse but generally more affluent and socially advantaged, and they include many of the most active and innovative of the latest cohorts of Europe's older people (King et al, 2000; Gustafson, 2001). The cohort has attracted the label the 'baby boomers' and the assertions that they are less family-oriented and more concerned with 'quality of life' than their predecessors (Giddens, 1991). In Europe the variable histories of fertility and 'modernisation' has reduced the term's validity and slowed its adoption. Certainly some international retirement migrants fashion new lifestyles, activities, roles and patterns of social participation in what they themselves perceive as positive approaches to old age (O'Reilly 2000a, 2000b; Huber and O'Reilly, 2004; Friedrich et al, 2005). Like all international migrants, they are also taking risks, by moving to countries with different languages, customs, institutions and social welfare and healthcare policies (Ackers and Dwyer, 2004). One reason for giving close attention to their situation is that little is yet known about how the decrements of old age – in vigour, health, income and social networks – are shaped by, and shape, people's living arrangements in an overseas country.

Alongside the two core groups, there are other older migrants about whom much less is known. The most apparent are the labour migrants who return to their native countries when they cease work (Cerase, 1974; Rodríguez and Egea, 2006). 'Return migrants' are themselves diverse, and their migrations constitute a wide continuum that straddles internal and international moves. Only a few of these moves have attracted systematic study and published accounts (King, 1986; Byron and Condon, 1996; Malcolm, 1996; Klinthall, 2006).

Social security and insurance agencies in Germany, the US and the UK publish statistics on the number of their clients receiving old-age benefits that are resident in other countries. From this indirect evidence, it is apparent that other types of migration in later life are more voluminous who either 'amenity-led' or 'return' retirement migration (Warnes, 2001). For both the Germans and the British, the largest overseas beneficiary populations are in the US, Canada and Australia. The clear inference is that there are substantial flows of family-joining migrants who follow their children's earlier migrations, and that their dispersion is influenced by long-established colonial, economic and overseas settlement connections. While the processes and consequences of family-joining migrations have been studied among recent intercontinental labour migrants into Europe and North America (Moon and Pearl, 1991; Pourat et al, 1999; Min et al, 2005), the comparable flows out of North West Europe have been neglected.

Research on migration and older migrants

Migration studies have burgeoned in recent years, and there are now probably more European researchers in the field than in either social gerontology or social policy. One of the largest multidisciplinary social science research programmes supported by the European Commission, International Migration, Integration and Social Cohesion (IMISCOE, see www.imiscoe.org/) involves 400 researchers from 22 European research institutes, and has a strong policy and practice orientation. Its principal academic and policy concerns are with labour migration and migrants, whether highly or low skilled. Another substantial Sixth Framework European Commission R&D (research and development) project has the objective of a major improvement in the quality, coverage and comparability of international migration data in Europe (Poulain et al, 2006). The associated issues of integration and community relations have also gained urgency and prominence (Joppke and Morawaska, 2003; Joppke, 2006).

Studies of older international migrants have proliferated since the mid-1990s and taken many forms. Two recent collections in *Ageing & Society* (vol 24, part 3, May 2004) and the *Journal of Ethnic and Migration Studies* (vol 32, part 8, September 2006) exemplify the field (Warnes et al, 2004; Warnes and Williams, 2006). One strand that focuses on 'retirement migration' has substantial antecedents, for *internal* retirement moves have featured in social science teaching and research for a generation, even in US regional economics, because the vigorous promotion of a 'retirement role' in low population density and stagnant 'sunbelt' counties has proven effective for economic regeneration (Serow and Haas, 1992). Recent publications have included the first substantial studies of retirement migration to overseas countries by US citizens (Banks, 2004; Migration Policy Institute, 2006; Sunil et al, 2007: forthcoming), impressive collections by Spanish researchers (for example, Rodríguez et al, 2006), and the first signs of a research literature on the phenomenon in South East Asia (Jones, 2006; Shinozaki, 2006).

Another strand has focused on the disadvantage and discrimination experienced by low-skilled labour migrants who have 'aged in place'. Such studies merge imperceptibly with the voluminous research on the socioeconomic circumstances and health of minority ethnic groups. Even 20 years ago in several European countries, there were reports of the particular health risk factors and problems of access to healthcare services of individual ethnic groups. Sandra Torres's (2001, 2004, 2006) critique has been widely noted. She identified a perverse sequence in Sweden by which the social services and healthcare agencies moved from unpardonable ignorance and neglect of the distinctive needs of older migrants to an over-reaction that problematised all such groups because they are migrants and 'other'. Such simplicities arise in many countries through a lack of detailed information about different groups, which reflects the great difficulty and cost of conducting research on multiple groups, with different languages. It is welcome when older migrants attract the attention of researchers, as a recent spate of German studies suggests, and publications from other Northern European countries confirm (for details see Warnes and Williams, 2006), but simply inventorying needs is only the beginning. Developing appropriate and effective welfare and service responses requires collaboration between the migrant group and its associations (that are best informed about their needs) and the public service agencies (that have the resources and professional expertise). Detailed R&D work is still comparatively rare in the UK, but several charitable foundations have funded specialist studies (for example, Chau, 2007), and the Policy Research Institute on Ageing and Ethnicity (PRIAE) conducts research and policy analysis in the field (see www.priae.org/). Research of special relevance to social policy has analysed the relationship between 'European citizenship' and national social security entitlements, as well as disputes between claimants and the agencies, which in turn have stimulated measures that increase the 'portability' of entitlements (Ackers and Dwyer, 2002, 2004; Dwyer, 2005; Dwyer and Papadimitriou, 2006).

Rising number of older migrants

Considerable efforts are being made in national statistical offices to improve and standardise data on international migration and foreign residents, but, except for those in North West European countries with 'continuous population registers', the available enumerations are partial, while the registers provide little beyond age, sex, nativity, ethnicity and the household of residence. It has, however, been possible to track the growth since the 1980s of older UK citizens resident in overseas countries to make comparisons with equivalent data for Germany and the US (Warnes, 2001). Early in 2006, the number of UK 'state pensioners' who received their payments at addresses in other countries exceeded one million. More precisely, the number paid at overseas addresses increased from 679,800 in March 1995 to 996,100 in March 2005, and to 1,025,600 on 7 January 2006. Partly reflecting the age difference in the eligibility age for a State Pension (60 years for women, and 65 for men), the majority (61.8%) of the beneficiaries were women. The annual growth rate during 1995-2005 was 3.9%; the rate for men (4.2%) was higher than that for women (3.7%).

As a proportion of all UK state pensioners, the overseas beneficiaries increased from 6.6% in 1995 to 8.6% in 2005 (see Figure 14.1). The male percentage was higher than the female percentage, especially in the early years of the review period. In 1995, men living abroad made up 7.2% of all male state pensioners, and women recipients formed 6.3% of the total. By 2005, the equivalent percentages were 9.0% and 8.4%. UK pensioners who live overseas include both young, active retiree couples and, a generally older group, widows and widowers living near or with children, or other relatives and friends. The balance between the two groups is unclear.

UK state pensioners are scattered through 230 overseas countries (and the Channel Islands and the Isle of Man) but are also highly concentrated in a few. In 2005, one quarter of the recipients abroad were in Australia, nearly one fifth in Canada, one sixth in the US, and over one tenth in

Figure 14.1: Percentage of UK state pensioners living overseas

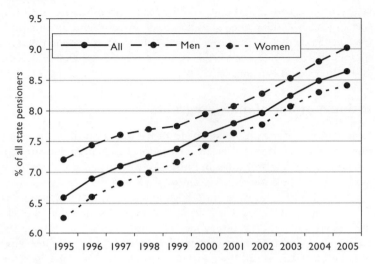

the Republic of Ireland. Those four countries accounted for exactly two thirds (66.6%) of the total. There were more than 10,000 recipients in only 11 countries, and more than 1,000 beneficiaries in only 36 countries (and in both Guernsey and Jersey). Table 14.1 displays the average annual growth rates in the number of UK state pensioners in the 20 countries with more than 4,000 recipients in 2005. The highest annual growth rate was in Nigeria, and the next highest in Sweden (15.4%) and in France and Spain (both with 9.8%). Four countries had decreases, the highest negative rate being in Zimbabwe (–4.6%), followed by Poland (–3.1%).

Previous analysis found differential growth rates in several country groups during the 1990s (Warnes, 2001). In particular, among the most popular destinations, the rates of growth were high to Mediterranean countries and low to Australia, Canada, New Zealand and South Africa. This reflects the changing overseas connections of the population, and the rising enthusiasm for 'amenity-seeking' retirement migrations to countries with warmer and brighter winters. The analysis is pursued in Table 14.2, which identifies four distinctive country groups. Between 1995 and 2005, the number of UK state pensioners in seven Southern European countries increased on average by 8.5% a year, whereas the increase in the number in Australia, Canada, New Zealand and South

Table 14.1: Numbers and growth rates of UK state pensioners in overseas countries (March 2005)

Country	Number (2005) (000s)	Share (2005) (%)	% increase (1995-2005)	Growth rate (1995-2005) %	Growth rate (1995-2005) Rank	Female: male ratio (2005)
Australia	239.7	24.1	38.2	3.3	23	1.42
Canada	149.9	15.0	22.2	2.0	28	1.58
US	123.9	12.4	44.7	3.8	18	1.88
Ireland	97.7	9.8	37.2	3.2	24	1.70
Spain	70.0	7.0	153.6	9.8	4	1.52
New Zealand	43.9	4.4	45.8	3.8	17	1.31
South Africa	37.6	3.8	19.0	1.8	31	1.59
Germany	32.0	3.2	61.6	4.9	15	2.33
Italy	31.4	3.2	79.4	6.0	13	1.45
France	30.5	3.1	154.2	9.8	3	1.44
Jamaica	21.7	2.2	19.9	1.8	30	1.33
Cyprus	9.8	1.0	117.8	8.1	8	1.45
Netherlands	7.1	0.7	42.0	3.6	20	1.77
Portugal	5.7	0.6	103.6	7.4	11	1.38
Pakistan	5.2	0.5	−18.8	−2.1	34	1.36
Austria	4.7	0.5	27.0	2.4	27	3.18
Barbados	4.6	0.5	109.1	7.7	10	1.04
Switzerland	4.6	0.5	84.0	6.3	12	1.71
Belgium	4.4	0.4	4.8	0.5	32	1.59
India	4.2	0.4	20.0	1.8	29	1.00

Notes: The tabulation is restricted to the 20 destination countries with at least 4,000 clients in 2005. The 'share' is the percentage of all customers abroad. The 'growth rate' is the average annual compound growth rate over the 10 years.

Source: DWP, International Pensions Centre, Newcastle-upon-Tyne, personal communication

Africa was only 2.8%. An even higher growth rate (10.9%) applied to Denmark, Norway and Sweden. Although a number of Caribbean islands have seen growing caseloads, and in January 2006 there were 23,021 recipients in Jamaica, the growth rate (2.8%) among six Caribbean countries was below the rate for all overseas destinations.

Table 14.2: Thousands of UK state pensioners in four country groups, the US and Ireland, growth statistics and the sex ratio (March 2005)

Country group	Denmark, Norway, Sweden	Southern Europe	Caribbean	Australia, Canada, Republic of South Africa, New Zealand	US	Ireland
Measure (000's)						
1995						
Both sexes	1.7	67.8	23.8	357.9	85.6	71.2
Men	(0.5)	(27.2)	(10.3)	(139.6)	(29.5)	(26.4)
Women	(1.1)	(40.5)	(13.6)	(218.3)	(56.2)	(44.7)
2000						
Both sexes	2.9	95.6	30.2	419.6	107	84.1
Men	(0.9)	(38.5)	(13.1)	(166.3)	(36.1)	(31.2)
Women	(1.9)	(56.9)	(17)	(253.3)	(70.9)	(52.9)

continued ...

Table 14.2 (continued)

Country group	Denmark, Norway, Sweden	Southern Europe	Caribbean	Australia, Canada, Republic of South Africa, New Zealand	US	Ireland
2005						
Both sexes	4.8	153.8	31.5	471.1	123.9	97.7
Men	(1.9)	(62.2)	(14.1)	(190.4)	(43)	(36.2)
Women	(2.9)	(91.6)	(17.4)	(280.8)	(80.9)	(61.5)
Increase 1995-2005 (%)	182.4	126.8	32.4	31.6	44.7	37.2
Mean annual % increase	10.9	8.5	2.8	2.8	3.8	3.8
Female:male ratio						
1995	2.20	1.49	1.32	1.56	1.91	1.69
2000	2.11	1.48	1.30	1.52	1.96	1.70
2005	1.53	1.47	1.23	1.47	1.88	1.70

Notes: The country groups in the first four columns respectively are: A. Denmark, Norway and Sweden. B. Cyprus, France, Greece, Italy, Malta, Portugal and Spain. C. Barbados, Dominican Republic, Grenada, Jamaica, St Lucia and Trinidad and Tobago. D. Australia, Canada, New Zealand and South Africa. The tabulation includes only countries with at least 1,000 clients in 2005.

Source: Department for Work and Pensions, International Pensions Centre, Newcastle-upon-Tyne, personal communication.

European Union social protection policies and procedures for migrants

Since the foundation of the EU in the 1952 European Coal and Steel Community and the 1958 Treaty of Rome, the principle of the 'free movement' of labour has been a cornerstone of its economic and industrial policies. By widening labour markets, it was known that rigidities in labour supply would be eroded and wages reduced, to the benefit of the national and European economies. Several contradictions have arisen, however, between 'free movement' and the principle that workers from any member state (and from 'third' countries if granted residence) are treated equally throughout the Union. Many if not most migrants bring dependants such as non-working spouses or partners and school-age children. Over time, other dependent relationships and complicated situations of partial and ex-dependency form, as with unemployed young adult children, divorced or estranged spouses and partners, and frail elderly parents. Consider just one scenario, of a young person aged 21 who was educated and 'socialised' in country A but is long-term unemployed and estranged from her or his parents. The parents and the adult child still live and work in country A but all are citizens of country B. Which nation's social security administration has a responsibility to provide income and housing benefits to the young person, A or B? Is this dependent on national citizenship, bilateral agreements between member states, or resolved by reference to EU agreements or citizenship principles?

Overcoming these cracks in the welfare system has required the coordination of state social insurance arrangements, as for the support of sick and injured migrant workers, and been partially achieved through innumerable individual settlements. Possibly one of the least noticed contributions to the promotion of migrants' welfare is the work of the international divisions of national social security agencies. Their core task is to negotiate their respective contributions to funding the benefits of a 'customer' who has made contributions to schemes in two or more nations. Hundreds of bilateral agreements have been made, and wider consortia formed, as with the Southern Cross Group that links Australia's social security system with those in 14 countries (see www.southern-cross-group.org/socialsecurity/bilateral.html). The principles and benefits to international migrants are explained on the websites of the major agencies (for example, www.ssa.gov/international/; www.hmrc.gov.uk/international/treaties1.htm; www.welfare.ie/schemes/employer/ssa.html). Details of the process and the achievements have been outlined in previous papers (King et al, 2000, chapter 7; Warnes, 1998, 2002).

As the decades have passed and welfare entitlements have been elaborated, the relative exclusion and vulnerability of labour migrants and their dependants have increasingly been exposed. The surge in and new forms of international migration since the 1960s, which manifest more intense global mobility, have exacerbated these limitations of late industrial systems of social protection. The ageing of labour migrants into retirement and of their children into adulthood, new large inflows of economic migrants, refugees and asylum seekers, the growing assertion of 'multiple identities and place affiliations' and the enlargement of the EU by the accession of countries with different welfare traditions and entitlements have made it imperative that the Union faces the paradoxes and inequities of co-extant European and national citizenship (Warnes, 1998; Joppke, 1999). So it is that over at least two decades, especially through the Maastricht, Amsterdam, Cologne, Lisbon and Nice summits, various social 'charters', 'codes' and 'policy agendas' have been elaborated. The process has exposed both tensions among the member states and increasingly obvious and malign contradictions between EU ideals, proclamations and actuality.

Progress among the EU member nations in developing the cross-border portability of social security rights has not until recently extended, except in very limited respects, to healthcare entitlements, even with the inception of EU citizenship. A combination of prudence and professional conservatism prevented the mutual recognition of national credentials to practise medicine, nursing and the allied professions, and there were only minimal concessions to the pan-European mission (Busse et al, 2002). By a European Council Regulation in June 1971 on the application of social security schemes, mechanisms were established by which "employed persons, self-employed persons and members of their families moving within the Community" could obtain healthcare in another member state, but only of two limited kinds:

> *Occasional care:* when residing temporarily in another member state, a person is entitled to care becoming necessary during their stay. To prove his/her entitlement in the home state, the patient should submit an E111 form in the host state (now replaced by the European Health Insurance Card – EHIC).

Planned care: patients moving to another member state specifically to obtain care need to gain prior authorisation from their competent institution in their home state. This authorisation, certified by an E112 form, must be given if the treatment is covered at home but cannot be provided there within medically justifiable time limits. Under these rules for coordination, the patient is treated in the host state (Bertinato et al, 2005, p 7).

The second provision has principally benefited the citizens of the Southern European countries (and Luxembourg) that have less comprehensive specialist medical services than the large, Northern countries. The former, the entitlement to 'emergency care', has reassured millions of tourists to the Mediterranean countries, and conditioned the strategies and decisions of Northern Europeans who retire to the south. They have been faced with a dilemma, whether to rely on the E111, or now the EHIC, entitlement and private health insurance, and to retain their full access rights to national healthcare services in their country of origin, or to declare themselves as permanent residents in their country of choice, become entitled to the local healthcare system (but also pay taxes), and thereby lose such entitlement in their country of origin.

As EU policy statements claim:

> ... high-quality health services are a priority issue for European citizens. Rights to healthcare are recognised in the Charter of Fundamental Rights, and health systems and health policies across the EU are becoming more interconnected than ever in the past. This is due to many factors, including the movement of patients and professionals (facilitated by rulings of the European Court of Justice), common public expectations across Europe, the dissemination of new medical technologies and techniques through information technology, and the forthcoming enlargement of the Union. This increased interconnection raises many health policy issues, including quality and access in cross-border care; information requirements for patients, health professionals and policy-makers; the scope for cooperation on health matters; and how to reconcile national policies with European obligations in general. (DG-HCP, 2006)

The situation changed dramatically in 1998 with two linked rulings by the European Court of Justice that patients could use internal market provisions to gain access to healthcare in other member states. As a consequence, the European Commission began to address the issue of patient mobility. The increasing reliance of the richer EU member states on medical staff trained in other countries has ignited the harmonisation of not only practitioners' credentials and care and treatment standards but also, to a degree, healthcare provision and entitlements. In July 2004, a 'high-level group' started work on practical aspects of collaboration between the member states' health services and medical care.

In 2006, the European Commission launched a broad public consultation on cross-border healthcare and cooperation between the health systems of the member states (DG-HCP, 2006). On the basis of the results, in November, European health ministers held a 'first round table discussion on health services' and specifically addressed: where greater legal certainty is required to facilitate cross-border healthcare in practice; areas where European action can support member states; what tools would be appropriate to tackle these issues; and the current impact of cross-border healthcare on accessibility, quality and financial sustainability of healthcare systems, for both 'sending' and 'receiving' countries. The Commission will put forward specific proposals during 2007.

Conclusion

Several social and economic changes during the opening years of the present century have brought immigration and community relations policies to the forefront of domestic politics in all major European countries. Practically every European is conscious of the criminal outrages committed by jihad terrorism since 2001, and of a new assertiveness among the millions of Muslim European residents of their religious and cultural identities. The ardent debates about the relative good sense of multiculturalism or of integration touch on major and minor aspects of quotidian life, from schooling to the allowable variations in corporate uniforms, and are now the main influence on migration policy. There are, however, several other pressing influences, not least of which is concern about low fertility and the near prospect of falling national populations. Some argue on economic grounds that we should encourage immigration to 'replace' the missing births; others argue that the arithmetic does not work, or that the 'social costs' are intolerable.

Furthermore, aggressive competition and deregulation in the airline industry continues to reduce the real cost of international travel, particularly within and between European countries, and this has awkwardly coincided with a radical enlargement of the EU. European political establishments are by and large keen for Eastern European countries to join, but their electorates deeply question the good sense of expanding the single labour market and the principle of free cross-border movement. There are also new pressures from affluent retirement migrants. Dutch retirees resident in Southern Europe have lobbied their government for the entitlements to medical care and subsidised and specialised housing provided in the Netherlands; they argue that the Mediterranean climate is healthier, reducing their need for medical care, and that it is cheaper to employ nursing home and care home staff in Southern Europe. British retirees in Spain, partly through Age Concern España and Help the Aged, have lobbied to be entitled to NHS care without delay or qualification if they return to the UK. Across North West Europe, migration policies are also influenced by the unexpectedly long period of strong economic growth and full employment, and heightened concern about competition from India and East Asian countries.

This constellation of factors has brought the debate about immigration and the change in Europe's population composition into the open. For decades, most mainstream politicians preferred not to engage with these difficult and volatile issues. Commercial voices in favour of managed labour immigration have considerable influence on central government and contest those who advocate minimal migration, such as Migration Watch. There are many signs of radical re-thinking in European governments. Quite unexpectedly, the Foreign and Commonwealth Office in London commissioned a major study of British citizens living abroad. As the quote below indicates, the resulting report well summarises the rationale:

> The UK government should follow the lead of several other countries and engage more with its diaspora. Such engagement would allow the UK to harness the potential of Britons living abroad to promote trade and investment links, develop overseas knowledge networks, and act as cultural ambassadors. More should also be done to promote the political participation of Britons living abroad and to make the most of returning Britons ... and to devise fair and workable rules on how long and under what conditions a Briton living abroad is entitled to British public services.

Such provision will not only ensure that those who are entitled to benefits receive them but will also help minimise the destitution experienced by some Britons living abroad who fall between the gaps of national entitlements. (Sriskandarajah and Drew, 2006, p x)

The integration of economic and welfare concerns and goals in this summary are exemplary. It is an invitation to social policy analysts to engage directly in questions of the welfare of immigrants and emigrants. The brief earlier reference to the erosion of 15 years' progress in tackling rough sleeping in London, through an unfortunate conjunction of mild paranoia about unemployed Romanian and Bulgarian migrants and narrow local government accounting, exemplifies a broader and growing challenge for social policy. There is every chance that the pace of social, economic and demographic change will be faster in the next few decades than in the last, and that an abiding element will be substantial international migration. As average living and welfare standards rise, partly through the contributions of international migrants, the case for integrating migration and social policy is strong. Maybe the felt injustices of both British retirement migrants in Southern Europe and of exploited labour migrants in our cities have, during the first decade of this century, combined to make social policy for migrants a priority.

Acknowledgements

The author thanks Helen Kelly and Jim Rynn of the International Pensions Centre, Newcastle-upon-Tyne, for their help and technical advice with the UK overseas pension data. The analysis and interpretation of these data are my own, and not those of the International Pensions Centre.

References

Ackers, L. and Dwyer, P. (2002) *Senior citizenship? Retirement, migration and welfare in the European Union*, Bristol: The Policy Press.

Ackers, L. and Dwyer, P. (2004) 'Fixed laws, fluid lives: the citizenship status of post-retirement migrants in the European Union, *Ageing & Society*, vol 24, no 3, pp 451-75.

Banks, S. (2004) 'Identity narratives by American and Canadian retirees in Mexico', *Journal of Cross-Cultural Gerontology*, vol 19, no 4, pp 361-81.

Bertinato, L., Busse, R., Fahy, N., Legido-Quigley, H., McKee, M., Palm, W., Passarani, I. and Ronfini, F. (2005) *Cross-border health care in Europe*, Policy brief, Copenhagen: WHO Regional Office for Europe.

Betty, C. and Cahill, M. (1999) 'British expatriates' experience of health and social services on the Costa del Sol', in F. Anthias and G. Lazaridis (eds) *Into the margins: Migration and social exclusion in Southern Europe*, Aldershot: Avebury, pp 83-113.

Bolzman, C., Poncioni-Derigo, R., Vial, M. and Fibbi, R. (2004) 'Older labour migrants' well being in Europe: the case of Switzerland, *Ageing & Society*, vol 24, no 3, pp 411-29.

Brockmann, M. and Fisher, M. (2001) 'Older migrants and social care in Austria', *Journal of European Social Policy*, vol 11, no 4, pp 353-62.

Burholt, V. (2004a) 'Transnationalism, economic transfers and families' ties: inter-continental contacts of older Gujaratis, Punjabis and Sylhetis in Birmingham with families abroad', *Ethnic and Racial Studies*, vol 27, no 5, pp 800-29.

Burholt, V. (2004b) 'The settlement patterns and residential histories of older Gujaratis, Punjabis and Sylhetis in Birmingham, England', *Ageing & Society*, vol 24, no 3, pp 383-410.

Busse, R., Drews, M. and Wismar, M. (2002) 'Consumer choice of healthcare services across borders', in R. Busse, M. Wismar and P. Berman (eds) *The European Union and health services – The impact of the Single European Market on member states*, Amsterdam: IOS Press, pp 231-48.

Byron, K. and Condon, S. (1996) 'A comparative study of Caribbean return migration from Britain and France: towards a context-dependent explanation', *Transactions, Institute of British Geographers*, vol 21, no 1, pp 91-104.

Cerase, F.P. (1974) 'Migration and social change: expectations and reality: a study of return migration from the United States to Italy', *International Migration Review*, vol 8, pp 245-62.

Chau, R. (2007) *The involvement of Chinese older people in policy and practice: Aspirations and expectations*, York: Joseph Rowntree Foundation.

Chau, R. and Yu, W.K. (2000) 'Chinese older people in Britain: double attachment to double detachment', in A.M. Warnes, L. Warren and M. Nolan (eds) *Care services for later life: Transformations and critiques*, London: Jessica Kingsley, pp 259-72.

DG-HCP (European Commission Directorate General on Health and Consumer Protection) (2006) *Developing a community framework for safe, high quality and efficient health services*, Brussels: DG-HCP (http://ec.europa.eu/health/ph_overview/co_operation/mobility/community_framework_en.htm).

Dwyer, P. (2005) 'Governance, forced migration and welfare', *Social Policy and Administration*, vol 39, no 6, pp 622-39.

Dwyer, P. and Papadimitriou, D. (2006) 'The social security rights of older international migrants in the European Union', *Journal of Ethnic and Migration Studies*, vol 32, no 8, pp 1301-19.

Friedrich, K., Kaiser, C. and Buck, C. (2005) 'Entornos de vida socioespacial y tramas sociales de los emigrantes de retiro alemanes en España: los ejemplos de Mallorca y la Costa Blanca' ('Aspirations and socio-spatial aspects of the ways of life of German migrant retirees in Spain: the examples of Mallorca and the Costa Blanca'), in V. Rodríguez, M.A. Casado-Díaz and A. Huber (eds) *Migración internacional de retirados en España* (*International retirement migrants in Spain*), Madrid: Consejo Superior de Investigaciones Científicas, pp 241-61.

Giddens, A. (1991) *Modernity and self-identity: Self and society in the late modern age*, Cambridge: Polity.

Gustafson, P. (2001) 'Retirement migration and transnational lifestyles', *Ageing & Society*, vol 21, no 4, pp 371-94.

Hardill, I., Spradbery, J., Arnold-Boakes, J.A. and Marrugat, M.L. (2005) 'Retirement migration: the other story, issues facing British migrants who retire to Spain', *Ageing & Society*, vol 25, no 5, pp 769-83.

Hilditch, M. (2007) 'Call to ignore A8 homeless', *Inside Housing*, 5 February (http://www.insidehousing.co.uk/news/article/?id=1448594).

Homeless Link (2007) *A8 nationals homelessness* (www.homeless.org.uk/inyourarea/london/policy/a8).

Huber, A. and O'Reilly, K. (2004) 'The construction of *Heimat* under conditions of individualised modernity: Swiss and British elderly migrants in Spain', *Ageing & Society*, vol 24, no 3, pp 327-52.

Jones, G.W. (2006) 'Challenges of ageing in East and Southeast Asia: living arrangements of older persons and social security trends', Paper presented at the 'Impact of Ageing: A Common Challenge for Europe and Asia' Conference, University of Vienna, 7-9 June (www.univie.ac.at/impactofageing/pdf/jones.pdf).

Joppke, C. (1999) *The domestic legal sources of immigrant rights: The United States, Germany and the European Union*, Working Paper SPS 99/3, Florence: European University Institute (www.iue.it/PUB/).

Joppke, C. (2006) *Immigrants and civic integration in Western Europe*, Montreal: Institute for Research on Public Policy (irpp@irpp.org).

Joppke, C. and Morawaska, E. (2003) *Towards assimilation and citizenship: Immigrants in liberal states*, Basingstoke: Palgrave Macmillan.

King, R. (1986) *Return migration and regional economic problems*, London: Croom Helm.

King, R., Warnes, A.M. and Williams, A.M. (2000) *Sunset lives: British retirement migration to the Mediterranean*, Oxford: Berg.

Klinthall, M. (2006) 'Retirement return migration from Sweden', *International Migration*, vol 44, no 2, pp 153-80.

Longino, C.F., Jr, Marshall, V.W., Mullins, L.C. and Tucker, R.D. (1991) 'On the nesting of snowbirds', *Journal of Applied Gerontology*, vol 10, pp 157-68.

Malcolm, E. (1996) *Elderly return migration from Britain to Ireland: A preliminary study*, Dublin: National Council for the Elderly.

Migration Policy Institute (2006) *America's emigrants: US retirement migration to Mexico and Panama*, Washington, DC: Migration Policy Institute.

Min, J.W., Moon, A. and Lubben, J.E. (2005) 'Determinants of psychological distress over time among older Korean immigrants and non-Hispanic white elders: evidence from a two-wave panel study', *Aging and Mental Health*, vol 9, no 3, pp 210-22.

Moon, J.H. and Pearl, J. (1991) 'Alienation of elderly Korean American immigrants as related to place of residence, gender, age, years of education, time in the US, living with or without children and living with or without spouse', *International Journal of Aging and Human Development*, vol 32, no 2, pp 115-24.

Nye, R.B. and Morpugo, J.E. (1955) *History of the United States, Vol 1: The Birth of the USA; Vol 2, The growth of the USA*, Harmondsworth: Penguin.

O'Reilly, K. (2000a) *The British on the Costa del Sol: Trans-national identities and local communities*, London: Routledge.

O'Reilly, K. (2000b) 'Trading intimacy for liberty: British women on the Costa del Sol', in F. Anthias and G. Lazaridis (eds) *Gender and migration in Southern Europe*, Oxford: Berg, pp 227-48.

Poulain, M., Perrin, N. and Singleton, A. (eds) (2006) *THESIM: Towards Harmonised European Statistics on International Migration*, Louvain-la-Neuve, Belgium: Presses Universitaires de Louvain.

Pourat, N., Lubben, J., Wallace, S.P. and Moon, A. (1999) 'Predictors of use of traditional Korean healers among elderly Koreans in Los Angeles', *The Gerontologist*, vol 39, no 6, pp 711-19.

Rodríguez,V.R. and Egea, C. (2006) 'Return and the social environment of Andalusian emigrants in Europe', *Journal of Ethnic and Migration Studies*, vol 32, no 8, pp 1377-93.

Rodríguez, V.R., Casado-Díaz, M.A. and Huber, A. (eds) (2006) *La Migración de Europeos Retirados en España*, Estudios de Política y Sociedad 23, Madrid: Consejo Superior de Investigaciones Científicas.

Serow, W.J. and Haas, W.H. III (1992) 'Measuring the economic impact of retirement migration: the case of Western North Carolina', *Journal of Applied Gerontology*, vol 11, no 2, pp 200-15.

Shinozaki, M. (2006) 'Japanese international retirement migration: a case study of Japanese retired couples in New Zealand', Master's thesis, Tokyo: Waseda University (extract available online at www.wiaps.waseda.ac.jp/initiative/2006/work/international_01/pdf/Group_02).

Silveira, E. and Allebeck, P. (2001) 'Migration, ageing and mental health: an ethnographic study on perceptions of life satisfaction, anxiety and depression in older Somali men in east London', *International Journal of Social Welfare*, vol 10, no 4, pp 309-20.

Sriskandarajah, D. and Drew, C. (2006) *Brits abroad: Mapping the scale and nature of British emigration*, London: Institute for Public Policy Research.

Sunil,T.S., Rojas,V. and Bradley, D.E. (2007) 'United States' international retirement migration: reasons for retiring to the environs of Lake Chapala, Mexico', *Ageing & Society*, vol 27, no 4.

Torres, S. (2001) 'Understandings of successful aging in the context of migration: the case of Iranian immigrants to Sweden', *Ageing & Society*, vol 21, no 3, pp 333-55.

Torres, S. (2004) 'Late-in-life immigrants in Sweden: who are they and what do they need?', in A.M. Warnes (ed) *Older migrants in Europe: Essays, projects and sources*, Sheffield: Sheffield Institute for Studies on Ageing, University of Sheffield, pp 59-62.

Torres, S. (2006) 'Elderly immigrants in Sweden: "otherness" under construction', *Journal of Ethnic and Migration Studies*, vol 32, no 8, pp 1341-58.

Trattner, W.I. (1974) *From Poor Law to welfare state: A history of social welfare in America*, New York, NY: The Free Press.

Warnes, A.M. (1998) 'Divided responses to ageing populations: apocalyptic demography, ideology and rational social administration', in R. Hudson and A.M. Williams (eds) *Divided Europe: Society and territory*, London: Sage Publications, pp 231-54.

Warnes, A.M. (2001) 'The international dispersal of pensioners from affluent countries', *International Journal of Population Geography*, vol 7, no 6, pp 373-88.

Warnes, A.M. (2002) 'The challenge of intra-union and in-migration to "Social Europe"', *Journal of Ethnic and Migration* Studies, vol 28, no 1, pp 134-52.

Warnes, A.M. and Williams, A. (2006) 'Older migrants in Europe: a new focus for migration studies', *Journal of Ethnic and Migration Studies*, vol 32, no 8, pp 1257-81.

Warnes, A.M., Friedrich, K., Kellaher, L. and Torres, S. (2004) 'The diversity and welfare of older migrants in Europe', *Ageing & Society*, vol 24, no 3, pp 307-26.

Wearn, R. (2007) 'Restrictions in force', *The Pavement News*, vol 17, January, p 4.

Yu, W.K. (2000) *Chinese older people: A need for social inclusion in two communities*, Bristol/York: The Policy Press/Joseph Rowntree Foundation.

FIFTEEN

Managing multiple life courses: the influence of children on migration processes in the European Union

Louise Ackers and Helen Stalford

Introduction

Traditional approaches to migration theorising, particularly in a European context, have tended to focus rather narrowly on a limited number of economic determinants and, in particular, the effect of wage differentials in shaping migration and location decisions. The emphasis on *the migration decision* has also tended to characterise migration as a one-time event, perhaps followed by a return move. In recent years, research has drawn attention to the role that a much wider range of factors play in shaping what are now conceptualised more accurately as migration *processes* or, in a European context 'mobilities'. This might include a more holistic appraisal of economic factors to encompass living costs and expenditures and their impact on family resources. In addition to this, research has encouraged us to consider the impact that personal and family relationships and obligations might have on migration behaviour, perhaps generating resistance to the 'pull' of economic considerations or, in other contexts, lubricating mobility. Concerns around spousal employment rights and the impact of dual career situations form the focus of an increasing body of research reflecting a move away from the individualistic and consensual 'male breadwinner' model towards acknowledging the role that couples play in migration decision making. Boyd critiques economic rationality models that "emphasise the movement of people as a result of rational calculations performed by individual actors", drawing attention to the role of partners and wives in particular (1989, p 640). A necessary development to this has been research exploring the impact of migration on family life (Mincer, 1978;

Litcher, 1980; Bailey and Cooke, 1998; Cooke, 2001; Ackers and Stalford, 2004; for a review of research in this area, see Kofman, 2004). Bailey and Boyle (2004), in their review of the multidisciplinary literature in this area, refer to the traditional assumption that migration decisions involving families are based on rational, economic logic. This implies a process by which the migrant worker parent (typically the male) weighs up the net economic gain to the family unit of moving. Similarly, Scott refers to the relationship between mobility and family/life course, suggesting that, "There is ... a work–life balance that matches the acquisition of mobility capital against familial priorities" (2006, p 1113).

Specific attention to the influence of children on migration processes has emerged more slowly. Where this is recognised, children tend to be viewed as the passive appendages or, indeed, intractable obstacles to their parents' migration. The child, in many ways, becomes one dimension of the adult decision makers' life course: what effect will having a child have on a couple's decision about whether or where to move? What impact will mobility have on their ability to care for young children, on their children's welfare and educational opportunity (and the associated costs) and, ultimately, on their economic prospects? While the shift in favour of understanding the relationship between mobility and life course is to be welcomed, not least to the extent that it recognises the influence of partners and children, the primary focus rests on the life course of the adult/s rather than on the interplay of multiple, parallel, life courses that intertwine to shape the increasingly complex, multifaceted and evolutionary transnational processes associated with mobility. Kofman, for instance, alludes to the importance of the (parents') life cycle as a key determinant of migration decisions and experiences, proposing that we understand migrant families in, "a different way ... as fluid and constantly being re-constituted and negotiated, adapting across spaces and through time" (2004, p 249). Equally important for the purpose of our analysis, however, is the stage at which the migration occurred in the life cycle of the child/ren, since age dictates, to a large degree, accessibility of and adaptability to a new learning or care environment, integration with peers, and the importance of environmental factors (such as leisure provision and safety) in deciding on a destination country or destination region within a country.

Aside from acknowledging the importance of the life course in shaping migration experiences, a second significant variable affecting migration, particularly that involving children, is context. While it is trite to note that family members' experiences vary according to the specific social, economic and geographical context in which the migration takes place, there is always a temptation to gloss over the significant contextual factors that can make a dramatic difference to the experiences of a seemingly homogeneous (and comparatively privileged) cohort of migrants such as those who move within the European Union (EU). It is useful (albeit perhaps a little crude) to group these contextual factors into three categories: the national (social policy) context; the professional context; and the personal context. The first factor relates to the degree of social welfare provision available to migrants in the host state, particularly the accessibility of childcare and the quality of educational provision. While, in an EU context at least, levels of social provision are bolstered by supranational legislation that guarantees all lawfully resident EU migrants equal access to social advantages on the same basis as nationals, whether or not migrants are in a better position once they move to the host state clearly depends on what is on offer in the host state and whether that is better or worse than what they left behind[1].

The professional context is also highly significant, not least because it dictates the extent to which migrants engage with the host state's welfare system. Under EU law, all EU migrant workers are guaranteed a basic equality of treatment with national workers in respect of employment opportunities, working conditions and remuneration[2]. However, many employment contracts (particularly in the corporate industries) supplement this with considerable occupational perks including assistance with housing and childcare, exclusive private education for children and generous healthcare and pension packages.

Finally, the personal context is, of course, relevant to migration experiences. The extent to which families move with or to join additional, informal support, for instance (in the form of maternal grandparents), may significantly alleviate the burden associated with securing appropriate and affordable childcare; and the existence of other social and cultural links with the host state may well mitigate the isolation commonly associated with migration processes (Kofman, 2004; Herman, 2006).

Research background

Bearing in mind the importance of life course and context to developing our understanding of migration processes, our analysis of the influence of children on migration behaviour draws on very specific research into the migration of highly skilled (science) professionals moving within the EU (hereafter, the MOBEX study)[3]. This research builds on and complements work conducted since the early 1990s on intra-EU mobility of different categories of EU nationals, including women (Ackers, 1998), children (Ackers and Stalford, 2004) and retired people (Ackers and Dwyer, 2002; Ackers and Groves, 2007: forthcoming). The selection of scientists in the MOBEX study was strategic; we wanted to focus on an occupational sector that places a very high premium on migration, and career progression in scientific research is closely intertwined with the willingness to tolerate repeated mobility (King, 2002; Ackers, 2003, 2005). Although this group cannot by any means be described as 'forced migrants' – to the extent that they have a degree of choice about whether to move – the majority will have considered the prospect of mobility at some stage and weighed up the 'risks' of immobility in terms of their ability to work effectively, to progress in their careers and to enjoy a fulfilling family life. An important dimension of this work, then, has been the extent to which these migrants take into account their families' (particularly their children's) interests in the migration process.

The contextual factors alluded to above are highly pertinent to the experiences of the MOBEX respondents. The study focused on skills flows between two 'sending' countries (Bulgaria and Poland) and two 'destination' countries (the UK and Germany), all with quite different welfare and educational systems, and all with quite different histories as far as their membership of the EU was concerned. At the time of the interviews, respondents from Poland had only recently gained access to the EU employment market under the free movement provisions[4]. Bulgaria was still awaiting accession to the EU at the time of the interviews, thereby excluding Bulgarian migrants from the more favourable remit of EU free movement law and policy[5].

Regarding the 'professional' context of their migration, the MOBEX sample of respondents could be described as 'free agent labour migrants' (Williams, 2006) to the extent that, as academic scientists, they move not only geographically but also between employment contracts. In effect they take the initiative to move as individual actors and shoulder the risks and costs associated with moving. This distinguishes them from company transferees, many of whom move within a 'protective bubble' often with significant corporate support with childcare, healthcare, education and housing and, in some cases, assistance with spousal employment (Ackers and Stalford, 2004; Beaverstock, 2005; Dickmann et al, 2006). Levels of remuneration for scientists vary markedly between countries but are generally significantly lower than comparable professional employment. Also, in common with many other highly skilled migrants, scientists tend to work in 'global cities' where living costs are very high. Scientific employment, particularly at the early stages of careers (when people are most mobile), usually takes the form of temporary contracts of between one and five years' duration[6]. Finally, the 'personal context' of scientific migration is that it typically attracts or generates a very high proportion of dual or 'same career' partnerships (Ackers, 2005, 2007). The majority of partnered scientists will have a partner who is also in full-time employment and usually working in science. Levels of internationalisation in science combine with this to generate a high proportion of international partnerships (couples in which the partners hold different nationalities). Consequently, many families already have strong personal links in and, by implication, a familiarity with the culture and language of the state to which they move because one or other partner is a national of that country (Scott, 2006).

While it is important to emphasise the importance of effective contextualisation in understanding migration processes, as well as the dangers of generalisation across occupational, economic and social categories, it is possible to draw from the MOBEX study and our past research on migration in Europe a number of issues that present common challenges to many migrant cohorts relating to the interests and welfare of family members, particularly children. This research strongly suggests that those who migrate with children consider a complex myriad of family-led factors that shift in prominence over the life course, demanding constant re-negotiation and re-evaluation, with the initial migration constituting just one stage in this process (Ackers and Stalford, 2004, pp 44-5). Admittedly, since this particular project examines migration from an adult perspective, it reveals less about the impact of such processes on children's experiences (although many respondents did reflect on their own childhood experiences of migration). Therefore, by juxtaposing the MOBEX findings with the findings of our previous work involving interviews with children, our aim in the following analysis is to tease out the most important challenges facing parents and children as a result of migration and to explore how these are negotiated throughout the life course of individual family members. The following discussion will examine how issues of context and life course operate in relation to two specific but highly important issues: care and education. The aim is to identify common strategies adopted by migrant parents that enable them to negotiate migration in a way that accommodates the needs of children at various points in the life course. In the process, the discussion will also consider the extent to which EU law and policy reflects and facilitates these practices.

Managing care transnationally

One critical factor shaping the mobility of workers with young children concerns the ability to access and pay for appropriate childcare in the host state. Previous research on the impact of migration on domestic caring arrangements has identified three obstacles to the successful combination of work/family life facing migrants: dislocation from informal and family support; diversity in levels of state support; and the dominant and decisive influence of male parents' careers (Ackers, 2004, p 379). This work underlines the importance of recognising the diversity of childcare needs among migrants that depend, to a large degree, on the age of the children and the dynamics of the family: "Care is a key determinant, emerging and re-emerging over the life-course, often in a most unpredictable fashion to challenge location decisions" (Ackers, 2004, p 378). Indeed, each stage of a child's life course, from post-natal care through pre-school and full-time education, poses new challenges to migrant workers who are faced with organising their professional obligations around the caring needs of their children in the face of limited familial support and a foreign, often inaccessible, welfare environment.

The inaccessibility of childcare can act as a mobility 'dampener'; workers feel less inclined to move if they feel they lack support of this nature in the destination state, and are effectively 'locked' either in the 'home' or receiving country. But concerns around care can equally act as a migration 'lubricant'; migrant families often *return* to their countries of origin to access vital familial and other informal support networks. Gamlen's research supports this view: "returns ... are frequently motivated by non-economic factors such as childrearing and care for the elderly ... and might be called 'breather periods' in which the migrant takes advantage of free public assistance with child rearing, healthcare or retirement in their home country" (2005, p 16). While Gamlen's recognition of the role of care in precipitating moves is welcome, it is perhaps inaccurate to describe such factors as 'non-economic' since the MOBEX study and our past research revealed many instances of a preference for informal arrangements precisely because of the prohibitive cost of crèche and other formal childcare facilities in the host state. Highly skilled workers often move on relatively low wages and with little corporate support, and express serious concerns around the provision and cost of childcare in the host countries (particularly in the UK). While this is a general concern for all migrant workers, the culture of long and unpredictable working hours coupled with ongoing work-related travel (often abroad) made this a problematic for the scientists we interviewed, particularly given that many were part of dual-career couples and had no option but to rely on formal childcare provision[7].

Extensive studies have been carried out to identify potential solutions to formal childcare costs and shortages within a single-nation and comparative context (Hantrais, 2003; OECD, 2005). It is only relatively recently, however, that childcare for workers has been explored in a migration context (Bailey et al, 2004; Stalford, 2005). This work has illustrated that the accessibility of childcare provision under domestic welfare regimes is influenced not only by economic factors but also by potent social and cultural factors. In that sense, those migrating from a member state that offers relatively generous and accessible childcare provision throughout the child's life course (such as Sweden) often find that moving to a country that endorses a more 'familistic' model of welfare (such as Spain, Greece or Portugal), or to one that offers a wide range of services but at a prohibitive cost (such as the UK) are less amenable to the demands of those without a network of family support to enable them to reconcile work and childcare responsibilities as effectively. These observations are supported by the findings of European Commission-funded research carried out in 2003:

> The attitude of governments towards families varies across countries and thus, public support appears to be quite different across the European arena. For example, in the UK, the choice of having children is considered a private one, one which has to be made by all parents, in general. As a result, family support is mainly targeted at poor or single parents. In other countries, the role of the government in providing support to families, is traditionally, much larger. When children are considered in a public manner, public policies are supposed to cover the cost of children regardless of family income. In France, the 'Duty of the Nation' towards families is embedded in the French Constitution. The provision of public services reflects the 'dual-earner' gender ideology. Nordic countries are the most evident adherents to this ideology. Their official gender-equality policies led them to support dual-earner families and female employment. In practice, this ideology has translated into extensive public care services. Possibly an exception can be made for France but in the rest of Continental Europe

... child care is largely left to the private sector to provide.
(EC, 2003, p 122)

While EU social policy has recognised the importance of childcare as a means of maximising labour market participation, particularly for women (European Council, 2002), it can only *encourage* member states to make childcare better, more affordable and more accessible. Moreover, the division of EU/national competence in respect of domestic social policy limits formal EU regulation to ensuring equality of treatment and does not seek to harmonise domestic welfare regimes. In that sense, once lawfully resident in the host state, all EU migrant workers and their family members are protected from any discrimination as far as access to public (including family-related) benefits is concerned[8]. However, as already noted, the ultimate value of equal access to rights as guaranteed by the free movement provisions depends largely on how they compare to the level of support available in the family's state of previous residence; these benefits may well turn out to be inferior, in which case, the ethic of equality underpinning EU free movement law does little to enhance the quality or level of social assistance available to migrant families. Moreover, it is important to remember that EU law only 'bites' where there is mobility between the 27 member states. Since many mobile highly skilled workers undertake periods of training in non-EU member states (such as North America), they are clearly subject to domestic immigration measures and, as such, may have more limited access to welfare provision than nationals of those countries.

Caring at a distance

A common strategy adopted by the MOBEX respondents to enable them to 'reconcile' demanding professional lives with their caring obligations was to separate the family unit. Previous research has identified that such dispersal is increasingly commonplace and, indeed, necessary in a globalised and fluid labour market and as opportunities for international experience (including leisure as much as work-related) become all the more available and affordable (Mason, 1998). While dispersal of adult siblings, parents and other relatives is now an accepted feature of life, particularly for the professionally mobile, separation of the *core* family unit (partners and children) is becoming increasingly commonplace[9]. Nine out of the 64 respondents interviewed for the research chose to leave their children behind (usually with the other parent or the child's grandparents) while they spent periods working in other countries[10].

Others benefited from the support of accompanying grandparents, although such arrangements were rare and usually short term.

Implicit in all of these decisions is a process of balancing up the benefits of economic and professional progression to the welfare of the family as a whole with the potentially damaging impact that temporary dispersal of the family unit might have on respondents' children and personal relationships. Some felt that the short-term nature of the employment contract was insufficiently secure to justify upheaval of the children[11]; others were uncertain as to whether the family would adapt to the new cultural and linguistic environment; and many respondents saw the move as an economic investment, such that by migrating alone, the workers' earnings would stretch much further (particularly in Poland and Bulgaria) if sent back to the family in the form of remittances (Glystos, 2002; Sana and Massey, 2005). A further common reason for the separation related to concerns around the impact that a move would have on the other partner's career, although this was a much more prominent concern as far as male partners were concerned[12]. There were some instances, therefore, where women left children behind in the care of their partners in the home state while they worked in another country for periods of up to two years.

In addition to short periods of parental absence, the research revealed quite complex arrangements that led to child siblings being separated from each other so that one or other could accompany the parent to the host state. There was generally quite a practical approach to these arrangements that were tailored to what parents perceived to be in their children's best interests at that particular point in each child's life course[13]. The following two Bulgarian scientists working in the UK describe how they essentially staggered the migration of the family over time, giving themselves a preparatory settling in period in the host state before the arrival of their two children, although in the first case the respondent's husband's life remained very much in Bulgaria:

> "I came here on my own; there was nobody and it was hard but I was very motivated. I took my younger daughter with me initially while [the older daughter] stayed with my husband [in Bulgaria] so the family was separate. Now my two daughters are here. My husband is coming over soon … but not for good. He still works in Bulgaria because he has got a good job there."

"When I started I came here on my own and the first year was very difficult because I didn't have my family here because we didn't have funding. I started working ... and that helped me to survive. And then I decided at the end of the first year to go back to Bulgaria because I didn't think I could survive. [But] then my husband decided to come and join me and ... he found a job.

Then the kids came over too and they built friendships here and now they feel much happier here. [In Bulgaria] they had been staying with my parents. It was a difficult time for them as well but we couldn't bring them. You don't take those risks with your children."

This 'policy of separation' is a common strategy adopted by EU migrant workers, both in the highly skilled and 'low'-skilled sectors, particularly in response to the increasing tendency for employers to engage workers on short-term contracts[14].

Building human and social capital: children's education and parental mobility

Bailey et al (2004, p 1624) comment that, "... families weigh up more than the immediate financial costs and benefits to partners and pay explicit attention to their children's educational portfolios when determining family migration". This is supported by Dickmann et al's research that claims that "two of the five most important factors for individuals were family-related including willingness of the spouse to move and children's educational needs" (2006, p 18). This was no less evident among the MOBEX respondents who identified their children's education as one of the most prominent considerations in the migration process. Many positively valued the prospects of moving with their children and the educational opportunities this might generate for them. Concerned about the economic and political situation at home and recognising the value of reputational capital and language skills, they often placed a premium on mobility for their children.

The weight attached to educational opportunities is clearly linked to the specific context within which people are contemplating moves. Dickmann et al found marked differences in the importance attached to education in their samples of Asian and British migrants: "Many interviewees from Asia outlined the positive effect a move would have on the education and language capabilities of their family (and sometimes themselves). In contrast, respondents from the UK saw the different educational systems and languages more as a barrier to mobility and perceived a potential disruption of family life" (2006, p 22).

Bulgarian and Polish respondents in our study expressed similar optimism about the potential benefits a western education would bring to their children's future economic and academic/career prospects. Much of this optimism is grounded in positive perceptions of the western education system, and particularly the merits of attaining fluency in the English language (as the language of the global economy)[15]. Their responses revealed that educational concerns increased and diminished in importance over the child's life course. In each of the cases presented below the decision to make an initial outward move had already been made, presumably taking into account the presence of children at that point in time. What is interesting is the influence of their children's educational circumstances in the ensuing period triggering a re-evaluation of mobility priorities, and often reconfiguring family relationships and location decisions quite significantly.

Andre's[16] first period of mobility had occurred many years beforehand when his two children were much younger. At this time he had 'reconciled' the needs of his then young children and his own career through the relatively common practice of short periods of separation. This enabled his family to remain in Bulgaria affording them some stability while enabling him to augment his salary and develop his career through regular trips to the UK. The decision to return to the UK for a longer period was very much influenced by concerns about his 17-year-old daughter's education:

> "From a personal point of view, I wanted very much for my daughter to have the opportunity to receive a good education in an English college so we discussed with my wife and we decided that it would be good to apply for this position and to have one of the daughters with me."

Asked whether he might consider a more permanent move in the future he replies:

> "No, I had never considered it mostly for personal reasons because the family and my wife is a teacher in biology but she doesn't speak English at all and she is now in Bulgaria

> so I'm here with one of my daughters and my wife and the
> other daughter are in Bulgaria."

Tereza had also made a series of short visits to the UK, on her own,
before she made the decision to bring her daughter over with her. She
explains how she initially planned to remain in the UK for two years,
leaving her husband and older daughter (who was an undergraduate at
the time) in Bulgaria. She was accompanied by her younger daughter
(then aged 11), believing that a period in the UK would benefit her
daughter's language skills. As her daughter reached an increasingly critical
point in her education, Tereza resolved to remain in the UK on a more
permanent basis:

> "Before my daughter goes to university I think I'd better be
> here. She's 15 and she has got her GCSEs now. After that, yes,
> she will have two years A-levels and after that university."

Similarly, in the following extracts, Irina and Jakob attribute their families'
decision to remain in the UK (rather than return to their country of
origin) to their children's educational needs and to their general social
and emotional well-being:

> "When we thought we would go back to Bulgaria it was
> the kids who were happy here and really wanted us to stay
> in the UK. They had their friendships and they had a good
> environment and were happy at school and that's what
> they wanted."

> "I would like to stay [in Germany] a bit longer … I don't
> know. To some extent I am forced [to stay]. My son is in
> the third class of the school and it will be hard for him if
> we have to go…."

These experiences reveal the complex and dynamic nature of migration
decision making, particularly where children are involved; while it
was the parents' professional aspirations that motivated the move
initially, subsequent mobilities are dictated primarily by concerns as
to the children's welfare and prospects. These concerns vary, as well, in
accordance with the age of the child/ren. Our past research involving
interviews with migrant children across the EU supports the widely held
perception that children generally adapt more easily to new cultural,

social and linguistic environments the earlier in their life cycle that the migration takes place (Ackers and Stalford, 2004). This observation is confirmed by the work of Bailey et al, who concluded in their study on dual-career couples that older children often act as a constraint on migration, and particularly long-distance moves (2004, p 1620). The findings of the MOBEX research provide further insight into this issue, suggesting that children's education has the strongest impact on return decisions; having moved with younger children, the respondents often expressed reluctance to move again or return home until their children had completed their secondary education.

That said, several EU policy developments have been instituted to counteract the 'dampening' impact of children's education on migration. The natural process of globalisation, encouraged by soft-law initiatives at EU level to promote cross-national exchange and integration in the education sector, have succeeded in eroding many of the linguistic and cultural barriers between nation states, so that theoretically, a child's age or stage in education should not act as a barrier to mobility. Moreover, the gradual, albeit modest replacement of nation-specific learning programmes with more international curricula (such as the International or European Baccalauréat), as well as the proliferation of private, international and foreign schooling across the EU, has circumvented much of the confusion associated with mutual recognition of educational qualifications that may have previously hindered access to schools or third-level education in other countries (at least within the EU) (Stalford, 2000). Access to this type of provision has become a common accompaniment ('carrot') to professional migration; globalised industries that depend on a mobile labour force routinely offer highly attractive relocation packages to encourage and facilitate skilled migration (Raghuram, 2004, p 310) and typically include generous support for exclusive international schooling for any accompanying children.

It would be erroneous, however, to presume that all children of highly skilled migrants enjoy a highly privileged status in this regard given that highly skilled migration is not confined to the multinational industrial sector. The focus of the MOBEX research on Eastern European migrant scientists, for instance, included a concentration of employment in the public (university)[17] sector that offers virtually no occupational perks such that any additional cost associated with private schooling was borne by the parents alone. Ivan's case illustrates this point. His move was almost entirely precipitated by the needs of his son. His wife, also a scientist, had moved in the first instance to take up a short-term position in the UK, leaving her son with Ivan in Bulgaria. She then encouraged the son to move to the UK to undertake his undergraduate degree at an English university, presumably to enhance his future employment prospects. At the time of interview Bulgaria had not acceded to the EU and their son was therefore required to pay expensive overseas tuition fees. This put pressure on Ivan to leave his permanent position in Bulgaria for a temporary research position in the UK in order to cover the costs of his son's education. While this decision might be construed as 'rational' and even profit maximising to the extent that it supports the son's future economic prospects, the sacrifices Ivan and his wife had made were significant, and their future financial and professional security decidedly uncertain.

It is interesting to reflect on the extent to which the concept of 'tied stayer' could be extended to some of these cases where parents become immobile as a result of their children's needs or plans. This description would seem to fit Ivan's situation and also that of another respondent, Vladimir, who moved from Bulgaria to the UK with his wife and child to work. The fact that they had settled well in the UK was placing pressure on Vladimir to stay even though he had not been able to secure a permanent position:

> "I came first so they came shortly after me and my son was five then so now he's finishing primary school and going to secondary [aged 11] ... in a sense he's more British than Bulgarian because in fact a big part of his conscious life was spent here. My wife was a PhD student in Bulgaria when we came here so she had to give up. She started a new one here and just finished this year and found a position.... I'm quite settled but that's unsettling for me. Because at the moment ironically I have the most shaky position in the family; my son is quite happy, he is enjoying his school activities and friends and my wife has a permanent position and I have a one-year contract.... It's limiting very much my options because I could go to another country where there are a lot of openings."

This case is yet another example of the fluid nature of mobility. The initial outward move was very much motivated by Vladimir's professional interests, even to the detriment of his wife's position who came to the UK as a 'tied mover' or 'trailing wife'. Six years later the tables have turned and his son's integration, coupled with the greater security attached to his wife's professional position, have tilted the balance in favour of remaining in the UK even if this restricts Vladimir's ability to move again and achieve a more secure position. At the time of interview he could perhaps be described as a 'tied stayer' with migration decisions, at that point in time, determined by his child's and wife's needs.

In most of the cases discussed above the parents were attempting to negotiate some kind of compromise between their own needs and the needs of a child or a number of children of similar age (and with similar educational needs). However, large differences in the age of siblings present mobile families with even more complex challenges in accommodating the demands of multiple life courses. Dessislava is a case in point: as a mother of two children, her approach to managing parenting and mobility had changed over time as their respective needs evolved. In the first instance she migrated from Bulgaria to Germany alone, leaving the children in the care of her mother and husband. As her older son approached 14 she decided to take him to Berlin with her, "because they had good programmes for foreigners in the schools ... a kind of international school with special classes to learn German". During this four-year period her younger son remained with his grandparents in Bulgaria. This arrangement enabled Dessislava to resolve her problems of finding childcare for the younger child while also enabling her older son to access the educational opportunity associated with mobility, even though the 'solution' implied long-term family dispersal. Ferro argues that the migration of "some but not all family members can constitute an important risk-reducing strategy" (2006, p 177). Although she is referring to the potential value of adult family members 'allocating resources in different labour markets', the same case could be made in relation to the family as a whole and the needs of both adults and children.

Conclusion

Our aim in this chapter has been to emphasise two important variables that shape the migration processes of families (life course and context), through a discussion of two substantive areas of entitlement that affect children: care and education.

We are aware, of course, of the methodological limitations of the research alluded to here, most of which does not involve interviews directly with children. The primary focus on adult perspectives arguably reveals more, therefore, about the impact of children on migration processes rather than the impact of migration processes on children. While recognising that children's perceptions and experiences of migration can differ dramatically from those of their parents, the findings indicate an acute awareness among parents of the benefits or disadvantages migration might bring, not only for their children's happiness and welfare in the short term, but also for their educational, economic and social opportunities in the long term.

Moreover, while the focus here on scientists' migration implies a somewhat narrow frame of analysis, it provides a useful lens through which to explore how various aspects of family life, and particularly issues relating to children, are negotiated in the context of migration. The focus on highly skilled migrant scientists is also pertinent because of its peculiarity as a sector that presents a stark choice between migration or professional stagnation. Implicit in the mobility expectation, however, are assumptions around parents' capacity to juggle their working commitments with the significant demands of parenting and care, and around appropriate support networks being in place, at either a formal or informal level to facilitate this process. This creates something of a paradox in that migration, which is widely regarded as the key to scientists' professional ascendance, may, ultimately, be the very factor that poses most obstacles to the effective reconciliation of work and family life. Indeed, concerns to secure their children's social well-being and academic prospects serve to effectively 'lock' migrants into geographical and economic spaces.

Member state sovereignty to determine levels of social provision including childcare and educational provision militates against any attempt (or, indeed, desire) to harmonise such issues, such that the social and welfare-related benefits or disadvantages of migration will always depend on whether migrants are moving to something better or worse than what they left behind. Moreover, legal and policy measures, however effective, have a limited impact on the range of personal and emotional factors that influence migration decisions, including relationships with kin, language, educational and cultural differentials, and the competing professional demands of partners. In many cases, this leads to a more complex configuration of family life resulting in the dispersal of the nuclear family over time and space. Paradoxically, therefore, separation of one or other parent from the family or of child siblings within the family has become a common strategy for accommodating multiple life courses where professional, personal and national factors impede the migration of the family as a unit.

Notes

[1] Directive 2004/38 [2004] OJ L158/77; corrigendum published as Directive 2004/58 at [2004] OJ L229/35 of 29 April 2004 on the right of citizens of the EU and their family members to move and reside freely within the territory of the member states amending Regulation (EEC) No 1612/68 and repealing Directives 64/221/EEC, 68/360/EEC, 72/194/EEC, 73/148/EEC, 75/34/EEC, 75/35/EEC, 90/364/EEC, 90/365/EEC and 93/96/EEC.

[2] EC Regulation 1612/68, OJ Special Edition 1968, No L257/2, p 475, amended by EC Regulation 312/76, OJ Special Edition 1968 L 257/2.

[3] 'Mobility and Excellence in the European Research Area: Promoting Balanced Growth in an Enlarging Europe'. Co-funded by the UK Economic and Social Research Council (ESRC) (under its Science and Society programme) and by the Anglo-German Foundation, this interdisciplinary study examines the relationship between scientific careers and mobility in the context of EU enlargement through in-depth interviews with 64 migrant scientists.

[4] Poland acceded to the EU along with nine other (including seven other Central and Eastern European) countries on 1 May 2004. All of the Central and Eastern European countries are subject to restrictions on the free movement of workers for a transitional period of up to a maximum of seven years (until 2011) during which time new migrant workers from these countries are subject to much more restrictive national immigration measures in almost all of the established member states. The UK, Ireland and Sweden were exceptional in their decision to allow all new migrant workers from these countries unlimited access to their labour markets from the date of accession, subject to minor administrative procedures. For further analysis see Dougan (2004); Hillion (2004); Adinolfi (2005); and Currie (2006).

[5] Until Bulgaria's accession in January 2007, Bulgarian workers and their families were subject to the conditions laid down in the Europe Agreement concluded with Bulgaria in 1995. These are broadly comparable to those rights available to the family members of EU migrant workers, provided such workers have been granted lawful access to the labour market of the host state: OJ L 358, 31/12/1994 P 0003-0222, Chapter I, Articles 38-9.

[6] For more discussion of the use of fixed-term employment in science careers see Ackers and Oliver (2006).

[7] Forty-eight respondents in the MOBEX sample had moved as part of a 'dual-career couple', of whom only seven were women.

[8] Article 7(2), Regulation 1612/68, above note 2 and Article 24 Directive 2004/38, above note 1. The same applied to Bulgarian migrant workers under the 1995 Europe Agreement until Bulgaria's accession to the EU on 1 January 2007.

[9] For an analysis of other 'strategies' adopted by migrant families to enable parents to manage work and caring obligations, see Wall and São José (2004).

[10] This was the recorded number of respondents who were separated from their partner and/or children at the time of the interview and does not necessarily reveal instances of previous separation among the remaining respondents.

[11] Seven respondents were employed on a contract of less than 12 months, 29 were employed on a temporary basis for between one and three years, and 10 were on a temporary contract for more than three years. Only 16 respondents from the sample were employed on a permanent basis. The remaining two respondents had migrated solely for the purposes of further study.

[12] The research found that men are much less likely to accompany their highly skilled partner to the host state unless they too benefit professionally from the move; in other words, they are unlikely to move for the sole purpose of providing domestic support while the woman pursues her career. This contrasts significantly with the habitual 'trailing wife' model that has revealed a much greater tendency (and indeed, expectation) among women to accompany and provide domestic support in the host state to enable the man to work there, often relinquishing their own successful careers back home in the process. For further discussion of this phenomenon, see Morokvasic and de Tinguy (1993); Kofman et al (2000); Erel (2003); and Raghuram and Kofman (2004).

[13] We will return to the importance of the life course in shaping migration and separation decisions in the context of education later in the discussion.

[14] This contrasts with EU law and policy that is traditionally premised on the archetypal 'trailing wife' model envisaging families moving as an indivisible unit, although more recent case law and legislation would suggest a gradual departure from this model. See Case C 413/99, *Baumbast and R v Secretary of State for the Home Department*, [2002] 3 CMLR; Case C-60/00 *Mary Carpenter v Secretary of State for the Home Department* [2002] ECR I-06279; and Article 12(3), Directive 2004/38, referred to above in note 1.

[15] This did not imply that the respondents did not value the education systems in their home country. Indeed many believed their home systems to be more rigorous and demanding as well as more disciplined (Ackers, 2007b). They were concerned for their children to access the reputational capital associated with western education and, in particular, with global centres of excellence at undergraduate level.

[16] All respondents' names have been changed to preserve anonymity.

[17] Forty-five respondents were employed in the higher education sector.

References

Ackers, H.L. (1998) *Shifting spaces: Women, citizenship and migration in the European Union*, Bristol: The Policy Press.

Ackers, H.L. (2003) *The participation of women researchers in the TMR programme of the European Commission: An evaluation*, Brussels: European Commission (DG12).

Ackers, H.L. (2004) 'Citizenship, migration and the valuation of care in the European Union', *Journal of Ethnic and Migration Studies*, vol 30, no 2, pp 373-96.

Ackers, H.L. (2005) 'Moving people and knowledge: assessing the impact of enlargement on scientific mobility within the European Union', *International Migration*, vol 43, no 5, pp 100-31.

Ackers, H.L. (2007) *Moving people and knowledge: Understanding processes of scientific mobility within an enlarging Europe*, Cheltenham: Edward Elgar.

Ackers, H.L. and Dwyer, P. (2002) *Senior citizenship? Retirement, migration and welfare in the European Union*, Bristol: The Policy Press.

Ackers, H.L. and Groves, K. (2007: forthcoming) 'European citizenship, individual agency and the challenge to social systems: a case study of retirement migration in the European Union', *Ageing and Society*.

Ackers, H.L. and Oliver, E.A. (2007) 'The effect of regulation in the area of fixed term contracts on the recruitment and retention of early career researchers in the UK', *International Studies of Management and Organization*, vol 37, no 1, pp 53-79.

Ackers, H.L. and Stalford, H. (2004) *A community for children?: Children, citizenship and migration in the European Union*, Aldershot: Ashgate.

Adinolfi, A. (2005) 'Free movement and access to work of citizens of the new member states: the transitional measures', *Common Market Law Review*, vol 42, p 469.

Bailey, A. and Boyle, P. (2004) 'Untying and retying family migration in the New Europe', *Journal of Ethnic and Migration Studies*, vol 30, no 2, pp 229-41.

Bailey, A., Blake, M. and Cooke, T. (2004) 'Migration, care and the linked lives of dual-earner households', *Environment and Planning*, vol 36, pp 1617-32, at p 1624.

Bailey, A.J. and Cooke, T.J. (1998) 'Family migration, migration history, and employment', *International Regional Science Review*, vol 21, no 2, pp 99-118.

Beaverstock, J.V. (2005) 'Transnational elites in the city: British highly-skilled inter-company transferees in New York City's financial district', *Journal of Ethnic and Migration Studies*, vol 31, no 2, pp 245-68.

Boh, K. et al (eds) (1989) *Changing patterns of European family life: A comparative analysis of 14 European countries*, London: Routledge.

Boyd, M. (1989) 'Family and personal networks in international migration: recent developments and new agendas', *International Migration Review*, vol 23, no 3, pp 638-70.

Cooke, T.J. (2001) '"Trailing wife" or "trailing mother"? The effect of parental status on the relationship between family migration and the labor-market participation of married women', *Environment and Planning*, vol 33, no 3, pp 419-30.

Currie, S. (2006) '"Free" movers? The post-accession experience of Accession-8 migrant workers in the UK', *European Law Review*, vol 31, no 2, pp 207-29.

Dickmann, M., Doherty, N. and Brewster, C. (2006) 'Why do they go? Individual and corporate perspectives on the factors influencing the decision to accept an international assignment', Paper to the Academy of Management Conference, Atlanta, August.

Dougan, M. (2004) 'A spectre is haunting Europe ... free movement of persons and the eastern enlargement', in C. Hillion (ed) *EU enlargement: A legal approach*, Oxford: Hart, p 111.

EC (European Commission) (2003) *The rationale of motherhood choices: Influence of employment conditions and of public policies*, Directorate General for Research, EUR 20792, Luxembourg, EC Directorate General for Research.

Erel, U. (2003) 'Skilled migrant women and citizenship', in M. Morokvasic, U. Erel and K. Shinozaki (eds) *Crossing borders and shifting boundaries. Vol I: Gender on the move*, Opalden: Leske and Budrich, p 261.

European Council (2002) *Barcelona Council Conclusions*, 15-16 March, SN 100/1/02 REV 1, Brussels: European Council.

Ferro, A. (2006) 'Desired mobility or satisfied immobility? Migratory aspirations among knowledge workers', *Journal of Work and Education*, vol 19, no 2, pp 171-200.

Gamlen, A. (2005) *The brain drain is dead, long live the New Zealand diaspora*, Centre on Migration, Policy and Society, Working Paper No 10, Oxford: University of Oxford.

Glystos, N. (2002) 'The role of migrant remittances in development: evidence from Mediterranean countries', *International Migration*, vol 40, no 1, pp 5-26.

Hantrais, L. (ed) (2003) *Policy relevance of 'family and welfare' research*, Brussels: European Commission.

Herman, E. (2006) 'Migration as family business: the role of personal networks in the mobility phase of migration', *International Migration*, vol 44, no 4, pp 191-230.

Hillion, C. (ed) (2004) *EU enlargement: A legal approach*, Oxford: Hart Publishing.

King, R. (2002) 'Towards a new map of European migration', *International Journal of Population Geography*, vol 8, no 2, pp 89-106.

Kofman, E. (2004) 'Family-related migration: a critical review of European studies', *Journal of Ethnic and Migration Studies*, vol 30, no 2, pp 243-62.

Kofman, E., Phizacklea, A., Raghuram, P. and Sales, R. (2000) *Gender and international migration in Europe: Employment, welfare and politics*, London and New York, NY: Routledge.

Litcher, D.T. (1980) 'Household migration and the labour market position of married women', *Social Science Research*, vol 9, pp 83-97.

Mason, J. (1998) *Living away from relatives: Kinship and geographical reasoning*, Working Paper No 7, Leeds: University of Leeds, Centre for Research in Family, Kinship and Childhood.

Mincer, J. (1978) 'Family migration decisions', *Journal of Political Economy*, vol 86, no 5, pp 749-73.

Morokvasic, M. and de Tinguy, A. (1993) 'Between East and West: a new migratory space', in H. Rudolph and M. Morokvasic (eds) *Bridging states and markets: International migration in the early 1990s*, Berlin: Sigma, pp 245-65.

OECD (Organisation for Economic Cooperation and Development) *Babies and bosses – reconciling work and family life*, vols 1-4, 2001-2005, available at: http://www.oecd.org/document/32/.

Raghuram, P. (2004) 'The difference that skills make: gender, family migration strategies and regulated labour markets', *Journal of Ethnic and Migration Studies*, vol 30, no 2, pp 303-21.

Raghuram, P. and Kofman, E. (2004) 'Out of Asia: skilling, re-skilling and deskilling of female migrants', *Women's Studies International Forum*, vol 27, no 2, pp 95-100.

Sana, M. and Massey, D. (2005) 'Household composition, family migration and community context: migrant remittances in four countries', *Social Science Quarterly*, vol 86, no 2, pp 509-28.

Scott, S. (2006) 'The social morphology of skilled migration: the case of the British middle class in Paris', *Journal of Ethnic and Migration Studies*, vol 32, no 7, pp 1105-129.

Stalford, H. (2000) 'Transferability of formal qualifications in the EU: the case of EU migrant children', in J. Shaw (ed) *Social law and policy in an evolving European Union*, London: Hart Publishing, pp 243-58.

Stalford, H. (2005) 'Parenting, care and mobility in the EU: issues facing migrant scientists', *Innovation, The European Journal of Social Science Research*, vol 18, no 3, pp 361-80.

Wall, K. and São José, J. (2004) 'Managing work and care: a difficult challenge for immigrant families', *Social Policy and Administration*, vol 38, no 6, pp 591-621.

Williams, A. (2006) 'Lost in translation? International migration, learning and knowledge', *Progress in Human Geography*, vol 30, no 5, pp 588-607.

Index

Page references for notes are followed by n